Learn Android Studio 3 with Kotlin

Efficient Android App Development

Ted Hagos

Apress®

Learn Android Studio 3 with Kotlin: Efficient Android App Development

Ted Hagos
Manila, National Capital Region, Philippines

ISBN-13 (pbk): 978-1-4842-3906-3   ISBN-13 (electronic): 978-1-4842-3907-0
https://doi.org/10.1007/978-1-4842-3907-0

Library of Congress Control Number: 2018962941

Managing Director, Apress Media LLC: Welmoed Spahr
Acquisitions Editor: Steve Anglin
Development Editor: Matthew Moodie
Coordinating Editor: Mark Powers

Cover designed by eStudioCalamar

Distributed to the book trade worldwide by Springer Science+Business Media New York, 233 Spring Street, 6th Floor, New York, NY 10013. Phone 1-800-SPRINGER, fax (201) 348-4505, e-mail orders-ny@springer-sbm.com, or visit www.springeronline.com. Apress Media, LLC is a California LLC and the sole member (owner) is Springer Science + Business Media Finance Inc (SSBM Finance Inc). SSBM Finance Inc is a **Delaware** corporation.

For information on translations, please e-mail rights@apress.com, or visit http://www.apress.com/rights-permissions.

Apress titles may be purchased in bulk for academic, corporate, or promotional use. eBook versions and licenses are also available for most titles. For more information, reference our Print and eBook Bulk Sales web page at http://www.apress.com/bulk-sales.

Any source code or other supplementary material referenced by the author in this book is available to readers on GitHub via the book's product page, located at www.apress.com/9781484239063. For more detailed information, please visit http://www.apress.com/source-code.

Printed on acid-free paper

For Adrianne and Stephanie.

Table of Contents

About the Author

Ted Hagos is the CTO and Data Protection Officer of RenditionDigital International, a software development company based out of Dublin, Ireland. Before he joined RDI, he had various software development roles and also spent time as trainer at IBM Advanced Career Education, Ateneo ITI, and Asia Pacific College. He spent many years in software development dating back to Turbo C, Clipper, dBase IV, and Visual Basic. Eventually, he found Java and spent many years there. Nowadays, he's busy with full-stack JavaScript and Android.

About the Technical Reviewers

Massimo Nardone has more than 24 years of experience in Security, Web/Mobile development, Cloud, and IT Architecture. His true IT passions are Security and Android.

He has been programming and teaching how to program with Android, Perl, PHP, Java, VB, Python, C/C++, and MySQL for more than 20 years.

He holds a Master of Science degree in Computing Science from the University of Salerno, Italy.

He has worked as a Project Manager, Software Engineer, Research Engineer, Chief Security Architect, Information Security Manager, PCI/SCADA Auditor and Senior Lead IT Security/Cloud/SCADA Architect for many years.

Technical skills include: Security, Android, Cloud, Java, MySQL, Drupal, Cobol, Perl, Web and Mobile development, MongoDB, D3, Joomla, Couchbase, C/C++, WebGL, Python, Pro Rails, Django CMS, Jekyll, Scratch, etc.

He worked as visiting lecturer and supervisor for exercises at the Networking Laboratory of the Helsinki University of Technology (Aalto University). He holds four international patents (PKI, SIP, SAML, and Proxy areas).

He currently works as Chief Information Security Officer (CISO) for Cargotec Oyj, and he is a member of ISACA Finland Chapter Board.

Massimo has reviewed more than 45 IT books for different publishers and has coauthored *Pro JPA in Java EE 8* (Apress, 2018), *Beginning EJB in Java EE 8* (Apress, 2018), and *Pro Android Games* (Apress, 2015).

Val Okafor is a software architect with expertise in Android development and resides in sunny San Diego, California. He has over 12 years of industry experience and has worked for corporations such as Sony Electronics, The Home Depot, San Diego County, and American Council on Exercise. Val earned his BSc in IT from National University, San Diego and his Masters in Software Engineering from Regis University, Colorado. He is the creator and principal engineer of Pronto line of mobile apps including Pronto Diary, Pronto Invoice, and Pronto Quotes.

His passion for software development goes beyond his skill and training; he also enjoys sharing his knowledge with other developers. He has taught Android development to over 5,000 students through Udemy, and his blog valokafor.com is considered an essential reading for Android developers. Val was also recently named among the first cohort of Realm MVP program because of his active participation in the Realm database community.

Acknowledgments

To Stephanie and Adrianne, for bearing with me for the past 9 months while I wrote this book. My thanks and my love.

To Mark Powers, for his understanding when I missed some of the writing deadlines and for keeping the schedule straight.

To Steve Anglin, for bringing me to Apress.

To everyone who made this book possible, Thank you. It truly feels great to hold one's printed book in one's hands. It's even more awesome the second time around.

Introduction

Welcome to the Kotlin edition of *Learn Android Studio 3*, This book will help you get started in your programming journey with the little green robot. You already bought the book, so you don't need to be convinced that programming for the mobile platform offers a lot of opportunity for software developers. Thank you for buying it, by the way.

Who This Book Is For

The book is aimed at beginning Android programmers, but it isn't for people who are completely new to programming. Ideally, you already are a Java programmer trying to get your feet wet in Android, and you wanna try the Kotlin language (coz all your dev friends told you it was cool). But in case you're not a Java developer or you don't have Android programming experience, don't sweat it. The book is friendly enough—I tried hard to write it that way—and approachable enough such that anyone with a passing knowledge of either C#, JavaScript, C, or C++ will be able to follow the code samples and the concepts presented in this book.

What's Different in the Kotlin Edition

All the code examples and the demo projects are mostly new. They're not a plain Kotlin port of the first edition's examples. I've also added new chapters; here they are:

- Collections

- Generics

- Higher Order Functions

- Broadcast Receivers

Some chapters in the first edition have been split into two or more chapters. I split them so that I can treat the subjects with more depth—for example, "Intents," "SharedPreferences," "Internal Storage," and "Fragments."

Organization and Treatment

The book is divided into two major parts. Chapters 1 to 7 are all about the Kotlin language, and Chapters 8 to 20 are about Android programming.

While you can use it as a reference book, I didn't write it that way. It's not meant as a substitute for the docs in `https://kotlinglang.org` or the Android developer guides `https://developer.android.com`. It's also not meant to be a "Definitive Guide" type of book where you can spend hours or days exploring every nook and cranny. Quite the contrary—I wanted it to be a "get started quick" type of book, like a recipe book, but without losing our grasp on the fundamental concepts.

Android and Kotlin are big subjects; I don't think there exists a "single best way" to present the materials for either of these two. So, I made certain bets on the instructional design. Here they are:

- **Bite-sized concepts**. The troublesome topics are broken down into a series of small steps so that you can solve them in isolation. When you can solve small problems, it gives you confidence to solve bigger ones. This approach helps a beginning programmer to grow in the direction of skill.

- **Conciseness**. I tried to keep each chapter as short as possible, so you can finish it in one sitting. Originally, I wanted each chapter to be a "20-minute read"; that was too ambitious, so, I gave up on it—but still, the chapters are short.

- **Multiple Learning Curves**. The book is about three topics: Android Studio, Android Programming, and Kotlin. Although Kotlin and Android programming may seem to have dedicated chapters for them, techniques on how to use Android Studio (and IntelliJ) are scattered throughout the book.

- **Balance between concept and code**. Admittedly, the treatment is biased (just a little bit) toward code. Programming is not a spectator sport; we learn by doing. Nonetheless, in every chapter, I tried to explain what the fundamental concepts are, what we're trying to do, what problems are we trying to solve, how we might solve those problems, and what does the solution look like—in code. Almost all of the chapters have one or more demo projects in them.

- **Verbose and complete code presentations**. Sometimes (most of the time actually), I presented the full source example, but only one or two lines of it are relevant. I erred on the side of caution (and verbosity) because it's easier for a beginner to understand the relevant codes if he can see it in relation to the whole program. So, you don't have to worry about, "Where do I put this code? Does this go inside function main or inside a class?"

- **Immediacy and coherence**. Like I said, I wanted this to be a "get started quick" or a "recipe" kind of book. So, instead of covering everything, including the kitchen sink, I chose to cover some topics and ignore others. I chose use-cases whose complexities are easy or moderate and covered topics that are only relevant for those use-cases. For example, in the BroadcastReceiver and Intent chapters, I didn't cover LocalBroadcastManager and PendingIntent. Cool as these topics are, they weren't relevant for the use-cases I chose. If I added more use-cases or demo-projects, that would have stretched the length of the chapter. It's a balancing act, you see.

- **Independent demo projects**. I designed them as such so that the demo project could be started (and followed) from scratch. There is no "putting it all together" project in the end. This way, the book can be conveniently used as a reference. If you pick a topic, it's almost self-contained, including the demo project.

In the end, I can only hope that the bets I made will pay off and that you will walk away as a slightly better programmer after reading the book.

Chapter Overviews

Chapter 1: "Getting into Kotlin" introduces the language. It tells you how to setup Kotlin in various ways on the three major platforms: macOS, Linux, and Windows. It also contains instructions on how to create, configure, and run a project in IntelliJ—this is the IDE I used to create all the Kotlin code samples for Chapters 1 through 7.

    Chapter 2: "Kotlin Basics" dives into the language fundamentals of Kotlin. You'll learn the basic building blocks of a Kotlin program (e.g., Strings, control structures, exception handling, basic data types). You'll also see some of Kotlin's features that are very different from Java, like its treatment of nullable and non-nullable types.

Chapter 3: "Functions." There's a whole chapter dedicated to functions because Kotlin's functions have something new up their sleeves. It has all the trimmings of a modern language like default and named parameters, infix functions, and operators; and with Kotlin, we can also create extension functions. Extension functions lets you add behavior to an existing class, without inheriting from it and without changing its source.

Chapter 4: "Working with Types." This chapter deals with object-oriented topics. You'll learn how Kotlin treats interfaces, classes, and access modifiers. We'll also learn about the new *data classes* in Kotlin. It also talks about *object declarations*—it's the replacement for Java's *static* keyword.

Chapter 5: "Lambdas and Higher Order Functions." Now we go to Kotlins's functional programming capabilities. It discusses how to create and use higher-order functions, lambdas, and closures.

Chapter 6: "Collections" walks through the classic collection classes of Java and how to use them in Kotlin.

Chapter 7: "Generics." Using generics in Kotlin isn't that much different from Java. If generics is old hat for you, then most of this chapter will be a review. But try to read through it still because it talks about *reified generics*, which Java doesn't have.

Chapter 8: "Android Studio Introduction and Setup." This chapter talks a bit about Android's history, its technical make-up, and the OS. It also walks you through the installation and setup of Android Studio.

Chapter 9: "Getting Started" gets you grounded on the fundamental concepts about Android programming. It talks about components, what they are, how they are organized, and how they come together in an Android app. In this chapter, you'll learn how the basic workflow of an Android project—how to create a project and run it on an emulator

Chapter 10: "Activities and Layouts." Here, we'll learn how to build a UI. Activity, Layout, and View objects are the building blocks for an Android UI.

Chapter 11: "Event Handling." You'll learn how to react to user-generated events like clicks and longclicks. We'll use some concepts that we learned in Chapters 4 and 5 (inner objects and lambdas) to help us write more compact and succinct event-handling code.

Chapter 12: "Intents." This chapter reviews some fundamental concepts on Android programming, specifically the concept of components, which dovetails to the topic of Intents. You'll learn how to use Intents to launch another Activity and pass data in-and-around Activities.

Chapter 13: "Themes and Menus." This is a short chapter. You'll learn how to add styles/themes to your app. We'll also work with some menus and the ActionBar.

Chapter 14: "Fragments." You'll learn how to use Android Fragments as a more granular composition unit for UI. We'll also see how to use Fragments to address changes in device orientation.

Chapter 15: "Running in the Background." Any non-trivial app will do something substantial like read from a file, write to a file, download something from the network, etc. These activities will likely take more than 16 ms to execute (you'll learn why 16 ms should be the upper limit and why you should not exceed it). When that happens, the user will see and feel "jank." This chapter discusses the various ways on how to run our code in a background thread.

Chapter 16: "Debugging" shows some of the things you can do to debug your apps in Android Studio 3. It goes through a list of the kinds of errors you might encounter while coding and what you can do in Android Studio to respond them.

Chapter 17: "SharedPreferences." When you need to save simple data, you can use the SharedPreferences API. This chapter walks you through detailed examples on how to do that.

Chapter 18: "Internal Storage." Just like in SharedPreferences, you can also store data using the Internal Storage API of Android. This chapter discusses internal and external storage.

Chapter 19: "BroadcastReceivers." Android has a way to make highly decoupled components talk to each other. This chapter talks about how BroadcastReceivers can facilitate messaging for Android components.

Chapter 20: "App Distribution." When you're ready to distribute your app, you'll need to sign it and list it in a marketplace like Google Play. This chapter walks you through the steps on how to do it.

How to Get the Most From This Book

I designed it like a workbook; it's best to use it like that. Most chapters have a "Demo Project" section. There are details on how to create a project—for example, what name should you use for the project, the minimum SDK to target, etc. The reason I included this information is so you can follow the coding exercise.

I used three kinds of blocks in the book: *Examples, Listings,* and *Figures.*

- **Examples** are commands that you would type in a terminal window.

- **Listings** contains program or code listing; it's something that you would type in a program file.

- **Figures** could be screenshots or diagrams. Some of the screenshots are annotated to point out a sequence of steps and how to do them on the IDE. I used Android Studio 3.1 and IntelliJ 2018.2 for the examples in this book; it's possible that by the time you read this book, you'll be using a different or higher version of these tools.

Programmers (mostly) learn by doing. If you work your way through the demo projects, I think the lessons will stick better. Remember that coding is like swimming or driving, you can read as many books as you want on the subjects, but if you don't go in the water or behind the wheel, you won't get anywhere.

Source Code

Source Code for this book can be accessed by clicking the **Download Source Code** button at www.apress.com/9781484239063.

PART I

The Kotlin Language

CHAPTER 1

Getting into Kotlin

What we'll cover:

- An introduction to the Kotlin language

- How to get Kotlin

- Installing Kotlin on macOS, Windows, and Linux

- Running a Kotlin program in the command line

- Creating and running a project in IntelliJ IDEA

This chapter introduces the Kotlin language and goes into some details on how to set up a development environment. You will find instructions on how to install Kotlin on macOS, Windows, and Linux. You'll also find instructions on how to install a Kotlin environment using just bare-bones command line. Each developer gravitates to certain kind of setup, and yours truly is not an exception. Here's the setup that I've used throughout the book:

- IntelliJ 2018 running on macOS (High Sierra). I used this throughout chapters 1 to 7

- Android Studio 3 on macOS (High Siera). I used this for the rest of the book

You don't need to follow my exact setup. We've taken pains to ensure that the instructions in this book works in Linux and Windows just as well as they do in macOS. Also, when I say Linux, I don't mean all the distributions of Linux. The fact is, I tested these codes only in Lubuntu 17. Why? Because that's the Linux distro that I'm most familiar with. I believe that most readers of this book (who use Linux) will also be familiar with this Linux distro (or any of its close cousins).

© Ted Hagos 2018
T. Hagos, *Learn Android Studio 3 with Kotlin*, https://doi.org/10.1007/978-1-4842-3907-0_1

Android Studio 3 and IntelliJ works on Windows 7, 8, and 10 (32- and 64-bit), but I only tested the exercises on Windows 10 64-bit—this is the only machine I have access to; and I believe that most readers who use Windows use this setup as well.

Lastly, let's discuss the JDK version. At the time of writing, JDK 10 is in early access. So the choices for JDK version was 8 or 9 (since JDK 7 ended its life sometime in 2015). I went with 9—no special reason, I think 8 would have worked just as well.

About Kotlin

Kotlin is a new language that targets the Java platform; its programs run on the JVM (Java Virtual Machine), which puts it in the company of languages like Groovy, Scala, Jython, and Clojure, to name a few.

Kotlin is from JetBrains, the creators of IntelliJ, PyCharm, WebStorm, ReSharper, and other great development tools. In 2011, JetBrains unveiled Kotlin; the following year, they open-sourced Kotlin under the Apache 2 license. At Google I/O 2017, Google announced first-class support for Kotlin on the Android platform. If you're wondering where the name Kotlin came from, it's the name of an island near St. Petersburg, where most of the Kotlin team members are located. According to Andrey Breslav of JetBrains, Kotlin was named after an island, just like Java was named after the Indonesian island of Java. However, you might remember that the history of the Java language contains references that it was named after the coffee, rather than the island.

Kotlin has many characteristics and capabilities as a language, and we have the whole first part of this book to explore those, but here are a few things that makes it interesting.

- **Like Java, it's object-oriented**. So, all those long hours you've invested in Java's OOP and design pattern won't go to waste. Kotlin classes, interfaces, and generics look and behave quite a lot like those of Java. This is definitely a strength because, unlike other JVM languages (e.g., Scala), Kotlin doesn't look too foreign. It doesn't alienate Java programmers; instead, it allows them to build on their strengths.

- **Statically and strongly typed**. Another area that Kotlin shares with Java is the type system. It also uses static and strong typing. However, unlike in Java, you don't have to always declare the type of the variable before you use it. Kotlin uses *type inference*.

- **Less ceremonious than Java**. We don't (always) have to write a class; top-level functions are OK. We don't need to explicitly write getters and setters for data objects; there are language features in Kotlin, which allows us to do away with such boiler-plate codes. Also, the natural way of writing codes in Kotlin prevents us from ever assigning *null* to a variable. If you want to explicitly allow a value to be *null*, you have to do so in a deliberate way.

- **It's a functional language**. Functions are not just a named collection of statements; you can use them anywhere you might use a variable. You can pass functions from a parameter input to other functions, and you can even return functions from other functions. This way coding allows for a different way of abstraction.

- **Interoperability with Java**. Kotlin can use Java libraries, and you can use it from Java programs as well. This lowers the barrier to entry in Kotlin; the interoperability with Java makes the decision to start a new project using Kotlin a less daunting enterprise.

There are many reasons to use Kotlin in your next project, but there are also counter-arguments to it. We won't list the pros and cons of why you should or why you shouldn't use Kotlin in your next project; but I'll discuss one reason why I would advise you to slow down and pause before you get all gung-ho about it.

It's still relatively new. Some people are convinced that it's approaching its "peak of inflated expectation" and will soon enter the "trough of disillusionment." Their main argument is that if you bet on Kotlin right now, you'll be saddled with learning curve problems and you'll be obligated to maintain that codebase—even if Kotlin disappears in a puff of smoke. In other words, you might carry it as a technical debt.

Kotlin's adoption will also come at some cost. You'll have to train your team on how to use it. No matter how experienced your team is, they will definitely lose some speed along the way—and that's a project management concern. Also, because Kotlin is new, there is no "Effective Kotlin" guide post yet, while Java programmers will always have their "Effective Java."

It will all boil down to your bet. If you bet that Kotlin will go the distance instead of quietly disappearing in the dark, then the bet would have paid off. If you're wrong about the bet, then you go down the arduous road of maintaining the codebase of a defunct language—a technical debt. Either that or you rework it back to Java.

Google has officially supported the language in Android Studio, and more and more developers are getting on the bandwagon. Adoption is growing. These are good signs that Kotlin won't go down quietly and might actually go the distance. Plus, it's a cool language.

Note   "Peak of inflated expectation" and "Trough of disillusionment" are part of the the "Hype cycle." The **hype cycle** is a branded graphical presentation developed and used by the American research, advisory, and information technology firm Gartner, for representing the maturity, adoption, and social application of specific technologies. You can read more about it at `https://gtnr.it/cycleofhype`.

Let's continue and build ourselves a dev environment.

Installing the Java SDK

Before we can use Kotlin, we need to install the JDK. If you already have an existing setup of the Java development kit, you can skip this section and jump to the next one (Installing Kotlin). The JDK installer is available for Windows, Linux, and macOS. You can download the currently stable version from the Oracle site, `http://bit.ly/java9download`.[1]

Figure 1-1 shows the download page for Oracle JDK. Choose the installer appropriate for your platform, then click the "Accept License Agreement" to proceed.

---

[1]Available from `http://www.oracle.com/technetwork/java/javase/downloads/jdk9-downloads-3848520.html`

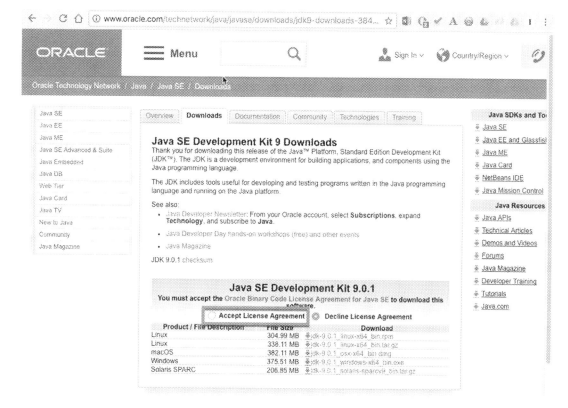

Figure 1-1. *Oracle JDK download page*

Installing on macOS

To install the JDK on macOS, double-click the downloaded **dmg** file and follow the prompts. The installer takes care of updating the system path, so you don't need to perform any further action after the installation.

When you're done with the installation, you can test if the JDK has been installed by launching the "Terminal.app" and trying out the Java command (*see* Listing 1-1).

Listing 1-1. Test the JDK tools on a macOS Terminal

```
$ java -version
$ javac -version
```

You'll know that you've installed the JDK without problems if the terminal outputs the version of java and javac as shown in Figure 1-2.

```
ted in ~
  java -version
java version "9.0.1"
Java(TM) SE Runtime Environment (build 9.0.1+11)
Java HotSpot(TM) 64-Bit Server VM (build 9.0.1+11, mixed mode)

ted in ~
  javac -version
javac 9.0.1

ted in ~
```

Figure 1-2. *java and javac on the Terminal.app*

Installing on Windows 10

You can install Android Studio 3 in Windows 7/8/10 (32- and 64-bit); but for the purpose of this book, I only used Windows 10 64-bit.

To install the JDK on Windows, double-click the downloaded zipped file, and follow the prompts. Unlike in macOS, you must perform extra configuration after the setup. You need to (1) include java/bin in your system path and (2) include a *CLASSPATH* definition in the *Environment Variables* of Windows. Table 1-1 walks you through the steps on how to do this.

Table 1-1. *JDK Configuration in Windows*

1	Include JAVA_HOME/bin to the system path	1. Click **Start ➤ Control Panel ➤ System** 2. Click **Advanced ➤ Environment Variables.** There are two boxes for variables, the upper box reads "User variables" and the lower box reads "System variables," the system PATH will be in the "System variables" box. 3. Add the location of the bin folder to the system PATH variable. 4. It is typical for the PATH variable to look like this: `C:\WINDOWS\system32;C:\WINDOWS;C:\Program Files\Java\jdk-9\bin;`
2	Create a *CLASSPATH* definition in Windows *Environment Variables*	While the **Environment Variables** window is still open, click the "New" button on the "User variables" section. Another dialog window will pop up with two text boxes that will allow you to add a new variable. Use the values below to populate the textboxes. 1. Name ➤ CLASSPATH 2. Value ➤ `C:\WINDOWS\system32;C:\WINDOWS;C:\Program Files\Java\jdk-9\jre\lib\rt.jar;`

Close the Environment Variables window and get a *cmd* window so we can test whether our changes have taken effect. When the cmd window is open, type the commands as shown in Listing 1-2.

Listing 1-2. Test the JDK tools on a Windows cmd shell

```
C:\Users\yourname>java -version
C:\Users\yourname>javac -version
```

If the cmd shell shows you the version of java and javac, then you have successfully installed and configured the JDK. If, on the other hand, you saw an error message (e.g., "Bad command or file name"), it means that JAVA_HOME\bin is still not part of the system path. You should revisit Table 1-1 and recheck your entries, then retest.

Installing on Linux

If you are a Linux user, you may have seen the tar ball and rpm options on the download, you may use that and install it like you would install any other software on your Linux platform or you may install the JDK from the repositories (see Listing 1-3). This instruction applies to Debian and its derivatives (e.g., Ubuntu, Mint, etc.).

Listing 1-3. Installing the JDK in Ubuntu Using a PPA

```
sudo add-apt-repository ppa:webupd8team/java
sudo apt-get update
sudo apt-get install oracle-java9-installer
sudo update-alternatives --config java
```

When the download finishes, you can test the installation by trying out the java and javac tools from the command line (see Listing 1-4). Open your favorite terminal emulator (e.g., *xterm, terminator, gnome-terminal, lxterminal*, etc.).

Listing 1-4. Test the JDK Tools on Linux

```
$ java -version
$ javac -version
```

If the install was successful, you should be able to see the version of java and javac in your system. Once the JDK is up and running, we can now get Kotlin.

Installing Kotlin

There are a couple of ways to get started in Kotlin coding. You can use the online IDE, which is the quickest because it won't require you to install anything. You may also try to download an IDE that has a plug-in for Kotlin (e.g., IntelliJ, Android Studio, or Eclipse). Finally, you can download the command line tools for Kotlin. If you don't want to install a full-blown IDE and simply use your trusty favorite editor, you can certainly do that with the command line tools. We won't explore each and every one of these options, but we'll take a look at the command line tools and IntelliJ.

Note   This book is about Android Studio, so you might be wondering why we won't use Android Studio to try out Kotlin. That's because this part of the book is about Kotlin only and not about Android programming (yet). I thought it best to focus more on the language and not be hampered by Android-specific topics when we do some coding exercises. Android Studio is based on IntelliJ anyway, so any IDE techniques we learn in this part of the book should carry over nicely when we get to part 2.

Installing the Command Line Tools

Even if you opt for the command line tools, there are a couple of choices for installation method. We can install it by (1) downloading a zipped file; (2) using SDKMAN if your OS and tooling supports it; or (3) using HomeBrew or MacPorts if you are on macOS. You only need to pick which one of these methods you are most comfortable with and go with that.

HomeBrew or MacPort

If you are on macOS and already using either brew or port, see either Listing 1-5 or 1-6 for the terminal commands to get Kotlin.

Listing 1-5. Install Kotlin Using HomeBrew

```
$ brew update
$ brew install kotlin
```

Listing 1-6. Install Kotlin Using MacPorts

```
$ sudo port install kotlin
```

Using a Zipped Installer

If you go to the Kotlin website, `http://kotlinglang.org` then "learn" ➤ "tutorials" ➤ "getting started" ➤ "working with the command line compiler", you'll find a web page[2] that might look like the one shown in Figure 1-3. The zipped installer can be downloaded by following the link "GitHub releases" (also shown in Figure 1-3).

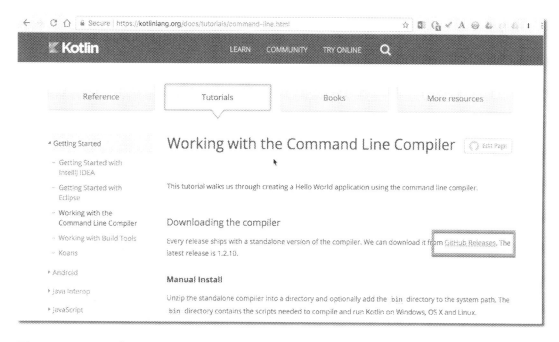

Figure 1-3. *Kotlin command line compiler page*

The link should take you to the GitHub page of JetBrains/Kotlin[3] (Figure 1-4). At the time of writing, Kotlin was on version 1.2.10; it might be a different version by the time you are reading this, but just download the latest stable version.

---

[2]Working with the command line compiler: `https://kotlinlang.org/docs/tutorials/command-line.html`

[3]JetBrains/Kotlin GitHub page: `https://github.com/JetBrains/kotlin/releases/tag/v1.2.10`

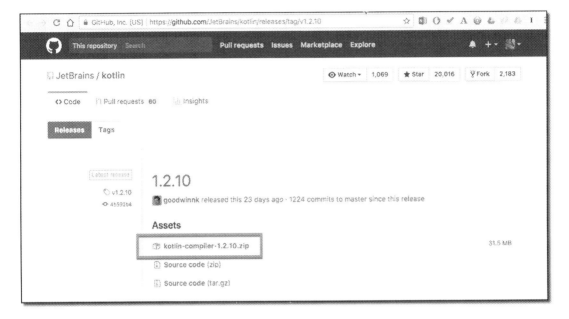

Figure 1-4. *GitHub page for the installer zipped file*

When the download finishes, unzip the installer file and put it somewhere in your system—preferably, a directory where you have read, write, and execute privileges. The file should unzip to a folder named "kotlinc". Next thing to do is to add the kotlinc/bin folder to the system path variable. The following sections will demonstrate how to do this on macOS, Linux, and Windows.

macOS and Linux

Copy the downloaded zipped file to your home directory and unzip it there. Listing 1-7 shows the command.

Listing 1-7. Unzip Kotlin Installer

```
$ cd ~
$ unzip ~/kotlin-compiler-1.2.10.zip
```

> **Note**   The unzip command is available in macOS by default, but for Linux systems, you might have to get it from the repositories first. Listing 1-8 shows the command on how to pull it from the repositories.

Listing 1-8. Getting the Unzip Tool

```
$ sudo apt get update
$ sudo apt-get install unzip
```

The installer file should unzip to a folder named "kotlinc", as shown in Figure 1-5.

```
ted in ~
 → unzip kotlin-compiler-1.2.10.zip
Archive:  kotlin-compiler-1.2.10.zip
   creating: kotlinc/
   creating: kotlinc/bin/
   creating: kotlinc/lib/
   creating: kotlinc/license/
   creating: kotlinc/license/third_party/
   creating: kotlinc/license/third_party/testdata/
  inflating: kotlinc/build.txt
  inflating: kotlinc/lib/allopen-compiler-plugin.jar
  inflating: kotlinc/lib/android-extensions-compiler.jar
  inflating: kotlinc/lib/android-extensions-runtime.jar
  inflating: kotlinc/lib/annotations-13.0.jar
  inflating: kotlinc/lib/kotlin-annotation-processing.jar
  inflating: kotlinc/lib/kotlin-annotations-android.jar
  inflating: kotlinc/lib/kotlin-annotations-jvm-sources.jar
  inflating: kotlinc/lib/kotlin-annotations-jvm.jar
  inflating: kotlinc/lib/kotlin-ant.jar
  inflating: kotlinc/lib/kotlin-compiler.jar
  inflating: kotlinc/lib/kotlin-daemon-client.jar
  inflating: kotlinc/lib/kotlin-jslib-sources.jar
```

Figure 1-5. *Unzipping the Kotlin installer*

Before we can use the command line tools, we need to add the "kotlinc/bin" folder to the system path variable as shown in Listing 1-9.

Listing 1-9. Adding kotlinc/bin to the System Path

```
$ export PATH=~/kotlinc/bin:$PATH
```

Press ENTER and the kotlinc command should now work. You can add the line shown in Listing 1-9 to your login script so that the Kotlin tools are available every time you open a terminal window.

Windows 10

Copy the Kotlin installer zipped file to your home directory and unzip it there. Use your favorite archive tool for unzipping. It should unzip to the following folder: `C:\Users\yourname\kotlinc`. Inside the kotlinc folder is the bin folder, which contains the various script and batch files that we need to use for compilation. This bin folder is what we need to add the Windows system path.

To add the kotlinc\bin folder to the system path, click the Windows **Start** button ➤ **Control Panel** ➤ **System**. Once the System dialog opens, click **Advanced** ➤ **Environment Variables**. There are two boxes for variables; the upper box reads "User variables" and the lower box reads "System variables". The system `PATH` will be in the "System variables" box. Append `kotlinc\bin` the `PATH` variable. Close the system dialog box to save your changes.

Using SDKMAN

SDKMAN can be used on macOS, Linux, Cygwin (Windows), FreeBSD, and other UNIX systems. If you have this already as part of your toolchain, you can use it to get the Kotlin compiler. If you don't have SDKMAN yet, it is simple to install. See Listing 1-10 to install SDKMAN.

Important   Before you can install SDKMAN from the command line, you will need to get the `curl` tool. If you don't have it yet, use your platforms package manager to get `curl`.

Listing 1-10. Installing SDKMAN From the Command Line

```
$ curl -s "https://get.sdkman.io" | bash
```

Follow the on-screen instructions to complete the installation. You will need to close the current terminal window and launch another one because the SDKMAN installer made changes to the login script. In order for those changes to take effect, you will need to open a new terminal window. When that's done, we can now install kotlin. See Listing 1-11 for the installation command.

Listing 1-11. Installing Kotlin via SDKMAN

```
$ sdk install kotlin
```

Coding With the Command Line Tools

Whichever way you chose to install the command line tools, by now you should already have a working Kotlin compiler. To try it out, get a terminal window and enter the command kotlinc. This will change your terminal prompt to a triple chevron (greater than sign); see Listing 1-12.

Listing 1-12. Kotlin REPL

```
$ kotlinc
Welcome to Kotlin version 1.2.10 (JRE 9.0.1+11)
Type :help for help, :quit for quit
>>>
```

This is the Kotlin REPL—short for Read, Eval, Print, Loop. It executes Kotlin commands interactively and shows you the results immediately. If you have used the console feature of modern browsers to enter JavaScript commands before, this is very similar to that. The REPL is a good way to learn the language interactively. It's also very useful during development because it allows you to try out expressions and statements without having to go through the full write-compile-run cycle. You might want to try out a couple of expressions and statements (see Listing 1-13).

Listing 1-13. Simple Expressions

```
>>> 5 * 3
15
>>> println("Hello there")
Hello there
for (i in 1 . . 3) {
. . .println(i)
. . .}
1
2
3
>>>
```

The REPL is very useful for trying out statements and even short snippets like the one shown in Listing 1-13, but if you need to try out longer programs, it will be more convenient to write it in a program file, compile, and run it, as you would Java programs. Let's try to see what that looks like in Kotlin.

First, create a file and name it "hello.kt"—Kotlin source files have an extension of ".kt". The contents of hello.kt is shown in Listing 1-14.

Listing 1-14. hello.kt

```kotlin
fun main(args: Array<String>) {
  print("Hello")
}
```

Kotlin has similarities with Java, so Listing 1-14 may look familiar, but you will also quickly notice some obvious things, so let's address those right now.

- **There is no class construct**. Kotlin doesn't need a class to execute function. The function, as shown in Listing 1-14, is known as a top-level function; the main function is special because, like the `public static void main()` of Java, the `fun main()` of Kotlin is the entry point of the application. The runtime will look for this function when you run a Kotlin file.

- **Function main has a slight different syntax**. Functions are defined with the keyword `fun`. The type declaration comes after the identifier (`args`); you'll get used to it. Also, Kotlin doesn't have a special syntax to define an array. Arrays are just types in Kotlin.

- **Function main has no return value**. Actually, it has, we just didn't write it in the example. The default return value for a function is `Unit`; it's like void in Java.

- **There is no semi-colon**. These are not necessary anymore.

The next step is to compile and run our source file. Listing 1-15 shows the commands to manage this.

Listing 1-15. Compile and Run hello.kt

```
kotlin hello.kt -include-runtime -d hello.jar
java -jar hello.jar
```

If you managed to type everything correctly as shown in the earlier listings and examples, you should see the "Hello World" message in your screen.

If you feel that command-line tools are not to your liking and you'd rather use a more feature-rich programming environment, you can try other IDEs like Eclipse, IntelliJ, or Android Studio 3 (AS3). We'll cover the installation and use of both IntelliJ and AS3 in this book. The next section will walk you through the setup of IntelliJ IDEA.

Installing IntelliJ

JetBrains created Kotlin, so as you would imagine it has excellent support for it. Android Studio is based on JetBrain's IntelliJ IDEA CE (Community Edition); however, Android Studio is free and OSS and is maintained by Google, not JetBrains.

We could have used AS3 even for the first part of this book; however, doing that would require that we deal with both Kotlin and Android components at the same time. I chose not to do it and instead focus solely on Kotlin. AS3 is based on IntelliJ IDEA anyway, so whatever learnings and skills we'll acquire on IntelliJ will commute nicely to AS3.

You can download IntellijJ IDEA from the JetBrains website (`http://www.jetbrains.com`) then come up to **tools** and come down to **IntelliJ IDEA** (see Figure 1-6). It will take you to a page where you can choose the appropriate installer for your platform. You will also be able to choose if you want to download the "Ultimate" or the "Community" edition. We will download the community edition.

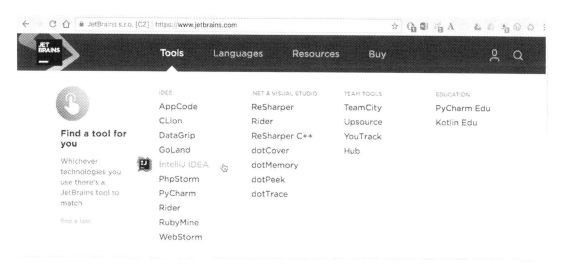

Figure 1-6. *IntelliJ IDEA download page*

If you are on **Windows**, you need to:

1. Double-click the *ideaIC.exe* that you downloaded

2. Follow the on-screen prompts to complete the installation

For **macOS**, do the following:

1. Double-click the *ideaIC.dmg* that you downloaded

2. Copy IntelliJ IDEA to the Applications folder

3. Run IntelliJ IDEA.

For **Linux**, the installation instruction is as follows:

1. Copy the tar.gz installer file into a directory where you have read, write, and execute privileges; for our purposes, we'll copy it into the home folder (see Listing 1-16).

Listing 1-16. Copy IntelliJ Installer to Your Home Folder

```
$ cd
$ cp ~/Downloads/ideaIC-2017.3.2.tar.gz .
```

2. Unpack the ideaIC.tar.gz, as shown in Listing 1-17.

Listing 1-17. Untar the Installer

```
tar –xzvf ideaIC.tar.gz
```

3. Add the ideaIC/bin to the system path, as shown in Listing 1-18.

Listing 1-18. Add ideaIC/bin to the System Path

```
$ export PATH=~/ideaIC-2017.3.2/bin:$PATH:.
```

4. Start IntelliJ IDEA by running idea.sh script, as shown in Listing 1-19.

Listing 1-19. Start idea.sh

```
$ sh idea.sh
```

Creating a Project

Launch IntelliJ if you haven't done so yet. It starts with a welcome screen, as shown in Figure 1-7. To get started, let's create a project.

Figure 1-7. *Welcome to IntellJ IDEA*

Clicking the "Create New Project" takes us to the "New Project" window (shown in Figure 1-8). Choose "Kotlin/JVM" and then click the "Next" button.

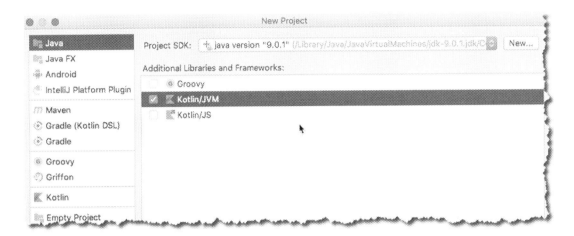

Figure 1-8. *New Kotlin/JVM Project*

This leads us to the second window of the "New Project" wizard where we need to enter some information, but most of them are pre-filled with default entries already, and we can simply accept the defaults. We do need to provide the "Project Name", unless you'd like to name your project "untitled" (which is the default value of the Project Name field—probably not a good idea).

In Figure 1-9, I used "kotlinproject" as the Project Name. I didn't change the default project location, which is "IdeaProjects" under the home folder. I also did not make any changes to the "Project SDK", which was detected by IntelliJ during the time of installation. To finish the project creation wizard, click the "Finish" button.

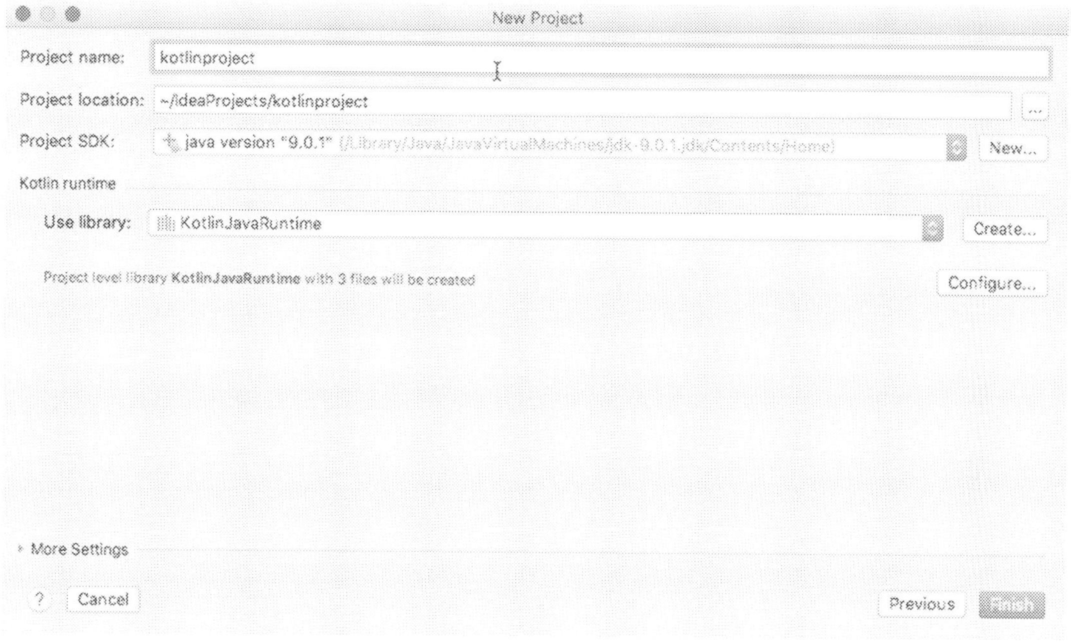

Figure 1-9. *New Project*

You'll be shown the "Tip of the Day" window (Figure 1-10) the very first time you launch IntelliJ. Tips are very useful in learning the capabilities of the IDE, but I prefer that they show up only when I summon them and not really pop up every time I launch the IDE. You can disable the "Tip of the Day" window showing up during launch time by unchecking the "Show tips on startup." Let's close it for now.

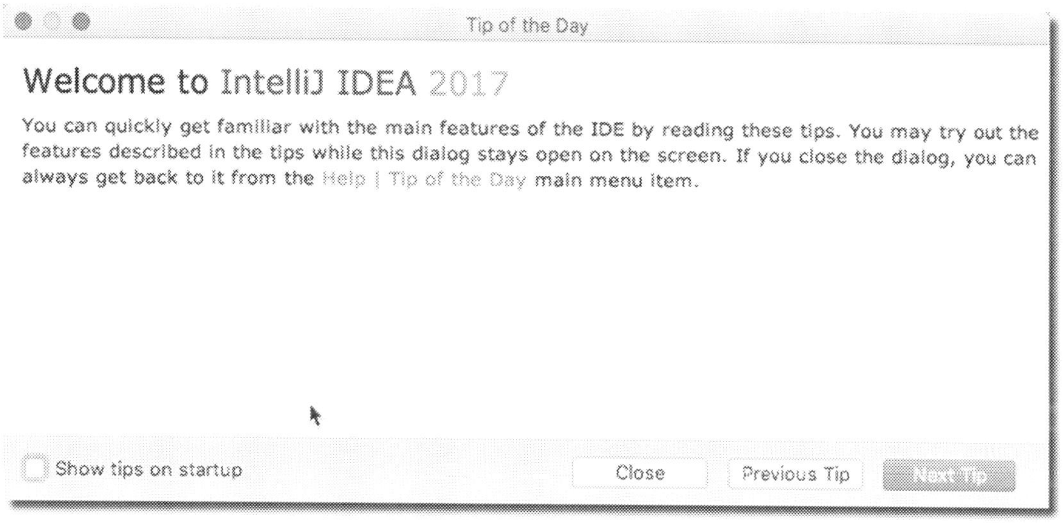

Figure 1-10. *Tip of the day*

When the tip of the day dialog is dismissed, we can see more fully our newly created project (Figure 1-11). The left-hand side of the IDE shows the "Project Tool window"; it doesn't have much right now because we haven't created anything yet.

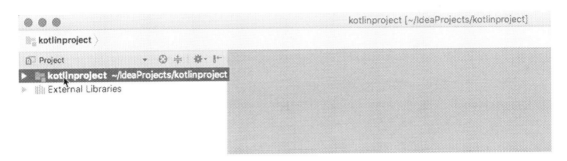

Figure 1-11. *Our Kotlin project in IntelliJ*

The Project Tool window allows us to change "views." All of the views show the same project, but each view arranges the contents a bit differently. You can change the view of the Project Tool window by clicking the dropdown button (see Figure 1-12). You should try out a couple of the views to familiarize yourself with them.

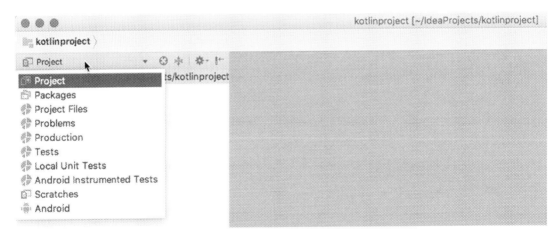

Figure 1-12. *Project tool window, Views*

For the rest of this section, we'll use the "Project" view. This view shows our files in a tree-like structure, pretty much like the file manager in your OS (see Figure 1-12). You can drill down and expand to see the contents of the folders, as shown in Figure 1-13.

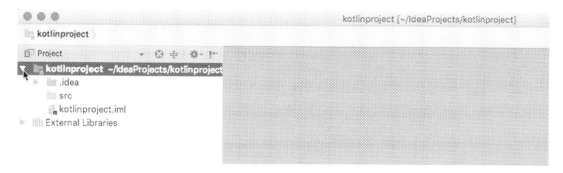

Figure 1-13. *Project tool window. Project view*

The "src" folder (short for "source") is where we will place our Kotlin source files. Right-click on the src folder and choose New ➤ Kotlin File/Class, as shown in Figure 1-14.

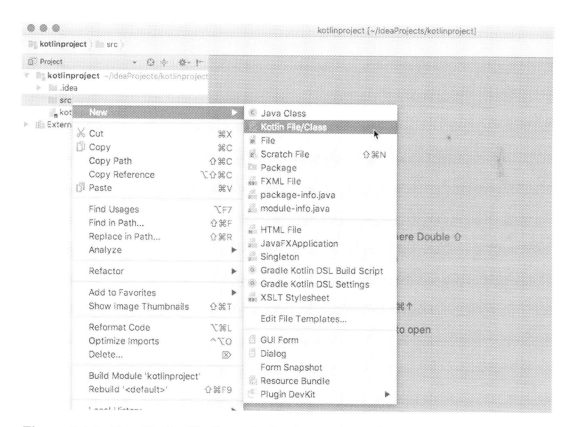

Figure 1-14. *New Kotlin file, from the Project tool window*

We'll create a Kotlin file for now and name it "Hello"; we don't have to write the ".kt" extension the Name field (see Figure 1-15)—the extension will be automatically added for us. Make sure that on the "Kind" field of the dialog window, the "File" option is selected (see Figure 1-15). Click the OK button to create the file.

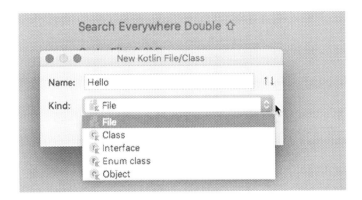

Figure 1-15. *New Kotlin File*

When the source file is created, you will see it under the src folder in the Project Tool window, and it will also be opened in the Main Editor window (see Figure 1-16).

Figure 1-16. *Hello.kt*

IntelliJ has excellent code hinting and autocomplete capabilities. When it recognizes something that you are typing, it tries to be helpful by giving you suggestions and hints (see Figure 1-15). As soon as you type enough character patterns that may be Kotlin keywords or constructs, the IDE offers suggestions. You can accept the currently suggested option (highlighted on pop-up window, shown in Figure 1-15) or use the mouse or arrow key to choose other auto-completion options.

The full code listing for this example is shown in Listing 1-20.

Listing 1-20. Hello.kt

```kotlin
fun main(args: Array<String>) {
  println("Hello World")
}
```

The next step is to run this program; you can manage this by invoking the Run menu on the main menu bar of IntelliJ. The main menu bar sits on top of the IDE, the top-level options are File, Edit, View all the way to Help. From the main menu bar, click **Run ➤ Run**. You will notice that there are two Run options on the main Run menu and that the first Run option is greyed out. Choose the other Run option, which is located four items down from the top. The first Run option is greyed out because we haven't defined any runtime configuration for the project. We could have edited the configuration and supplied the name of the runtime class, but we don't have to do it. Choosing the second run option pops out a dialog window (see Figure 1-17) and will ask us for the name of the runtime class for the current project. "HelloKt" is the class we will choose as the runtime class for this project.

Note   The name of our source file is "Hello.kt" but the Kotlin compiler will not generate "Hello.class"; instead, it will generate the byte code "HelloKt.class". You should keep this in mind when working with Kotlin class files.

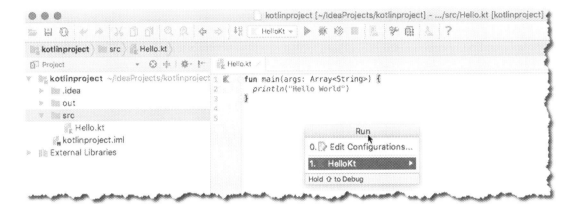

Figure 1-17. *Running Hello.kt*

The IDE will compile "Hello.kt" into "HelloKt.class" and run afterward. The results will be displayed in the "Run" tool window (see Figure 1-18).

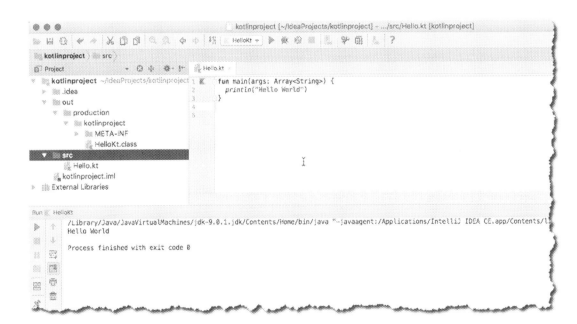

Figure 1-18. *Result of Running Hello.kt*

Now that we've successfully run a top-level function, let's add a class to the app and do a more object-oriented version of the code sample. To add a class, right-click the "src" folder on the Project tool window (Figure 1-19) and choose **New ➤ Kotlin File/Class**.

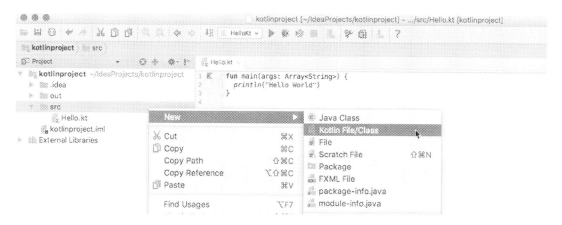

Figure 1-19. *Adding a new File/Class to the project*

When the "New Kotlin File/Class" dialog window pops up, choose "Class" (Figure 1-20); let's name it "Greeter".

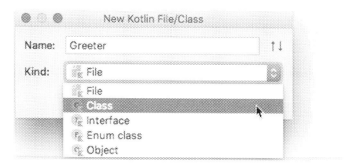

Figure 1-20. *New Kotlin class*

Edit the Greeter class on the main editor window (Figure 1-21).

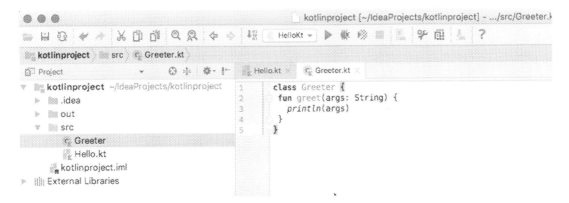

Figure 1-21. *Greeter class*

Then edit Hello.kt as shown in Figure 1-22. After making the changes, run "Hello.kt" again. From the main menu bar, **Run ➤ Run**; alternatively, you can use Shift + F10 to run the code.

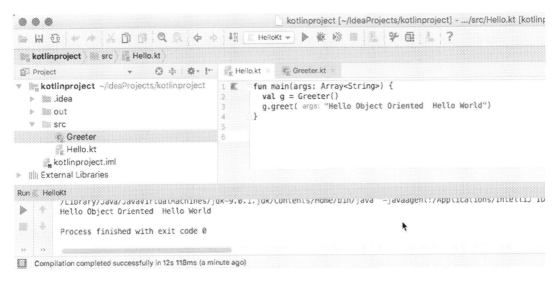

Figure 1-22. *Running main with the Greeter class*

Figure 1-21 shows the output of our updated code(s). That concludes all the coding activities for this chapter. As you can probably tell by now, IntelliJ has excellent support for the Kotlin language; you don't have to use it if you prefer to code Kotlin programs using a different editor. But if you choose to use it, we might as well take a quick tour of the IDE so we can use it better. That's what the next section is all about.

The IntelliJ IDE

Figure 1-23 shows the various parts of the IDE. You need to have an open project for you to see something similar on your desktop.

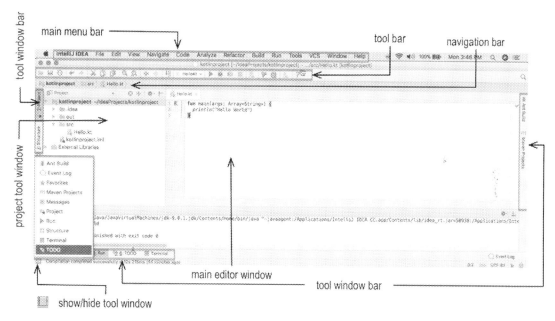

Figure 1-23. *IntelliJ IDEA IDE*

Table 1-2 discusses the parts of the IDE, as it relates to Figure 1-22.

Table 1-2. *IntelliJ IDE*

Main Menu bar	There are many ways to accomplish any task in the IDE; you can use the various keyboard shortcuts or the context menus, but the most comprehensive means of navigation will be on the main menu bar. This bar sits on the very top of the IDE.
Tool Window bar	The tool window bar runs along the perimeter of the IDE window. It contains the individual buttons you need to activate specific tool windows.
Show/hide tool window	This is a fast shortcut to view the various tool windows in IDEA. The tool windows can also be viewed or hidden from the main menu bar, **View ➤ Tool Windows.**
Main Editor window	This is the most prominent window, and it has the most screen real estate. The editor window is where you can create and modify project files and source files.
Tool bar	The tool bar lets you do a wide range of actions (e.g., save files, run the app, open the AVD manager, open the SDK manager, undo, redo actions, etc.).
Navigation bar	It allows you to navigate the project files. This is just a more compact view of the "Project files" window. It's a horizontally arranged collection of arrow boxes that resembles some sort of breadcrumb navigation that you can find on some websites. You can open your project files either through the navigation bar or the project tool window.
Project tool window	Shows you the files in your project. If you want to open a particular file, double-click that file from this window and it will be opened in the main editor window. You can also use context menus on the items in this window. Context menus allows for alternative ways to accomplish task in the IDE (e.g., adding a class file, running codes, debugging, etc.).

Chapter Summary

- Kotlin is the newest programming language for Android, and it has first-class support on Android Studio 3.

- There are many ways to install the Kotlin command line compiler and runtime on macOS, Linux, and Windows.

- Various IDEs have support for the Kotlin language; on some of them, you'll have to get a plug-in, and on some, it's supported out of the box.

- Kotlin looks similar to Java, but it also has differences.

- IntelliJ has excellent support for Kotlin—well, JetBrains created Kotlin after all.

In the next chapter, we'll look at the following:

- Program elements (e.g., literals, variables, expressions, keywords, operators, etc.) —all kinds of stuff that makes up our code

- What types of data can we use in Kotlin

- Why is there a Nullable type in Kotlin, and what is it in the first place?

- Control structures, so that you can loop and branch

- Exception handling and why you don't have to write try-catch anymore in Kotlin (spoilers)

CHAPTER 2

Kotlin Basics

What we'll cover:

- Program elements

- Basic types

- Immutability

- Strings

- Nullable types

- Control structures

- Exception handling

Kotlin isn't all that different from Java. While it introduced quite a few features, you'll find that Kotlin and Java are more similar than they are different. This is good news to Java programmers because it means the learning curve for Kotlin isn't that steep.

You'll need to get used to a few new things, like expressions and statements in Kotlin (they are quite the reverse from Java; e.g., assignments are statements in Kotlin but they are expressions in Java). In this chapter, we'll cover some Kotlin basics that we can use as foundation knowledge in the coming chapters.

Program Elements

When learning a new language, a proper language, like French, Spanish, etc., you'll probably start with parts of speech and the rules that govern them. It'd be easier to approach a language if we had some basic understanding of how its parts come together. A Kotlin program contains literals, variables, expression, keywords, and a whole lot of other things, we'll explore some of them in this section.

© Ted Hagos 2018
T. Hagos, *Learn Android Studio 3 with Kotlin*, https://doi.org/10.1007/978-1-4842-3907-0_2

Literals

Kotlin provides literals for the basic types (numbers, character, Boolean, String).

Listing 2-1. Literal Examples

```
var intLiteral = 5
var doubleLiteral = .02
var stringLiteral = "Hello"
var charLiteral = '1'
var boolLiteral = true
```

In Listing 2-1, the values `5`, `.02`, `"Hello"`, `'1'`, and `true` are literals of Integer, Double, String, Character, and Boolean types, respectively.

Variables

A variable is something that we use to manipulate data or, more precisely, a value. Values are things that you can store, manipulate, print, push, or pull from the network. For us to be able to work with values, we need to put them inside variables. A variable in Kotlin is created by declaring an identifier using the `var` keyword followed by the type, like in the statement

```
var foo: Int
```

In this statement, `foo` is the identifier and `Int` is the type. Kotlin specifies types by placing it to the right of the identifier and is separated from it by a colon.

Now that the variable is declared, we can assign a value to it, like so:

```
foo = 10
```

and then, use it in a function, like the following:

```
println(foo)
```

We can declare and define variables on the same line, like in Java. Here's the *var foo* example again.

```
var foo: Int = 10
println(foo)
```

We can still shorten the assignment statement above by omitting the type (Int). See the sample code:

```
var foo = 10
println(foo)
```

We don't always have to declare or write the type of the variables; Kotlin is smart enough to figure out the type when you assign a literal value to variable; it's called *type inference*. On the occasions that we explicitly tell Kotlin the type of variable, notice that it is on the right side of the variable name (foo), while in Java, it's the other way around, the variable type is on the left side of the identifier. The reason Kotlin did not follow the Java convention of putting the type to the left of the identifier is because in Kotlin, we don't always write the *type*.

```
var foo = 10 // compiler knows 10 is an integer literal
var boo = .02 // double literal makes boo a double type
```

Kotlin uses another keyword to declare variables, the val keyword. Variables declared with this keyword can be initialized only once within the execution block where they were defined. That makes them effectively constants; think of val as the equivalent of the final keyword in Java—once you initialize it to a value, you can't change it anymore, they're *immutable*. While variables that were created using var are *mutable*, they can be changed as many times as you want.

Val variables are declared and initialized just like *var* variables:

```
val a = 10 // declaration and initialization on the same line
```

They can also be declared and initialized at a later time, like the statements here:

```
val a: Int
a = 10
```

Just remember that variables that are declared with the val keyword are final and cannot be re-assigned once you've initialized them to a value. The code snippet here will not work:

```
val boo = "Hello"
boo = "World" // boo already has a value
```

If you think you need to change the value of the variable boo at a later time, change the declaration from val to var.

IntelliJ Tip   If you try to re-assign the value of a variable that was declared using the *val* keyword, IntelliJ will give you enough visual hints that "val cannot be reassigned" even before you try to compile the code.

Expressions and Statements

An expression is a combination of operators, functions, literal values, variables, or constants and always resolves to a value. It also can be part of a more complex expression. A statement can contain expressions, but in itself, a statement doesn't resolve to a value. It cannot be part of other statements. It's always a top-level element in its enclosing block.

For the most part, what you learned in Java about expressions and statements holds true in Kotlin, but there are slight differences. As we go further along, I'll point out the differences between Java and Kotlin when it comes to statements and expressions. Some of these differences are:

Assignments are **expressions in Java,** but they are **statements in Kotlin**. That means you cannot pass assignment operations as argument to loop statements like *while*. See Listing 2-2.

Listing 2-2. Assignment Operation As Argument to While

```
while ((rem = a % b) != 0) {
 a = b
 b = rem
}
println(b)
```

Kotlin won't let you compile because the while statement expects an expression and assignments are not expressions. To make the previous code example (Listing 2-2) work in Kotlin, you'll have to write it another way, as shown in Listing 2-3.

Listing 2-3. Using the While Loop in Kotlin

```
var foundGcf = false

while(!foundGcf) {
 rem = a % b
 if (rem != 0) {
 a = b
 b = rem
 }
 else {
 foundGcf = true
 }
}
println(b)
```

Listing 2-3 is a bit more verbose than what you may be used to (in Java), and it has more characters to type but the intent of the code is clearer and plainer to see.

Another notable difference between Kotlin and Java when it comes to expressions and statements is that in Kotlin, most control structures (except for, do, and do/while) are expressions, while in Java they are statements.

Keywords

Keywords are reserved terms that have special meaning to the compiler, and as such, they cannot be used as identifiers for any program elements such as classes, variable names, function names, and interfaces.

Kotlin has hard, soft, and modifier keywords. The hard keywords are always interpreted as keywords and cannot really be used as identifiers. Some examples of these are as, break, class, continue, do, else, false, while, this, throw, try, super, and when.

Soft keywords act as reserved words in certain context where they are applicable; otherwise, they can be used as a regular identifier. Some examples of soft keywords are the following: file, finally, get, import, receiver, set, constructor, delegate, get, by, and where.

Finally, there are modifier keywords. These things act as reserved words in modifier lists of declarations; otherwise, they can be used as identifiers. Some examples of these things are the following: `abstract`, `actual`, `annotation`, `companion`, `enum`, `final`, `infix`, `inline`, `lateinit`, `operator`, and `open`.

IntelliJ Tip   If you use IntelliJ, you don't have to memorize the list of keywords. The IDE will give you enough visual hints if you accidentally use a keyword as an identifier.

Whitespace

Like Java, Kotlin is also a tokenized language; whitespace is not significant and can be safely ignored. You can write your codes with extravagant use of whitespace, like

```
fun main(args: Array<String>) {
 println( "Hello")
}
```

or you can write it with very little of it, like the following example:

```
fun main(args: Array<String>) {println("Hello")}
```

Either way, the compiler doesn't care, so write your codes for the benefit of humans who may be unlucky enough to maintain our codes. Forget the compiler—it doesn't care about whitespace anyway. Use whitespaces to prettify the code and make it readable, probably something like

```
fun main(args: Array<String>) {
 println("Hello")
}
```

Operators

Like in Java and other programming languages, Kotlin supports a variety of operators and symbols that we can use to formulate expression and statements. Table 2-1 shows some of them.

Table 2-1. *Kotlin Operators and Symbols*

Operators or Symbol	What It Means
+, -, *, /, %	These are the usual mathematical operators—they do exactly what you expect them to do. No difference with Java at all. But we need to note that the asterisk or star symbol (*) is also used to pass an array to a vararg parameter.
=	The equal symbol is used for the assignment statement (assignment is a statement in Kotlin, while in Java, it's an expression).
+=, -=, *=, /=, %=	These are augmented assignment operators. The += can be used like this a += 1, which is short for a = a + 1; the -= can be used like a -= 1, which is short for a = a -1, and so on.
&&, ||, ! logical 'and', 'or', 'not' operators	When you need to construct complex or compound logical operations, you will use these operators. The short-circuit *and* (&&) behaves similarly as in Java. When one of the operands evaluates to false, the other operand will no longer be evaluated and the whole expression evaluates to false. While logical 'and' does not perform short-circuit evaluation; think of it as the equivalent of the & operator in Java. The short-circuit or (||) acts the same as in Java. Kotlin doesn't have the single pipe operator; instead, it has the 'or' operator, which performs a logical OR without short-circuiting.

(continued)

Table 2-1. (*continued*)

Operators or Symbol	What It Means

==, !=	These are equality operators. Since Kotlin doesn't have primitive types (like in Java), you can use these operators to compare any type, basic or otherwise:
	
	``kotlin
	fun main(args: Array<String>) {
	var a = "Hello"
	var b = "Hello"
	if (a == b) { // this evaluates to true
	println("$a is equal to $b")
	}
	}
	``
	
	In Java, we wouldn't be able to do object comparisons like this using the double equals operator. Objects (like *Strings*) should use the .equals() method if we want to test for equality. In Kotlin, however, we don't need to worry about such things. We use the double equals operator to compare *Strings*. Kotlin translates this internally to call to .equals() method.

===, !===	Referential equality is checked by the === operation (and its negated counterpart !==). a === b evaluates to true if and only if a and b point to the same object. For example,
	
	``kotlin
	var p1 = Person("John")
	var p2 = Person("John")
	
	if(p1 === p2) { // false
	println("p1 == p2")
	}
	``
	
	In the above example, p1 and p2 do not point to the same object; hence, the triple equals will not evaluate to true.

<, >, <=, >=	Comparison operators. Kotlin translates these to calls to compareTo()—no primitive types, remember?

(*continued*)

Table 2-1 (*continued*)

Operators or Symbol	What It Means
[ ] [,]	Index access operators are used as a convenience way to access elements of a list or the values of map. Instead of using the Java-style `get(index)` or `get(key)`, we can use array-indexing to retrieve the items.

```
fun main(args: Array<String>) {
val fruits = listOf("Apple", "Banana", "Orange")
println(fruits.get(2)) // Banana
println(fruits[2]) // Banana
}
```

Blocks

Often, you may need to write a bunch of statements and you will need to group them together. Blocks allow us to do just that. The lexical symbol for blocks are a pair of curly braces; they are also sometimes called French or squiggly braces. Blocks can be found on many Kotlin constructs such as classes, like the following code:

```
class Person(val name: String) {

}
```

when defining interfaces, such as

```
interface Human {
 fun walk()
 fun talk()
}
```

in functions, like

```
fun main(args: Array<String>) {
 greet("John")
}
```

```kotlin
fun greet(name:String) {
 println("Hello $name")
}
```

in looping constructs, like the *while loop*

```kotlin
var counter = 0
while (counter++ != 5) {
 println("counter $counter")
}
```

when using the *try-catch* construct

```kotlin
val num = "1"

val ans = try {
 Integer.parseInt(num)
}
catch(e:Exception) {
 e.printStackTrace()
}
```

and any other control structure that may need to group statements.

Comments

Comments are useless to the compiler; it ignores them. But they are useful to other people (and you) who will read the codes. This makes them an excellent tool to make the code more understandable because you can use comments to dump your thought processes at the time you are writing the code. It clarifies and conveys your intentions. There are three ways to write comments, they are:

1. **Single-line comments**, also known as inline comments. These are written using two forward slashes. The compiler will ignore everything to the right of the slashes until the end of the line, see the example:

    ```kotlin
    // This statement will be ignored
    var a = 0 // so will this line
    ```

2. **Multiline comments**, also known as C-style comments. They are called as such because they came primarily from the C language. This style is useful if your comments span multiple lines. See the example:

```
/*
 Everything inside the pair of these slashes
 and asterisks will be ignored by the
 compiler
*/
```

3. **KDoc** is like Javadoc, it starts with /** and it ends with */. This form of commenting is very similar to the multiline comment (above), but this is used to provide API documentation to Kotlin codes. Listing 2-4 illustrates how to use the KDoc syntax.

Listing 2-4. KDoc Syntax

```
/**
This is an example documentation using KDoc syntax

@author Ted Hagos
@constructor
*/
class Person(val name: String) {
 /**
 This is another KDoc comment
 @return
 */
 fun foo(): Int{

 }
}
```

IntelliJ Tip   You can comment on multiple lines of code in IntelliJ by selecting the lines you want to comment on and use one of the the keyboard shortcuts to comment out codes.

In Windows and Linux, these keys are:

```
CTRL + / — comment using //
CTRL + Shift + / — comment using /* */
```

In macOS, the keys are:

```
⌘ + / — comment using //
⌘ + ⌥ + / — comment using /* */
```

Basic Types

Kotlin has some basic types, but they are not the same as Java's primitive types because all types in Kotlin are objects. They're just called basic types because they are in very common usage. These types are numbers, characters, booleans, arrays, and string—we'll look at them in this section.

Numbers and Literal Constants

There are built-in types to handle numbers (shown in Table 2-2). They may be represented as primitive values during runtime, but for all intents and purposes, they don't appear to the programmer as primitives. They appear as bona fide objects, with member functions and properties.

Table 2-2. *Kotlin's Number Built-In Type*

Type	Bit Width
Double	64
Float	32
Long	64
Int	32
Short	16
Byte	8

Kotlin handles numbers very close to how Java handles them but with some notable differences. For example, widening conversions are not implicit anymore; you will need to perform the conversions deliberately.

```
var a = 10L // a is a Long literal, note the L postfix
var b = 20

var a = b // this won't work
var a = b.toLong() // this will work
```

When whole numbers are used as literal constants, they are automatically *Ints*. To declare a *Long* literal, use the L postfix, like

```
var a = 100 // Int literal
var b = 10L // Long literal
```

You can use underscores in numeric literals to make them more readable. This feature was introduced in Java 7 and its later versions.

```
var oneMillion = 1_000_000
var creditCardNumber = 1234_5678_9012_3456
```

Literals with decimal positions are automatically *Doubles*. To declare a float literal, use the F postfix, like

```
var a = 3.1416 // Double literal
var b = 2.54 // Float literal
```

Every number type can be converted to any of the number types. That means all *Double, Float, Int, Long, Byte,* and *Short* types support the following member functions:

- toByte() : Byte

- toShort() : Short

- toInt() : Int

- toLong() : Long

- toFloat() : Float

- toDouble() : Double

- toChar() : Char

Characters

Characters in Kotlin cannot be treated directly as numbers. You can't do things like the following:

```
fun checkForKey(keyCode:Char) {
 if (keyCode == 97) { // won't work, keyCode is not a number
 }
}
```

Character literals are created by using single quotes, like

```
var enterKey = 'a'
```

Like in Java, you can use escape sequences such as \t, \b, \n, \r, \", \", \\, and \$ and if you need to encode any other character, you can use the Unicode syntax (e.g., \uFF00).

Let's not forget that *Characters* are objects in Kotlin, so you can call member functions on them. Listing 2-5 shows a snippet that demonstrates some usage scenarios.

Listing 2-5. Member Functions of the Character Type

```
val a = 'a'

println(a.isLowerCase()) // true
println(a.isDigit()) // false
```

```
println(a.toUpperCase()) // A

val b: String = a.toString() // converts it to a String
```

Booleans

Booleans are represented by the literals `true` and `false`. Kotlin doesn't have the notion of truthy and falsy values, like in other languages such as Python or JavaScript. It means that for constructs that expect a *Boolean* type, you have to supply either a *Boolean* literal, variable, or expression that will resolve to either `true` or `false`.

```
var count = 0

if (count) println("zero") // won't work
if ("") println("empty") // won't work either
```

Arrays

Kotlin doesn't have an array object like the one created in Java using the square braces syntax. The Kotlin array is a generic class—it has a type parameter. We've been using Kotlin arrays for quite some time now because the small code snippets and the "Hello World" example in the previous chapter have featured the use of *Arrays*. The argument to the main function is actually an *Array* of *String*. Let's see that main function again, just as a refresher.

```
fun main(args:Array<String>) {

}
```

There are a couple of ways to create an array. They can be created using the `arrayOf()` and `arrayOfNulls()` functions, and finally, they can be created using the *Array* constructor. Listing 2-6 provides some sample codes on how to work with them.

Listing 2-6. Working With the Array Type

```kotlin
fun main(args: Array<String>) {

 var emptyArray = arrayOfNulls<String>(2) ❶
 emptyArray[0] = "Hello" ❷
 emptyArray[1] = "World"

 for (i in emptyArray.indices) println(emptyArray[i]) ❸

 for (i in emptyArray) println(i) ❹

 var arrayOfInts = arrayOf(1,2,3,4,5,6) ❺
 arrayOfInts.forEach { e -> println(e) } ❻

 var arrayWords = "The quick brown fox".split(" ").toTypedArray() ❼
 arrayWords.forEach { item -> println(item) }

}
```

❶ We used the `arrayOfNulls` function to create an array that has two elements.

❷ We can assign values to specific elements of the array. We just need specify the position of the element in the array using its index. This syntax of accessing the element of the array is the same as in Java.

❸ We can use the for loop to traverse the contents of the array. In this example, we used the `indices` to access the element of the array.

❹ This is a more direct way of accessing the element of the array. An Array object has an iterator, so we can use that iterator to get to the array element right away.

❺ This creates an array of Ints using the `arrayOf()` function.

❻ This example uses the `forEach` function to traverse the elements of the array. Using the `forEach` function is considered more idiomatic (and more efficient).

❼ This creates an array using an ArrayList(arrayWords). The List arrayWords was created by invoking the `split()` member function of the String.

Strings and String Templates

Much of what we've learned about Java Strings are still applicable in Kotlin; hence, this section will be short.

The easiest way to create a String is to use the escaped string literal—escaped strings are actually the kind of strings we know from Java. These strings may contain escape characters like \n, \t, \b, etc. See the code snippet below.

```
var str: String = "Hello World\n"
```

Kotlin has another kind of string that is called a raw string. A raw string is created by using triple quote delimiter. They may not contain escape sequences, but they can contain new lines, like

```
var rawStr = """Amy Pond, there's something you'd
 better understand about me 'cause it's important,
 and one day your life may depend on it:
 I am definitely a mad man with a box!
 """
```

A couple more things we need to know about Kotlin strings are as follows:

1. They have iterators, so we can walk through the characters using a *for loop*:

   ```
   val str = "The quick brown fox"
   for (i in str) println(i)
   ```

2. Its elements can be accessed by the indexing operator (str[elem]), pretty much like *Arrays*

   ```
   println(str[2]) // returns 'e'
   ```

3. We can no longer convert numbers (or anything else for that matter) to a String by simply adding an empty String literal to it:

   ```
   var strNum = 10 + "" // this won't work anymore
   var strNum = 10.toString() // we have to explicitly convert now
   ```

We can still use `String.format` and `System.out.printf` in Kotlin; after all, we can use Java codes from within Kotlin. It's still possible to write programs like the code snippet shown in Listing 2-7.

Listing 2-7. Using String.format and printf

```
var name = "John Doe"
var email = "john.doe@gmail.com"
var phone = "(01)777-1234"

var concat = String.format("name: %s | email: %s | phone: %s", name, email,
phone)
println(concat)
// prints
// name: John Doe | email: john.doe@gmail.com | phone: (01)777-1234
```

The preferred way to do string composition in Kotlin is by using string templates, like

```
var concat = "name: $name | email: $email | phone: $phone"
println(concat)
// prints
// name: John Doe | email: john.doe@gmail.com | phone: (01)777-1234
```

Kotlin strings may contain template expressions. These are pieces of code that are evaluated. The result of the evaluation is inserted (concatenated) into the String. A template expression starts with a dollar sign ($) followed by an expression. See Listing 2-8 for examples.

Listing 2-8. Using Template Expressions

```
fun main(args:Array<String>) {
 var name = "John Doe"

 println("Hello $name") ❶
 println("The name '$name' is ${name.length} characters long") ❷
 println("Hello ${foo()}") ❸
}

fun foo(): String {
 return "Boo"
}
```

❶ Shows the basic use of a template string. The template expression is created by using the $ symbol immediately followed by an identifier. The value of the identifier is evaluated, resolved, and finally inserted into the body of the String where the template expression is declared.

❷ In this example, the `name.length` is enclosed in curly braces. This is because the $ symbol is right-associative—it will evaluate the expression that is immediately to its right. That won't work in our situation because we don't want to evaluate the `name` variable; what we want to resolve instead, is `name.length`—hence, the need to enclose it in curly braces.

❸ We're not limited to simple variables; we can even write functions inside template expressions.

Controlling Program Flow

Program statements are executed sequentially by default, one after the other, in a linear fashion. There are constructs that can cause programs to deviate from a linear flow. Some can cause the flow to fork or branch, and other constructs can cause the program flow to go around in circles, like in a loop. These constructs are the subject of this section.

Using ifs

The basic form of the *if* construct is

```
if (expression) statement
```

where *expression* resolves to Boolean. If the expression is true, the statement will be executed; otherwise, the statement will be ignored and program control will flow to the next executable statement. When you need to execute more than one statement, you can use a block with the *if* construct, like

```
if (expression) {
 statements
}
```

Let's see how it looks in code.

```
val theQuestion = "Doctor who"
val answer = "Theta Sigma"
val correctAnswer = ""

if (answer == correctAnswer) {
 println("You are correct")
}
```

So far, the *if* construct in Kotlin behaves exactly as it does in Java. It also supports the *else if* and the *else* clause, as shown in following snippet:

```
val d = Date()
val c = Calendar.getInstance()
val day = c.get(Calendar.DAY_OF_WEEK)

if (day == 1) {
 println("Today is Sunday")
}
else if (day == 2) {
 println("Today is Monday")
}
else if ( day == 3) {
 println("Today is Tuesday")
}
```

The new thing about Kotlin's *if* is that it's an expression, which means we can do things like

```
val theQuestion = "Doctor who"
val answer = "Theta Sigma"
val correctAnswer = ""

var message = if (answer == correctAnswer) {
  "You are correct"
}
else{
  "Try again"
}
```

The *String* on the first block of the *if* construct will be returned to the `message` variable if the condition is true; otherwise, the *String* on the second block will be the returned value. We can even omit the curly braces on the blocks, since the blocks contain only single statements.

```
var message = if (answer == correctAnswer) "You are correct" else "Try
again"
```

The code example above would probably remind you of the ternary operator in Java. By the way, Kotlin doesn't support the ternary operator, but don't worry since you don't need it. The if construct is an expression, if you feel you need to write code that requires the ternary operator, just follow the preceding code example.

The when Statement

Kotlin doesn't have a *switch* statement, but it has the *when* construct. Its form and structure is strikingly similar to the *switch* statement. In its simplest form, it can be implemented like this:

```
val d = Date()
val c = Calendar.getInstance()
val day = c.get(Calendar.DAY_OF_WEEK)

when (day) {
 1 -> println("Sunday")
 2 -> println("Monday")
 3 -> println("Tuesday")
 4 -> println("Wednesday")
}
```

when matches the argument (the variable `day`) against all branches sequentially until it encounters a match; note that unlike in *switch* statements, when a match is found, it doesn't flow through or cascade to the next branch—hence, we don't need to put a *break* statement.

The *when* construct can also be used as an expression, and when it's used as such, each branch becomes the returned value of the expression. See the code example:

```
val d = Date()
val c = Calendar.getInstance()
val day = c.get(Calendar.DAY_OF_WEEK)

var dayOfweek = when (day) {
 1 -> "Sunday"
 2 -> "Monday"
 3 -> "Tuesday"
 4 -> "Wednesday"
 else -> "Unknown"
}
```

Just remember to include the *else* clause when *when* is used as an expression. The compiler thoroughly checks all possible pathways and it needs to be exhaustive, which is why the *else* clause becomes a requirement.

You're not limited to numeric literals; you can use a wide variety of types for the branches, as shown in Listing 2-9.

Listing 2-9. How to Write Branches Inside the When Construct

```
fun main(args: Array<String>) {

 print("What is the answer to life? ")
 var response:Int? = readLine()?.toInt() ❶

 val message = when(response){
 42 -> "So long, and thanks for the all fish"
 43, 44, 45 -> "either 43,44 or 45" ❷
 in 46 .. 100 -> "forty six to one hundred" ❸
 else -> "Not what I'm looking for" ❹
 }

 println(message)
}
```

❶   `readLine()` reads an input from the console. Don't worry about the questions marks for now; we'll get to that in the coming sections.

❷   The branch conditions may be combined with a comma.

❸   We can check if it's a member of a range or a collection.

❹   The *else* clause is required when *when* is used as an expression.

The while Statement

The *while* and *do . . while* statements work exactly as they do in Java—and like in Java, these are also statements and not expressions. We won't spend too much time on *while* and *do . . while* loops here.

A basic usage of the while loop is shown here, just as a refresher.

```kotlin
fun main(args: Array<String>) {
 var count = 0
 val finish = 5

 while (count++ < finish) {
 println("counter = $count")
 }
}
```

for loops

Kotlin doesn't have the traditional *for loop* of Java 7 and below—the one that looks like the following:

```
for (int i = 0; i < 10; i++) {
 statements
}
```

Kotlin's *for loop*, instead, works on things that have an iterator. If you've seen the *for each* loop in JavaScript, C#, or Java 8, Kotlin's is a lot closer to that. A basic example is shown in Listing 2-10.

Listing 2-10. Basic for Loop

```
fun main(args: Array<String>) {

 val words = "The quick brown fox".split(" ") ❶

 for(word in words) { ❷
 println(word) ❸
 }
}
```

---

❶ The `split()` method of the String class returns an *ArrayList* type, we can iterate over that.

❷ For each item (`word`) in the collection (`words`), we;

❸ print the item.

If you need to work with numbers on the *for loop*, you can use *Ranges*. A range is a type that represents an arithmetic progression of integers. Ranges are created with the `rangeTo()` function, but we usually use it in its operator form (..). To create a range of integers from 1 to 10, we write like this:

```
var zeroToTen = 0..10
```

We can use the `in` keyword to perform a test of membership.

```
if (9 in zeroToTen) println("9 is in zeroToTen")
```

To use ranges in for loops, we can start with something that looks like the code shown in Listing 2-11.

Listing 2-11. Using Ranges in for Loop

```
fun main(args: Array<String>) {
 for (i in 1..10) {
 println(i)
 }
}
```

Exception Handling

Kotlin's exception handling is very similar to Java: it also uses the *try-catch-finally* construct. Whatever we've learned about Java's exception handling commutes nicely to Kotlin. However, Kotlin simplifies exception handling by simply using unchecked exceptions. What that means is writing *try-catch* blocks is now optional. You may or may not do it. Let's consider the code shown in Listing 2-12.

Listing 2-12. I/O Operations Without Try-Catch Blocks

```
import java.io.FileReader ❶

fun main(args: Array<String>) {

 var fileReader = FileReader("README.txt") ❷

 var content = fileReader.read() ❸
 println(content)

}
```

❶ We can use Java's standard library in Kotlin.

❷ This one may throw the "*FileNotFoundException*".

❸ And this could throw the "*IOException*", but Kotlin happily lets us code without handling the possible *Exceptions* that may be thrown.

Although Kotlin lets us get away with not having to handle exceptions, we still can do that, and for some situations, we may really have to. When that happens, just write the exception handling code the way you did in Java; see Listing 2-13 for an example.

Listing 2-13. Kotlin's Try-Catch Block

```
import java.io.FileNotFoundException
import java.io.FileReader
import java.io.IOException

fun main(args: Array<String>) {

 var fileReader: FileReader
```

```
try {
fileReader = FileReader("README.txt")
var content = fileReader.read()
println(content)
}
catch (ffe: FileNotFoundException) {
println(ffe.message)
}
catch(ioe: IOException) {
println(ioe.message)
}
}
```

Handling Nulls

A common source of bugs and expensive rework activities in Java may be attributed to the way programmers handle null values. Some of us are really diligent, and such defensive programmers that this discussion may not be necessary anymore. But not all programmers are created equal, and for most of us, we need to be reminded to mind the possibility of *NullPointerExceptions*. Handling of null values is such a big concern in Java that Kotlin made a very deliberate decision to introduce the concept of a *Nullable* type. In Kotlin, when we declare a variable like

```
var str: String = "Hello"
str = null // won't work
```

we will never be able to set the value of this variable to null. We may assign it a different *String* value, but Kotlin guarantees that str will never be null. If, for some reason, you really need this variable to be null, you have to explicitly tell Kotlin that str is a *Nullable* type. To make a *String* (or any type) Nullable, we use the question mark symbol as postfix to the type, like

```
var str: String? = "Hello"
```

After declaring a type as *Nullable*, we now have to do some things that Kotlin used to do for us. For non-*Nullable* types, Kotlin ensures that it's pretty safe to use them in operations such as assignment, printing, inclusion in expressions, etc. When we make types *Nullable,* Kotlin assumes that we know what we're doing and that we're responsible enough to write the necessary guard conditions to prevent *NullPointerExceptions.* Kotlin assumes we'd do something like the code shown in Listing 2-14.

Listing 2-14. Demonstration of Nullable Types

```
fun main(args: Array<String>) {
 var a = arrayOf(1,2,3)
 printArr(null)
}

fun printArr(arr: Array<Int>?) { ❶
 if(arr != null) { ❷
 arr.forEach { i -> println(i) } ❸
 }
}
```

❶ We're declaring Array<Int> to be Nullable. This means we can pass null to printArr().

❷ Because arr is no longer guaranteed to be non-null, we have to manually check for null values before we do some operations that involve the arr local variable.

❸ If arr is not null, we can safely perform this operation.

Kotlin introduced an operator that we can use to handle *Nullable* types. It's called the safe-call operator, which is written as the question mark symbol followed by a dot ?.

We can replace the entire if block, which performs the null checking, with just one statement:

```
arr?.forEach { i -> println(i) }
```

What the safe call does is to first check if arr is null; if it is, it won't go through the forEach operation. Only when arr is not null will the array be traversed.

Listing 2-15 shows the refactored code for Listing 2-14.

Listing 2-15. Safe Call Operator

```
fun main(args: Array<String>) {

 var a = arrayOf(1,2,3)
 printArr(null)
}

fun printArr(arr: Array<Int>?) {
 arr?.forEach { i -> println(i) }
}
```

Kotlin's default behavior regarding nullability of objects should prevent many of us from doing things that will disgrace ourselves because it doesn't allow variables to be null by default. However, if we think we know what we're doing and certain situations would force us to use *Nullable* types, we can still do that. Just remember to use the safe call operator; it's idiomatic compared to performing null checks using *ifs*.

Chapter Summary

- Kotlin's program elements are not that different from Java; it also has operators, blocks, statements, expressions, etc. In Kotlin, however, some constructs that are considered statements in Java are expressions in Kotlin, and some that were considered expressions in Java are statements in Kotlin (e.g., the assignment operation).

- Kotlin's basic types are not the same as primitive types of Java. Everything in Kotlin is an object.

- There are two ways to declare a variable in Kotlin. When the var keyword is used, the variable is mutable. When the val keyword is used, the variable is immutable.

- Strings in Kotlin have iterators. Also, they're easier to compose and combine with the help of template expressions.

- When variables are declared in Kotlin, they are by default non-Nullable, unless we declare them otherwise.

- Kotlin doesn't have a switch statement, but it's got a when construct.

- In Kotlin, we don't have to write try-catch anymore because it basically uses unchecked Exceptions.

In the next chapter, you'll find out:

- How to (easily) create functions in Kotlin

- Why we don't need to do tons of method overloads in Kotlin

- How we can move away from writing Utility functions and instead use Kotlin's Extension functions (Java doesn't have this)

CHAPTER 3

Functions

What we'll cover:

- Declaring functions
- Default parameters
- Named parameters
- Extension functions
- Infix functions
- Infix operators

Kotlin's functions are almost the same as Java methods, although it's closer in behavior to functions in JavaScript, because in Kotlin, functions are more than just a named collection of statements. In Kotlin, functions are first-class citizens; you can use a function wherever you could use a variable. You can pass them as parameters to other functions, and you can return functions from other functions as well. But before we can dive into that topic, we need to start with the basics of Kotlin functions—for example, how they are declared, how they treat parameters, how different (or similar) they are from Java methods, plus a couple of other details. That's what we'll cover in this chapter.

Declaring Functions

Functions can be written in three places. You can write them (1) inside a class, like methods in Java—these are called *member functions*; (2) outside classes—these are called *top-level* functions; and (3) they can be written inside other functions—these

© Ted Hagos 2018
T. Hagos, *Learn Android Studio 3 with Kotlin*, https://doi.org/10.1007/978-1-4842-3907-0_3

are called *local* functions. Regardless of where you put the function, the mechanics of declaring it doesn't change much. The basic form a function is as follows:

```
fun functionName([parameters]) [:type] {
  statements
}
```

The function is declared using the reserved word *fun* followed by an identifier, which is the function name. The function name includes the parentheses where you can declare optional parameters. You may also declare the type of data the function will return, but this is optional since Kotlin can infer the function's return type by simply looking at the function's body declaration. What follows is the pair of curly braces with some statements inside the function's body.

You should name your functions following the same guidelines as if you are writing Java methods—namely, the function name (1) shouldn't be a reserved word; (2) mustn't start with a number; and (3) shouldn't have special characters in them. And finally, from a stylistic perspective, its name should contain a verb or something signifying an action—as opposed to when you are naming a variable where the name contains a noun. Listing 3-1 shows a basic declaration of a function that takes a *String* and *Int* parameters. For purposes of comparison, Listing 3-3 shows the equivalent Java code for Listing 3-1.

Listing 3-1. displayMessage Function

```
fun displayMessage(msg: String, count: Int) {
  var counter = 1
  while(counter++ <= count ) {
    println(msg)
  }
}
```

The `displayMessage()` in Listing 3-1 is a non-productive function; it doesn't return anything—notice the absence of a *return* keyword in the body of the function. In Java, when a function doesn't return anything, we still indicate that the return type is void (see Listing 3-3). In Kotlin, however, we don't really have to do that since Kotlin is capable of type inference—it can figure it out for itself. But as an academic exercise, let's rewrite Listing 3-1 verbosely to completely tell the compiler what kind of return type `displayMessage()` has. See the code example in Listing 3-2.

Listing 3-2. displayMessage With an Explicit Return Type

```
fun displayMessage(msg: String, count: Int) : Unit {
  var counter = 1
  while(counter++ <= count ) {
    println(msg)
  }
}
```

The only difference between Listing 3-1 and 3-2 is the *Unit* return type of the displayMessage() function. *Unit* corresponds to Java's *void*.

Listing 3-3. DisplayMessage in Java

```
public class DisplayMessage {

  public static void main(String []args) {
    displayMessage("Hello", 3);
  }

  static void displayMessage(String msg, int count) {
    int counter = 1;
    while(counter++ <= count) {
      System.out.println(msg);
    }
  }
}
```

To invoke the displayMessage() function, we call it by its name and pass the appropriate parameters, as shown in Listing 3-4.

Listing 3-4. Calling the displayMessage Function

```
fun main(args: Array<String>) {
  displayMessage("Hello", 3) ❶ ❷
}

fun displayMessage(msg: String, count: Int) {
  var counter = 1
```

```
  while(counter++ <= count ) {
    println(msg)
  }
}
```

---

❶ "Hello" is passed to the msg argument of displayMessage()

❷ 3 is passed to the count argument of displayMessage(); like in Java, arguments passed to a function are matched to its parameters in the order they were defined, starting from left going to the right.

To make functions productive (return something), just put a *return* statement somewhere in the body of the function and declare the function's return type. See Listing 3-5 for an example.

Listing 3-5. getSum, A Productive Function

```
fun main(args: Array<String>) {
  println(getSum(listOf(1,2,3,4,5,6)))
}

fun getSum(values: List<Int>) : Int { // return type is Int
  var total = 0;
  for (i in values)  total += i
  return total                          // return value
}
```

You can return anything from functions; we're not limited to the basic types. See Listing 3-6 for another example.

Listing 3-6. Using Pairs As a Return Type

```
fun bigSmall(a: Int, b:Int) : Pair<Int, Int> { ❶

  if(a > b) return Pair(a,b) ❷
  else {
    return Pair(b,a) ❸
  }
}
```

```
fun main(args: Array<String>) {
  var (x,y) = bigSmall(5,3) ❹

  println(x)
  println(y)
}
```

---

❶   This function is telling the compiler that it returns a *Pair*. A *Pair* is a data class that represents a, well, generic pair. If you've used Python before, this might remind you of tuples.

❷   If parameter *a* is greater than *b*, then we create the *Pair* using parameter *a* as the first component, and b as the second component, then we return it to the caller.

❸   If parameter *a* is less than *b*, then we create the *Pair* using parameter *b* as the first component, and *a* as the second component, and then we return it to the caller.

❹   A Pair can be returned to two named variables on the left-hand side of the assignment statement. This destructuring declaration allows us to save multiple values to multiple variables all at once. In this case, variable *x* will receive the first component of the returned Pair and variable *y* will receive the second component of the *Pair*.

Single Expression Functions

Earlier in the chapter, we did say that functions follow the basic form

```
fun functionName([parameters]) [:type] {
  statements
}
```

There is a second form of writing functions in Kotlin that allows for a more concise syntax. There are situations when we can omit (1) the *return* statement; (2) curly braces; and (3) the *return type* altogether. This second form is called *single expression* functions. As you may have inferred from its name, the function only contains a single expression, as shown in the code snippet here:

```
fun sumInt(a: Int, b: Int) = a + b
```

A single expression function omits the pair of curly braces and instead uses an assignment operator in its place. It also doesn't need the return statement anymore because the expression on the right-hand side of the assignment automatically becomes the returned value. Finally, a function like this doesn't need an explicit return type because the compiler can infer the type that's returned from the value of expression. The omission of the explicit return type is not in any way a hard rule. You may still write an explicit return if that's what you prefer, like so:

```
fun sumInt (a: Int, b: Int): Int = a + b
```

Default Arguments

Function parameters can have default values in Kotlin, which allows the caller (of the function) to omit some arguments on the call site. A default value can be added to function's signature by assigning a value to a function's parameter. An example of such a function is shown in Listing 3-7.

Listing 3-7. connectToDb

```
fun connectToDb(hostname: String = "localhost",
                username: String = "mysql",
                password:String = "secret") {
}
```

Notice that "localhost", "mysql", and "secret" were assigned to hostname, username, and password, respectively. This function can be invoked like this:

```
connectToDb("mycomputer","root")
```

Any and all arguments to call the connectToDb() function can be omitted because all of its parameters have default values. But in this case, we omitted only the third one.

We can even call the function without passing any arguments to it, like so:

```
connectToDb()
```

Kotlin's ability to provide default arguments to functions allows us to avoid creating function overloads. We couldn't do this in Java, which is why we had to resort to method overloading. Overloading functions is still possible in Kotlin, but we'll probably have fewer reasons to do that now, all thanks to default parameters.

Named Parameters

Let's go back to Listing 3-7. If we call that function and provided all the arguments, the call might look like this:

```
connectToDb("neptune", jupiter", "saturn")
```

This is a valid call because all of the parameters of connectToDb() are Strings, and we passed three String arguments. Can you spot the problem? It isn't clear from the call site which one is the username, the hostname, or the password. In Java, this problem of ambiguity was solved by a variety of workarounds, including commenting the call site.

```
connectoToDb(/* hostname*/, "neptune,
             /* username*/ "jupiter",
             /*password*/ "saturn")
```

We don't have to do this in Kotlin because we can name the argument at the call site.

```
connecToDb(hostname = "neptune",
           username = "jupiter",
           password = "saturn")
```

It's important to remember that when we start specifying the argument name, we need to specify the names of all the arguments after that in order to avoid confusion. Besides, Kotlin wouldn't let us compile if we did that. For example, a call like this

```
connectToDb(hostname = "neptune",
            username = "jupiter",
            "saturn")
```

isn't allowed because once we name the second argument (username), we need to provide the name of all the arguments that come after it. And in the example call above, the second argument is named but not the third one. On the other hand, a call like this

```
connectToDb("neptune",
            username = "jupiter",
            password = "saturn")
```

is allowed. It's okay that we didn't name the first argument, because Kotlin would have treated this as a regular function call and use the positional value of the argument to resolve the parameter. And then we named all the remaining arguments.

Variable Number of Arguments

Functions in Kotlin, like in Java, can also accept an arbitrary number of arguments. The syntax is a bit different from Java, instead of using three dots after the type **...** , we use the *vararg* keyword instead. Listing 3-8 shows an example on how to declare and call a *vararg* function.

Listing 3-8. Demonstration of a Variable Argument Function

```
fun<T> manyParams(vararg va : T) { ❶
  for (i in va) { ❷
    println(i)
  }
}

fun main(args: Array<String>) {
  manyParams(1,2,3,4,5) ❸
  manyParams("From", "Gallifrey", "to", "Trenzalore") ❹
  manyParams(*args) ❺
  manyParams(*"Hello there".split(" ").toTypedArray()) ❻
}
```

❶ The `vararg` keyword lets us accept multiple parameters for this function. In this example, we declared a function that has a typed parameter; it's generic. We didn't have to declare it as generic in order to work with variable arguments—we just chose to so that it could work with a variety of types.

❷ This is a simple looping mechanism so that we can print each item in the argument.

❸ We can pass `Ints`, and we can pass as many as we want because `manyParams` accepts variable number of arguments.

❹ It works with `Strings` as well.

❺ Like in Java, we can pass an array to a function that accepts variable arguments. We need to use the spread operator * to unpack the array. It's like passing the individual elements of the array one by one, manually.

❻ The `split()` member function will return an *ArrayList*, you can convert it to an *Array*, then use the spread operator so you can pass it to a *vararg* function.

Extension Functions

In Java, if we needed to add functionality to a class, we could either add methods to the class itself or extend it by inheritance. An *extension function* in Kotlin allows us to add behavior to an existing class, including the ones written in Java, without using inheritance. It essentially lets us define a function that can be invoked as a member of the class, but the function is implemented outside the class. To demonstrate this, let's start with a simple code, chanthofy, terminatorify (shown in Listing 3-9); it's a contrived application but it should set the grounds for us to explore extension functions.

Listing 3-9. homerify, chanthofy, terminatorify

```
fun main(args: Array<String>) {
  val msg = "My name is Maximus Decimus Meridius"
  println(homerify(msg))
  println(chanthofy(msg))
  println(terminatorify(msg))

}

fun homerify(msg: String) = "$msg -- woohoo!"
fun chanthofy(msg: String) = "Chan, $msg , tho"
fun terminatorify(msg: String) = "$msg -- I'll be back"
```

The application in Listing 3-9 features three functions that take a String argument, add some Strings to it, and then return them back to the caller; it's simple. It is usable as it is, but we can probably consolidate it a bit more by putting all the three functions in a common class, which will become our utility class. Such a class might look something like the code in Listing 3-10.

Listing 3-10. Our Very Own StringUtil Class

```
fun main(args: Array<String>) {
  val msg = "My name is Maximus Decimus Meridius"

  val util = StringUtil()
  println(util.homerify(msg))
  println(util.chanthofy(msg))
  println(util.terminatorify(msg))
}
```

```
/*
  The StringUtil class consolidates our three methods as member functions.
  This is a very common Java practice
*/
class StringUtil {
  fun homerify(msg: String) = "$msg -- woohoo!"
  fun chanthofy(msg:String) = "Chan, $msg , tho"
  fun terminatorify(msg: String) = "$msg -- I'll be back"
}
```

We can already use the code in Listing 3-10; in fact, this is a very common practice in Java. It's considered a good idea to consolidate methods that are somewhat related into a utility class (like our very own StringUtil class in Listing 3-10), although Java programmers might have implemented homerify(), chanthofy(), and terminatorify() as static methods, and not instance methods, as we did here. That's a small matter, and we can safely ignore it. The point is, in Kotlin, instead of writing a utility class for our three methods, we can rewrite our methods in a much simpler way (see Listing 3-11).

Listing 3-11. homerify As an Extension Function

```
fun String.homerify() = "$this -- woohoo!"
```

It looks deceptively simple, but this is really all it takes to write an extension function. Extension functions introduce the concept of a *receiver* type and a *receiver* object. In Listing 3-11, the *receiver* type is *String*; it's the class to which we'd like to add our extension function. The *receiver* object is the instance of that type, which in our examples is "*My name is Maximus Decimus Meridius*". When you attach an extension function to a type, such as a *String* in our case, the extension function can reference the receiver object using the keyword *this*. For all intents and purposes, an extension functions appears to be just like any member function defined on the *receiver* type. So, it makes sense for the extension function to be able to reference *this*. Listing 3-12 shows the full code for our extended String class.

Listing 3-12. Extended String Class

```
fun main(args: Array<String>) {
  val msg = "My name is Maximus Decimus Meridius"

  println(msg.homerify())
  println(msg.chanthofy())
  println(msg.terminatorify())

}

fun String.homerify() = "$this -- woohoo!"
fun String.chanthofy() = "Chan, $this , tho"
fun String.terminatorify() = "$this -- I'll be back"
```

It's perfectly alright to still write utility functions in Kotlin, but with extension functions at our disposal, it seems more natural to use them because it increases the semantic value of our code. It feels more natural to use extension function syntax.

Infix Functions

"Infix" notation is one of the notations used in math and logical expressions. It's the placement of operator between operands (e.g., *a* + *b*; the plus symbol is "infixed" because it's between the operands *a* and *b*). In contrast, operations can follow "post fixed" notation where the expression is written like so *(+ a b)* or they can be "post fixed," in which our expression is written like this *(a b +).*

In Kotlin, member functions can be "infixed," which allow us to write codes like the following:

```
john say "Hello World"
```

If *john* is a variable that points to an object of type *Person* (we'll see the definition in a little while) and *say* is a method that takes a *String* argument like "Hello World", then the statement above is a more natural way of writing something like

```
john.say("Hello World")
```

To begin our exploration of infix functions, let's start by implementing the codes that will allow us to call the say() member function using the traditional dot notation. And then we'll write the codes that will let us use the infixed version. Listing 3-13 shows the classic implementation of the *Person* class, which we can call using the dot notation.

73

Listing 3-13. Person Class Without infix Function

```
fun main(args: Array<String>) {
  val john = Person("John Doe")
  john.say("Hello World")
}

class Person(val name : String) {
  fun say(message: String) = println("$name is saying $message")
}
```

No surprises here, these kinds of call are where most of us cut our teeth in Java programming. This doesn't need any further commentary. Now, let's see the implementation that allows us to call the *say* method in an "infixed" way.

Listing 3-14. Person Class With an infix Function

```
fun main(args: Array<String>) {
  val john = Person("John Doe")
  john say "Hello World"
}

class Person(val name : String) {
  infix fun say(message: String) = println("$name is saying $message")
}
```

The only thing you need to do in order to use the say() function in an "infixed" way is to add the infix keyword in the beginning of the function, as shown in Listing 3-14. Having said that, you cannot convert every function to become an infix. A function can be converted to infix, only if

- it's a member function (part of a class) or an extension function, and

- it accepts exactly one parameter (only). If you're thinking of a loophole like, "I could probably define a single parameter in my function and use vararg," that won't work. Variable arguments are not allowed to be converted to infix functions.

By the way, you cannot call an infix function using named parameters, like this

```
john say msg = "Hello World" // won't work
```

Remember that infix functions take only a single argument; it doesn't make much sense to name the argument at the call site.

Infix functions, when used judiciously, allow for more intuitive coding because they can hide program logic behind a keyword-like syntax. You can create some sort of a meta-language with infix notation; just be careful not to overdo it.

Operator Overloading

The topic of operator overloading may seem a bit out of place in a chapter that is all about *functions*. But in Kotlin, this topic dovetails nicely into a discussion of infix functions because of their shared mechanics in implementation, as we will see shortly.

Operator overloading allows us to appropriate the use of some standard operators, like the math operators' *addition, subtraction, division, multiplication*, and *modulo*. For example, we can write a code that allows the use of the plus sign to, say, add two *Employee* objects, or any other custom type. Consider the code in Listing 3-15.

Listing 3-15. Adding Two Employee Objects

```
fun main(args: Array<String>) {

  var e1 = Employee("John Doe")
  var e2 = Employee("Jane Doe")
  var e3 = e1 + e2
  println(e3.name)
}
```

Somehow, we intuitively know what the statement e3 = e1 + e3 means; if we add one employee object to another, then we should get the combined information or state of employees *e1* and *e2*—if that is the kind of thing you want to be able to do in code. Programmatically, we know this statement should not work because the addition operator doesn't know anything about Employee objects, much less how to perform the add operation on them. However, in Kotlin, we can teach the addition operator how to add two Employee objects. This is shown in Listing 3-16.

Listing 3-16. class Employee

```
class Employee(var name: String) {

    infix operator  fun plus(emp: Employee) : Employee { ❶
     this.name += "\n${emp.name}" //
     return this
  }
}
```

---

❶ This is very similar syntax to an *infix function*, as we've seen in previous section. The only thing new here is the *operator* keyword.

We already know what the infix keyword will do to the function. The fact that *plus* is an *infix-ed* function, allows us to write code like this (see Listing 3-16):

```
var e1 = Employee("John Doe")
var e2 = Employee("Jane Doe")

var e3 = e1 plus e2
```

However, the function name *plus* isn't an ordinary function name. It isn't just another name that we thought about and made up. It has a special meaning to Kotlin. The *plus* function name is a *fixed identifier* that corresponds to the math operator +. And when this special function name is combined with the keywords *infix* and *operator*, it allows us to write codes like this

```
var e3 = e1 + e2
```

Kotlin allows us to override quite a number of operators, and it's not limited to just math operators. Table 3-1 shows some of them. It's not a complete list, but it should give you an idea of how much you can overload.

Table 3-1. *Operators That can be Overloaded and Their Corresponding Function Names*

Operator	Function name	Expression	Translated to
+	Plus	a + b	a.plus(b)
-	Minus	a - b	a.minus(b)
/	Div	a / b	a.div(b)
*	Times	a * b	a.times(b)
%	rem	a % b	a.rem(b)
..	rangeTo	a .. b	a.rangeTo(b)
++	inc	a++	a.inc()
--	dec	a--	a.dec()
+=	plusAssign	a += b	a.plusAssign(b)
-+	minusAssign	a -= b	a.minusAssign(b)
/=	divAssign	a /= b	a.divAssign(b)
*=	timesAssign	a *= b	a.timesAssign(b)
%=	remAssign	a %= b	a.remAssign(b)
>	compareTo	a > b	a.compareTo(b) > 0
<	compareTo	a < b	a.conpareTo(b) < 0
>=	compareTo	a >=	a.conpareTo(b) >= 0
<=	compareTo	a<= b	a.conpareTo(b) <= 0

Operator overloading is a specific case of polymorphism where different operators, like math operators, can have different implementations depending on the arguments (or type of operands), as we've seen demonstrated in Listings 3-14 and 3-15. The use of operator overloading, when done correctly, can produce codes that are easier to understand because they are written in the language of the *business* or *object domain*. They have higher semantic values.

Kotlin isn't the first language to implement operator overloading. It's been done by languages like C++ before. It should be noted that the use or, more aptly, the overuse and abuse of operator overloading has led to much criticism. Precisely because if you can redefine the actions and behavior of well-known operators like plus, minus, etc., it can lead to unwieldy code. So, exercise good judgment when you take the route of *operator overloading*.

Chapter Summary

- Kotlin functions can be written in three places. Like in Java, they can be a member of the class, but they can also be written as a top-level construct. Third, they can be written embedded in other functions—we did not delve into local functions in this chapter, but we will consider this topic at some length in later chapters.

- Kotlin makes it easier to declare and call functions by adding support for default parameters, named parameters, and even variable numbers of arguments. The combination of positional, named, and default parameters allows us to move away from excessive use of parametric overloading, like what we did in Java.

- Extension functions offer a new way to extend behaviors of existing types. We can add the extra behavior outside the class but we can call the extension function as if it was baked right into the class definition.

- Infix functions and Infix operators let us increase the semantic values of our codes by allowing to us write function invocations without using the dot notation. By allowing function calls to be *infix*-ed, the resulting code becomes more expressive and closer to the language of the domain.

In the next chapter, we'll look the OOP side of Kotlin. We'll learn how Kotlin deals with classes, constructors, and interfaces. We'll also learn about the new data classes in Kotlin.

CHAPTER 4

Working with Types

What we'll cover:

- Interfaces
- Classes
- Data classes
- Access modifiers
- Object declarations

Kotlin, like Java, is a class-based, object-oriented language. It uses interfaces and classes to define custom types. The way Kotlin works with types will feel very similar to the way we've worked in Java, but there are also some areas where Kotlin will not feel like we're in familiar ground. In this chapter, we'll explore those similarities and differences.

Interfaces

The basic form of an interface in Kotlin, like in Java, looks something like the code in Listing 4-1.

Listing 4-1. Interface Fax

```
interface Fax {
  fun call(number: String) = println("Calling $number")
  fun print(doc: String) = println("Fax:Printing $doc")
  fun answer()
}
```

© Ted Hagos 2018
T. Hagos, *Learn Android Studio 3 with Kotlin*, https://doi.org/10.1007/978-1-4842-3907-0_4

79

It still uses the *interface* keyword, and it also contains *abstract* function(s). What's remarkable about Kotlin interfaces are that they can (1) contain properties and (2) have functions with implementations—in other words, concrete functions. Although, Java 8 did allow for *default* implementations in Java, so that last one is no longer unique to Kotlin, but still pretty useful, as we shall see later. Don't worry too much about interfaces having properties—you'll get used to it. Although we won't deal with properties in this section (yet), we'll get to them in a later section (classes). To implement an interface, Kotlin uses the colon operator, as shown in Listing 4-2.

Listing 4-2. class MultiFunction Implementing Fax

```
class MultiFunction : Fax { ❶
  override fun answer () { ❷

  }
}
```

❶ The colon operator is used, instead of Java's *implements* keyword. The colon is used for inheriting classes as well.

❷ We have to provide an implementation for the answer() function because it didn't have an implementation in the interface definition. On the other hand, we don't have to provide implementation for call() and print() because they have an implementation in the interface definition. You may also note that we are using the override keyword in this function. Its use is necessary in order to clarify to the compiler that we don't intend to hide or overshadow the answer() function in the interface definition. Rather, we intend to replace it, so it can be polymorphic. We want to provide our own behavior for the answer() function in this class.

You might be wondering why Kotlin would allow us to provide implementations inside *interfaces*. Aren't *interfaces* supposed to contain only *abstract functions* and leave the implementations to the classes that will implement the *interface*? That way, you can enforce contracts between types. Well, during the early days of Java, that was precisely the way interfaces were used; they were purely an *abstract construction*. However, as of Java 8, you can already provide *default implementations* on *interfaces*.

There are some practical reasons why this was allowed. Default implementations on interfaces would allow us to evolve the interfaces over time. Imagine if we wrote *interface Foo* today with member functions *a()*, *b()*, and *c()*, and this was released to other developers. In the future, if we added function *d()* to *interface Foo*, all codes that used *Foo* would now break. However, if we provide a *default implementation* for *d()*, then the existing codes don't have to break. This is one of the use-cases where a function implementation on an interface might be useful.

Diamond Problem

A *"diamond problem"* happens when a class inherits from, say, two super types, and both super types implement exactly the same function or method. See Listing 4-3 for a code example.

Listing 4-3. Diamond Problem

```
interface A {
  fun foo() {
    println("A:foo")
  }
}

interface B {
  fun foo() {
    println("B:foo")
  }
}

class Child : A, B {

}
```

The code shown in Listing 4-3 won't compile because it's not clear what will be the behavior of function *foo()* when invoked from an instance of the *Child* class; *foo()* is defined by *interfaces A* and *B* and both interfaces provide default implementation for the function. This is known as the "diamond problem." A class inherits from two supertypes, and a behavior is defined on more than one of the types from where the *class* descends. In Listing 4-3, if we invoked *foo()* from an instance of *Child*, it is ambiguous which behavior it would exhibit—whether it would print "A:foo" or "B:foo". In Kotlin, the way to resolve this is to let the *Child* class provide an implementation of the conflicted function—in this case, function *foo()*. Listing 4-4 shows the solution.

Listing 4-4. Diamond Problem, Solved

```kotlin
interface A {
  fun foo() {
    println("A:foo")
  }
}

interface B {
  fun foo() {
    println("B:foo")
  }
}

class Child : A, B {
  override fun foo () {
    println("Child:foo")
  }
}

fun main(args: Array<String>) {
  var child: Child = Child()
  child.foo()
}
```

Invoking Super Behavior

Like Java, Kotlin's functions can call the functions of its supertype if it has an implementation. Also, like in Java, Kotlin uses the *super* keyword to accomplish this. The *super* keyword in Kotlin means the same as it did in Java—it's a reference to the instance of the *supertype*. To invoke a function on a supertype, you'll need three things: (1) the super keyword; (2) name of the supertype enclosed in a pair of angle brackets; and (3) the name of function you want to invoke on the supertype. It looks something like the code snippet here:

```kotlin
super<NameOfSuperType>.functionName()
```

Let's expand our Fax and Multifunction example from earlier in the chapter.

Listing 4-5. Printable, Fax, and MultiFunction

```
interface Printable {
  fun print(doc:String) = println("Printer:Printing $doc")
}

interface Fax {
  fun call(number: String) = println("Calling $number")
  fun print(doc: String) = println("Fax:Printing $doc")
  fun answer() = println("answering")
}

class MultiFunction : Printable, Fax {

  override fun print(doc:String)  {
    println("Multifunction: printing")
  }
}
```

Listing 4-5 shows the Fax and MultiFunction example from earlier. We've added a new interface called *Printable,* and it also defines a print() function. Our revised code listing shows the *MultiFunction* class inheriting from both *Fax* and the new *Printable* interfaces. The *MultiFunction* class overrides the print() function; it has to, because the print() function is inherited from both *Printable* and *Fax* interfaces, and it has default implementations on both.

The overridden print() function in *MultiFunction* has a simple *println* statement. To demonstrate how to call a function on the supertype, we will invoke the print() function on both supertypes from within the overridden print() in *MultiFunction*. Listing 4-6 shows us how to do this.

Listing 4-6. MultiFunction, Calling Functions on Supertype

```
class MultiFunction : Printable, Fax {

  override fun print(doc:String)  {
    super<Fax>.print(doc)
    super<Printable>.print(doc)
    println("Multifunction: printing")
  }
}
```

Now, when we invoke the print() function, it will call the print() in *Fax*, then in *Printable*, and finally, whatever statements are left in the overridden print() in *MultiFunction*. Listing 4-7 shows the full codes for this example.

Listing 4-7. MultiFunction, Printable, and Fax

```
interface Printable {
  fun print(doc:String) = println("Printer:Printing $doc")
}

interface Fax {
  fun call(number: String) = println("Calling $number")
  fun print(doc: String) = println("Fax:Printing $doc")
  fun answer() = println("answering")
}

class MultiFunction : Printable, Fax {

  override fun print(doc:String)  {
    super<Fax>.print(doc)
    super<Printable>.print(doc)
    println("Multifunction: printing")
  }
}

fun main(args: Array<String>) {
  val mfc = MultiFunction()
  mfc.print("The quick brown fox")
  mfc.call("12345")
}
```

Classes

A class is defined using (1) the *class* keyword; (2) an identifier, which will be its name; (3) an optional header; and (4) an optional body. Listing 4-8 shows a basic class.

Listing 4-8. A basic class in Kotlin

```kotlin
class Person() {
}
```

The header of the class is the pair of parentheses. The header may contain parameters, but in this example, it doesn't have any. The pair of curly braces comprises the body of the class. Both the header and the class body are optional, but most of the codes we will use this in book will include both of them.

To instantiate the Person class, we can write something like the following:

```kotlin
var person = Person()
```

If not for the noticeable absence of the new keyword, it looks a lot like how we would create objects in Java. The pair of parentheses after the type name (*Person*) is a call to a *no-arg* constructor (ctor). Let's go back a bit to Listing 4-8 and take a closer look at the header portion of the class definition. This is one of the few areas where Kotlin looks and feels a bit different from Java. Java classes didn't have headers, but Kotlin does. This header is actually a constructor definition.

Constructors

Kotlin classes can have more than one constructor in their definitions. This isn't very different from Java since its classes can also contain more than one ctor. However, Kotlin makes a distinction between a primary ctor and a secondary one. A primary ctor is written on the header part of the class, like the one you've seen in Listing 4-8, while secondary ctor(s) are written in the body. Listing 4-9 shows a class with a primary constructor.

Listing 4-9. Person Class with Primary Constructor

```kotlin
class Person constructor(_name: String) { ❶
  var name:String    ❷
  init {             ❸
    name = _name     ❹
  }
}
```

❶   When a constructor is written on the class header, like this, it's primary ctor. This way of writing a ctor is essentially the same as in our example in Listing 4-8, except that Listing 4-8 doesn't contain the *constructor* keyword, and that in here (Listing 4-9), our ctor is taking in a parameter.

❷   This is a member variable that will hold the value of _name.

❸   This is an *initializer* block that is similar to Java's *initializer*. This gets executed whenever an instance of a class is created. You can have more than one initializer block in your class, and when that happens, *initializers* will be executed in the order they were defined in the class. An *initializer* block is a pair of curly braces prefixed by the keyword `init` You would normally use them when the only constructor you have is a primary constructor, because primary constructors cannot contain any code (whether statement or expressions).

❹   We can access arguments that were passed to the primary ctor from an initializer block.

When the primary ctor doesn't have (or need) annotations or visibility modifiers, we can omit the *constructor* keyword, like so:

```kotlin
class Person (_name: String) {
  var name:String
  init {
    name = _name
  }
}
```

We can further simplify and shorten the code by joining the init block and declaration of the name variable in a statement. Kotlin is smart like that.

```kotlin
class Person (_name: String) {
  var name:String = _name
}
```

Constructors may also be defined inside the body of the class, just like the way it was done in Java. When they are written as such, they are called secondary constructors. Listing 4-10 shows a sample code with a secondary ctor.

Listing 4-10. Employee Class, with Secondary Constructor

```
class Employee {
  var name:String
  constructor(_name: String) {
    name = _name
  }
}
```

Notice in Listing 4-11 that we didn't have to use the *init* block because the initialization of the name member variable was done in constructor body. A secondary ctor, unlike a primary ctor, can contain code.

Listing 4-11. class Employee, with Two Secondary Constructors

```
class Employee  {
  var name:String = ""     ❶
  var empid:String = ""

  constructor(_name: String) : this(_name, "1001") ❷
  constructor(_name:String, _id: String) {         ❸
    name = _name
    empid = _id
  }
}
```

---

❶ We have to initialize our member variables because Kotlin won't be able to tell what we are doing the initialization.

❷ A secondary constructor needs to have the *constructor* keyword. This ctor doesn't have a body; it's okay to write it like that. Furthermore, this ctor invokes another ctor—one that accepts two arguments.

❸ Another secondary constructor is defined for the Employee class. This one takes in two parameters: a name and an employee id.

You can overload your constructors in Kotlin, like we did in Java, as you can see in Listing 4-11. And also, as in Java, we can invoke other constructors using the *this* keyword. The *this* keyword in Kotlin is the same as in Java, it refers to an instance of yourself—no surprises there. Notice, though, how we used the *this* construct to delegate the call to another secondary constructor. You need to chain the *this* call to the constructor definition using a colon (see bullet 2 of Listing 4-11).

While Kotlin allows us to do parametric polymorphism on constructors via overloading, this isn't really idiomatic Kotlin because the same result can be achieved using Kotlin's ability to provide default values for function parameters. See Listing 4-12 for a simplified version of the Employee class example.

Listing 4-12. Simplified Employee class

```kotlin
class Employee (_name:String, _empid:String = "1001")  {
  val name = _name
  val empid = _empid
}
```

The code in Listing 4-12 is shorter and more concise. Furthermore, by moving the constructor parameters to the primary constructor, it allowed us to declare the member variables using *val* rather than *var*. The use of immutable variables is a preferred technique in Kotlin because it reduces coding errors overall. You can't accidentally change a property's value if it's immutable in the first place.

Inheritance

Kotlin classes are *final* by default, as opposed to Java classes that are "open" or non-final. The code, as shown in Listing 4-13, won't compile because the Person class is *final*.

Listing 4-13. Person and Employee class

```kotlin
class Person {
}

class Employee : Person() {
}
```

In order for our code sample to compile, we have to explicitly tell Kotlin that class *Person* is *open*, which signifies that we intend for it to be extended or inherited (see Listing 4-14). This default behavior of Kotlin classes is considered to be the correct behavior and good practice. To paraphrase a quote from Joshua Bloch's *Effective Java*

(Addison-Wesley, 2008): *"design and document for inheritance, otherwise prohibit it."*
This effectively means that all classes and methods that you don't intend to be extended
or overridden ought to be declared as *final*. In Kotlin, this is the automatic behavior.
Listing 4-14 shows the Person class again, but this time, it has the open modifier, which
signifies that class *Person* can be extended.

Listing 4-14. Person and Employee class

```kotlin
open class Person {
}

class Employee : Person() {
}
```

The behavior of being *final* as a default behavior isn't just for classes; member
functions are like that too in Kotlin. When a function is written without the *open*
modifier, it is final.

Listing 4-15. Method Overriding

```kotlin
open class Person(_name:String) {
  val name = _name

  open fun talk() {  ❶
    println("${this.javaClass.simpleName} talking")
  }
}

class Employee(_name:String, _empid:String = "1001") : Person(_name) {
  val empid = _empid

  override fun talk() { ❷
    super.talk() ❸
    println("Hello")
  }

  override fun toString():String{  ❹
    return "name: $name | id: $empid"
  }
}
```

❶ Functions need to be specifically marked as open so that they can be overridden by subtypes.

❷ Subtypes need to mark the function with the *override* keyword in order to make it polymorphic. IntelliJ is smart enough to prevent compilation from happening when it senses that you are defining a function on the subtype that has an exact signature on the supertype without using the *override* keyword.

❸ We can call the super behavior from here; this effectively invokes the talk() function in class *Person*.

❹ We're overriding the toString() function. This behavior was inherited from the *Person* class, which in turn it inherited from class *Any*. You can think of class *Any* as the analog for the *java.lang.Object*.

You need to keep in mind that when a function has been marked as *open*, it will remain open for overriding by its direct subtypes and even its indirect subtypes unless the function is marked as *final* again. To illustrate this point, let's consider Listing 4-16.

Listing 4-16. class Person, Employee, and Programmer

```
open class Person(_name:String) {
  val name = _name

  open fun talk() { ❶
    println("${this.javaClass.simpleName} talking")
  }
}

open class Employee(_name:String, _empid:String = "1001") : Person(_name) {
  val empid = _empid

   override fun talk() { ❷
    super.talk()
    println("Employee overriding talk()")
  }

  override fun toString():String{
    return "name: $name | id: $empid"
  }
}
```

```
class Programmer(_name:String) : Employee(_name) {
  override fun talk() { ❸
    super.talk()
    println("Programmer overriding talk()")
  }
}
```

❶ talk() function is marked as open for the first time.

❷ We can override talk() from here.

❸ We can still override talk() from here even if class Employee did not mark the function as
    open. Function talk() stays implicitly open through the inheritance hierarchy, unless it will be
    marked as final somewhere in the inheritance chain.

Listing 4-17 demonstrates how to make a function "closed" again in the midst of the
inheritance chain.

Listing 4-17. How to Make a Function Final, Again

```
open class Person(_name:String) {
  val name = _name

  open fun talk() {
    println("${this.javaClass.simpleName} talking")
  }
}

open class Employee(_name:String, _empid:String = "1001") : Person(_name) {
  val empid = _empid

   override fun talk() {
    super.talk()
    println("Employee overriding talk()")
  }

  final override fun toString():String{ ❶
    return "name: $name | id: $empid"
  }
}
```

```
class Programmer(_name:String) : Employee(_name) {
  override fun talk() { ❷
    super.talk()
    println("Programmer overriding talk()")
  }
}
```

---

❶ Seeing the final and override keyword on the same line does seem a bit odd, but it's perfectly legal. What it means is that we are overriding the function and at the same time "closing" it for further inheritance. The final keyword in this function affects only subtypes of the Employee class, but not the Employee class itself.

❷ This won't compile anymore.

Properties

A property in a class or object is traditionally created by defining a member variable and providing accessor methods for it. These methods will usually follow some naming conventions where the name of the member variable will be prefixed by *get* and *set*.

Listing 4-18. Person Class in Java with a Single Property

```
class Person {
  private String name;

  public String getName() {
    return this.name;
  }
  public void setName(String arg) {
    this.name = arg;
  }

  public static void main(String []args) {
    Person person = new Person();
    person.setName("John Doe");
    System.out.println(person.getName());
  }
}
```

Listing 4-18 shows a simple Java class that defines a single property called name. This is done by defining a member variable that will be kept private so that access to this state will only be controlled via the accessors—getName() and setName(). This kind of coding is idiomatic in Java because it doesn't have native language support for properties. We can still follow this style of coding in Kotlin, but we don't have to because Kotlin has language support for properties.

If we were to re-write Listing 4-18 in Kotlin, it would look like the code in Listing 4-19.

Listing 4-19. Person class With a Single Property

```
class Person(_name:String) { ❶
  val name:String = _name ❷
}

fun main(args: Array<String>) {
  var person = Person("John Smith")
  println(person.name) ❸
}
```

❶   A constructor takes in a parameter. This allows us to set the name of the object at the point of creation.

❷   We have access to parameters from via the constructor from here.

❸   This may look like we are directly accessing the name member variable, but we are not. This actually calls the get accessor method.

The Person class definition in Listing 4-19 can further be simplified to that in Listing 4-20.

Listing 4-20. Simplified Person class

```
class Person(val name:String)

fun main(args: Array<String>) {
  var person = Person("John Smith")
  println(person.name)
}
```

The code here is the most concise way of defining a property in Kotlin. It's also considered idiomatic. Notice the changes we made in the code:

1. The parameter in the primary constructor now has a *val* declaration. This effectively makes the constructor parameter a property. We could have used *var*, and it would work just as well.

2. We no longer need to differentiate the identifier in the constructor parameter with the member variable; hence we dropped the leading underscore in the _name variable.

3. We can drop the entire body of the class since we don't need it anymore. The class body only contains the code to transfer the value of the constructor parameter to the member variable. Since Kotlin will automatically define a backing field for the constructor parameter, we don't have to do anything anymore in the class body.

The code in Listing 4-20 shows the most basic way to define data objects in Kotlin (Java programmers refer to them as POJOs or plain old java object). By simply using either *val* or *var* in the primary constructor parameters, we can automagically define properties with proper mutator methods. However, there will still be situations when you will need to exercise more control over the "getting" and "setting" process of these properties. Kotlin allows us to do that as well.

We can take over the automatic process of "getting" and "setting" by doing the following:

1. Declare the property in the body of the class, not in the primary constructor.

2. Provide getter and setter methods in the class body.

The full syntax for declaring a property is as follows:

```
var <property name>:[<property type>][=<initializer>]
  [<getter>]
  [<setter>]
```

Listing 4-21 shows some basic usage of custom accessor methods.

Listing 4-21. Custom Accessor Methods

```kotlin
class Employee {
  var name: String = ""    ❶
    get() {  ❷
      Log("Getting lastname") ❸
      return field  ❹
    }
    set(value) {  ❺
      Log("Setting value of lastname")
      field = value ❻
    }
}

fun Log(msg:String) {
  println(msg)
}

fun main(args: Array<String>) {
  var emp = Employee()
  emp.name = "John Doe"   ❼
  println(emp.name) ❽
}
```

❶ We declare and define the *property* inside the class body, instead of capturing it as parameter in the primary constructor. We initialize it to an empty String first.

❷ The syntax for get() looks a lot like the syntax for defining a *function,* except we don't write the *fun* keyword before it.

❸ This is where you write your custom code. This statement will be executed every time someone tries to access the name property.

❹ The *field* keyword is a special one. It refers to the *backing field,* which Kotlin automatically provides when we define a property called name. The name member variable isn't a simple variable; Kotlin makes an automatic *backing field* for it, but we don't have direct access to that variable. We can, however, access it via the *field* keyword, like what we did here.

❺ The value parameter corresponds to the value that will be assigned to the property after the Employee object has been created (see bullet ❼).

❻   After we've performed our custom logic, we can now set the value of the field.

❼   This will trigger our set accessor logic, see bullet ❺.

❽   This will trigger our get accessor logic, see bullet ❷.

You might be wondering why we use the *field* keyword in the *getter* and *setter* method. Why couldn't we just code the accessor methods like we did in Java (see Listing 4-22)? This is the wrong way to code getter and setter for properties.

```
class Employee {
  var name: String = ""
    get() {
      Log("Getting lastname")
      return this.name         ❶
    }
    set(value) {
      Log("Setting value of lastname")
      this.name = value   ❷
    }
}
```

❶   This results in a recursive call, which will eventually throw *StackOverflowError.*

❷   So will this

In Listing 4-22, the expression this.name doesn't really access the member variable name. Instead, it calls the default accessor methods that Kotlin provides automatically when you define a property for the class. So, calling this.name from within an accessor function will result in a tailspin of recursive calls, and eventually the runtime will throw a *StackOverflowError.* To prevent this from happening, you should use the field keyword when referring to the *backing field* of a property name from within an accessor function.

Data Classes

When POJOs are created, sometimes they get to be stored on collections (e.g., *ArrayList, HashMap, HashSet,* etc.). And in order to utilize these POJOs correctly, in Java, we needed to override the equals(), hashCode(), and toString() methods. Remember that in Java, so that we can use properly when they are stored in collections—specifically collections that are sensitive to the hashCode.

In the previous section, we've seen how easily we can create the analog of POJOs in Kotlin. We can simply define properties in our classes and we should be good to go. For simple use-cases, the data objects that we created in the previous section should be good enough. But when you need to do things like store value objects in collections or compare objects with one another for content equality, you'll find that classes with properties aren't enough. To utilize value objects properly from within collection objects, we need to be able to compare objects with each other reliably. In Java, we use to solve this kind of problem by overriding some methods of the java.lang.Object—namely, the equals() and hashCode() methods. These methods are the key players when we're doing object comparison.

Listing 4-22. Comparing Two Employee Objects

```
class Employee(val name:String)

fun main(args: Array<String>) {

  val e1 = Employee("John Doe")
  val e2 = Employee("John Doe")

  println(e1 == e2) // output is false
}
```

Remember that in Kotlin, the double equals operator actually invokes the equals() function of the operands being compared—and since everything in Kotlin is an object, they all have the equals() function since it's inherited from the supertype *Any*. If we let the Employee class stand as it does in Listing 4-22, it will use the implementation of the equals() function from class *Any*, and it doesn't know how to compare Employee objects. To resolve this, we can override the equals() method and provide an implementation on how to compare Employee objects.

Note   Like Java, Kotlin follows a single-rooted class inheritance. If we don't specify a superclass in a class definition, the class will implicitly extend *Any*. This class is the supertype of all non-nullable types in Kotlin.

To fix the code in Listing 4-22, we would normally have to override the equals() and hashCode() functions as shown in Listing 4-23.

Listing 4-23. Overriding the hashCode() and equals() Functions

```
import java.util.*

class Employee(val name:String){
  override fun equals(obj:Any?):Boolean { ❶
    var retval = false
    if(obj is Employee) { ❷
      retval  = name == obj.name ❸
    }
    return retval
  }
  override fun hashCode(): Int { ❹
    return Objects.hash(name)
  }
}

fun main(args: Array<String>) {

  val e1 = Employee("John Doe")
  val e2 = Employee("John Doe")

  println(e1)            ❺
  println(e1 == e2)      ❻
}
```

❶ The equals() function in class *Any* is *open*, we can override it.

❷ We check first if we are comparing an *Employee* object to another *Employee* object. The *is* keyword performs two functions: (1) it checks if *obj* is actually an instance of *Employee*, and (2) it automatically casts *obj* to an *Employee* object.

❸ Obj is automatically casted to an *Employee* object. The *is* keyword already did that. Now, we can safely compare the name member variables of the two objects.

❹   Overriding the `hashCode()` function is usually needed if you intend to store this object in collections where comparisons of hash code is material (e.g., *HashSet*, *HashMap*, etc.). For our small example, it's not necessary. But it's a good practice to override the `hashCode()` function whenever you override the `equals()` function.

❺   Invokes the `toString()` function of the *Employee* object. The `toString()` function is found on the supertype *Any*. The default implementation of `toString()` gives us an output of something like this "Employee@ae805cc4".

❻   Now, this prints "true".

This kind of coding practice is very common in Java, and for that reason, quite a few IDEs have capabilities to generate the boilerplate code of toString(), equals(), and hashCode(). While we can still do these things in Kotlin, we don't have to. The only thing we need to do in Kotlin is to make Employee a data class. Listing 4-24 shows us how.

Listing 4-24. Employee Data Class

```kotlin
data class Employee(val name:String) ❶

fun main(args: Array<String>) {
  val e1 = Employee("John Doe")
  val e2 = Employee("John Doe")

  println(e1)        ❷
  println(e1 == e2)  ❸
}
```

❶   To make any class in Kotlin a *data class*, just use the keyword *data* on the class declaration.

❷   We get an added bonus of a nicer `toString()` output with data classes. This one now prints "Employee(name=John Doe)".

❸   Also, the `equals()` comparison returns true.

Visibility Modifiers

Kotlin uses almost the same keywords as Java for controlling visibility. The keywords *public*, *private,* and *protected* mean exactly the same in Kotlin as they do in Java. But, the default visibility is where the difference lies. In Kotlin, whenever you omit the visibility modifier, the default visibility is *public*.

Listing 4-25. Class Foo

```
class Foo {
  var bar:String = ""
  fun doSomething() {

  }
}
```

In Listing 4-25, class Foo and its members are visible publicly. If you want to change the visibility to something less permissive, you have to declare that explicitly. In contrast, Java's default visibility is *package-private*, meaning it's only available to classes that are on the same package. Kotlin doesn't have a *package-private* equivalent because Kotlin doesn't use packages as a way to manage visibility. Packages in Kotlin are simply a way to organize files and prevent name clashes.

In place of Java's package-private, Kotlin introduces the *internal* keyword, which means it is visible in a *module*. A module is simply a collection of files, it can be (1) an IntelliJ module or project; (2) an Eclipse project; (3) a Maven project; or (4) a Gradle project. To demonstrate the some of the visibility modifiers in action, see Listing 4-26.

Listing 4-26. Demonstrating Visibility Modifiers

```
internal open class Foo {  ❶
  private fun boo() = println("boo")
  protected fun doo() = println("doo")
}

fun Foo.bar() { ❷
  boo() ❸
  doo() ❹
}
```

```
fun main(args: Array<String>) {
  var fu = Foo()
  fu.bar()
}
```

❶   Class *Foo* is marked as *internal*, which makes it visible only in classes and top-level functions
     that are within the same module and whose visibility are also marked *internal.*

❷   This is an error. The *extension function* is marked as *public,* but the receiver of the function
     (Foo) is marked as internal. Class *Foo* is less visible than the extension function; hence, Kotlin
     doesn't allow us.

❸   boo() is private to the class, so we can't reach it from here.

❹   doo() is protected, we can't reach it from here.

To make Listing 4-26 run without problems, we need to fix the visibility errors.
Listing 4-27 shows the solution.

Listing 4-27. class Foo, Corrected Visibility Errors

```
internal open class Foo {
  internal fun boo() = println("boo")
  internal fun doo() = println("doo")
}

internal fun Foo.bar() {
  boo()
  doo()
}

fun main(args: Array<String>) {
  var fu = Foo()
  fu.bar()
}
```

Access Modifiers

The access modifiers of Kotlin are *final, open, abstract,* and *override*. They affect inheritance. We've used *final, open,* and *override* earlier in the chapter, so the only keyword we haven't used is *abstract*. The abstract keyword has the same meaning in Kotlin as it does in Java. It's applicable to classes and functions.

When you mark a class as *abstract*, it becomes implicitly *open* as well, so you don't need to use the *open* modifier, it becomes redundant. Interfaces don't need to be declared as *abstract* and *open*, since they are implicitly, already, *abstract* and *open*.

Object Declarations

Java's *static* keyword did not make the cut in Kotlin's list of keywords. There is no *static* equivalent in Kotlin; in its place, Kotlin introduces the *object* and *companion* keywords.

The *object* keyword allows us to define both a class and its instance all at the same time. More specifically, it defines only a single instance of that class, which makes this keyword a good way to define *singletons* in Kotlin. Listing 4-28 shows the basic usage for the *object* keyword.

Listing 4-28. Using the Object Keyword to Define a Singleton

```
object Util {
  fun foo() = println("foo")
}

fun main(args: Array<String>) {
  Util.foo() // prints "foo"
}
```

We substitute the *object* keyword in place of the *class* keyword. What this effectively does is define the class and create a single instance of it. To invoke the functions defined in this object, we prefix the dot (.) with the name of the object—pretty much like how we would call static methods in Java.

Object declarations can contain most of the things you can write in class, like initializers, properties, functions, and member variables. The only thing you cannot write inside an object declaration is a constructor. The reason for this is because you don't need a constructor. The object declaration creates an instance already at the point of definition, so a constructor is not necessary. Listing 4-29 shows some basic usage and definition for an object declaration.

Listing 4-29. Initializers, Properties, Functions, and Member Variables in Object Declarations

```
object Util {
  var name = ""
    set(value) {
      field = value
    }

  init {
    println("Initializing Util")
  }

  fun foo() = println(name)
}

fun main(args: Array<String>) {
  Util.name = "Bar"
  Util.foo() // prints "Bar"
}
```

Chapter Summary

- Kotlin interfaces are almost similar to that of Java, except that you can declare properties in interfaces, although they still are not allowed to have backing fields. Like Java 8, Kotlin interfaces can have *default* implementations.

- Kotlin classes are defined a bit differently than their Java counterparts. Classes are, by default, final and public.

- Kotlin has two kinds of constructors: you can define primary and secondary constructors. Primary constructors are a good way to create simple value objects. However, to create really useful value objects, Kotlin's data classes are a good way to go.

- Kotlin has almost the same mechanism for controlling visibility like Java, except that Kotlin replaced Java's *package-private* with the *internal* keyword.

In the next chapter, we'll dip our toes into the world of functional programming.

CHAPTER 5

Lambdas and Higher Order Functions

What we'll cover:

- Higher order functions

- Lambda

- Closures

- With and apply

In Chapter 2, we discussed the mechanics of Kotlin functions, and you've already seen how similar they are to Java functions; you've also seen how different they are. In this chapter, we'll get back to the discussion of functions, but a different kind of function—the kind that supports *functional programming*. You may have used lambdas in Java 8; similarly, Kotlin also has support for lambdas. In this chapter, we'll explore these two topics.

Higher Order Functions

Higher order functions are functions that operate on other functions, either by taking them in as parameters or by returning them. The term *higher order functions* comes from the world of Math where there is a more formal distinction between functions and other values.

Before we can get into a discussion about "Why would we need higher order functions?" we'll need to attend to its mechanics. We need to know how to write them and what they look like. The discussion on the "why" of higher order functions may even

© Ted Hagos 2018
T. Hagos, *Learn Android Studio 3 with Kotlin*, https://doi.org/10.1007/978-1-4842-3907-0_5

come in later chapters, when we get to Android programming where there are plenty of opportunities to put higher order functions to good use.

Listing 5-1 below shows an example of a function that takes in another function as parameter.

Listing 5-1. A Function That Accepts Another Function

```
fun executor(action:() -> Unit) {
  action()
}
```

Notice how the parameter is written in Listing 5-1, *action* is the name of the parameter and its type is written as ()-> Unit, which means that it's type is *function*. A *function type* is written with a pair of parentheses, followed by the arrow operator (a dash plus the greater than sign) and then followed by a type that the function is supposed to return. In our example in Listing 5-1, our function parameter doesn't return anything—hence it's declared as *Unit*.

This may look strange at first, especially if you haven't used a language where functions are treated the same way that variables are treated. In Kotlin, like any language that supports higher order functions, functions are first class citizens. We can pass (or return) functions from anywhere we can pass (or return) variables. Wherever you can use a variable, you can also use a function.

Let's go back to Listing 5-1. If we wanted the *action* parameter to be of type *String*, then we could have written something like that in Listing 5-2.

Listing 5-2. If Action Was of Type String

```
fun executor(action:String) {
  action()
}
```

But that's not the case; we want *action* to be of type *function*. In Kotlin, a function isn't just a named collection of statement, it's also a type. So, just like *String, Int,* or *Float,* we can declare a variable to be of type *function*. A function type has three components: (1) the parenthesized parameter type list; (2) the arrow operator; and (3) the return type.

In Listing 5-1, the parenthesized parameter type list is empty, but it won't always be the case. It's empty right now because the function we intend to pass to executor() doesn't accept any parameters. The return type of executor() is Unit because the function we intend to pass to it doesn't return any value—that also, will not always be the case, you may want to return an Int or String sometimes.

Now that we understand how to declare a parameter to be of function type, let's take a look at how to declare and define a variable to be of function type. See Listing 5-3.

Listing 5-3. How to Declare and Define a Function Type

```
val doThis:() -> Unit  = {
  println("action")
}
```

The LHS (left-hand side) doesn't require much explanation, we're simply declaring a variable named doThis to be of *type function*, and this function doesn't return anything, so it's declared return type is Unit. The RHS (right-hand side) looks like a function without a header (the *fun* keyword and the function name), this is a lambda. We'll get to lambdas in the next section. Going back to our code examples, Listing 5-4 shows how to put executor() and doThis together.

Listing 5-4. Complete Code for doThis and executor() Examples

```
val doThis:() -> Unit  = { ❶
  println("action")
}

fun executor(action:() -> Unit) { ❷
  action() ❸
  action.invoke() ❹
}

fun main(args: Array<String>) {
  executor(doThis) ❺
}
```

❶ doThis is declared and defined as a *function type*. The implementation of the function is given as a lambda expression on the RHS. The body of the function doesn't return anything; hence the return type specified for the function is Unit.

❷ executor() is a function that accepts another function as a parameter; this parameter is named action and its type is *function*, which is written as () → Unit. More specifically, this *function type* doesn't return anything—that's why it's declared as Unit.

❸ By appending a pair of parentheses on the name of the parameter, we get to invoke the function.

❹ This is another way of invoking the action function, but calling it like action()is more idiomatic and, hence, preferred.

❺ Inside the main function, we get to call executor() and we pass doThis. Note that we're not passing doThis()with the parentheses. We don't want to invoke doThis and then pass the resulting value to executor(). What we want is to pass doThis not as a resulting value, but as a function definition. The idea is to invoke doThis within the body of the executor()function.

In Listing 5-4, we wrote doThis as a property whose value is a lambda. This is perfectly fine, but it might not feel like a natural way to write functions. Another way to write Listing 5-4 is shown in Listing 5-5.

Listing 5-5. Another Way of Writing the doThis and executor() Examples

```
fun doThis() { ❶
  println ("action")
}

fun executor(action:() -> Unit) {
  action()
}

fun main(args: Array<String>) {
  executor(::doThis) ❷
}
```

❶ doThis is now defined in the usual way that we write functions, with the fun keyword and the name of the function in the header.

❷ ::doThis is invoked with a double colon. This means we are resolving the function within the current *package*.

Lambda and Anonymous Functions

Lambdas and anonymous functions are called *function literals*. These are functions that are not declared but, rather, passed immediately as an expression—more often than not, to a higher order function. Because of this they don't need a name. We've used lambda expressions earlier in this chapter. In Listing 5-3, we defined a property called *doThis* whose type is a function, but it's a rather verbose way of working with a function type. We actually don't need to explicitly write the return type of the function because Kotlin can infer it for us. Listing 5-6 shows a more concise version of Listing 5-3.

Listing 5-6. Concise Version of Listing 5-3

```
val doThis = {
  println("action")
}
```

As you've seen in the previous section, this kind of code is intended to be passed along as an argument to a higher order function. But you can actually use this without passing it to a higher order function. To invoke it, you may do something like the following—presumably inside function main or any other top-level function

```
doThis()
```

or something like this

```
doThis.invoke()
```

The former looks more natural; it's also considered more idiomatic, so we should probably use that. Anyway, lambda expressions aren't meant to be used like this. They really shine when used within the context of higher order functions. In Listing 5-5, we used the full syntactic form of the lambda expressions when we passed a named lambda expression to a higher order function. While you can certainly do that, it may not be the usual way you'll encounter lambda expressions in the wild. Listing 5-7 is a rewrite of Listing 5-5, but this time, instead of declaring and defining a named lambda, we will simply pass it as an argument to the higher order function *executor*, as seen in Listing 5-7.

Listing 5-7. Pass a lambda to a Higher Order Function

```
fun main(args: Array<String>) {
  executor(
    { println("do this") } ❶
  )
}

fun executor(action:() -> Unit) {
  action()
}
```

❶ This is the *function literal*. In Listing 5-5, we passed doThis, which was a property whose value was a lambda expression. In this example, we are passing the lambda expression itself directly to the higher order function. A lambda expression is enclosed in a pair of curly braces— just like the body of a function.

Parameters in Lambda Expressions

Consider the code in Listing 5-8. If we were to write it as a lambda, it would look like Listing 5-9.

Listing 5-8. Simple Function to Display a String

```
fun display(msg:String) {
  println("Hello $msg")
}
```

Listing 5-9. display Function Written As lambda

```
{ msg:String -> println("Hello $msg") }
```

You'll notice that the entire function header, the keyword *fun* and the function name, is completely gone, and the parameter list was relocated inside the lambda expression. The whole expression is enclosed in a pair of curly braces. In a lambda expression, the parameter list is written on the left-hand side of the arrow operator and the body of the function is found on the right. You will also notice that the parameters in a lambda expression don't need to be inside a pair of parentheses because the arrow operator separates the parameter list from the body of the lambda.

Also, in Listing 5-9, you can omit the type declaration of String in the parameter, so it can be written like in Listing 5-10.

Listing 5-10. Omitted Type Declaration in Parameter List

```
{ msg -> println("Hello $msg") }
```

In some cases where the lambda expression takes only one parameter, like our code example shown in Listing 5-10, Kotlin allows us to omit the parameter declaration and even the arrow operator. We can rewrite Listing 5-10 in an even shorter way (see Listing 5-11).

Listing 5-11. The Implicit It

```
{ println("Hello $it") }
```

The *it* parameter name is generated if the context expects a lambda that has only one parameter and if its type can be inferred. Listing 5-12 shows the full code on how to declare and use a lambda expression within the context of a higher order function. Now we have the *functional programming* version of the Hello World example.

Listing 5-12. Full Code for the lambda Example

```
fun main(args: Array<String>) {
  executor({ println("Hello $it") })
}

fun executor(display:(msg:String) -> Unit) {
  display("World")
}
```

Writing and using lambdas with more than one parameter isn't much different from our single parameter example, as long as you write the parameter list on left side of the arrow operator. See Listing 5-13 for an example.

Listing 5-13. lambdas With More Than One Parameter

```
fun main(args: Array<String>) {
  doer({ x,y -> println(x + y) })
}

fun doer(sum:(x:Int,y:Int) -> Unit) {
  sum(1,2)
}
```

There may be occasions when a higher order function will take in some other parameters together with function types. Such a function could look like Listing 5-14.

Listing 5-14. Higher Order Function With Multiple Parameters

```
fun executor(arg: String = "Mondo", display:(msg:String) -> Unit) {
  display(arg)
}
```

We can invoke this function with this

```
executor("Earth", {println("Hola $it")})
```

And since *executor's* first parameter has a default value, we can still invoke it like this

```
executor({println("Hola $it")})
```

Kotlin allows us to be a bit more precise in our syntax with lambdas. In cases where the lambda is expected as the last parameter in a higher order function, we can write the lambda outside the parentheses of the invoking function, like this:

```
executor() { println("Hello $it")}
```

And if the lambda is the only parameter, we can even omit the parentheses entirely, like this one:

```
executor { println("Hello $it")}
```

The simplification may not seem like a big deal right now, but I believe you'll appreciate the syntactical improvements later as you write more and more lambda expressions. The Kotlin Standard library makes heavy use of these things.

Closures

When you use a lambda expression inside a function, the lambda can access its *closure*. The closure is comprised of the local variables in the outer scope as well as all the parameters of the enclosing function. See Listing 5-15 for an example.

Listing 5-15. lambda Accessing Its Closure

```
fun main(args: Array<String>) {
  executor(listOf(1..1000).flatten()) ❶
}

fun executor(numbers:List<Int>) {
 var sum = 0;
 numbers.forEach {        ❷
   if ( it % 2 == 0 ) {
     sum += it            ❸
   }
 }
  println("Sum of all even numbers = $sum")
}
```

❶ We're passing a list of *Ints* to the executor() function. Using the *rangeTo* function in operator form (..) is a handy way to generate a list of integers from 1 up to 1000. But you'd have to use the flatten() function to make it a list of *Ints*.

❷ forEach is a higher order function; it takes in a lambda, which allows us to walk through items in the list. The forEach only has one parameter, and we can access that single parameter using the implicit it parameter name.

❸ The sum variable is part of the *closure*; it's within the function body where the lambda is defined. Lambdas have access to their *closures*.

> **Note**   In Java lambdas, you can only access a variable in its closure if that same variable is final. There is no such restriction in Kotlin.

with and apply

Lambdas are used heavily in Kotlin, they have their footprint all over Kotlin's library. In this section, we'll take a look at the functions *with* and *apply* from the standard library, specifically from Standard.kt. These functions demonstrate the capabilities of Kotlin's lambdas and what makes them stand out from their Java counterparts. Kotlin lambdas have the ability to call methods of a different object without additional qualifiers in the body of the lambda. These kinds of lambdas are called *lambdas with receivers*.

The functions *with* and *apply* are of particular interest not because they allow us to perform multiple operations on the same object without repeating the object's name—which is a welcome feature-but because they look like they were baked into the language, which they're not. They simply are functions that were made special by *extension functions* and *lambdas*.

Listing 5-16 shows the definition of a simple class and how to set some of its properties. The creation of an *Event* instance and the setting of its various properties are happening inside *function main*. Notice that for every property we set, we have to explicitly resolve the property back to the object reference, and this might be just fine—after all, this was how we coded in Java, this chore is, sort of, expected.

Listing 5-16. class Event

```
import java.util.Date

data class Event(val title:String) {
  var date = Date()
  var time = ""
  var attendees = mutableListOf<String>()

  fun create() {
    print(this)
  }
}
```

```
fun main(args: Array<String>) {

  val mtg = Event("Management meeting")

  mtg.date = Date(2018,1,1)
  mtg.time = "0900H"
  mtg.attendees.add("Ted")

  mtg.create()
}
```

If we were to use the *with* function to refactor the code, it would look like one in Listing 5-17.

Listing 5-17.   Using the With Function

```
fun main(args: Array<String>) {

  val mtg = Event("Management meeting")

  with(mtg) {
    date = Date(2018,1,1)
    time = "0900H"
    attendees.add("Ted")

  }
}
```

The *with* function takes in an object (*mtg*) and a lambda. Inside the lambda, we can work with the *mtg* object without the need to explicitly reference it. This is made possible because the *mtg* object was made into a *receiver* of the lambda—remember the extension functions in Chapter 3? And because *mtg* is the receiver, inside the lambda, the *this* keyword points to the *mtg* object. We could have explicitly referenced *this* in our code, but that wouldn't be any better than when we first started with this example. By omitting the explicit reference to *this*, the resulting code is much cleaner. Also, the convention to put the lambda outside the parentheses definitely works in this situation because it makes the construct look as if *with* is a part of the Kotlin language.

The *apply* function can achieve the same thing; it's almost very similar to the *with* function except that it returns the receiver (the object passed to it)—the *with* function doesn't.

```
fun main(args: Array<String>) {

  val mtg = Event("Management meeting")

  mtg.apply {                    ❶
    date = Date()                ❷
    time = "0900H"
    attendees.add("Ted")
  }.create()                     ❸
}
```

❶ Apply is an extension function and the *mtg* object becomes its *receiver.*

❷ And because the *mtg* object is the *receiver*, *this* refers to the *mtg* object.

❸ When the lambda returns, it returns the *receiver*, which is a *mtg* object; hence, we can chain some calls into it.

There are many more functions in Standard.Kt like *run, let, also*, etc., but these two examples using with and apply should give us an idea of what lambdas are capable of.

Chapter Summary

- Functions in Kotlin are more than just a named collection of statements. They are also a type. A *function type* can be used anywhere else that other types can be used—functions are first-class citizens in Kotlin.

- Lambdas and anonymous functions are function literals. They're like regular functions, but they don't have a name. They can be passed around (to other functions) immediately as an expression.

- Kotlin lambdas, unlike their Java lambdas (at least Java 9, as of this writing), can mutate variables in its closure.

- Higher order functions are functions that operate on other functions. They can accept function types as parameters, or return function types.

In the next chapter, we'll explore Kotlin's Collection classes.

CHAPTER 6

Collections and Arrays

What we'll cover:

- Arrays
- Collections
- Filter and Apply

One of the real-world analogies for collections would be a purse or a pouch filled with various things such as coins. The coins would be the *items* and the pouch itself is the *collection.* So, based on this analogy, we can say that a collection is a *container* of sorts that may have zero, one, or many items in it. You might remember that we already have something like that—an array. The array fits this description exactly because it can contain zero, one, or many items inside it. If this is the case, do we really need to learn about other containers? In this chapter, we'll take a look at arrays, collections, and some of the functions within the Kotlin collections framework.

Arrays

Coming from Java, you'll need to step back a bit before working with Kotlin arrays. In Java, these are special types; they have first-class support on the language level. In Kotlin, arrays are just types; more specifically, they are parameterized types. If you wanted to create an array of Strings, you might think that the following snippet might work:

```
var arr = {"1", "2", "3", "4", "5"}
```

This code wouldn't make sense to Kotlin—it doesn't treat arrays as a special type. If we wanted to create an array of Strings like the example, we can do it in a couple of ways. Kotlin has some library functions like *arrayOf, emptyArray,* and *arrayOfNulls* that we

© Ted Hagos 2018
T. Hagos, *Learn Android Studio 3 with Kotlin*, https://doi.org/10.1007/978-1-4842-3907-0_6

can use to facilitate array creation. Listing 6-1 shows how to create and populate an array using the *emptyArray* function.

Listing 6-1. Using the emptyArray Function

```
var arr = emptyArray<String>();
arr += "1"
arr += "2"
arr += "3"
arr += "4"
arr += "5"
```

Adding elements to a Kotlin array isn't as verbose as it is in Java, but don't be fooled by nice syntax. Arrays are still fixed-size at the time of creation, even here in Kotlin. Adding an element to an array is done by creating a new array that is bigger than the old array and then copying the elements of the old array into the new one. So, you see, it's still an expensive operation—even if we have a nice sugary syntax. Listing 6-2 shows how to use the *arrayOfNulls* function to do the same thing.

Listing 6-2. Using the arrayOfNulls Function

```
var arr2 = arrayOfNulls<String>(2)
arr2.set(0, "1")
arr2.set(1, "2")
```

The integer argument of the arrayOfNulls function is the size of the array to be created. Unlike the empty array in Listing 6-1, this function gives you a chance to provide a size for the array you're about to create. By the way, you can still use bracket syntax for Kotlin arrays, the *get* and *set* methods of *Arrays* are just convenience functions. Listing 6-3 shows the use of the bracket syntax together with the new *get* and *set* functions.

Listing 6-3. Get and Set Methods of Array

```
var arr2 = arrayOfNulls<String>(2)

// arr2.set(0, "1")
// arr2.set(1, "2")

arr2[0] = "1"
arr2[1] = "2"
```

```
println(arr2[0]) // same as arr2.get(0)
println(arr2[1])
```

Another way to create an array is using the *arrayOf* function. Listing 6-4 shows the snippet.

Listing 6-4. Using the arrayOf Function

```
var arr4 = arrayOf("1", "2", "3")
```

This function is probably the closest syntax we can get to the Java array literal, which is probably why it is used by programmers more commonly. You can pass a comma-separated list of values to the function, and that automatically populates the newly created array.

Finally, arrays can be created using the Array constructor. The constructor takes in two arguments, the first of which is the size of the array to be created and the second argument is a lambda function that can return an initial value of each element.

Listing 6-5. Using the Array Constructor

```
var arr3 = Array<String>(5, {it.toString()})
```

In most situations when you need to work with arrays of numbers, using the *Array* class should suffice. You need to remember, however, that `Array<Int>,` for example, represents the ints as Integer objects rather than integer primitives. So, if you need to squeeze a bit more performance juice out of your code and really use the primitive number types, you can use the specialized array types of Kotlin.

The specialized classes like *ByteArray, IntArray, ShortArray,* and *LongArray* represent arrays of primitive types (like the ones in Java). These types let you work with arrays without the boxing and unboxing overhead of *Arrays* that uses the object counterparts of the number primitives. These specialized types actually do not inherit from *Array*, but they have the same sets of methods and properties. Also, they have specialized factory functions that make them easier to work with. See Listing 6-6 for an example.

Listing 6-6. Special Array Types

```
var z = intArrayOf(1,2,3)
var y = longArrayOf(1,2,3)
```

```
var x = byteArrayOf(1,2,3)
var w = shortArrayOf(1,2,3)

println(Arrays.toString(z))
println(Arrays.toString(y))
println(Arrays.toString(x))
println(Arrays.toString(w))
```

I used the `Arrays.toString()` function so that we'll get a human-readable output when printing the contents. If you simply print the array without the helper function, it looks like gibberish, like this

```
println(z) // outputs [Ljava.lang.String;@6ad5c04e
```

Traversing arrays can be done in a couple of ways. First, you can use the trustworthy *for* loop, as shown in Listing 6-7.

Listing 6-7. Using a for Loop to Process Each Array Element

```
for (i in z) {
  println("$i zee")
}
```

Or you could use the *forEach* function, like so.

```
y.forEach { i -> println("$i why") }
```

If you need to keep track of both the index and the element of the array, you can use the *forEachIndexed* function, as shown in Listing 6-8.

Listing 6-8. Using the forEachIndexed Function to Traverse the Array

```
x.forEachIndexed { index, element ->
  println("$index : $element")
}
```

Before we leave the subject of arrays, we need to remember that if you don't want any duplication on the contents of the array, you'll have to write that program logic yourself. Uniqueness of contents is not something that arrays will guarantee.

While arrays are very useful in many situations, they do have limitations, as you've seen in the previous discussions. Adding new elements to arrays, while the syntax is friendly, is still an expensive operation. You can't print them out without the use of helper functions (although this is not a big deal). Finally, it doesn't have a facility for constraining the elements (e.g., enforcing uniqueness). For some situations these limitations may not be a big deal, but for some situations, these may be deal-killers. So, when we come up to the limitations of the arrays, we are coming up on the territory of Collections—they help us deal with such limitations.

The availability of the collections framework as part of the development kit may not be such a big deal for you. After all, you came from Java and it has an impressive collections framework. But you need to remember that before languages like Java, C#, Python, etc., there were no collections frameworks. Programmers had to write their own program logic in order to deal with problems like resizable arrays, last-in first-out access, hash tables or hash maps, etc. These aren't simple storage issues, but rather, they are data structure issues. It's quite difficult to implement this data structure logic on your own; there are a lot of edge cases to get right. Although there might still be legitimate reasons to implement your own data structures (probably for performance reasons), in most cases, you'd be better off to use the built-in collections framework.

Collections

The Kotlin collections are actually direct instances of the collections in the JDK. There's no conversion of wrapping involved. So, if you didn't skimp on your study of collections while you were in Java, that will certainly come in handy now. Although Kotlin didn't define its own collections code, it did add quite a few convenience functions to the framework, which is a welcome addition because it makes the collections easier to work with.

Before we go to the code examples and more details, something needs to be said regarding why it is called a collections framework. The reason it's called a framework is because the data structures are very diverse, in and of themselves. Some of them put constraints on how we go through the collection; they impose certain order of traversal. Some of the collections constrain the uniqueness of the data elements; they won't allow you to put duplicates. And some of them let us work with the collections in pairs—like in a dictionary entry, you'll have a key with a corresponding value.

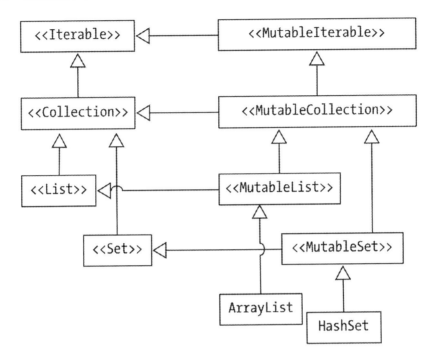

Figure 6-1. *Collections Framework*

Figure 6-1 shows the hierarchy of the Kotlin collections framework. At the top of the hierarchy are the interfaces *Iterable* and *MutableIterable*—they are the parents of all the collection classes we will work with. As you may have noticed in the diagram, each Java collection has two representations in Kotlin: a read-only one and a mutable one. The mutable interfaces map directly to the Java interfaces while the immutable interfaces lack all of the mutator methods of their mutable counterparts.

Kotlin doesn't have a dedicated syntax for creating lists or sets, but it does provide us with library functions to facilitate creation. Table 6-1 lists some of them.

Table 6-1. *Kotlin Collections and Their Creation Functions*

Collection	Read-Only	Mutable
list	listOf	mutableListOf, arrayListOf
set	setOf	mutableSetOf, hashSetOf, linkedSetOf, sortedSetOf
map	mapOf	mutableMapOf, hashMapOf, linkedMapOf, sortedMapOf

Note   Although the map class doesn't inherit from either *Iterable* or *MutableIterable* (Figure 6-1), it's still represented in Kotlin as two distinct versions: a mutable and an immutable one.

Lists

A list is a type of collection that has a specific iteration order. It means that if we added a couple of elements to the list, and then we stepped through it, the elements would come out in a very specific order—it's the order by which they were added or inserted. They won't come out in a random order or reverse chronology, but precisely in the sequence they were added. It implies that each element in the list has a placement order, an index number that indicates its ordinal position. The first element to be added will have its index at 0, the second will be 1, the third will be 2, and so on. So, just like an array, it is zero-based. Listing 6-9 shows the basic usage for a list.

Listing 6-9. Basic Usage of Lists

```kotlin
fun main(args: Array<String>) {

  val fruits = mutableListOf<String>("Apple") ❶
  fruits.add("Orange")        ❷
  fruits.add(1, "Banana")     ❸
  fruits.add("Guava")

  println(fruits)  // prints [Apple, Banana, Orange, Guava]

  fruits.remove("Guava")      ❹
  fruits.removeAt(2)          ❺

  println(fruits.first() == "Strawberries") ❻
  println(fruits.last() == "Banana")        ❼

  println(fruits) //  prints [Apple, Banana]
}
```

❶ Creates a mutable list, the constructor function allows us to pass a variable argument that will be used to populate the list. In this case, we only passed one argument—we could have passed more.

❷ Adds an element to the list; "Orange" will come right after "Apple" since we did not specify the ordinal position for the insertion.

❸ Adds another element to the list, but this time, we told it where exactly to put the element. This one bumps down the "Orange" element and then inserts itself. Naturally, the ordinal position or the index of all the elements that come after it will change.

❹ You can remove elements by name. When an element is removed, the element next to it will take its place. The ordinal position of all the elements that comes after it will change accordingly.

❺ You can also remove elements by specifying its position on the list.

❻ You can ask if the first() element is equal to "Strawberries".

❼ You can also test if the last() element is equal to "Banana".

Sets

Sets are very similar to lists, both in operation and in structure, so all of the things we've learned about lists apply to sets as well. Sets differ from lists in the way they put constraints on the uniqueness of elements. They doesn't allow duplicate elements or the same elements within a set. It may seem obvious to many what the "same" means, but Kotlin, like Java, has a specific meaning for "sameness." When we say that two objects are the same, it means that we've subjected the objects to a test for structural equality. Both Java and Kotlin define a method called equals(), which allows us to determine equivalence relationships between objects. This is generally what we mean by "sameness." Listing 6-10 shows some basic operations with sets.

Listing 6-10. Basic Usage for Sets

```
val nums = mutableSetOf("one", "two")   ❶
nums.add("two")                         ❷
nums.add("two")                         ❸
nums.add("three")                       ❹

println(nums) // prints [one, two, three]
```

```
val numbers = (1..1000).toMutableSet()  ❺
numbers.add(6)
numbers.removeIf { i -> i % 2 == 0 }    ❻

println(numbers)
```

---

❶   Creates a mutable set and initializes it by passing a variable argument to the creator function.

❷   This doesn't do anything. It won't add "two" to the set because the element "two" is already in the set.

❸   No matter how many times you try to add "two," the set will reject it because it already exists.

❹   This, on the other hand, will be added because "three" doesn't exist in the elements yet.

❺   Creates a mutable set from a range. This is a handy way of creating a set (or a list) with many numeric elements.

❻   This demonstrates how to use a lambda to remove all the even numbers in the set.

Maps

Unlike lists or sets, maps aren't a collection of individual values; rather, they are a collection of pairs of values. Think of a map like a dictionary or a phone book. Its contents are organized using a key-value pair. For each key in a map, there is one and only one corresponding value. In a dictionary example, the key would be the *term*, and its value would be the *meaning* or the *definition* of the term.

The keys in a map are unique. Like sets, maps do not allow duplicate keys. However, the values in a map are not subjected to the same uniqueness constraints; two or more pairs in map may have the same value. Listing 6-11 show some basic usage for maps.

Listing 6-11. Basic Operations on a Map

```
val dict = hashMapOf("foo" to 1)   ❶
dict["bar"] = 2                    ❷

val snapshot: MutableMap<String, Int> = dict  ❸
snapshot["baz"] = 3                           ❹

println(snapshot)                  ❺
println(dict)                      ❻
println(snapshot["bar"]) // prints 2  ❼
```

❶ Ca mutable map

❷ Adds a new key and value to the map

❸ Assigns the `dict` map to a new variable. This doesn't create a new map. It only adds an object reference to the existing map.

❹ Adds another key-value pair to the map

❺ Prints {bar = 2, baz = 3, foo=1}

❻ Also prints {bar = 2, baz = 3, foo=1}, because both `snapshot` and `dict` points to the same map.

❼ Gets the value from the map using the key

Now that we've seen some examples of basic usage of collections, you probably have noticed that they share some common characteristics—maybe not 100% as with the map, but the list and the set have quite a lot of overlap. One good thing about working with the collections framework is the uniformity or regularity of certain operations throughout the entire collection. The skills and knowledge that we learn from working with lists, for example, commutes or translates nicely across sets and maps as well. Because of this, it's a good idea to be familiar with the collections protocol. Table 6-2 lists some of the more common operations on collections.

Table 6-2. *Common Operations on Collections*

Function or Property	Description
`Size`	Tells you how many elements are in the collection. Works with lists, sets and maps.
`isEmpty()`	Returns True if the collection is empty, False if it's not. Works with lists, sets, and maps.
`contains(arg)`	Returns True if arg is within the collection. Works with lists, sets, and maps.
`add(arg)`	Add arg to the collection. This function returns true if arg was added—in the case of a list, arg will always be added. In the case of a set, arg will be added and return true the first time, but if the same arg is added the second time, it will return False. This member function is not found on maps.
`remove(arg)`	Returns True if arg was removed from the collection, returns False is the collection is unmodified.
`iterator()`	Returns an iterator over the elements of the object. This was inherited from the Iterable interface. Works with lists, sets, and maps.

Collections Traversal

By now, we already know how to work with basic collections. We know how to create them and add and remove items from them. Another skill we will need to work effectively with collections is the ability to loop through them or traverse them. To do that, let's go back to Figure 6-1 and recall the inheritance structure of the collections framework.

In Figure 6-1, you'll notice that *Collections* inherits the *Iterable* interface. An *iterable* defines something that can be iterated over or stepped over. When a class inherits an Iterable interface, whether directly or indirectly, it means we can pull an iterator out of it and step through its elements one by one. And in each step, we can also pull the value of each element—it's up to your program logic what you want to do with those values; you can transform them, use them in an arithmetic operation, or persist it in a storage, for example.

We can use a variety of ways to step through the elements in a collection. We can use the trusty *while* and *for* loops, if you prefer, but using the more modern *forEach* is more idiomatic—and a bit in vogue. Listing 6-12 shows how to step through a list using *while* and for *loops.*

Listing 6-12. Using while and for Loops for Collections

```
val basket = listOf("apple", "banana", "orange")
var iter = basket.iterator()
while (iter.hasNext()) {
  println(iter.next())
}

for (i in basket) {
  println(i)
}
```

Listing 6-12 is probably something close to how you worked with collections in Java, so it should look familiar. Listing 6-13 shows the equivalent codes when using the *forEach* function.

Listing 6-13. Using forEach

```
fruits.forEach { println(it) } ❶
nums.forEach { println(it) }   ❷

// for maps

dict.forEach { println(it) }   ❸
dict.forEach { t, u -> println("$t | $u") } ❹
```

❶ The lambda expression of the forEach has an implicit it parameter. The it parameter is the value of the current element. What this statement means is for each item in *fruits*, do what's inside the lambda, which in our case is just println().

❷ Same thing works for *sets*

❸ Same thing works for *maps*

❹ This is a variation of bullet 3 above, but this one allows us to work with the *key* and *value* separately.

Filter and Map

Filter and map are part of the essential skills you need to master in order to work with collections efficiently. Filtering allows us to work with the elements of a collection selectively. It narrows down the field. It basically returns a subset of the original collection. A map, on the other hand, allows us to transform either the elements or the collection itself.

Let's say, for example, that we have a list of numbers—integers to be precise, like this

```
val ints = (1..100).toList()
```

The variable ints contains a list of integers from 1 up until 100, in increments of 1. If we wanted to work with only the even numbers in this list, we could do so by (1) creating a new list; (2) iterating over the ints list and performing a modulo check for even numbers; and then (3) if the current element being processed is an even number, we add it to the new list. That code might look like Listing 6-14.

Listing 6-14. Using a for Loop to Sieve Out the Even Numbers

```kotlin
val evenInts2 = mutableListOf<Int>()
for (i in ints) {
  if (i % 2 == 0) {
    evenInts2.add(i)
  }
}
```

Listing 6-14 is what might be called the "imperative" way of filtering out things. Nothing wrong with it—it's a little verbose, that's all. But it's perfectly readable, even by someone just starting out in programming. However, in Kotlin, the more idiomatic way of narrowing down collections is by using the *filter* function. If we were to do this using filters, it would like this

```kotlin
val evenInts = ints.filter { it % 2 == 0 }
```

I do not even put a Listing label on it anymore because it's unnecessary—it's just one line. The filter function is a standard function in the collections library. You already know that the expression in the curly braces is a lambda. However, for filters, the more apt term is a lambda predicate. A lambda predicate is also a function literal, but the expression inside has to yield a Boolean value.

Going back to our example, the filter is invoked against a collection—for example, a list of ints. The result of filter operation is a smaller list or a subset. The list is trimmed down by iterating over each element and testing them against the condition specified in the lambda predicate. Any item that passes the test of the predicate will be included in the resulting subset.

Let's continue our example and work with our smaller list of even integers. Let's say that what we want now is to square each element in our list of even integers. This requires us to manipulate and transform each element in the list and then return a new list that contains the transformed elements. If we were to solve this using a for loop, it would look like Listing 6-15.

Listing 6-15. Generate a List of Squared Ints Using a for Loop

```
val squaredInts2 = mutableListOf<Int>()
for (i in evenInts2) {
  squaredInts2.add( i * i )
}
println(squaredInts2)
```

Or we could have solved it using the *forEach* function in Collections. It would have looked like Listing 6-16.

Listing 6-16. Generate a List of Squared Ints Using forEach

```
val squaredInts2 = mutableListOf<Int>()
evenInts2.forEach { squaredInts2.add(it * it) }
```

This is actually looking much better, but transforming elements in a collection is really the province of the map function. So, let's solve the squared integers problem using maps. Listing 6-17 shows the code.

Listing 6-17. Using the Map Function

```
val squaredInts = evenInts.map { it * it}
println("Sum of squares of even nos <= 100 is ${squaredInts.sum()}")
```

The only relevant statement in Listing 6-17 is the first one. The second statement just prints out the sum of all the even numbers from 1 up to 100. Also, the second line showcases another built-in function in the collections framework, the sum() function. It's pretty obvious what it does—it sums up the values in the collection.

Chapter Summary

- When working with a group of values, we can use either Arrays or Collections. Use arrays for simple data structures, but when you need to dynamically size your group of data or you need to put more constraints to it, such as a uniqueness constraint, you might be better served by Collections.

- Arrays in Kotlin are unlike the ones in Java; they don't enjoy special treatment. In Kotlin, Arrays are just classes.

- Kotlin provides specialized classes for arrays if you feel you need to work with arrays without the overhead of boxing and unboxing.

- Kotlin Collections are very similar to Java collections, but each of the Java collection classes is represented in two ways: a mutable and an immutable one.

- Kotlin collections have built-in functions like filter, map, and sum, which makes working with collections a bit easier.

In the next chapter, we'll explore how Kotlin deals with Generics.

CHAPTER 7

Generics

What we'll cover:

- Using generics

- Constraints

- Variance

- Reified generics

Ah, Generics. That devious topic that emerges even in beginner texts. This subject trips up a lot of beginners because it's tricky to understand and even trickier to explain. But we need to deal with it because without Generics, it's difficult to work with Collections.

For the most part, Kotlin generics works the same way as Java generics; but they have some differences. In this chapter, we'll look at how to work with generics and how similar (or different) Kotlin's generics is from that of Java's—also, don't worry too much about the complexities of generics, we won't do anything too crazy in this chapter.

Why Generics

Generics came to Java around 2004, when JDK 1.5 was released. Before generics, you could write codes like that in Listing 7-1.

Listing 7-1. Using a Raw List, Java

```
List v = new ArrayList();
v.add("test");
Integer i = (Integer) v.get(0); // Run time error
```

© Ted Hagos 2018
T. Hagos, *Learn Android Studio 3 with Kotlin,* https://doi.org/10.1007/978-1-4842-3907-0_7

You might say, "But why would you do something as careless and patently idiotic as that? You could clearly see from Listing 7-1 that we put a String in the ArrayList; so, just don't do any operation that's not appropriate for a String. Problem solved." It may not always be as easy as that. The sample code is clearly contrived, and it's easy to spot the error right now, but if you're doing something non-trivial, it may not always be obvious what the List contains.

The other point to notice about the sample code—and it's actually the main point— is that the code will compile without problems. You'll only discover the error at runtime. There was no way for the compiler to warn us that we're about to do something that isn't type-safe. This is the main problem that generics is trying to solve: type-safety.

Going back to Listing 7-1, we know that the variable v is a List. It would have been more useful if we knew what kinds of things were stored on that list. It's in these situations where generics is helpful. It allows us to say things like "this is a list of Strings" or "this is a list of Ints"—and the compiler knows that beforehand; and because the compiler knows it, it can prevent us from doing inappropriate things like casting a String to an Int or subtracting with Strings, etc. Listing 7-2 shows how to use generics in our code.

Listing 7-2. List, with Generics: Java

```
List<String> v = new ArrayList<String>();
v.add("test");
Integer i = v.get(0); // (type error)  compilation-time error
```

Now that the compiler has foreknowledge about what kinds of things are in the List, it can prevent us from doing unsupported operations on the List.

The codes in Listings 7-1 and 7-2 are both valid in Java, which means you have the option not to use generics in Collections (*raw types*). Java has to do this because it needs to maintain backward compatibility with codes that were written prior to JDK 5. Kotlin, on the other hand, doesn't need to maintain any compatibilities with legacy codes. So, in Kotlin, you cannot use *raw types*. All Kotlin Collections require type parameters. You always have to use generics.

Terminologies

Generic programming is a language feature of Kotlin. With it, we can define classes, functions, and interfaces that accept type parameters. The parameterized type allows us to re-use the algorithm to work with different types; it truly is a form of *parametric polymorphism*. Figure 7-1 shows where the type parameters and type arguments are in a generic class.

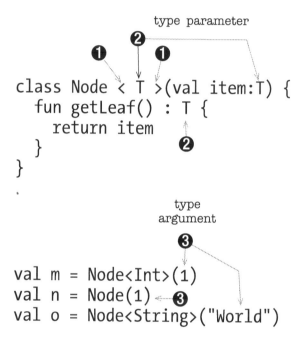

Figure 7-1. *Type arguments and type parameters*

---

❶ **Angle brackets**. When a class has angle brackets at the end of its name, it's called a generic class (there are also generic functions and interfaces).

❷ **Type parameter**. It defines the type of data that this class can work with. You can think of it as being part of the class implementation. Right now, we're using the letter **T** to symbolize the type parameter, but this is arbitrary. You can call it anything you want, it can be any letter or a combination of letters; I'd stick to **T** if I were you, because it's the convention many developers follow. You can use **T** throughout the code inside the class as if it's a real type. It's a *placeholder* for a type. In this example, we used *T* as type for the **item** property and as return type for the **getLeaf** function.

❸ **Type argument**. In order to use the generic class, you to have provide the **type argument**. Now that we're creating an instance of the Node class, **T** will be substituted by *type argument* (*Int* and *String*, in this illustration).

You've seen generics code in the previous chapters, specifically in *Chapter* 6 *(Collections)*. All of Kotlin's collections classes use generics. As I said before, there are no raw types in Kotlin. It's not possible to create just a *List*—you have to be specific what kind of *List* it is (e.g., a "list of Strings" **List<String>** or "a list of Ints" **List<Int>).**

Using Generics in Functions

To create a generic function, declare the type parameter before the function name. Then, you can use the type parameter anywhere in the function.

Listing 7-3. fooBar, Generic Function

```
fun <T> fooBar(arg:T) : String { ❶
  return "Heya $arg"  // ❷
}

println(fooBar("Joe"))  // prints "Heya Joe"
println(fooBar(10))     // prints "Heya 10"
```

❶   The type parameter **T** is used as the type of the function parameter **arg.**

❷   We're just returning the **arg** concatenated in String.

That's pretty simple to follow. We just used the type param in one place, and the function is returning a String, no matter what type the param is. For another example, see Listing 7-4.

Listing 7-4. A More Complex fooBar Function

```
fun <T> fooBar(arg:T) : T { ❶
  var retval:T = 0 as T
  when (arg) {
    is String -> {          ❷
      retval = "Hello world" as T  ❸
    }
```

```
    is Number -> {
      retval = 100 as T
    }
  }
  return retval
}
```

---

❶ In this example, we used the *type parameter* as a type for **arg** (parameter to **fooBar** function) and as a return type of the function itself.

❷ We're testing if **arg** is of String type. If it is, we're also effectively casting it to a String; smart cast, remember?

❸ We're returning "Hello world", and we are casting it (forcibly) as **T**. We cannot return a "String" type right here, because fooBar expects to return type **T** to its caller, not String.

You can also use generics for extension functions. If you're making a function that works with Lists, you probably want it to work with any kind of List, not just Strings or Ints. Listing 7-5 shows how to use generics in an extension function.

Listing 7-5. Generics in Extension Function

```
fun <T> List<T>.getIt(index:Int): T { ❶
  return this[index] ❷
}

fun main(args: Array<String>) {

  val lfruits = listOf("Apples", "Bananas", "Oranges") ❸
  val lnumbers = listOf(1,3,5)      ❹
  val lnumlist = (1..100).toList().filter { it % 5 == 0 } ❺

  println(lnumlist.getIt(5))
  println(lfruits.getIt(1))
}
```

❶ You can use the type parameter in the *receiver* **(List<T>)** and the return type of the extension function.

❷ Let's not do anything fancy; let's just return an item given an index. In a production code, you might want to actually check if the index exists, before you return it. In case you forgot what **this** refers to, it refers to the List itself (it's the receiver object).

❸ Our extension function works with a list of Strings.

❹ It also works with a list of Ints.

❺ This one is a bit fancy, but in the end, it still returns a List, so our extension function should still work.

Using Generics in Classes

Like in Java, you can create Kotlin generic classes by putting a pair of angle brackets after the name of the class and placing the type parameter between the angle brackets. After that, you can use the type parameter anywhere in the class. Listing 7-6 shows, annotates, and explains how to write a generic class.

Listing 7-6. Writing a Generic Class

```
class Node<T>(val item:T) {      ❶
  fun getLeaf() : T {            ❷
    return item
  }
}

fun main(args: Array<String>) {
  val m = Node<Int>(1)             ❸
  val n = Node(1)                  ❹
  val o = Node<String>("World")    ❺
}
```

❶ Type parameter is declared right after the name of the class, **Node<T>**. We're using the **T** as the type for parameter **item.**

❷ We're also using **T** as the return value of the function **getLeaf.**

❸ We're passing an Int to the constructor of Node. We can be verbose and specify Int as the as the type parameter, **Node<Int>.**

❹ Node can infer what the type parameter is, so we can skip the angle brackets. It's okay to write it this way, too.

❺ And because it's a generic class, it works with Strings too.

You can constrain or restrict the types that can be used as type arguments for a class or function. Our Node class, at the moment, should work with any type, because the default parent (or *upper bound*) for the type parameter, if you don't specify a constraint, is **Any?** (Nullable type, so the question mark is included).

When you specify an upper-bound constraint for a type parameter, that will limit the types you can use to instantiate the class. For example, if we wanted our Node class to accept only Ints, Doubles, or Floats, we could use Number as the upper-bound constraint. See Listing 7-7 for the code sample.

Listing 7-7. Node Class, with Constraint

```
class Node<T:Number>(val item:T) { ❶
  fun getLeaf() : T {
    return item
  }
}

fun main(args: Array<String>) {
  val m = Node<Int>(1)            ❷
  val n = Node(1.0F)              ❸
  val o = Node<String>("World")   ❹
  val p = Node(1.0)              ❺
}
```

❶ Now we're putting a constraint on the type parameter **<T:Number>**. The only types we can use to instantiate this class has to be subtypes of **Number**.

❷ Int is subtype of Number, so it's okay.

❸ Float is also okay.

❹ This wouldn't work anymore; IntelliJ will tell you that "Type argument is not within bounds".

❺ This should still work for Double, since it is a child class of number.

If you don't have any restriction other than nullability of the type argument, you can simply use **Any** as the upper-bound for the type parameter; see Listing 7-8.

Listing 7-8. Prevent Null Type Arguments

```
class Node<T:Any>(val item:T) {
  fun getLeaf() : T {
    return item
  }
}
```

Variance

We'll need to review some of our object-oriented programming (OOP) basics to prepare us for a discussion on variance. Hopefully, we can jog your memory and remember some of the fundamental principles of OOP.

OOP is a boon to developers; because of it, we can write codes like Listing 7-9.

Listing 7-9. Assign an Int Variable to Number Type

```
val a:Int =  1
val b:Number = a

println("b:$b is of type ${b.javaClass.name}")
```

We can also write functions like Listing 7-10.

Listing 7-10. Function That Accepts a Number Type

```
foo(1)
foo(100F)
foo(120)

fun foo(arg:Number) {
  println(arg)
}
```

The codes in Listings 7-9 and 7-10 are possible because of the *Liskov Substitution Principle* (LSP). It's one of the more important parts of OOP — where a parent type is expected, you can use a subtype in its place. The reason we use a more generalized type (like **Number**, in Listing 7-10), is so that in the future, if we need to, we can write an implementation of a subtype and insert into an existing and working code. This is the essence of the **Open Closed Principle** (which states that a class must be open to extension but closed to modification).

Note   The **Liskov Substitution Principle** and **Open Closed Principle** are part of the SOLID design principles. It's one of the more popular sets of design principles in OOP. SOLID stands for (S) Single Responsibility (O) Open Closed (L) Liskov Substitution (I) Interface Segregation and (D) Dependency Inversion

---

Let's take another example, see Listing 7-11.

Listing 7-11. Employee, Programmer, and Tester

```
open class Employee(val name:String) {
  override fun toString(): String {
    return name
  }
}

class Programmer(name:String) : Employee(name) {}
class Tester(name:String) : Employee(name) {}
```

```
fun main(args: Array<String>) {
  val employee_1 :Employee = Programmer("Ted")   ❶
  val employee_2 :Employee = Tester("Steph")     ❷

  println(employee_1)
  println(employee_2)
}
```

❶   employee_1 is of type **Employee**, we're assigning a **Programmer** object to it. Which is okay.
     Programmer is a *subtype* of Employee.

❷   Same thing here, the type **Tester** is a subtype of **Employee**, so the assignment should be okay.

No surprises here, the Liskov principle is still at work. Even if you put Programmer and Employee on a List, the type relationship is preserved.

Listing 7-12. Employee and Programmer in Lists

```
val list_1: List<Programmer> = listOf(Programmer("James"))
val list_2: List<Employee> = list_1
```

So far, so good. What about this next code; do you think it will work? (See Listing 7-13.)

Listing 7-13. Group of Employees and Programmers

```
class Group<T>
val a:Group<Employee> = Group<Programmer>()
```

This is one of the tricky parts of generics. Listing 7-13, as it currently stands, won't work. Even if we know that **Programmer** is a subtype of **Employee**, and that what we're doing is type-safe, the compiler won't let us through because the second statement in the code has a problem.

When you're working with generics, always remember that by default **Group<Employee>, Group<Programmer>,** and **Group<Tester>** don't have any type relationship—even if we know that Tester and Programmer are subtypes of Employee. By default, the type parameter in the class **Group<T>** is *invariant*. For the second statement (in Listing 7-13) to work, **Group<T>** has to be *covariant*. We'll solve in Listing 7-14.

Listing 7-14. Classes Employee, Programmer, Tester, and Group

```
class Group<out T>     ❶

open class Employee(val name:String) {
  override fun toString(): String {
    return name
  }
}
class Programmer(name:String) : Employee(name) {}
class Tester(name:String) : Employee(name) {}

fun main(args: Array<String>) {
  val a:Group<Employee> = Group<Programmer>() ❷
}
```

---

❶ When you put the **out** keyword before the type parameter, that makes the type parameter *covariant.*

❷ This code works because, **Group<Programmer>** is *now* a subtype of **Group<Employee>**, thanks to the **out** keyword.

From these examples, we can now generalize that if type Programmer is a subtype of Employee and **Group<T>** is covariant, then **Group<Programmer>** is a subtype of **Group<Employee>.** Also, we can generalize that generic class, like Group, is invariant on type parameter, if for the given types **Employee** and **Programmer**, **Group<Programmer>** isn't a subtype of **Group<Employee>.**

Now we've dealt with *invariant* and *covariant*. The last terminology we need to deal with is *contravariant*. If the type parameter of **Group<T>** is contravariant, for the same given types Employee and Programmer, then we can say that **Group<Employee>** is a subtype of **Group<Programmer>**—it's quite the reverse of *covariant.*

Listing 7-15. Use the in Keyword for Contravariance

```
class Group<in T> ❶

open class Employee(val name:String) {
  override fun toString(): String {
    return name
```

```
  }
}
class Programmer(name:String) : Employee(name) {}
class Tester(name:String) : Employee(name) {}

fun main(args: Array<String>) {
  val a:Group<Programmer> = Group<Employee>()  ❷
}
```

---

❶   The **in** keyword makes the type parameter **<T>** contravariant, which means;

❷   Type **Group<Employee>** is now a subtype of **Group<Programmer>**.

Subclass vs Subtype

Alright. I suspect that what you've read in the last 10 minutes left a bitter taste in your mouth. How can it happen that **Programmer** is a subtype of **Employee**, **List<Programmer>** is a subtype of **List<Employee>**, but **Group<Programmer>** is not a subtype of **Group<Employee>?** Let's try to answer that by going back to the concept of class, types, subclass, and subtypes.

We think of a class as somewhat synonymous to a type, and generally that's true—for non-generic classes at least, and for most of the time. We know that a class has at least one type—it's the same type as that of the class itself. Go back to that time when you were first studying Java classes—your teacher, mentor or probably a favorite author must have defined a type of an object like this: "It's the sum total of all its public behavior, otherwise known as the object's methods or contract," or something like that. Let's just say it's the set of behavior that the object has.

Going back to "a class has at least one type," well, it can have more. Just look at Figure 7-2.

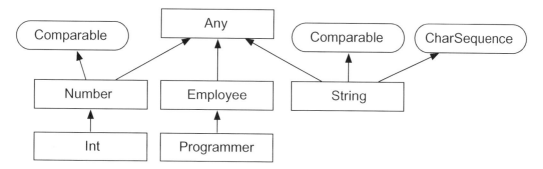

Figure 7-2. *Hierarchy for a bunch of classes and interfaces*

From Figure 7-2, we can say:

- **Any** is at the top of the class chart; class **Any** is the equivalent of java. lang.Object.

- **Employee** is a subclass of **Any**. Employee has two types: the one that it inherited from Any, and itself—because the Employee class can define its own set of behavior (methods), so that counts as one type.

- **Programmer** is a subclass of **Employee,** which is a subclass of **Any,** which means Programmer has three types: one from Any, another from Employee, and another coming from the Programmer class itself.

- **Number** is a subtype of **Any**, but it also implements the **Comparable** interface. So, Number has three types: one from Any, another one from itself, and another from the Comparable interface. We can say that Number is a subtype of Any and it's also a subtype of Comparable—whatever you expect the Comparable to do, the Number can do; whatever Any can do, Number can also do. This is basic OOP.

- The **String** class has four types: one from **Any**, another from **Comparable**, another one from **CharSequence,** and finally, from its own class.

From the statements and the diagram, it's okay to use subclass and subtype interchangeably. There's not much difference between the two. Their difference will become apparent when we start considering nullable types.

The case of the nullable type is an example where a subclass is not the same as a subtype. See Figure 7-3.

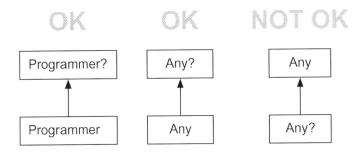

Figure 7-3. *Nullable types*

When you put a question mark after the name of a type, it becomes the nullable version of that type. In Kotlin, we can create two types from the same class: the nullable and the non-nullable version. We can't really say **Programmer** is a subclass of **Programmer?** because there is just one class definition for Programmer, but **Programmer** (the non-nullable version) is a subtype of **Programmer?** (the nullable one). Similarly, **Any** is a subtype of **Any?** but **Any?** is not a subtype of **Any**—the reverse direction isn't true.

It's okay to write

```
var j:Programmer? = Programmer("Ted") // assign non-null to nullable
Programmer
j = null. // then we assign a null to j
```

But it's not okay to write

```
var i:Programmer = j // assign j (which is null) to non-nullable Programmer
```

Now we come to generics. Figure 7-4 should help us illustrate the next set of concepts we need to grapple with.

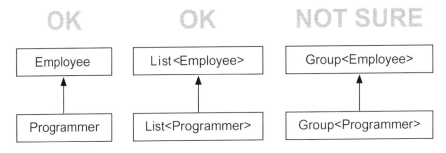

Figure 7-4. *Generic types*

We know the first relationship **Employee** is the supertype of **Programmer**. We also know **List<Employee>** will accept **List<Programmer>**; we tested this in Listing 7-12—you're probably not quite sure why it works, so I'll circle back to this point after we deal with the third set of boxes.

Now, given the codes

```
class Group<T>
val a:Group<Employee> = Group<Programmer>() // not sure
```

Why is it that we can't reliably answer the question "Is **Group<Employee>** a supertype of **Group<Programmer>**?"

It's because while **Group** is a class, **Group<Employee>** is not, and by extension, **Group<Programmer>** is not a subclass of **Group<Employee>**—if you're thinking of List<Employee> and List<Programmer> right now, stop. I did say I'll circle back to that. Stick with Group<Employee> and Group<Programmer> first. Table 7-1 should help us summarize some of these things.

Table 7-1. *Class vs. Type*

	Is It Class	Is It a Type
Programmer	Yes	Yes
Programmer?	No	Yes
List	Yes	Yes
List<Programmer>	No	Yes
Group	Yes	Yes
Group<Programmer>	No	Yes

Now we can establish that Group<Employee> has no type relationship with Group<Programmer>, even if class Employee has a type relationship with Programmer. The type parameter in Group<T> is, by default, *invariant* (no type relationship). In order to change the variance of <T> you need to use either **out** (to make it covariant) or **in** (to make contravariant) keyword.

So, if we want Group<Programmer> to be a subtype of Group<Employee> we need to write the **Group** class like this:

```
class Group<out T>
val a:Group<Employee> = Group<Programmer>() // this is ok now
```

Now we can circle back to List<Employee> and List<Programmer> question. Why and how does it work? Why is it okay to write this?

```
var m:List<Employee> = listOf(Programmer("Ted"))
```

The simple answer lies in the definition of the List interface, I copied the source code of the List interface in Listing 7-16 for your convenience; I stripped all the comments.

Listing 7-16. Excerpt of the List Interface Source Code

```
public interface List<out E> : Collection<E> { ❶
    override val size: Int
    override fun isEmpty(): Boolean
    override fun contains(element: @UnsafeVariance E): Boolean
    override fun iterator(): Iterator<E>
    override fun containsAll(elements: Collection<@UnsafeVariance E>):
    Boolean
    public operator fun get(index: Int): E
    public fun indexOf(element: @UnsafeVariance E): Int
    public fun lastIndexOf(element: @UnsafeVariance E): Int
    public fun listIterator(): ListIterator<E>
    public fun listIterator(index: Int): ListIterator<E>
    public fun subList(fromIndex: Int, toIndex: Int): List<E>
}
```

---

❶   Type parameter is covariant. List uses the **out** keyword before the type parameter **E**.

The reason why it's okay to assign List<Programmer> to List<Employee> is because the type parameter on List<E> is *covariant*. Hence, if type **Employee** is a supertype of **Programmer**, and **List<E>** is covariant, then **List<Programmer>** is a subtype of **List<Employee>**.

So, now that we understand types and subtypes a bit better, like in a Quentin Tarantino movie, I'd like you to go back some 20 minutes ago and read the section on "Variance" again.

Reified Generics

Let's deal with the meaning of "reify" first. It means "to make something real," and the reason we're using rify and generics on the same statement is because of Java's *type erasure*.

Type erasure means exactly what you think it means. Java, and Kotlin as well, erases generic type information at runtime. There are good reasons for this, but unfortunately, we're not going to discuss those reasons why the language design is like that—but we will discuss its effects. Because of type erasure, you can't perform any reflection activity and you can't do any runtime check on a type, if it's generic. See Listing 7-17 for an example.

Listing 7-17. Check for Type at Runtime

```
fun checkInfo(items:List<Any>) {
    if(items is List<String>) {        ❶
      println("item is a list of Strings")
    }
  }
}
```

---

❶   This won't compile. The error is "*Cannot check for instance of erased type.*"

The **is** keyword doesn't work on generic types at runtime; the smart cast breaks because of type erasure. If you have some confidence about what the runtime type of the List will be, you can make a speculative decision and cast it using the **as** keyword, like this:

```
val i = item as List<String>
```

The compiler will let you through, but this is a dangerous thing to do. Let's consider one more example where we can build a stronger case as to why we need to retain type information at runtime.

Let's say I have a List of objects, Programmer and Tester objects. I want to create a function where I can pass a type parameter and filter the list using that type parameter. I want the function to return the filtered list. Listing 7-18 shows us a code sample on how this might be done—the code sample won't work of course, because of the type erasure issue, but just read through it first, and we will fix it later.

Listing 7-18. Filtering a List Using a Type Parameter

```
fun main(args: Array<String>) {
  val mlist = listOf(Programmer("Ted"), Tester("Steph"))    ❶
  val mprogs = mlist.typeOf<Programmer>()                   ❷

  mprogs.forEach {                                          ❸
    println("${it.toString()} : ${it.javaClass.simpleName}")
  }
}
fun <T> List<*>.typeOf() : List<T> {                       ❹

  val retlist = mutableListOf<T>()                         ❺
  this.forEach {
    if (it is T) {                                         ❻
      retlist.add(it)                                      ❼
    }
  }
  return retlist                                           ❽
}
open class Employee(val name:String) {
  override fun toString(): String {
    return name
  }
}
class Programmer(name:String) : Employee(name) {}
class Tester(name:String) : Employee(name) {}
```

❶ Let's create a list of Programmer and Tester objects.

❷ Let's call an extension function (of the List type) called **typeOf**. We're passing **Programmer** as a type argument, which means we want this function to return only a list of Programmers objects.

❸ We're just iterating through each item of the list. We print the *name* property and the Java simpleName.

❹ Now we come to the definition of the extension function. We're defining a type parameter <T>, we're using **T** as the return type of this function. Also, we want this function to work with any kind of List—hence the syntax.

❺ Let's define a mutable list; we'll use this to hold the filtered list.

❻ This is the code that won't compile because we don't know what kind of List this is anymore at runtime. Kotlin, like Java, erases the type information. But let's assume for a moment that Kotlin does retain generic type information; if that's the case, then this code is okay.

❼ If the condition is okay, let's add the current item to the return value.

❽ Finally, let's return the filtered list.

Listing 7-18 would have worked perfectly if only **List.typeOf** could remember, at runtime, what kind of list it was. To solve this problem, we'll use the *inline* and *reified* keyword. Listing 7-19 shows us how to do this.

Listing 7-19. How to Use Reified and Inline in a Function

```
inline fun <reified T> List<*>.typeOf() : List<T> { ❶

  val retlist = mutableListOf<T>()
  this.forEach {
    if (it is T) {
      retlist.add(it)
    }
  }
  return retlist
}
```

❶ Make the function **inline** and use the **reified** keyword before the type parameter. After doing this, the function can retain type information at runtime.

You can only reify inline functions. When you inline a function, the compiler will replace every call to that function with its actual bytecode (not just the address of the function). It's like copying and pasting the bytecode of the function wherever the function is called. This is how the compiler knows the exact type that you used as the type argument. Hence, the compiler can generate the bytecode for the specific class that was used as the type argument.

So, if we make a call like this:

```
val mprogs = mlist.typeOf<Programmer>()
```

If we reverse-engineer the bytecodes that compiler will generate for our reified function, it might look like Listing 7-20.

Listing 7-20. Reified Function

```
val retlist = mutableListOf<Programmer>()
this.forEach {
  if (it is Programmer) {
    retlist.add(it)
  }
}
return retlist
```

As you can see, we're not testing if **it is T** anymore—we're testing if **it is Programmer**. The generated bytecode references a specific class (Programmer), not a type parameter (T). This is the reason why reified functions are not affected by type erasure. This, of course, will increase the size of your runtime program, so use it sparingly. Listing 7-21 shows the full and revised code of the reified example.

Listing 7-21. Filtering a List Using a Type Parameter

```
fun main(args: Array<String>) {
  val mlist = listOf(Programmer("Ted"), Tester("Steph"))
  val mprogs = mlist.typeOf<Programmer>()

  mprogs.forEach {
    println("${it.toString()} : ${it.javaClass.simpleName}")
  }
}
```

```kotlin
inline fun <reified T> List<*>.typeOf() : List<T> {

  val retlist = mutableListOf<T>()
  this.forEach {
    if (it is T) {
      retlist.add(it)
    }
  }
  return retlist
}

open class Employee(val name:String) {
  override fun toString(): String {
    return name
  }
}
class Programmer(name:String) : Employee(name) {}
class Tester(name:String) : Employee(name) {}
```

Chapter Summary

- Generic programming lets us reuse algorithms.

- All Collections in Kotlin uses generics.

- Kotlin doesn't have raw types, like Java.

- There are three variances you need to know about: (1) invariance; (2) covariance; and (3) contravariance.

- Kotlin, like Java, erases generic type information at runtime; but if you want to retain type information, inline your functions and use the reified keyword.

This is the end of book's Kotlin part. In the next chapter, we'll start our discussion of Android programming. We'll kick it of by setting up the Android Studio development environment.

PART II

Android Programming with Kotlin

CHAPTER 8

Android Studio Introduction and Setup

What we'll cover:

- Overview of Android

- History

- Tooling

- Setup

Android could mean many things to different people, but since you're holding this book, I assume you're interested in the part of Android that's suited for developers. Android is a platform that's comprised of an operating system, software libraries, application frameworks, software development kit, pre-built applications, and a reference design. Both the platform and its development eco-system have evolved over time.

In this chapter, we'll take a look at Android's history and architecture. We'll also discuss Android Studio and how to set it up.

History

Android came to life sometime in 2003 when a company named Android Inc. was founded by Andy Rubin. At that time, Google was already backing Android Inc. but didn't own it yet. Google acquired Android Inc. sometime in 2005; then in 2007, the Open Handset Alliance came to life, and the Android OS was officially *opensourced*. During this time, Android had not reached version 1.0 just yet and it was far from mainstream. Android reached version 1.0 in 2008—the dessert names weren't part of the culture just yet, but it wouldn't be long before they were.

© Ted Hagos 2018
T. Hagos, *Learn Android Studio 3 with Kotlin*, https://doi.org/10.1007/978-1-4842-3907-0_8

The following two years, 2009 to 2010, saw a torrent of rapid releases: Cupcake, Donut, Froyo, éclair, and Gingerbread versions were released during this period.

2011 was a major milestone because up until that point, the Android OS remained confined to mobile phones. Honeycomb, the successor to Gingerbread, was the first Android version to be installed on tablets. There was a bit of controversy with Honeycomb because Google did not release its code to open source immediately.

Table 8-1 shows a brief summary of Android's history.

Table 8-1. *Android's History*

2003	Android Inc., founded by Andy Rubin and backed by Google, was born
2005	Google bought Android Inc.
2007	Android was officially open-sourced. Google turned over its ownership to the Open Handset Alliance (OHA)
2008	version 1.0 was released
2009	versions 1.1, 1.5 (Cupcake), 1.6 (Donut), and 2.0 (Eclair) were released
2010	versions 2.2 (Froyo) and 2.3 (Gingerbread) were released
2011	versions 3.0 (Honeycomb) and 4.0 (Ice cream sandwich) were released
2012	version 4.1 (Jellybean) was released
2013	version 4.4 (KitKat) was released
2014	versions 5.0-5.1 (Lollipop) were released; Android became 64-bit
2015	version 6.0 (Marshmallow) was released
2016	versions 7.0-7.1.2 (Nougat) were released
2017	version 8 (Oreo) was released
2018	version 9 (Android P, beta) was released

Architecture

The most visible part of Android, at least for developers, is its operating system (OS). An OS is a complex thing, but for the most part, it is what stands between a user and the hardware. That is an oversimplification, but it will suffice for our purposes. By "user," I don't literally mean an end user or a person. What I mean by it is an application, a piece of code that a programmer creates, like a word processor or an e-mail client.

Take the e-mail app, for example: as you type each character on the keys, the app needs to communicate to the hardware for the message to make its way to your screen and hard drive, and eventually send it to the cloud via your network. It is a more involved process than I describe it here, but that is the basic idea. At its simplest, an OS does three things:

1. manages hardware on behalf of applications

2. provides services to applications like networking, security, memory management, etc.

3. manages execution of applications; this is the part that allows us to run multiple applications, seemingly, almost at the same time

Figure 8-1 shows the logical architecture of the Android platform.

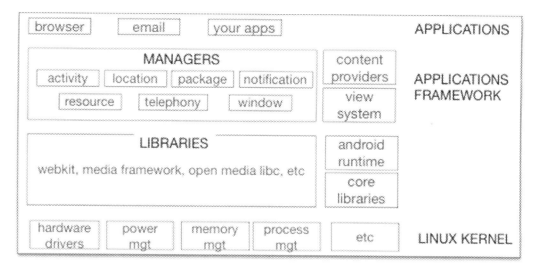

Figure 8-1. *Android's logical architecture*

At the lowest level of the diagram is the Linux kernel. It's responsible for interfacing with the hardware, among other things. It's also responsible for various services like memory management and execution of processes.

Linux is a very stable OS and is quite ubiquitous; you can find this OS in wide use. It can run on things as small as watches or as large as server farms. Android has an embedded Linux inside it that handles hardware interfacing and some other kernel functions.

On top of the Linux kernel are low-level libraries like SQLite, OpenGL, etc. These are not part of the Linux kernel but are still low level and, as such, are written mostly in C/C++. On the same level, you will find the android runtime (android class libraries + dalvik virtual machine), which is where Android applications are run.

Next up is the application framework layer. It sits on top of both the low-level libraries and the android runtime because it needs both. This is the layer that we will interact with as application developers because it contains all the libraries we need to write apps.

Finally, on top is the application layer. This is where all our applications reside, both the ones we write and the ones that come prebuilt. It should be pointed out that prebuilt applications that come with the device do not have any special privileges over the ones we will write. If you don't like the e-mail app of the phone, you can write your own and replace it. Android is democratic like that.

Android Studio IDE

Developing applications for Android was not always as convenient as today. When Android 1.0 was released sometime in 2008, what developers got by way of development kit was no more than a bunch of command line tools and Ant build scripts. Building apps with Vim, Ant, and other command line tools wasn't so bad if you were used to that kind of thing, but many developers were not used to that. The lack of IDE capabilities like code hinting, project setups, and integrated debugging was somewhat a barrier to entry.

Thankfully, the android development tools (ADTs) for the Eclipse IDE was released, also in 2008. Eclipse was, and still is, a favorite and dominant choice of IDE for many Java developers. It felt very natural that it would also be the go-to IDE for Android developers.

From 2009 up until 2012, Eclipse remained the choice of IDE for development. The android SDK has also undergone both major and incremental changes in structure and in scope. In 2009, the SDK manager was released; we use this to download tools, individual SDK versions, and android images that we can use for the emulator. In 2010, additional images were released for the ARM processor and X86 CPUs.

2012 was a big year because Eclipse and ADT was finally bundled, this was a big deal because until that time, developers had to install Eclipse and the ADT separately, and the installation process wasn't always smooth. So, the bundling of the two together made it a whole lot easier to get started with Android development. 2012 is also memorable because it marked the last year of Eclipse being the dominant IDE for android.

In 2013 Android Studio was released; to be sure, it was still on beta, but the writing on the wall was clear. It will be the official IDE for Android development. Android Studio is based on JetBrains's IntelliJ. IntelliJ is a commercial Java IDE that also has a community (non-paid) version. It would be this version that would serve as the base for Android Studio.

There are quite a few JVM languages, but Java has always been the go-to language for Android development—until 2017, when it was announced at Google I/O that Android will have first-class support for Kotlin. Android Studio 3 (AS3) automatically has support for Kotlin.

Setup

The JDK is a required software for Android Studio, but since we've already covered the JDK installation in Chapter 1, we'll proceed to the installation of AS3. The installer is available for macOS, Windows, and Linux; the download page is at `http://bit.ly/getas3`—the page should be able to detect what OS you are using and will display the appropriate installer for you. You will be asked to agree to some terms and conditions before you can proceed with the download. Read it, understand it, and agree to it so you can carry on. After that, the AS3 installer will be downloaded in a zipped file.

For macOS, you need to do the following:

1.   Unpack the installer zipped file.

2.   Drag the application file into the Applications folder.

3.   Launch AS3.

4.   AS3 will prompt you to import some settings if you have a previous installation. You can import that—it's the default option.

Note   If you have an existing installation of Android Studio, you can keep using that version and still install the preview edition. AS3 can coexist with your existing version of Android Studio; its settings will be kept in a different directory.

For Windows, you need to do the following:

1. Unzip the installer file.

2. Move the unzipped directory to a location of your choice, for example *C:\Users\myname\AndroidStudio*

3. Drill down to the *AndroidStudio* folder; inside it, you'll find *studio64.exe*. This is the file you need to launch. It's a good idea to create a shortcut for this file—if you right-click on studio64.exe and choose "*Pin to Start Menu*," you can make AS3 available from the Windows Start menu. Alternatively, you can also pin it to the Taskbar.

The Linux installation requires a bit more work than simply double-clicking and following the installer prompts. In future releases of Ubuntu and its derivatives, this might change and become as simple and frictionless as its Windows and macOS counterparts, but for now, we need to do some tweaking. The extra activities on Linux are mostly because AS3 needs some 32-bit libraries and hardware acceleration.

Note   The installation instructions in this section are meant for Ubuntu 64-bit and other Ubuntu derivatives (e.g., Linux Mint, Lubuntu, Xubuntu, Ubuntu MATE, etc.). I chose this distribution because I assumed that it was a very common Linux flavor; hence, readers of this book would be using that distribution.

If you are running a 64-bit version of Ubuntu, you will need to pull some 32-bit libraries in order for AS to function well.

To start pulling the 32-bit libraries for Linux, run the following commands on a terminal window:

```
sudo apt-get update && sudo apt-get upgrade -y
sudo dpkg --add-architecture i386
sudo apt-get install libncurses5:i386 libstdc++6:i386 zlib1g:i386
```

When all the prep work is done, you need to do the following:

1. Unpack the downloaded installer file. You can unpack the file using command line tools or using the GUI tools. You can, for example, right-click on the file and select the *"Unpack here"* option, if your file manager has that.

2. After unzipping the file, rename the folder to *AndroidStudio*.

3. Move the folder to a location where you have read, write and execute privileges. Alternatively, you can also move it to */usr/local/AndroidStudio*.

4. Open a terminal window and go to the AndroidStudio/*bin* folder, then run *./studio.sh*.

5. At first launch, AS3 will ask you if you want to import some settings. If you have installed a previous version of Android Studio, you may want to import those settings.

Android Studio Configuration

If this is the first time you've installed AS3, you might want to configure a couple of things first before diving into coding work. In this section, I'll walk you through the following:

- Getting some more software that we'll need in order to create programs that target specific versions of Android

- Making sure we have all the SDK tools we need; and optionally

- Changing the way we get updates for AS3

Launch AS3 if you haven't done so yet, then click "Configure," as shown in Figure 8-2. Choose "Preferences" from the dropdown list.

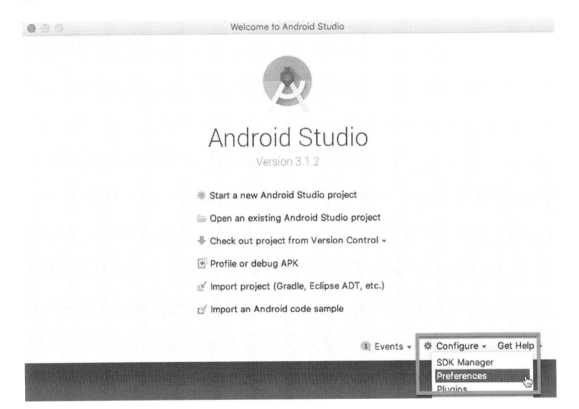

Figure 8-2. *Go to preferences from the AS3 opening screen*

You will see the "Preferences" window, as shown in Figure 8-3. On the left-hand side of the window, click "Android SDK."

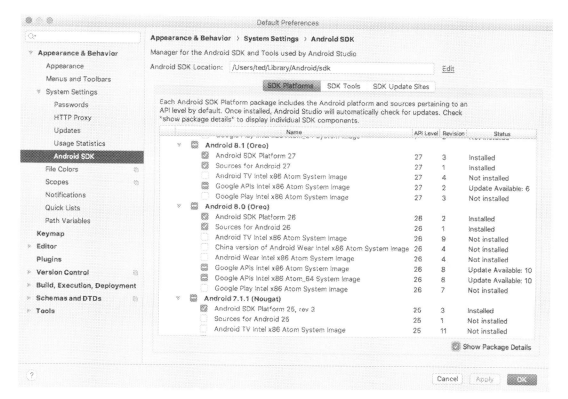

Figure 8-3. *SDK platforms*

When you get to the SDK window, enable the "Show Package Details" option so you can see a more detailed view of each API level. We don't need to download everything in the SDK window. We will get only the items we need.

SDK levels or platform numbers are specific versions of Android. Android 8 or "Oreo" is API levels 26 and 27, Nougat is API levels 24 and 25. You don't need to memorize the platform numbers, at least not anymore because AS3 shows the platform number with the corresponding Android nickname.

You may download "Nougat" and "Oreo" if you wish; those are API levels 24, 25, 26, and 27. For our purposes, please download "Marshmallow"—it is API level 23. This is the version that we will mostly use throughout the book. Make sure that together with the platforms, you will also download "Google APIs Intel x86 Atom_64 System Image." We will need those when we get to the part where we test run our applications.

Choosing an API level may not be a big deal right now, because at this point, we're simply working with practice apps. When you plan to release your application to the public, you may not be able to take this choice lightly though. Choosing a minimum

SDK or API level for your app will determine how many people will be able to use your application. At the time of writing, 25% of all Android devices are using "Marshmallow," 22% are using "Nougat," and 4% are using "Oreo." These stats are from dashboard page of developer.android.com. It's a good idea to check these statistics from time to time; you can find it here `http://bit.ly/droiddashboard`.

Going back to our configuration, when you're happy with your selection, enable the tick boxes for the API and images that you'd like to download, then click "SDK Tools" — it's right next to the "SDK Platforms" button as shown in Figure 8-4.

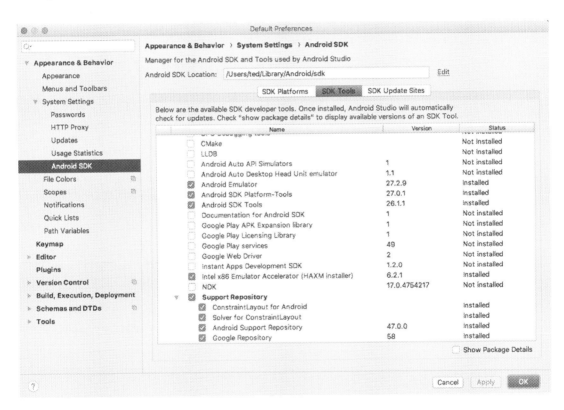

Figure 8-4. *SDK tools*

You don't generally have to change anything on this window, but it wouldn't hurt to check if you have the tools, as shown in Table 8-2, marked as "Installed."

Table 8-2. *SDK Tools*

Tool	Description
Android SDK Build Tools	This contains important tools like adb, which will help us do diagnostics and debugging; sqlite3, which we can use when we create applications that use databases; plus a couple of other tools.
Android SDK Platform Tools	This contains important tools like adb, which will help us do diagnostics and debugging; sqlite3, which we can use when we create applications that use databases; plus a couple of other tools.
Android SDK Tools	This includes essential Android tools like ProGuard. You don't need to deep dive into the details of these tools (for now). Just make sure this box is ticked and we're good to go.
Android Emulator	You will definitely use this. This is a device emulation tool. We will use this to test our applications in a virtual device.
Support Repository	If you want to write code that targets Android Wear, Android TV, or Google Cast, you want to download this. This also contains local Maven repository for support libraries. The support repository also allows you to use new features on older Android versions.
HAXM Installer	If you are using a macOS, or a PC with Intel processor, you can use this. It is an accelerator for the Android Emulator.

Note   If you are on the Linux platform, you cannot use HAXM, even if you have an Intel processor. KVM will be used in Linux instead of HAXM.

Once you're happy with your selection, click the "OK" button to start downloading the packages.

The last configuration check we will do is the "Update Channel." It's on the same "Preferences" window. Click the "Updates" item on the right-hand side to show the "Updates" settings, as shown in Figure 8-5.

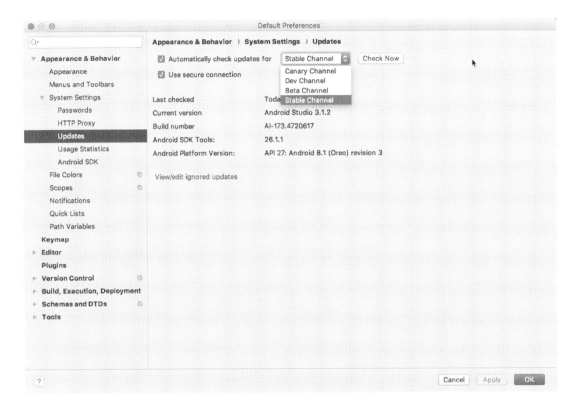

Figure 8-5. *Updates*

AS3, just like any Android Studio installation, is configured by default to get updates from channel where you originally downloaded the installer. Since we downloaded the installer from the stable channel, it will get its update from that channel by default. You can change the channel to either one of these four:

- **Canary channel:** this is bleeding edge releases, it could be updated every week. You don't want to use this for production codes.

- **Dev Channel:** just like the Canary channel but a bit more stable. You still don't want to use this for production.

- **Beta channel:** this contains release candidates. The devs are basically waiting for feedback before it gets fed to the stable channel.

- **Stable Channel:** this is official stable release and is suited for production work.

Hardware Acceleration

As you write your apps, it will be useful to test and run it from time to time in order to get immediate feedback and find out if it is running as expected, or if it is running at all. To do this, you will use either a physical or a virtual device. Each option has its pros and cons, and you don't have to choose one over the other. In fact, you will have to use both options eventually.

An Android Virtual Device, or AVD, is an emulator where you can run your apps. Running on an emulator can sometimes be slow—this is the reason why Google and Intel came up with HAXM. It is an emulator acceleration tool that makes testing your app a bit more bearable. This is definitely a boon to developers. That is if you are using a machine that has an Intel processor that supports virtualization and that you are not on Linux. But don't worry if you're not lucky enough to fall on that part of the pie; there are ways to achieve emulator acceleration in Linux, as we'll see later.

macOS users probably have it the easiest, because HAXM is automatically installed with AS3. They don't have to do anything to get it—the AS3 installer took care of that for them.

Windows users can get HAXM either by:

- Downloading it from `https://software.intel.com/en-us/android`. Install it like you would any other Windows software, double-click, and follow the prompts.

- Alternatively, you can get HAXM via AS3's SDK manager; this is the recommended method.

For Linux users, the recommended software is KVM instead. KVM (Kernel-based Virtual Machine) is a virtualization solution for Linux. It contains virtualization extensions (Intel VT or AMD-V).

To get KVM, we need to pull some software from the repos. But before doing anything else, you need to do two things:

1. Make sure that virtualization is enabled on your BIOS or UEFI settings. Consult your hardware manual on how to get to these settings. It usually involves shutting down the PC, restarting it, and pressing an interrupt key like F2 or DEL as soon as you hear the chime of your system speaker, but like I said, consult your hardware manual.

2. Once you have made your changes, and rebooted to Linux, find out if your system can run virtualization. This can be accomplished by running the following command from a terminal `egrep -c '(vmx|svm)' /proc/cpuinfo`. If the result is a number higher than zero, that means you can go ahead with the installation.

To install KVM, type the commands, as shown in Listing 8-1, on a terminal window.

Listing 8-1. Commands to Install KVM

```
sudo apt-get install qemu-kvm libvirt-bin ubuntu-vm-builder bridge-utils
sudo adduser your_user_name kvm
sudo adduser your_user_name libvirtd
```

You may have to reboot the system to complete the installation.

Chapter Summary

- Android is complete development platform. It includes an OS, application framework, applications, software development kit, pre-built applications, and a reference design

- The release cadence for Android is approximately 12 months; we get a new version every year.

- AS3 automatically includes support for Kotlin.

- Hardware acceleration for the emulator is something you might want to look into. It will shave off a lot of waiting time during development and testing.

Here's what's in store for the next chapter:

- What's inside an Android app? We'll explore what makes up an app; Android calls them components, and there are several of them. We'll take a look at each one of them.

- We'll create our first project. We'll step through the processes (and the screens) on how get a simple project up and running in Android Studio.

- We'll build an emulator—it's what you use to test an app. Android devs call it AVD, which is short for Android Virtual Device.

- We'll look the some part of the Android Studio IDE. It's always good to know the nooks and crannies of your tools.

CHAPTER 9

Getting Started

What we'll cover:

- Android components
- Creating a project
- Creating an android virtual device
- The Android Studio IDE

Applications in android are not quite the same as apps written for the desktop. They might have some striking similarities as far as appearances go, but structurally they differ quite a lot. The EXE files contain all the routines and subroutines the application needs within it. From time to time it may rely on some dynamically loaded library, but the executable file is pretty much self-contained. Android apps are not quite like that, they are made up of loosely coupled components that communicate with each other using a message-passing mechanism that is quite unique to the Android platform.

In this chapter, we'll take a closer look at what's inside an Android application. We will also try to familiarize ourselves with Android Studio 3 by creating and running a sample application. Finally, we'll take a brief tour of the Android Studio 3 IDE.

What's in an App

An android app is not a monolithic package like an EXE file in Windows. It is a bundle of loosely assembled components and other resources and they are held together inside an Android Package file or *APK*. Figure 9-1 shows the logical structure of a hypothetical application.

© Ted Hagos 2018
T. Hagos, *Learn Android Studio 3 with Kotlin*, https://doi.org/10.1007/978-1-4842-3907-0_9

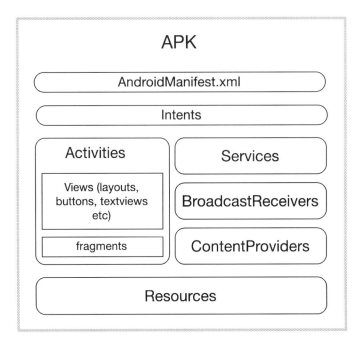

Figure 9-1. *What makes up an app*

The app depicted in Figure 9-1 is a big application—it's got everything in it, including the kitchen sink. Your applications don't need to include all of these things, like our hypothetical app in here; but yours will definitely include some of them.

Activities, Services, BroadcastReceivers, and ContentProviders are called *Android components.* They are the key building blocks of an application. They are high-level abstractions of useful things like showing a screen to a user, running a task in the background, broadcasting an event so that interested applications may respond to them, etc. Components are pre-coded or pre-built classes with very specific behavior, and we use them in our application by extending them so that we can add the behavior that will be unique to our application.

Building an Android app is a lot like building a house. Some people build houses the traditional way—they assemble beams, struts, floor panels, etc. They build the doors and other fittings from raw materials by hand, like an artisan. If we built android applications this way, it could take us a long time and it might be quite difficult. The skill necessary to build applications from the scratch could be out of reach for some programmers. In Android, applications are built using components. Think of it as pre-fabricated pieces of a house. The parts are manufactured in advance, and all it requires is assembly.

An **Activity** is where we put together things that the user can see. It's a focused thing that users can do. For example, an Activity may be purposely made to enable a user to view a single email or fill up a form. It's where the user interface elements are glued together. As you can see in Figure 9-1, inside the Activity, there are *Views* and *Fragments*. Views are classes that are used to draw content into the screen; some examples of View objects are buttons and textviews. A Fragment is similar to an Activity in that it's also a composition unit but a smaller one. Like Activities, they can also hold View objects. Most modern apps use Fragments in order to address the problem of deploying their app on multiple form factors. Fragments can be turned on or off depending on available screen real estate and/or orientation.

Services are classes that allow us to run program logic without freezing up the user interface. Services are codes that run in the background; they can be very useful when your app is supposed to download a file from the web, or maybe play music.

BroadcastReceivers allow our application to listen for specific messages from either the Android system or from other applications—yes, our apps can send messages and broadcast systemwide. You might want to use BroadcastReceivers if you want to display a warning message when the battery dips to below 10%, for example.

ContentProviders allow us to create applications that may be able to share data to other applications. It manages access to some sort of central data repository. Some ContentProviders have their own UI but some don't. The main reason why you would use this component is to allow other applications access to your app's data without them going through some SQL acrobatics. The details of database access are completely hidden from them (client apps). An example of a pre-built application that is a ContentProvider is the "Contacts" app in Android.

Your application may need some visual or audio assets; these are the kinds of things we mean by "Resources" in Figure 9-1.

The AndroidManifest is exactly what its name implies—it's a manifest and it's in XML format. It declares quite a few things about the application, like

- The name of app

- Which Activity will show up first when the user launches the app

- What kind of components are in the app. If it has activities, the manifest declares them—names of classes and all. If the app has services, their class names will also be declared in manifest.

- What kinds of things can the app do? What are its permissions? Is it allowed to access the internet or the camera? Can it record GPS locations? And so on.

- Does it use external libraries?

- What version(s) of Android will this app run on?

As you can see, the manifest is a busy place, there's a lot of things to keep an eye on. But don't worry too much about this file. Most of the entries here are automatically taken care of by the creation wizards of AS3. One of the few occasions you will interact with it is probably when you need to add permissions to your app.

Component Activation

Android is gung-ho about loose coupling. An application is just a collection of components held together by a manifest file. Each of these components can be activated by sending a message to it. This approach to program interactivity is quite unique because it's very user-centric. It gives the user a lot of power to make choices on how they manipulate and create data.

Let's take a common usage scenario for an Android device. A user opens the "Contacts" application and chooses the contact detail of John Doe, for example. This contact could have an e-mail address, a mobile phone, and a twitter name, let's say. The user could tap on each and every one of John's contact points, and each time, Android will launch a different application; the default e-mail client, a dialer, and a downloaded Twitter app. The user probably doesn't care which application was launched or how many applications are currently open; he just wants to send a message. If this user doesn't like the e-mail app or the default twitter client, he could delete these apps and replace them with something else, and he should be back in business.

For this kind of program interaction to happen, Android needed to architect the platform, focusing heavily on loose coupling and pluggability. A component, like the Contacts app should not know any specific detail about what app it should use when an e-mail address or a mobile phone number is tapped. The resolution for what kind of app to use for a specific kind of data should not be hardwired into the Contacts app; otherwise, the user won't be able to exercise his choice on which app to use when sending e-mails or tweets.

This is where Intents come in. When a component has data or information that is beyond its capability to service, it can go out to the Android platform using Intents and ask around if there's any application that can (or wants) to fulfill the request. There are two kinds of Intent: an implicit and an explicit one. The Intent we are talking about in the e-mail and twitter example is called an explicit Intent. We'll get into this a bit more in later chapters.

Android Intents is a component activation mechanism. They are a message-passing mechanism that you can use if you want to activate any Android component, be it an Activity, Service, ContentProvider, or BroadcastReceiver. To activate any component, you will need to create an Intent and pass it to the component you want to activate. In an application that has more than one Activity, Intents are used to switch control or focus from one Activity to another.

Creating a Project

Now that we have some working idea about what goes inside an Android app, let's try to create a sample project and try out the IDE. Launch AS3 if it isn't open yet. Figure 9-2 shows the Welcome screen of Android Studio 3.

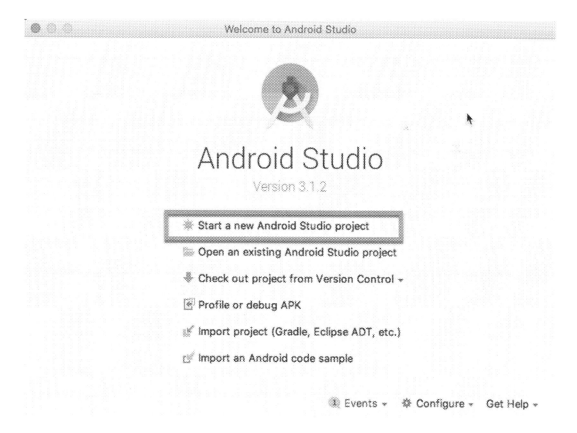

Figure 9-2. *AS3 welcome screen*

Click "Start a new Android Studio Project," as shown in Figure 9-2. It may be a good idea to check if you have an internet connection. AS3 uses the Gradle build tool; when the creation wizard finishes, Gradle will pull several files from internet repositories. Figure 9-3 shows the next screen.

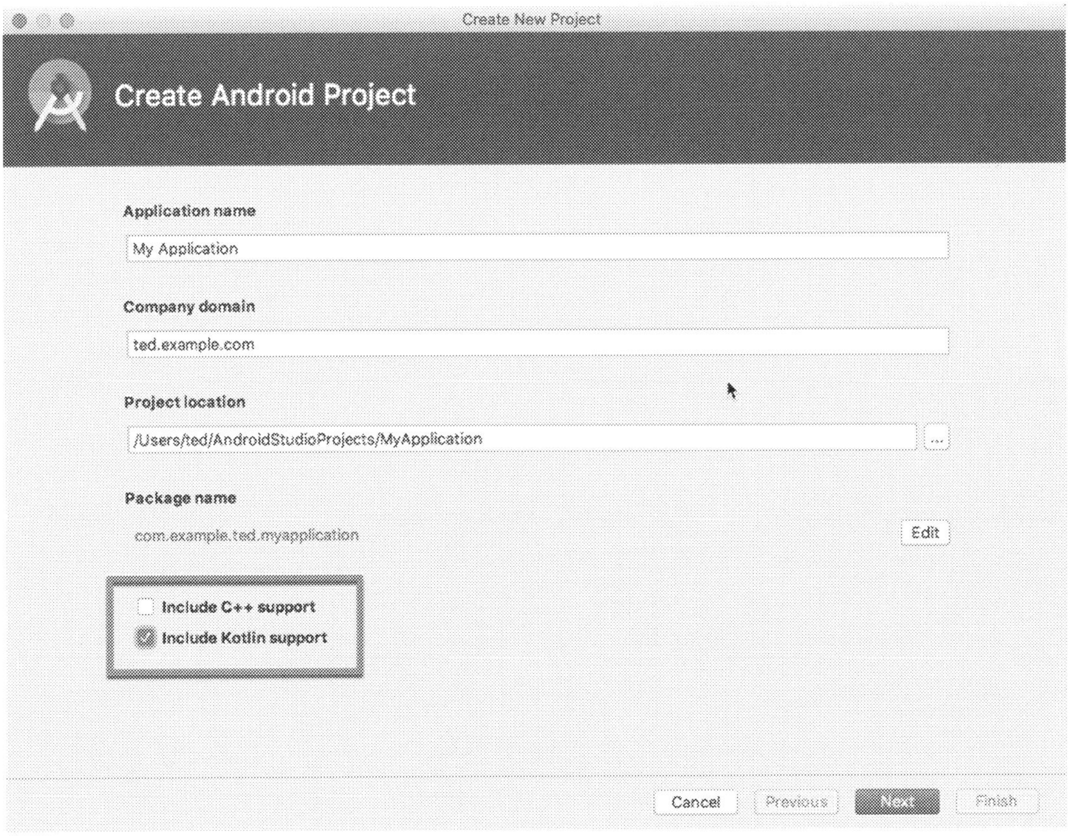

Figure 9-3. *Create new project*

As you can see in Figure 9-3, you'll need to fill in some information about the project (e.g., app name, company domain, and project location). The default value for application name is "My Application"; you can leave the default value.

I filled up the company domain; you can too, if you prefer. It's usually the website of your company. This information will be used in the project and will become its package name in reverse-DNS notation. So, our class will be stored in a package named *com. example.ted*.

The project location is the location of the folder where AS3 will store your project. You can also leave this with the default value.

It's important that the "Include Kotlin support" tick box is enabled because we're going to use Kotlin as our programming language. Click "Next."

Figure 9-4 shows the next screen. In here, you will be asked to choose the Android version that your application is expected to run on. Tick only "Phone and Tablet" and choose API 23.

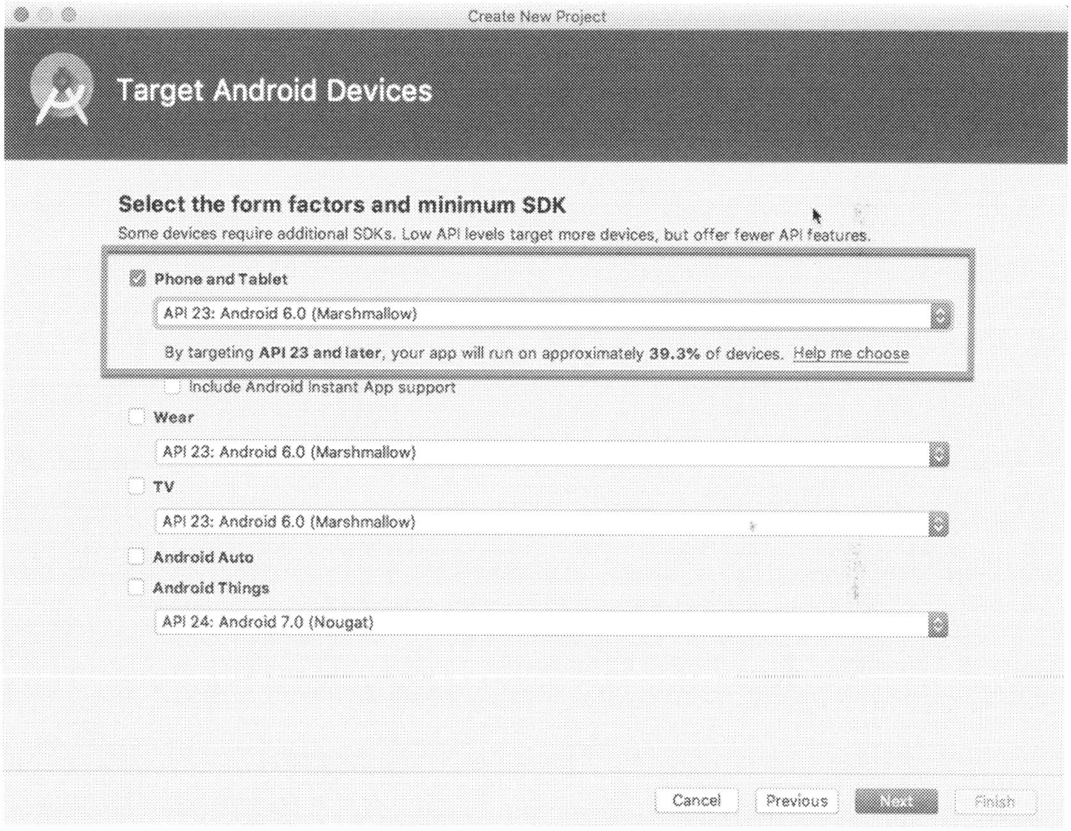

Figure 9-4. *Target Android devices*

Figure 9-5 shows the next screen; a small pop-up might appear reminding you that you need to install "Instant Apps." Click "No" for now. "Instant Apps" is a Google Play feature that allows users to use or try out apps without installing them. If the users like the app, then they can purchase it, if necessary, from the App Store. We will completely ignore this for now. Click "Next."

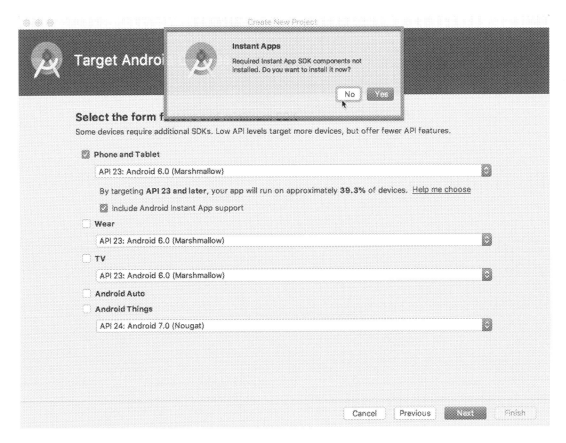

Figure 9-5. *Instant apps*

On the next screen, as shown in Figure 9-6, we are asked to add an Activity to the app. You have a couple of choices, but for our purpose, choose "Empty Activity." Click "Next."

Figure 9-6. *Choose an activity*

The last screen on the project creation wizard is shown in Figure 9-7. We're asked to fill in the activity name and the layout name. We'll leave everything in their default values. Click "Next."

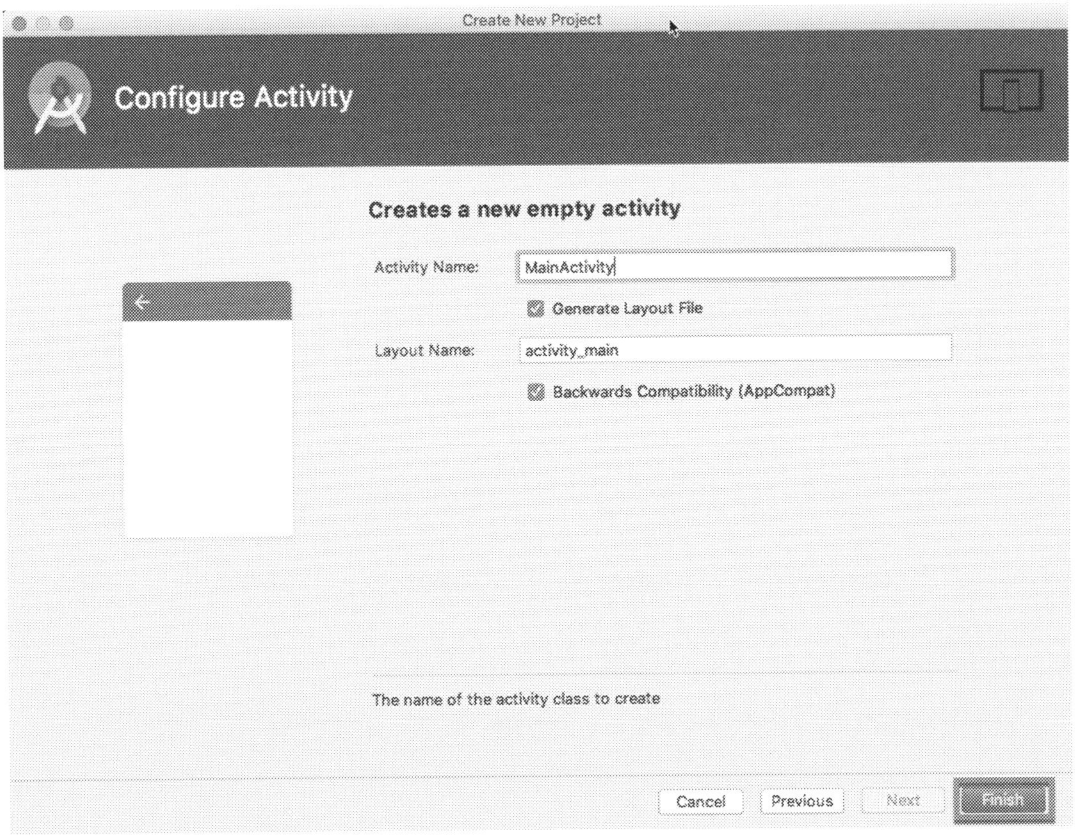

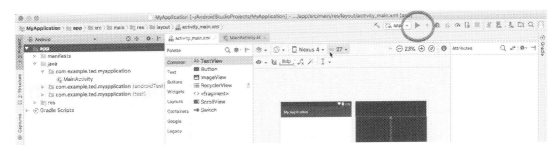

Figure 9-7. *Configure activity*

Figure 9-8 shows our newly created project in the main Window of AS3. After Clicking the "Next" button in Figure 9-7, it will take a while before things settle in because the Gradle tool will build the project, and as it tries to do that, it will pull quite a few files from the repositories.

Figure 9-8. *Main AS3 with an open project*

We won't try to change anything in this project right now. Our goal is to simply take AS3 for a test drive and get acquainted with the various steps of project creation. The project creation wizard generated an activity with a couple of views in it already. The next step in our test drive is to run the project in an emulator. To do that, click the Run icon in the toolbar (encircled in Figure 9-8).

When you click the Run icon, the "Select Deployment Target" screen will appear, as shown in Figure 9-9. This screen shows all running Android Virtual Devices (AVDs). It also shows all the connected physical Android Devices, if you plugged any.

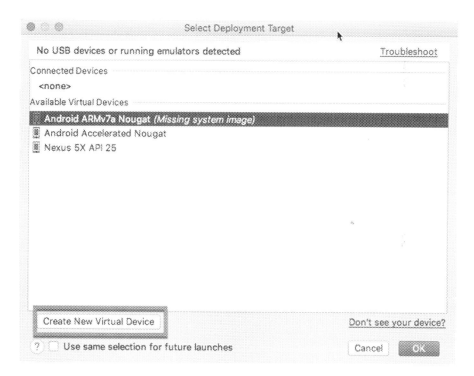

Figure 9-9. *Select deployment target*

As you can see, I've created a couple of virtual devices already. In your case, you might not see anything under the "Available Virtual Devices" since you have a fresh installation. Click "Create New Virtual Device."

In Figure 9-10, you can choose the form factor for your virtual device. I chose the Nexus 5x. Click "Next."

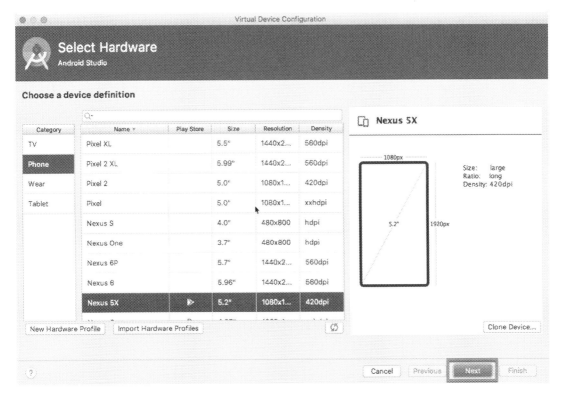

Figure 9-10. *Select hardware*

Figure 9-11 shows our options for the system image. A system image is a copy of the Android OS that we can run on an emulator. Our project was created with the target SDK value of API 23 ("Marshmallow"). It's okay to choose a system image that is higher than API 23, but for our purpose, let's actually download the API 23 system image.

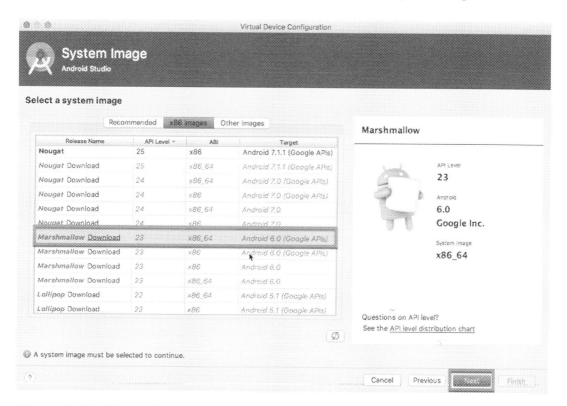

Figure 9-11. *System image*

Click the middle tab that's labeled "x86 Images," as shown in Figure 9-11, and look for API level 23, x86_64 with the Google APIs. Click the "Download" link.

Figure 9-12 shows the Component installer window, it displays the progress of the download. As soon as it finishes, click "Finish" to dismiss the window.

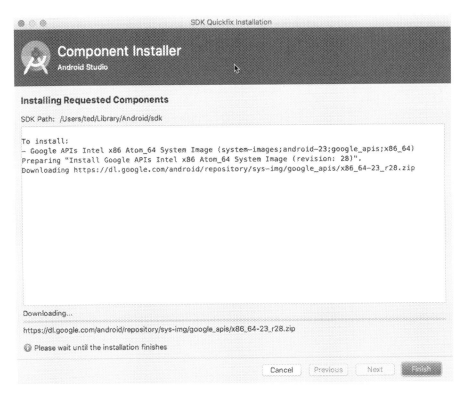

Figure 9-12. *Component installer*

We're back to System Image window again, as shown in Figure 9-13. You'll notice that the "Download" link is no longer visible beside the "Marshmallow" label and that the row is now selectable. While the Marshmallow row is selected, Click "Next."

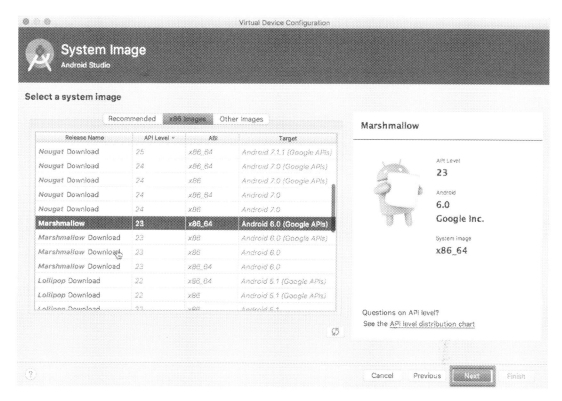

Figure 9-13. *System image*

Figure 9-14 shows the final configuration screen for the AVD creation. I'll leave everything in their default value, including the AVD name. Click "Finish."

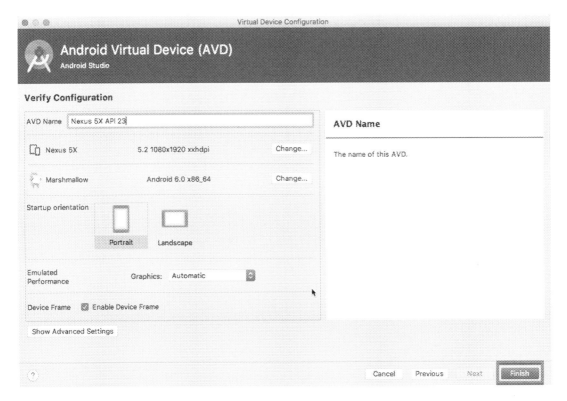

Figure 9-14. *Android Virtual Device*

We're back to the "Select Deployment Target" screen (Figure 9-15), but this time around, we have our newly created AVD (Nexus 5X API 23) showing up in "Available Virtual Devices." Select the AVD we just created and click "OK."

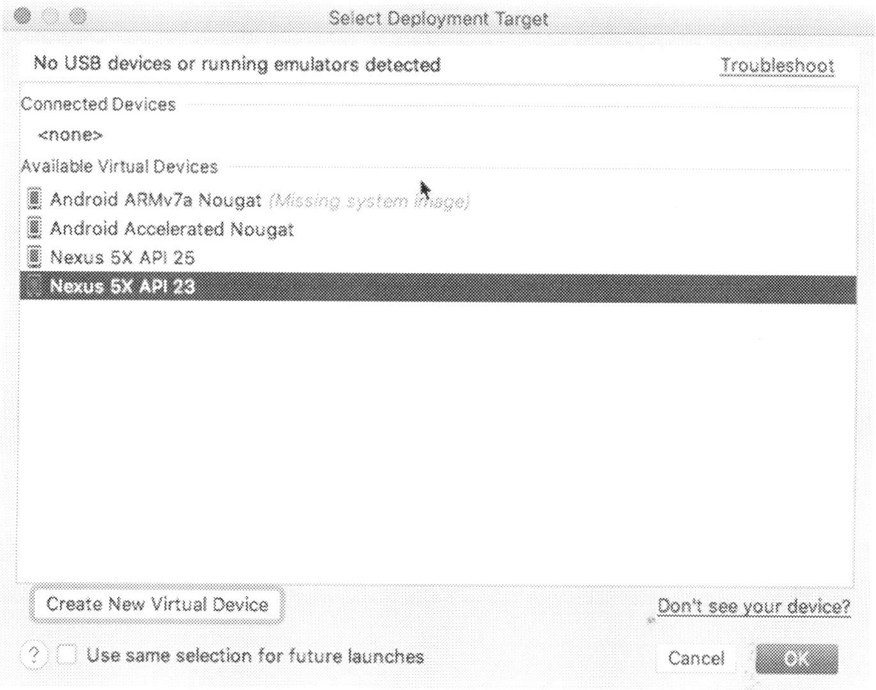

Figure 9-15. *Select deployment target*

AS3 might prompt you to install "Instant Run", as shown in Figure 9-16. We want to install this because it will speed up our development time. Instant run allows us to push code changes to the AVD without building a new APK. That will save us time. Click "Install and Continue."

Instant Run

Instant Run requires that the platform corresponding to your target device (Android 6.x (Marshmallow)) is installed.

Proceed without Instant Run   Install and Continue

Figure 9-16. *Instant run*

AS3 will create the APK for the app and will push it to the AVD right after. When that's done, you should be able to see the app running in the AVD, as shown in Figure 9-17.

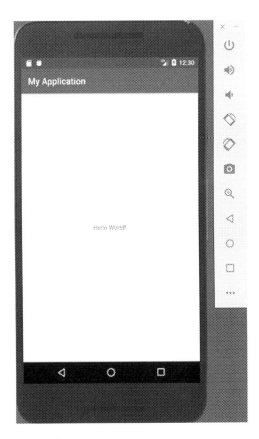

Figure 9-17. *Android Virtual Device*

The IDE

Let's take some time to familiarize ourselves with the IDE. It's best to get some bearings before diving deep into coding. Android Studio is based on IntelliJ, and we used IntelliJ for our Kotlin studies in the earlier chapters, so AS3 should look familiar. Figure 9-18 shows the AS3 IDE with an opened project.

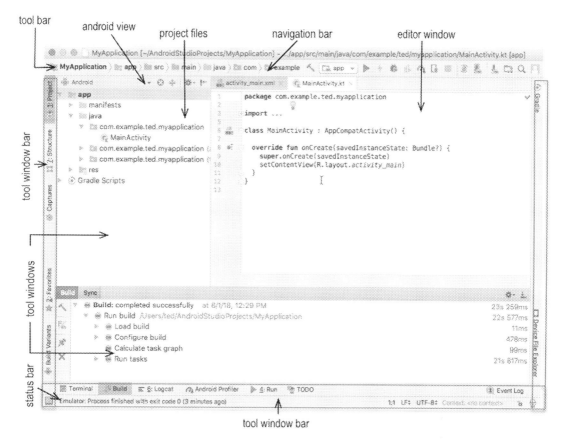

Figure 9-18. *AS3 IDE with an opened project*

The **Editor window** is the most prominent window and has the most screen real estate. The editor window is where you can create and modify project files. It changes its appearance depending on what you are editing. If you're working on a program source file, this window will show just the source files. When you are editing layout files, you may see either the raw XML file or a visual rendering of the layout.

Each project in Android Studio contains one or more modules with source code files and resource files. The types of modules includes Android app modules, library modules, and, sometimes, Google app modules. By default, AS3 displays the **Project Files** in *Android View*, as shown in Figure 9-18. The Android View is organized by modules to provide quick access to the project's most relevant files. You change how you view the project files by clicking the down arrow on top of the Project window, as shown in Figure 9-19.

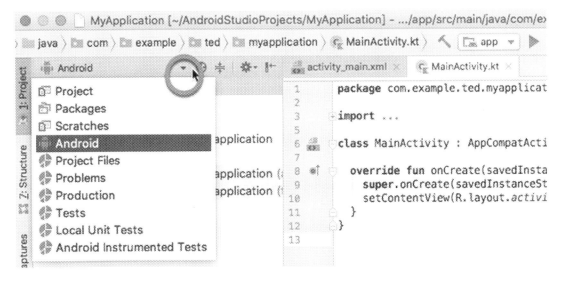

Figure 9-19. *How to switch views in the Project window*

The **Navigation bar** lets you navigate the project files. This is just a more compact view of the "Project files" window. It's a horizontally arranged collection of chevrons that resembles some sort of breadcrumb navigation that you can find on some websites. You can open your project files either through the navigation bar or the project tool window.

The **Tool bar** lets you do a wide range of actions (e.g., save files, run the app, open the AVD manager, open the SDK manager, undo, redo actions, etc.).

The **Tool windows** gives you access to very specific tasks (e.g., look at the project files, view all the TODO annotations, view the logcat window, access the profiler, etc.). Each of the tool windows are expandable and collapsible. You can pop them open when you need them, then tuck it away when you're done.

The **Tool window bar** runs along the perimeter of the IDE window. It contains the individual buttons you need to activate specific tool windows.

The **Status Bar** is that part of the IDE that shows what's going on with your project and with AS3 itself. It displays context-sensitive messages, such as error messages, running processes, repository messages, etc.

Main Menu

Android Studio offers many way of navigating the IDE, but the primary way of navigation is the Main Menu. Figure 9-20 shows the AS3 Main Menu; it sits at the top of the IDE and provides the most complete way of navigation. It contains commands for opening, creating projects, refactoring code, running and debugging apps, keeping files under version control, and so much more.

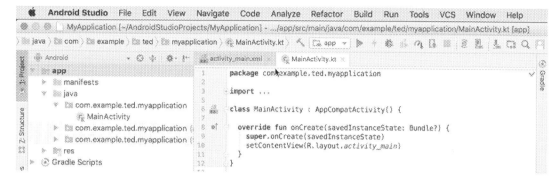

Figure 9-20. *Main menu of Android Studio*

Keyboard Shortcuts

As your application grows, you may want to try a quicker way to navigate AS3. Here are some keyboard shortcuts to get you started.

Table 9-1. *Some Keyboard Shortcuts*

Task	Linux and Windows	macOS
Search within a file	CTRL + F	⌘ + F
Search everywhere	CTRL + Shift + F	CTRL + ⌘ + F
Save all	CTLR + S	⌘ + S
Override methods	CTRL + O	CTRL + O
Implement methods	CTRL + I	CTRL + I
Basic code completion	CTRL + Space	CTRL + Space
Build	CTRL + F9	⌘ + F9
Build and Run	Shift + F10	CTRL + R
Apply changes (with Instant Run)	CTRL + F10	CTRL + ⌘ + R

The list of keyboard shortcuts shown in Table 9-1 is obviously not complete. The Android Developer website maintains a page that has a comprehensive list of Android Studio keyboard shortcuts; you can find it here http://bit.ly/ androidstudiokbshortcuts.

There are certain actions or option in AS3's Main Menu that don't have a default mapping to the keyboard (e.g., entering a full screen view). In such cases, you may map a keyboard shortcut of your own choosing to a menu action. You can do this in the *keymap settings* for AS3.

To open the keymap setting, choose **File ➤ Settings** (on macOS, **Android Studio ➤ Preferences**) from the Main Menu and navigate to the keymap pane, as shown in Figure 9-21.

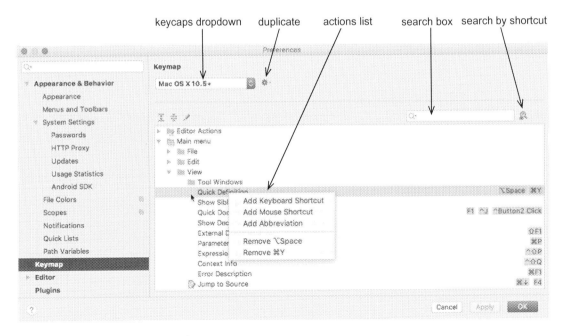

***Figure 9-21.** Keymap settings*

- **Keymaps dropdown** lets you select the desired keymap, it switches between the preset keymaps.

- **Actions list**. Right-click on an action to modify it. You can add additional keyboard shortcuts for the action, add mouse shortcuts to associate an action with a mouse click, or remove current shortcuts. If you are using a preset keymap, modifying an action's shortcuts will automatically create a copy of the keymap and add your modifications to the copy.

- You can use the **Search Box** to search for a keyboard shortcut using the *action name*.

- **Search by shortcut**. You can type the keyboard short cut in this search window to find the action name.

Customizing Code Style

On the same *Settings* (*Preferences* in macOS) window, you can also customize the coding style and a lot more other settings like editor font and color scheme, etc.

To customize the coding style, open the preferences window, if it isn't opened yet. Click **File ➤ Settings** (on macOS, **Android Studio ➤ Preferences**) on the Main Menu. The code style window is under the *Editor* menu on the right-hand side of the Preferences window, as shown in Figure 9-22.

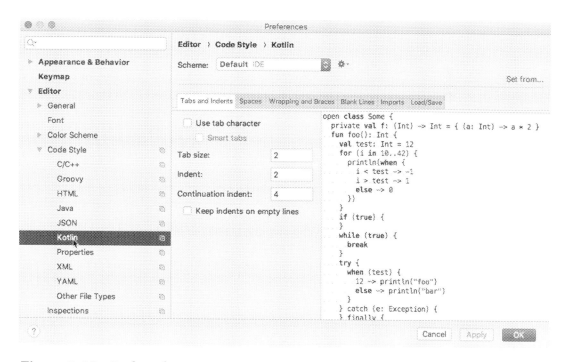

Figure 9-22. Code style

Now you can tune your editor whichever way you want. The settings are very self-explanatory, just tweak it to your liking—or, if you are working on a team, tweak the settings according the issued coding style guide.

Chapter Summary

- An Android app is made up of components that are loosely assembled that are held together by AndroidManifest.xml.

- You can set application permissions in the Android manifest file.

- An app may contain a combination of components such as Activities, Services, BroadcastReceivers, and ContentProviders.

- Components communicate to each other using Intents.

In the next chapter, we will start looking at how to build user interfaces with Activities and layouts. We'll learn how Android uses XML as a layout resource and how these XML resources get converted and rendered into objects at runtime using a process called inflation—this, and so much more.

CHAPTER 10

Activities and Layouts

What we'll cover:

- Activities and layouts

- View and ViewGroup objects

- Activity lifecycle

- Kotlin Android Extension

Most programs need an entry point or a beginning routine where all execution begins. Even the simple "Hello World" in previous examples required a main function as an entry point. Android programs are the same, it also needs its own version of the "function main." But the entry point of an Android program isn't just a function called "main"—it's a bit more involved than that. In this chapter, we'll explore the structure of a basic app. We'll take a look at how to build a user interfaces and discover what makes them tick.

Application Entry Point

A simple app that shows a screen to the user requires at least three things. It needs (1) an Activity class that acts as the main program file; (2) a layout file that contains all UI definitions; and (3) a Manifest file, which ties all the project's contents together. If you still remember working with JavaBean's manifest file, the Android manifest is a bit like that. It describes the contents of the project.

When an application is launched, the Android runtime creates an Intent object and inspects the manifest file. It's looking for a specific value of the `intent-filter` node; the runtime is trying to see if the application has a defined entry point, something like a "main function." Listing 10-1 shows an excerpt from a manifest file.

© Ted Hagos 2018
T. Hagos, *Learn Android Studio 3 with Kotlin*, https://doi.org/10.1007/978-1-4842-3907-0_10

Listing 10-1. Excerpt from AndroidManifest.xml

```
<activity android:name=".MainActivity">
 <intent-filter>
   <action android:name="android.intent.action.MAIN" />
   <category android:name="android.intent.category.LAUNCHER" />
 </intent-filter>
</activity>
```

Listing 10-1 shows the declaration for one Activity. If the app has more than one activity, you will see several definitions like Listing 10-1—one for each Activity. The first line of the definition has an attribute called `android:name`. This attribute points to the class name of an Activity. In this example, the name of the class is "MainActivity."

The second line declares the *intent-filter*; when you see something like `android.intent.action.MAIN`, on the intent-filter node, it means the Activity is the entry point for the application. When the app is launched, this is the Activity that will interact with the user.

Activity Class

The main Activity class is responsible for the initial interaction with the user. This is a Kotlin class, and in it, we can, and often, do the following:

- Choose which UI file to use. When we call the `setLayout(xml:file)` function from inside the Activity, it will bind the Activity to xml:file. This is called "Layout binding." When the Activity binds to the layout, the screen will be filled with user interface elements that users can touch or swipe.

- Get references to view objects. View objects are also called widgets or controls. When we have a programmatic reference to the view objects, we can manipulate them, change their properties, or associate them with an event. This is called *View binding*.

The Activity class inherits from android.app.Activity in one way or another. In our examples, they inherit from AppCompatActivity; this is a child of FragmentActivity, which in turn is a child of android.app.Activity. We use the AppCompatActivity class so we can put modern UI elements like ToolBars in our project, and still run them on older versions of Android where ToolBars are otherwise unsupported—hence, the "Compat" in the name AppCompatActivity.

When the runtime launches an app that eventually launches an Activity, it creates and tracks what's happening to the Activity. Each Activity has a very thorough life cycle, and each life cycle event has an associated function that we can use to customize the behavior of the application.

Figure 10-1 shows the stages of the Activity's life cycle. Each box shows the state of the Activity on a particular stage of existence. The name of the function calls are embedded in the directional arrows that connect the stages.

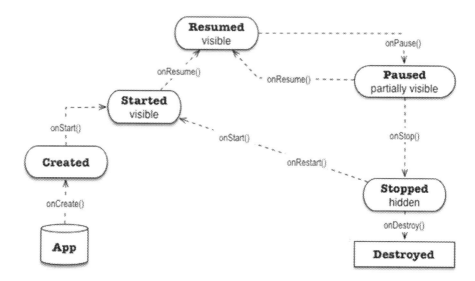

Figure 10-1. *Activity Life Cycle*

When the runtime launches the app, it calls the onCreate() function of the main Activity, which brings the state of the Activity to "created." You can use this function to perform initialization routines like preparing event handling codes, etc.

The Activity will proceed to the next state, which is "started"; the Activity is visible to the user at this point, but it's not yet ready for interaction. The next state is "resumed"; this is the state where the app is interacting with the user.

If the user clicks on anything that may launch another Activity, the runtime will pause the current Activity and it will enter the "paused" state. From there, if the user goes back to the Activity, the onResume() function is called and the Activity is running again. On the other hand, if the user decides to open a different application, the runtime may "stop" and eventually "destroy" the application.

Layout File

A layout file contains view objects that are arranged in an XML hierarchy. The user interface elements like buttons or text fields are written inside an XML file. Some people may cringe at the thought of composing the UI by hand using only an XML editor. But you don't have to worry because AS3 makes it easy to compose user interfaces. We can work with the layout file either in text mode (hand editing the XML), or we can work with it in design mode (WYSIWYG).

Figure 10-2 shows a layout file displayed in two possible modes: text mode and design mode. You can switch the modes by clicking on the tabs "Text" or "Design" on the left lower part of the main editor window. When you change an element by editing the XML, AS3 automatically updates the rendition of the design view. Similarly, when you make a change in the design view, the XML file gets updated.

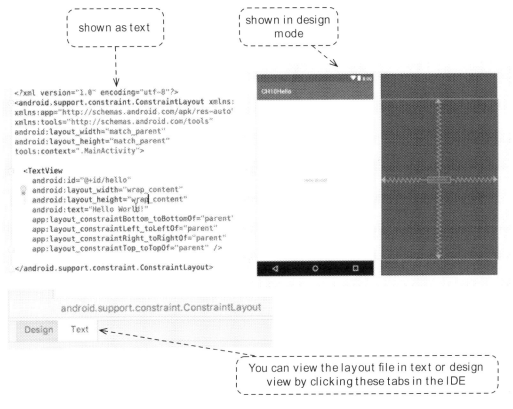

Figure 10-2. *Layout file shown in both text and design mode*

Listing 10-2 shows a typical layout file. It's what the project creation wizard will produce if you chose to create an "empty" activity.

Listing 10-2. activity_main.xml

```
<?xml version="1.0" encoding="utf-8"?>
<android.support.constraint.ConstraintLayout xmlns:android=http://schemas.
android.com/apk/res/android
  xmlns:app=http://schemas.android.com/apk/res-auto
  xmlns:tools=http://schemas.android.com/tools
  android:layout_width="match_parent"
  android:layout_height="match_parent"
  tools:context=".MainActivity">

  <TextView
    android:layout_width="wrap_content"
    android:layout_height="wrap_content"
    android:text="Hello World!"
    app:layout_constraintBottom_toBottomOf="parent"
    app:layout_constraintLeft_toLeftOf="parent"
    app:layout_constraintRight_toRightOf="parent"
    app:layout_constraintTop_toTopOf="parent" />

</android.support.constraint.ConstraintLayout>
```

A simple layout file generally has two parts: a declaration of a container and the declarations of each UI element inside of it. In Listing 10-2, the second line (which is also the root of the XML document) is the container's declaration. The TextView element is declared as a child node of the container. This is how containers and UI elements are arranged in a layout file.

View and ViewGroup Objects

A view object is a composition unit. You build a UI by arranging one or more view objects alongside each other, or sometimes embedded in each other. There are two kinds of views as the Android library defines it, a "view" and a "view group." An example of a View object is a button or a text field. These objects are meant to be composed alongside other views, but they are not meant to contain child views—they are meant to stand alone.

201

A ViewGroup, on the other hand, can contain child views—it's the reason why they're sometimes called containers.

Figure 10-3 shows the class hierarchy of some of the more common UI elements. Every item in a user interface is a child of the *android.view.View* class. We can use prebuilt user interface elements in the Android SDK such as TextView, Button, ProgressBars, etc., or, if need be, we can construct custom controls (widgets or views are sometime called "controls") by either (1) sub-classing existing elements like TextViews; (2) subclassing the View class itself and completely drawing a custom widget from scratch; or (3) sub-classing the ViewGroup and embedding other widgets in it—this is known as a *composite view* (the RadioGroup in Figure 10-3 is an example of such).

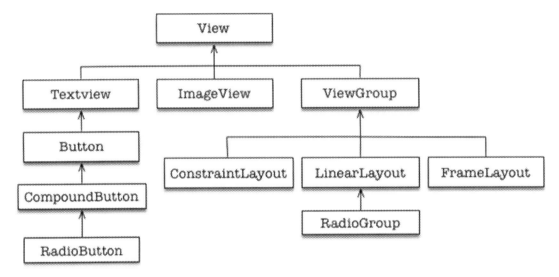

Figure 10-3. *ViewGroup class hierarchy*

Each view object ultimately becomes a Java object at runtime, but we work with them as XML elements during design time. We don't have to worry about how Android inflates the XML into Java objects because that process is invisible to us—it happens behind the scenes. Figure 10-4 shows a logical representation of Android's compilation process.

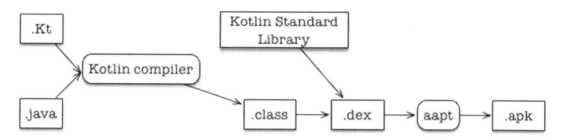

Figure 10-4. *Android compilation process*

The Kotlin compiler transforms the program source files into Java byte codes. The resulting byte codes are combined with the Kotlin Standard Library to form a DEX file. A DEX file is a Dalvik Executable—it's the executable format that the Android Runtime (ART) understands. Before the dex files and other resources gets wrapped into an Android package (APK), it also produces as a side effect a special file named "R.class." We use the R.class to get a program reference to the UI elements that we defined in the layout file.

Containers

Apart from creating composite views, the ViewGroup class has another use. They form as the basis for layout managers. A layout manager is a container that's responsible for controlling how child views are positioned on the screen, relative to the container and to each other. Android comes with a couple of pre built layout managers. Table 10-1 shows us some of them.

Table 10-1. *Layout Managers*

Layout Manager	Description
LinearLayout	positions the widgets in single row or column, depending on the selected orientation. Each widget can be assigned a weight value that determines the amount of space the widget occupies compared to the other widgets.
TableLayout	arranges the widgets in a grid format of rows and columns
FrameLayout	stacks child views on top of each other. The last entry on the XML layout file is the one on top of the stack.
RelativeLayout	Views are positioned relative to other views and the container by specifying alignments and margins on each view.
ConstraintLayout	The ConstraintLayout is the newest layout. It also positions widgets relative to each other and the container (like RelativeLayout). But it accomplishes the layout management by using more than just alignments and margins. It introduces the idea of a "constraint" object which anchors a widget to target. This target could be another widget or a container; or another anchor point. This is the layout we will use for most of our examples in this book.

Now that we have some working knowledge about activities and layouts, let's explore them at the code level in the next section.

Hello World

Let's create a new application with an empty activity. If you want to follow along and work on the code examples, the project information is shown in Table 10-2.

Table 10-2. *Project Information for the Hello App*

Project Detail	Value
Application name	CH10Hello
Company domain	Use your website name
Kotlin support	Yes
Form factor	Phone and Tablet only
minimum SDK	API 23 Marshmallow
Type of activity	Empty
Activity name	MainActivity
Layout name	activity_main

When the project is created, you will see a bunch of files in the project window, but we're only interested in three. Figure 10-5 shows the location of (1) the main program file; (2) the manifest; and (3) the main layout file in the project file window.

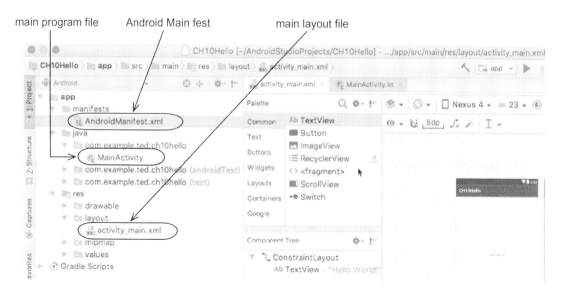

Figure 10-5. *CH10Hello project*

The main layout file, named *activity_main.xml*, is found in *app ➤ res ➤ layout* folder. All user interface elements are written in a layout file.

The main program file, *MainActivity.kt*, is found in *app ➤ java ➤ package name* folder. This is the Kotlin file that contains the class that extends an Android Activity. If you want to do something as a reaction to a user-generated event, this is where we write that program logic. Don't let the "java" folder throw you off, all source files, whether Java or Kotlin, are stored in the "java" folder. There is no "kotlin" folder.

The manifest file describes the essential information about the app to the Android build tools: Android OS and Google play. Looking at Figure 10-5, it appears as if the manifest file is in *app ➤ manifests ➤ AndroidManifest.xml*. You need to remember that what we're looking at is the "Android View" of the Project window. It's a logical representation of the project files, it's not the literal arrangements of the files with respect to the root folder of the project. If you want to see the actual location of the project files, switch to "Project view," as shown in Figure 10-6.

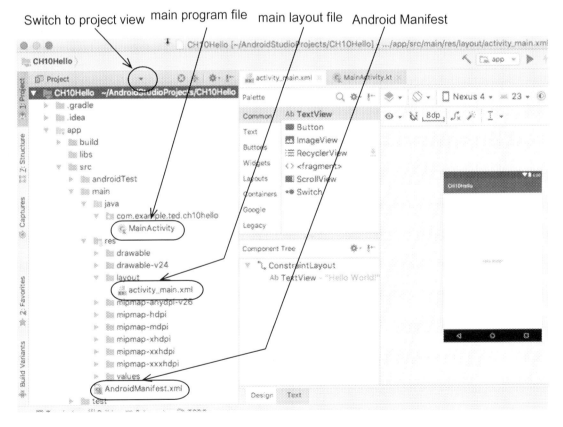

Figure 10-6. *CH10Hello, in project view*

The Project view shows the actual location of all the project files. It looks a lot busier than the "Android view," but if you need to locate any file under the project, this view could be useful. Now we can revert back to "Android view," which is what we'll use throughout most of the book.

Let's take a closer look at the generated layout and MainActivity files. The codes are shown in Listings 10-3 and 10-4, respectively.

Listing 10-3. activity_main.xml

```
<?xml version="1.0" encoding="utf-8"?>
<android.support.constraint.ConstraintLayout ❶
xmlns:android="http://schemas.android.com/apk/res/android"
xmlns:app="http://schemas.android.com/apk/res-auto"
xmlns:tools="http://schemas.android.com/tools"
android:layout_width="match_parent"
android:layout_height="match_parent"
tools:context=".MainActivity">

  <TextView                              ❷
    android:id="@+id/hello"
    android:layout_width="wrap_content"
    android:layout_height="wrap_content"
    android:text="Hello World!"
    app:layout_constraintBottom_toBottomOf="parent" ❸
    app:layout_constraintLeft_toLeftOf="parent"
    app:layout_constraintRight_toRightOf="parent"
    app:layout_constraintTop_toTopOf="parent" />

</android.support.constraint.ConstraintLayout>
```

❶ Root node of layout file, which also declares what kind of layout manager is in effect. In this case, we are using the ConstraintLayout manager

❷ Declaration of the a TextView object. It's a child node of the layout manager.

❸ Defines one of the constraints of the TextView object. It says, there's an anchor point to the bottom of the TextView and it anchored to the bottom of the container.

Listing 10-4. MainActivity.Kt

```
package com.example.ted.ch10hello

import android.support.v7.app.AppCompatActivity
import android.os.Bundle

class MainActivity : AppCompatActivity() {

  override fun onCreate(savedInstanceState: Bundle?) { ❶
    super.onCreate(savedInstanceState)
    setContentView(R.layout.activity_main) ❷
  }
}
```

❶ The very first of the Activity life cycle methods. The runtime may or may not pass a `Bundle` object to the function. A bundle object typically contains data from a previous Activity state (e.g., when you're collecting data from the user, you may want to save them in a Bundle when the Activity gets to a "paused" state so that if the user is interrupted—usually by another Activity— you won't have to ask the user to input the data again because it's already in the Bundle).

❷ The `setContent()` function binds this Activity to a specific layout file. The "R" class was generated by the *aapt* tool during the Android build process; it contains a programmatic reference to everything we declared in the *app ➤ res* folder. In this statement, we're associating MainActivity.Kt with `R.layout.activity_main`.

Now that we know what the project wizard gave us, let's make changes to the application.

Modifying Hello World

We'll make some minor changes to both the layout file and the Activity. We'll do the following:

1. Change the text in the current TextView control.

2. Add a Button to the screen, we will put the button right below the TextView.

3. Add a function to the Activity. The function will increment the current value of the TextView.

4. We'll associate our new function to the Button, so that every time we click the button, the value of the TextView will increase by 1.

Figure 10-7 shows the general layout of our project inside AS3. Currently, we're looking at activity_main.xml in design mode. While in this mode, we can see the view palette, design surface, and blueprint surface.

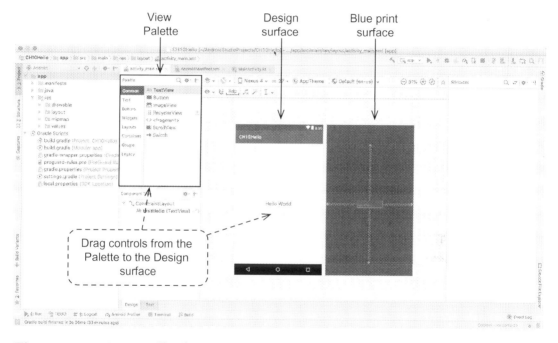

Figure 10-7. *CH10Hello shown in design view*

To add a Button control, drag and drop the Button from the View palette to the design surface as shown in Figure 10-8—you can also drop it in the blueprint surface, that will work as well.

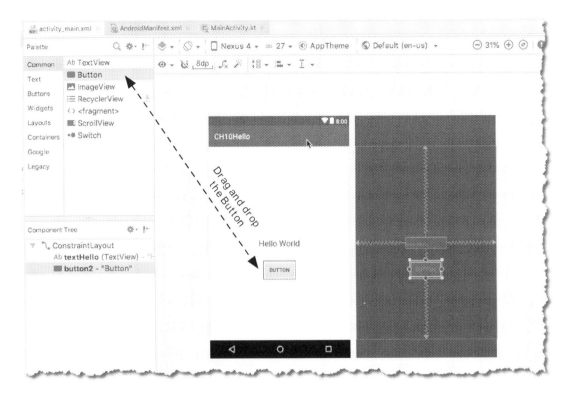

Figure 10-8. *Drag and drop controls from the view palette*

The Button control doesn't have any constraint yet because we didn't put any. Constraints are not automatically added when you add a control to the design surface. The TextView has constraints because that was generated by the wizard when we created the project. Figure 10-9 shows the runtime and design time rendition of our project as it currently stands.

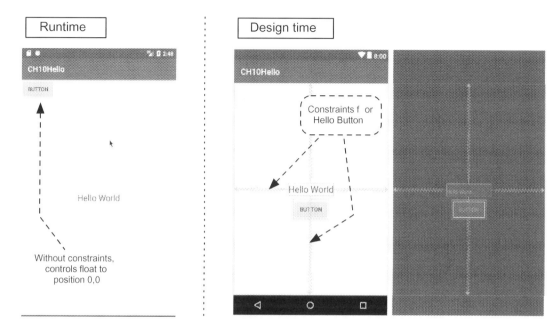

Figure 10-9. *Button without constraint*

The Hello TextView is nicely centered in the screen because it has four anchor points (constraints). The Button appears right below the Hello text in design time, but in runtime, it's on position 0,0 (top left) of the screen—this is how controls are positioned at runtime when they don't have constraints.

Let's start fresh. Remove all existing constraints in the design surface. You can do this by selecting all the controls and clicking the "clear constraints" button, as shown in Figure 10-10.

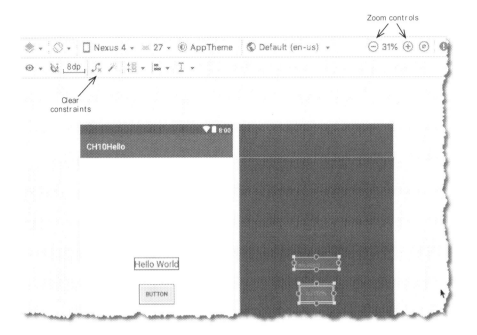

Figure 10-10. *Clear constraints*

When all the constraints are removed, reposition the controls on the design surface in the way you would like them to appear during runtime. Next, select all the controls again—you can do this by clicking and dragging the mouse around the controls.

To "magically" add all the constraints for our controls, click "Infer constraints," as shown in Figure 10-11. AS3 will try to best guess the needed constraints for the controls that will match your arrangement in the design surface.

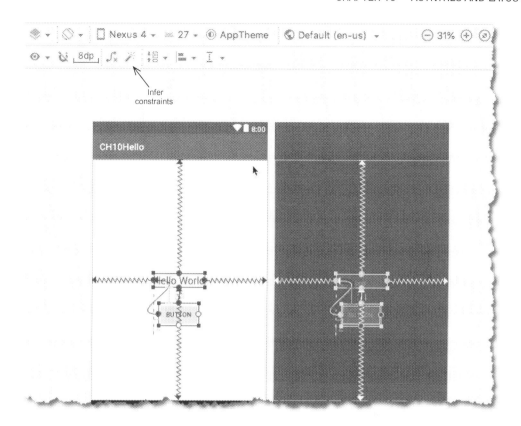

Figure 10-11. *Inferred constraints*

The properties of the controls can be set in the "Attributes" window. We need to change some properties of the TextView and the Button controls. The properties of an object will appear on the attributes window when the object is selected in the design surface, as shown in Figure 10-12.

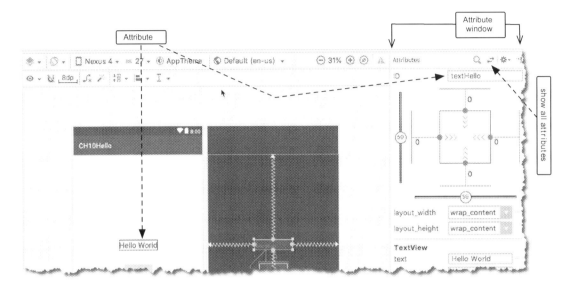

Figure 10-12.   *Attributes window*

The attributes window contains all of the properties for the selected view object, but it doesn't show all of them by default. It shows only the properties we commonly use. To view all the properties, click the "view all attributes" button, as shown in Figure 10-12.

Change the "ID" property of the TextView to "textHello", as shown in Figure 10-12. Next, change the "textApperance" to "Material.LARGE"—you have to scroll down a bit in the attributes window, so you can see the "textApperance" property.

The ID property of a view object is important because it makes the view object accessible from our code (the Activity class).

The next attribute we need to change is the Button's onClick property. Select the Button, then find the "onClick" property. You may have to show all the attributes of the Button and scroll down until you get to the onClick property.

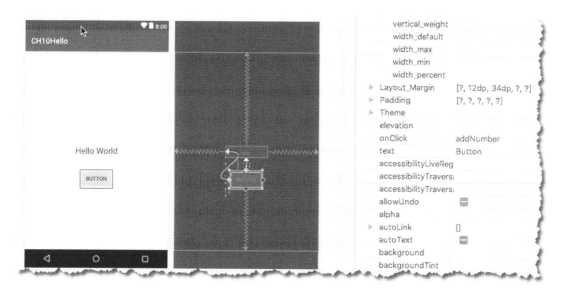

Figure 10-13. *Button's onClick property*

Type "addNumber" in the Button's onClick property, as shown in Figure 10-13. This action will associate the click event of the Button to the addNumber() function in MainActivity class. Of course, we haven't written the function yet, but it's okay, because we'll implement it shortly.

We've finished our work in the layout file. Now we can work on MainActivity class. Open MainActivity.Kt in the main editor and make the following changes as shown in Listing 10-5.

Listing 10-5. MainActivity.Kt

```kotlin
class MainActivity : AppCompatActivity() {

  override fun onCreate(savedInstanceState: Bundle?) {
    super.onCreate(savedInstanceState)
    setContentView(R.layout.activity_main)

    findViewById<TextView>(R.id.textHello).text = "1"

  }
}
```

No surprises here. The last statement in the onCreate() function gets the reference to the textHello object and sets the text property to "1." This is already a big improvement. Remember that in Java, this statement would have looked like Listing 10-6.

Listing 10-6. How to Set a Property During Runtime, in Java

```
TextView helloText = (TextView) findViewById(R.id.textHello);
helloText.setText("1")
```

In Kotlin, we get that nice getter and setter syntactic sugar. But we can still cut some more boiler-plate code. AS3 comes automatically with the Kotlin Android Extensions plug-in, and it's already declared in the module level "build.gradle" file whenever a new project is created. Figure 10-14 shows the build.gradle file and its contents.

Gradle has replaced Apache Ant as the build tool. You generally don't need to change anything in the gradle file because the default contents are just fine, most of the time.

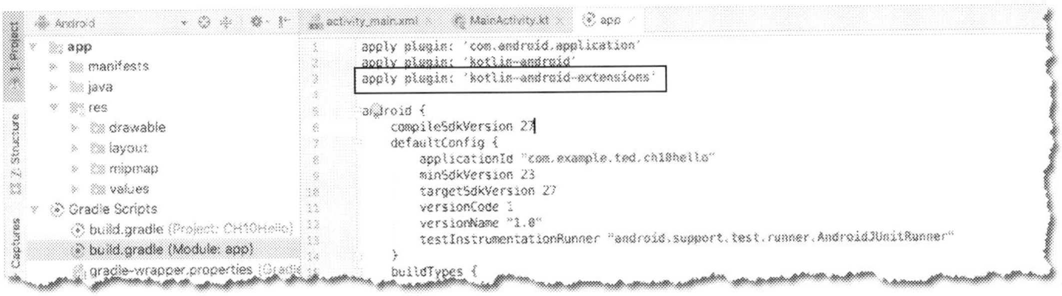

Figure 10-14. *build.gradle, module level*

Going back to the code, Listing 10-7 shows the full program for MainActivity.Kt, which implements the logic for incrementing the value of textHello whenever the Button is clicked.

Listing 10-7. MainActivity.Kt

```
import android.support.v7.app.AppCompatActivity
import android.os.Bundle
import android.view.View
import android.widget.TextView
import kotlinx.android.synthetic.main.activity_main.* ❶
```

```
class MainActivity : AppCompatActivity() {

  override fun onCreate(savedInstanceState: Bundle?) {
    super.onCreate(savedInstanceState)
    setContentView(R.layout.activity_main)

    textHello.text = "1" ❷

  }

  fun addNumber(v: View) {   ❸
    val currVal = textHello.text.toString().toInt() ❹
    val nextVal = currVal + 1
    textHello.text = nextVal.toString() ❺
  }
}
```

❶ This statement imports the Kotlin Android Extension. You may not have to type this yourself— AS3 adds it automatically as soon as try to do view binding using the ID of a view object.

❷ We don't have to use findViewById() anymore; we don't even have to use the R.class to qualify the ID of the view object. The Android Kotlin Extensions exposes the views to our code with a lot less ceremony. This results in a much cleaner code. Notice also that we get the nice getter and setter syntax that was added by Kotlin.

❸ The addNumber() function is associated with the *onClick* event of the Button control. This function is an *event handler*—when the Button is clicked, this function will be called. It needs to accept a View object as a parameter because that's a requirement for an event handler. The function needs to have access to the view object that raised the event.

❹ textHello.text returns the current value of textHello as CharSequence type. The toString() converts it to a String type that we can convert to an Int using the toInt() function. We need the value as Int because we will use it in a Math operation.

❺ This statement sets the text property of textHello to a new value.

When you're done with the edits, run the application on an AVD. Figure 10-15 shows the project running on an emulator.

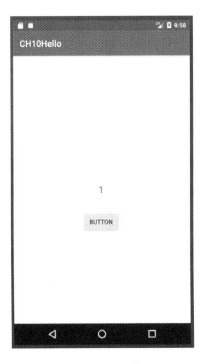

Figure 10-15. *CH10Hello running on an emulator*

Chapter Summary

- The entry point for an Android application requires three files: the manifest file, the layout file, and an Activity class

- The AndroidManifest file declares all the contents of the Android project. The manifest may be able to designate an Activity class that will serve as the application's entry point.

- A layout file describes the UI structure of a screen. Each element is described as an XML node, but the XML file is inflated during runtime. The inflation process produces the Java object representations of the UI elements.

- All UI elements inherits from the android.view.View class.

- Composite views can be constructed by inheriting from the ViewGroup class.

- Layout managers provide ways to arrange UI elements in a screen. The Android SDK has plenty of pre-built managers we can use out of the box.

- The Kotlin Android Extensions allow us to simplify view-binding codes by exposing the properties and functions of view elements. We don't need to use findViewById anymore.

In the next chapter, we'll learn how to:

- Work with some basic View elements like Buttons and Toasts

- Use Kotlin's Android Extensions to get references to View objects; it replaces ButterKnife

- Handle clicks and long clicks; we'll do both long-form using the full syntax of object expressions and the short-cut way using lambda expressions

CHAPTER 11

Event Handling

What we'll cover:

- Listener objects

- Anonymous inner objects

- Use of lambdas in event handlers

In the last chapter, we already did some event handling. The part of the exercise where we wrote a function that will increment the value of a text view each time a button is clicked is an exercise on declarative event handling. To bind a function name to a click event, we simply set a View's **android:onClick** attribute to the name of a function. This is a simple and low-ceremony way to handle events, but it is limited to only the "click" event. When you need to handle events like long-clicks or gestures, you need to use event listeners—this is the topic of this chapter.

Introduction to Event Handling

The user interacts with your app by touching, clicking, swiping, or typing something. The Android framework captures, stores, processes, and sends these actions to your app as *event objects*. We can respond to these events by writing functions that are specifically designed to handle them. Functions that handle events are written inside *listener objects*—and there's quite a few of them. Figure 11-1 shows a simplified model of how user actions are handled by the Android framework and your app.

© Ted Hagos 2018
T. Hagos, *Learn Android Studio 3 with Kotlin*, https://doi.org/10.1007/978-1-4842-3907-0_11

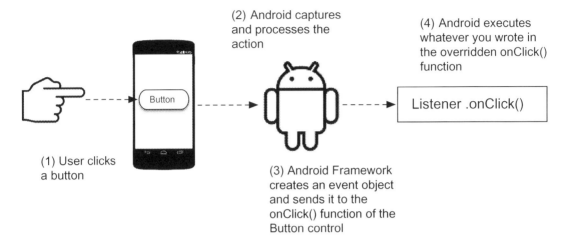

(2) Android captures and processes the action

(4) Android executes whatever you wrote in the overridden onClick() function

Button

Listener .onClick()

(1) User clicks a button

(3) Android Framework creates an event object and sends it to the onClick() function of the Button control

Figure 11-1. *Simplified event handling model*

When a user does something with your app, like clicking a button, the Android framework catches that action and turns it into an event object. An event object contains data about the user's action (e.g., which button was clicked, what was the location of button when it was clicked, etc.) Android sends this event object to your application and it calls a specific function that corresponds with the user's action. If the user *clicked* the button, Android will call the onClick() function on the Button object, if the user clicks the same button but holds it a bit longer, then the onLongClick() function will be called. View objects, like the Button, can respond to a range of events like clicks, keypresses, touch or swipes, etc. Table 11-1 lists some of the common events and their corresponding event handlers.

Table 11-1. *Common Listener Objects*

Interface	Function	Description
View.OnClickListener	onClick()	This is called when the user either touches and holds the control (when in touch mode), or focuses upon the item with the navigation keys then presses the ENTER key
View.OnLongClickListener	onLongClick()	Almost the same as a click, but only longer
View.OnFocusChangeListener	onFocusChange()	When the user navigates onto or away from the control
View.OnTouchListener	onTouch()	Almost the same as click action but this handler lets you find out if the user swiped up or down. You can use this to respond to gestures
View.OnCreateContextMenuListener	onCreateContextMenu()	Android calls this when a ContextMenu is being built, as a result of a sustained long click

To set up a listener, the View object can set or, more aptly, register a *listener object*. Registering a listener means you are telling the Android framework which function to call when the user interacts with the View object. Figure 11-2 shows an annotated code for registering handlers.

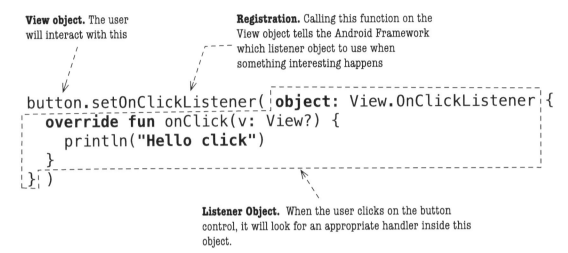

Figure 11-2. *Annotated event registration and handling code*

The **setOnClickListener** is a member function of the android.view.View class, which means every child class of View has it. This function expects an **OnClickListener** object as an argument—this object becomes the listener for the button control. When the button is clicked, the codes inside the **onClick** function are run.

We created the listener object by creating an object expression that inherits from **View.OnClickListener**. This type is declared as a nested interface in the View class. Object expressions are the Kotlin equivalent of Java's anonymous inner classes. In Java, we wrote codes like thseat in Listing 11-1.

Listing 11-1. onClick Listener in Java

```
button.setOnClickListener(new View.OnClickListener() {
  @Override
  public void onClick(View view) {
    System.out.println("Hello click");
  }
}});
```

In Kotlin, an anonymous inner class is created using an object expression, as shown in Listing 11-2.

Listing 11-2. onClick Listener in Kotlin

```
button.setOnClickListener(object: View.OnClickListener {
  override fun onClick(v: View?) {
    println("Hello click")
  }
})
```

Listing 11-2 is actually a verbose way of writing an object expression. Kotlin's support for lambdas can simplify our existing code to something like that in Listing 11-3.

Listing 11-3. onClick Listener Using lambdas

```
button.setOnClickListener {
  println("Hello")
}
```

Now that we have enough working knowledge about events, let's explore them further by creating a new project. Table 11-2 shows the project details.

Table 11-2. *Project Information for the CH11EventAnonymousclass*

Project Detail	Value
Application name	CH11EventAnonymousClass
Company domain	Use your website name
Kotlin support	Yes
Form factor	Phone and Tablet only
minimum SDK	API 23 Marshmallow
Type of activity	Empty
Activity name	MainActivity
Layout name	activity_main
Backwards compatibility	Yes. AppCompat

This project will contain only two controls: the TextView that came with the project when we used the wizard and a Button view, which we are yet to add. The Button will intercept the events click and long-click using an anonymous inner object.

Open the **activity_main.xml** file in the main editor if it's not open yet. You can find it in the Project Explorer window under the *app > res > layout* folder.

Add a button to the design surface and add some constraints to it. You can add a Button control to the layout by dragging it from the palette and onto the design surface, as shown in Figure 11-3.

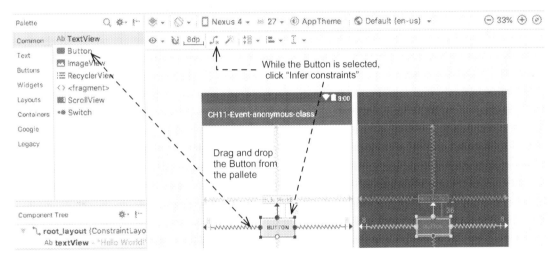

Figure 11-3. *Add a button control to the design surface*

While the button control is selected, click the "Infer constraints" on the constraints toolbar (also shown in Figure 11-3).

You might notice a yellow warning triangle somewhere in the upper-right corner of the layout editor (shown in Figure 11-4). Click the warning box.

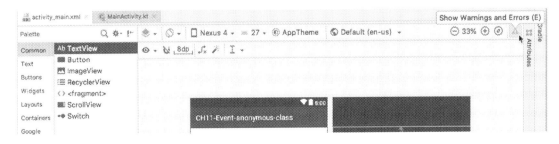

Figure 11-4. *Show warnings and error button*

Figure 11-5 shows the message tool window. It contains some explanation as to why we got the warning and a button prompt for a suggested fix.

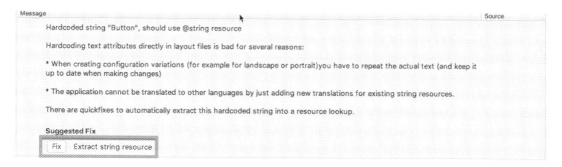

Figure 11-5. *Suggested fix*

AS3 is complaining because the newly added Button has a hard-coded value in its *text property*. Listing 11-4 shows (a snippet of) activity_main.xml before the "fix." Right now, the *android:text* property has a value of "Button," a string literal.

Listing 11-4. activity_main.xml, Button Element, Before the Fix

```
<Button
  android:id="@+id/button"
  android:text="Button"
/>
```

Androids prefer that we write attribute values, like the *text property* of the Button, in a resource file, rather than hard-coding them. Click the "Fix" button so AS3 can automatically extract the string resource. This action opens the Extract Resource window (see Figure 11-6).

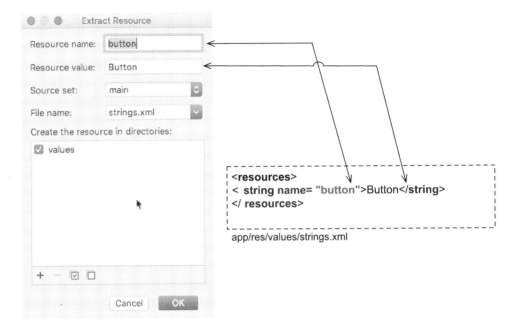

Figure 11-6. *Extract resource*

Our project has a string resource file in **app/res/values/strings.xml**. It provides textual resource values for the app. Android wants us to store all the string literals in this resource file instead of hard-coding them as you've seen in Listing 11-4.

The "Resource name" becomes the "name" attribute of the newly created string resource, and the "Resource value" becomes, well, the value of the string resource. This value is what will show up in the Button's text. Click "OK" to complete the action.

Listing 11-5 shows the content of activity_main.xml after the fix. The value of android:text is now set to "@string/button." The @ sign means we should not use the value of this string directly but instead look up a resource named "button" in the strings resource file.

Listing 11-5. activity_main.xml, Button Element, After the Fix

```
<Button
  android:id="@+id/button"
  android:text="@string/button"
/>
```

Last thing we need to do on the layout file is to assign an **id** attribute to the layout container. The layout container, by default, doesn't have an id attribute. We need to assign an id to it because we will refer to it later in our code. Switch to design mode and click somewhere inside the layout container (as shown in Figure 11-7). In the attributes panel, edit the **id** property. In this example, the **id** of the layout container is "root_layout."

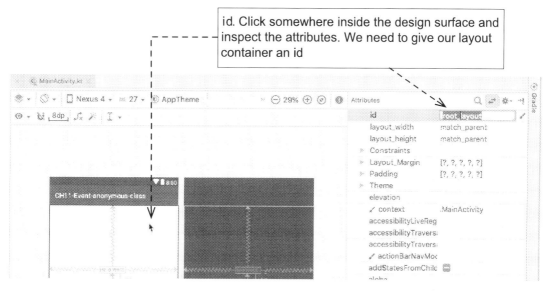

Figure 11-7. *Change the id attribute of the layout container*

Listing 11-6 shows the modified contents of our layout file.

Listing 11-6. Complete Listing for activity_main.xml

```xml
<?xml version="1.0" encoding="utf-8"?>
<android.support.constraint.ConstraintLayout xmlns:android="http://schemas.
android.com/apk/res/android"
  xmlns:app="http://schemas.android.com/apk/res-auto"
  xmlns:tools="http://schemas.android.com/tools"
  android:id="@+id/root_layout"      ❶
  android:layout_width="match_parent"
  android:layout_height="match_parent"
  tools:context=".MainActivity">
```

```
<TextView
    android:id="@+id/textView"
    android:layout_width="wrap_content"
    android:layout_height="wrap_content"
    android:text="Hello World!"
    app:layout_constraintBottom_toBottomOf="parent"
    app:layout_constraintLeft_toLeftOf="parent"
    app:layout_constraintRight_toRightOf="parent"
    app:layout_constraintTop_toTopOf="parent"
    app:layout_constraintVertical_bias="0.353" />

<Button
    android:id="@+id/button"
    android:layout_width="wrap_content"
    android:layout_height="wrap_content"
    android:layout_marginEnd="8dp"
    android:layout_marginStart="8dp"
    android:layout_marginTop="36dp"
    android:text="@string/button"      ❷
    app:layout_constraintEnd_toEndOf="parent"
    app:layout_constraintStart_toStartOf="parent"
    app:layout_constraintTop_toBottomOf="@+id/textView" />
```

`</android.support.constraint.ConstraintLayout>`

---

❶ The android:id of the layout container is now set to +@id/root_layout. Later in our code, we can refer to this control as just root_layout .

❷ The android:text property now has a value of @string/button; it's no longer hardcoded. It now gets its value from the strings.xml resource file.

Now we can work on the program file. Open *MainActivity.Kt* in the main editor. You can launch it by double-clicking on the file app/java/com.example.../MainActivity.Kt in the Project window.

We want the button to respond to both clicks and long-clicks. To do this, we need to set up two separate listeners for the same button—we could have created two buttons and assigned a listener to each, but I feel that the exercise is more instructive if we bind the two listeners to the same button.

The Activity doesn't need to be visible to the user before we set up the listeners; it only needs to be on the "created" state. This is why we'll set up the listeners in the onCreate() callback function. Let's deal with the click event first, then we'll handle the long-click. Listing 11-7 shows the code for the OnClickListener.

Listing 11-7. OnClickListener

```
button.setOnClickListener(object : View.OnClickListener {
    override fun onClick(v: View?) {
    }
})
```

By the way, as you type these codes, you might see some errors or warnings, like the one shown in Figure 11-8.

Figure 11-8. *AS3 hints*

In the Figure 11-8, AS3 warned of an unresolved "button" reference. To fix this error, we can either manually type the required import statements or we can use AS3's "Quick Fix" feature. To use the Quick Fix, click anywhere in unresolved reference—in our case, the "button" identifier—then press the keys **OPTION + ENTER** if you're on macOS; **ALT + ENTER** if you're on Windows or Linux.

AS3 will present some options if there's more than one way to resolve the issue. You can scroll through the options and choose which one you want to use.

Figure 11-9 shows the options on how to the fix the unresolved reference error. We'll pick the last option—this import statement is the Kotlin Android Extensions (KAE). KAE's magic sauce is that it exposes the IDs of all the view elements in your layout as extension properties of the Activity class. So, if you have a Button view in **activity_main.xml** whose ID is "button," you can simply use that ID in the Activity class like a regular variable—you don't need to use **findViewById()** anymore.

Figure 11-9. *AS3 hinting on an import*

Once you've typed the event handler as shown in Listing 11-7 and also in Figure 11-10, you'll notice that AS3 is hinting us to convert the listener object to a lambda expression.

```
button.setOnClickListener(object: View.OnClickListener {
    override fun onClick(v: View?) {
    }
})
```
Convert to lambda more... (⌘F1)

Figure 11-10. *Convert to lambda hint*

To use the Quick Fix, click anywhere in "OnClickListener," as shown in Figure 11-11, and press OPTION + ENTER or ALT + ENTER, then choose "Convert to lambda."

Figure 11-11. *Convert to lambda quick fix*

The lambda-simplified version removed some of our codes—the parentheses of setOnClickListener, the object expression, and the overridden onClick function are all gone, leaving us with just the following code:

```
button.setOnClickListener {  }
```

Next thing to do is to put a Toast message inside the onClick handler. Listing 11-8 shows a simple Toast message inside the click handler. A Toast is a small pop-up message that automatically disappears after some time. You can use it to send small feedback messages to the user. Listing 11-8 shows how to construct a Toast message inside the OnClickListener.

Listing 11-8. Toast Message

```
button.setOnClickListener {
  Toast.makeText(this, "Hello World", Toast.LENGTH_LONG).show()
}
```

Showing a Toast message is a two-step process. First step is to create a Toast message using the **makeText()** function. It takes three parameters: (1) the Context of the application, which in our case is the instance of MainActivity; (2) the message to show; and (3) how long to show the message. Second step is to make it visible by calling the **.show()** function.

Let's move on to the long-click listener. The code for this listener is shown in Listing 11-9.

Listing 11-9. OnLongClickListener

```
button.setOnLongClickListener(object: View.OnLongClickListener {
  override fun onLongClick(v: View?): Boolean {

    return true
  }
})
```

Reducing the code in Listing 11-9 to its lambda version gives us the following code:

```
button.setOnLongClickListener { true }
```

To test the long-click handler, let's use SnackBar rather than Toast. SnackBar is similar to Toast but it appears at the bottom of the screen. You can make it disappear after some timeout too, like Toasts, or you can make the user swipe it. SnackBar is more capable than Toast because you can include some actions in the message, like a small dialog box.

Before you can use SnackBar in your project, you need to modify the project's build. gradle file. See Listing 11-10 for the changes you need to make.

Listing 11-10. /app/build.gradle

```
dependencies {
    implementation 'com.android.support:design:27.1.1' ❶
    implementation fileTree(dir: 'libs', include: ['*.jar'])
    implementation"org.jetbrains.kotlin:kotlin-stdlib-jre7:$kotlin_version"
    implementation 'com.android.support:appcompat-v7:27.1.1'
    implementation 'com.android.support.constraint:constraint-layout:1.1.2'
    testImplementation 'junit:junit:4.12'
    androidTestImplementation 'com.android.support.test:runner:1.0.2'
    androidTestImplementation 'com.android.support.test.espresso:espresso-
    core:3.0.2'
}
```

❶ You need to add this to the project's **build.gradle** file (app level) before you can use SnackBar.

After that, you need to "Sync" the gradle file. A yellow strip will appear on the upper portion of the main editor, and on the upper-right corner, there will be a link to "Sync" the file. Click it, as shown in Figure 11-12.

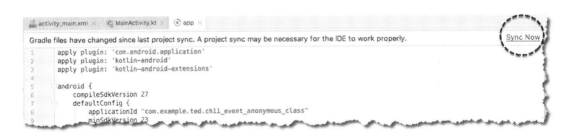

Figure 11-12. *Sync the build.gradle file*

After that, you can now use the SnackBar element. Listing 11-11 shows how to construct a SnackBar inside a long-click handler.

Listing 11-11. SnackBar Message Inside OnLongClickListener

```
button.setOnLongClickListener {
  Snackbar.make(root_layout, "Long click", Snackbar.LENGTH_LONG).show()
  true
}
```

SnackBar's make function requires three parameters: (1) a parent view; root_layout is the ID of our layout container; (2) a message to show; and (3) how long to show the message.

The last line in OnLongClickListener is actually a return statement, but we omitted the "return" because the handler is in lambda form—and in this form, the last expression on the block is returned.

The onLongClick() callback function has a Boolean signature—it returns either true or false. In our example, we returned true, which tells the Android runtime that the event has already been consumed and there is no need for other event handlers (like onClick) to handle it again. Had we returned false, the onClick handler would have kicked in right after onLongClick. Listing 11-12 shows the full code for MainActivity.

Listing 11-12. MainActivity.Kt, Annotated

```
package com.example.ted.ch11_event_anonymous_class  ❶

import android.support.v7.app.AppCompatActivity
import android.os.Bundle
import android.support.design.widget.Snackbar
import android.test.ViewAsserts
import android.view.View
import android.widget.Toast
import kotlinx.android.synthetic.main.activity_main.*  ❷

class MainActivity : AppCompatActivity() {  ❸

  override fun onCreate(savedInstanceState: Bundle?) {
    super.onCreate(savedInstanceState)
    setContentView(R.layout.activity_main)  ❹
```

```
button.setOnClickListener {
  Toast.makeText(this, "Hello World", Toast.LENGTH_LONG).show()
}

button.setOnLongClickListener {
  Snackbar.make(root_layout, "Long click", Snackbar.LENGTH_LONG).show()
  true
}
}
}
```

❶ Package declaration for our project. This comes from the "company domain" entry during project creation.

❷ Import statement for the Kotlin Android Extension (KAE). The KAE turns all the View elements in activity_main.xml into an extension property. Hence, we can refer to any View element using just their ID.

❸ We're extending from AppCompatActivity, so we can use modern elements like SnackBar and still run the app on earlier versions of Android.

❹ This statement binds MainActivity to activity_main.xml, our layout file.

If you run the app on the emulator, you'll see something like Figure 11-13.

Toast. A toast provides simple feedback about an operation in a small popup. It only fills the amount of space required for the message and the current activity remains visible and interactive. Toasts automatically disappear after a timeout

Snackbars provide lightweight feedback about an operation. They show a brief message at the bottom of the screen on mobile and lower left on larger devices. Snackbars appear above all other elements on screen and only one can be displayed at a time. They automatically disappear after a timeout or after user interaction elsewhere on the screen, particularly after interactions that summon a new surface or activity. Snackbars can be swiped off screen

Figure 11-13. *Completed project running in the emulator*

Chapter Summary

- You can set the **android:onClick** attribute to a name of a function if you want to handle simple click events.

- Listener objects has to be registered to the Android runtime if you want to intercept certain events.

- There are many kinds of listener objects, and they are listed as nested interfaces in the View class.

- Using the Kotlin Android Extension simplifies our coding. It exposes the IDs of all the Views in the layout file as extension properties of MainActivity—we don't need to use **findViewById()** anymore.

- Lambdas cleans up our event handling codes.

In the next chapter, we'll take a look at one of Android's most important part: Intents. Android, as an architecture, cannot exist without it. It's the glue that binds together all the loosely coupled components in Android.

CHAPTER 12

Intents

What we'll cover:

- Intent overview

- Explicit and implicit Intents

- Passing data between activities

- Returning results from Intents

Android's architecture is quite unique in the way it builds application. It has this notion of components instead of just plain objects. And the way that Android makes these components interact is something that can only be found in the Android platform. Android uses Intents as a way for its components to communicate—it uses it to pass messages across components. In this chapter, we'll look at Intents: what they are and how we use them.

What Intents Are

An Intent is "an abstract description of an operation to be performed.[1]" It's a uniquely Android concept because no other platform uses the same thing as a means of component activation. In the earlier chapters, we looked at what's inside an Android application. You might remember that an app is just a bunch of "components" (see Figure 12-1) that are loosely held together, and each component is declared in a manifest file.

---

[1]https://developer.android.com/reference/android/content/Intent

© Ted Hagos 2018
T. Hagos, *Learn Android Studio 3 with Kotlin*, https://doi.org/10.1007/978-1-4842-3907-0_12

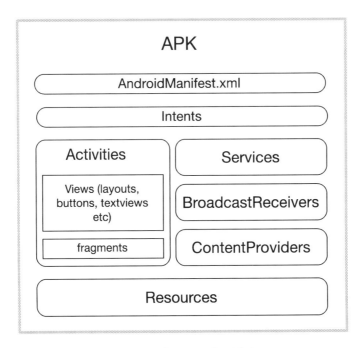

Figure 12-1. *Logical representation of an Android App*

What if youl need your components to talk to each other (e.g., launch another Activity)? How do you think we should manage that? If you have any experience with desktop programming, you might do something like the code in Listing 12-1.

Listing 12-1. Wrong Way to Activate Another Activity

```
class MainActivity : AppCompatActivity {

  button.setOnClickListener(object: View.OnClickListener {
    override fun onClick(v: View?) {
      SecondActivity(). // Won't work
  }
  })
}

class SecondActivity : AppCompatActivity {}
```

Listing 12-1 may appear to be a simple and direct way to launch another Activity, but unfortunately, it's wrong and it won't work. An Activity is not a simple object—it's a component. You cannot activate a component just by instantiating it. To launch an Activity, you need to create an Intent object and launch it using the startActivity() function. The code is shown in Listing 12-2.

Listing 12-2. How to Activate Another Activity

```
button.setOnClickListener {
  val intent = Intent(this@MainActivity, SecondActivity::class.java) ❶ ❷
  startActivity(intent) ❸
}
```

❶ **this@MainActivity** The first parameter of the Intent constructor is a `Context` object. We passed `this@MainActivity` because the Activity class is a subclass of `Context`, so we can use that. Alternatively, we also could have used `getApplicationContext()`; an Application context would have been accepted just as well.

❷ **SecondActivity::class.java**. The second parameter is a `Class` object. It's the class of the Component to which we want to deliver the message. This a *reflection* syntax. As you may already know, *reflection* allows us inspect the structure of our programs during runtime. `SecondActivity::class` would refer to the runtime reference of SecondActivity if it were a Kotlin class (KClass), but it's not. SecondActivity is a Java class (Android libraries are still in Java), hence we refer to it as `SecondActivity::class.java`

❸ We launch the Activity by calling `startActivity()` and passing the intent object to it.

The Android platform is gung-ho on loose coupling, and component activation is smacked in the middle of its architecture. An application is just a collection of components held together by a manifest file, and each of these components can be activated by sending a message to it. The basic idea is that none of the components talks directly to another. If one component, like an Activity, wants to talk to another component, it needs to send a request to the Android runtime and let the runtime resolve that request. You can think of an Intent as a message-passing mechanism within Android: it glues the components together.

Loose Coupling

You might be tempted to think that Android was over-architected because, why go to these lengths just to launch another screen? Why couldn't we just create an instance of an object and be done with it—it is a well-known programming idiom already. Why do we have to replace this with component activation?

Well, Android's approach to program interactivity is quite unique because it's very user-centric. It gives the user a lot of power to make choices on how they manipulate and create data. Mobile users are generally task-focused rather than app-focused; they don't really care which application does what, as long as it gets done.

Let's take a common usage scenario for an Android device. A user opens the "Contacts" application and chooses the contact detail of Ted Hagos, for example. This contact could have an e-mail address, a mobile phone, and a twitter name, let's say. The user could tap on each of Ted's contact points, and each time, Android will launch a different application; the default e-mail client, a dialer, and a downloaded Twitter app. The user probably doesn't care which application was launched or how many applications are currently open; he just wants to send a message. If this user doesn't like the e-mail app or the default twitter client, he could delete these apps and replace them with something else, and he should be back in business. Figure 12-2 shows a simple storyboard on using the Contacts app.

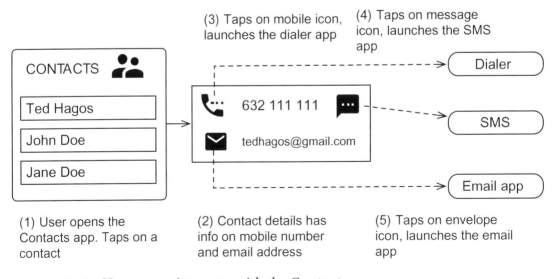

Figure 12-2. *How a user interacts with the Contacts app*

For this kind of program interaction to happen, Android needed to architect the platform, focusing heavily on loose coupling and pluggability. A component, like the Contacts app, should not know any specific detail about what app it should use when an e-mail address or a mobile phone number is tapped. The resolution for what kind of app to use for a specific kind of data should not be hardwired into the Contacts app; otherwise, the user won't be able to exercise his choice on which app to use when sending e-mails or tweets.

This is where Intents come in. When a component needs to complete a task that is beyond its capability to service, it can go out to the Android platform using Intents and ask around if there's any application that can (or wants to) fulfill the request.

Two Kinds of Intent

There are two kinds of Intent: an implicit and an explicit one. An analogy might be helpful to illustrate the difference between these two kinds of Intent. Let's say that we'll ask someone to buy some sugar. If we gave an instruction like "could you please buy some sugar," with no further details, this would be equivalent to an implicit Intent because that person could buy the sugar anywhere. On the other hand, if we gave instructions like "could you please go to the ABC store on third street and buy some sugar," this would be equivalent to an explicit Intent. The earlier code sample in Listing 12-2 is an example of an explicit Intent.

Implicit Intents are very powerful because they allow your application to take advantage of other applications. Your app can gain functionalities that you did not write yourself. You can, for example, create an Intent that opens the Camera, shoots and save a photo—without writing any Camera specific code.

Intents Can Carry Data

Intents can do much more than launch other Activities; you can also send and receive data with it. Assuming we have two Activities named *MainActivity* and *SecondActivity* and when a Button View object is clicked within MainActivity, we want to launch and send some data to SecondActivity. To send data to SecondActivity, you need to:

1. Create an Intent—for the purposes of our example here, it will be an explicit Intent.

2. Add data to the intent using the **putExtra** method.

3. Launch the other Activity by calling the **startActivity** method; at this point, the Android runtime will launch *SecondActivity*.

4. Within the **onCreate** method of *SecondActivity*, we can extract the data from the Intent by using the **getExtra** method.

Figure 12-3 shows a simple sequence diagram on how this all works.

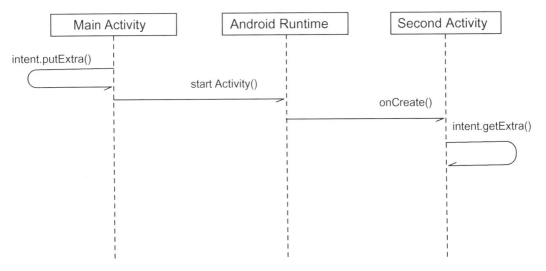

Figure 12-3. *How to send data to another Activity*

Note   Most of the function calls in Android like **startActivity**, **onCreate**, etc. are asynchronous—that's why the arrows used in the sequence diagram are half-stick arrows. The sequence of calls as shown in Figure 12-3 (and in the other sequence diagrams) are approximations only, they may not actually happen in that order.

To represent these steps in code, it might look like Listing 12-3.

Listing 12-3. Code Snippet from MainActivity

```
button.setOnClickListener {
  val intent = Intent(this@MainActivity, SecondActivity::class.java)
  intent.putExtra("main_activity_data", editText.text.toString())
  startActivity(intent)
}
```

The parameters of the **putExtra** method is a key-value pair; the first parameter is the key or name and the second parameter is the value. The name parameter will always be of String type but the second parameter (value) may not be of String type always. The **putExtra** method is overloaded, it can accept a range of types for the second parameter. If you type slowly enough in Android Studio, you might see the options shown in the code hinting while you are typing the **putExtra** method; see Figure 12-4.

```
button.setOnClickListener { it: View!
    val intent = Intent( packageContext: this@MainActivity, SecondActivity::class.java)
    intent.putExtra( name: "main_activity_data", editText.text.toString())
    intent.putEx|
    st m   putExtra(name: String!, value: Int)                          Intent!
}        m   putExtra(name: String!, value: Byte)                       Intent!
butt     m   putExtra(name: String!, value: Char)                       Intent!
    va   m   putExtra(name: String!, value: Long)                       Intent!  .java)
    va   m   putExtra(name: String!, value: Float)                      Intent!
         m   putExtra(name: String!, value: Short)                      Intent!
    bu   m   putExtra(name: String!, value: Double)                     Intent!
    bu   m   putExtra(name: String!, value: Boolean)                    Intent!
    in   m   putExtra(name: String!, value: Bundle!)                    Intent!
    st   m   putExtra(name: String!, value: String!)                    Intent!
}        —   putExtra(name: String!  value: IntArray!)                  Intent!
}
         ^↓ and ^↑ will move caret down and up in the editor >>              π
override fun onActivityResult(requestCode: Int, resultCode: Int, data: Intent?) {
```

Figure 12-4. *Code hinting in AS3 showing the overloaded putExtra()*

In Listing 12-3, we put a String in the second parameter of **putExtra;** we can use other types as well (e.g., basic types like *Int, Byte, Char, Float, Short,* etc.). We can also use *Bundles, Parcelables,* or *Serializables.*

After calling the **putExtra** method on the Intent, the next step is to call **startActivity**. That will trigger the Intent resolution mechanism of the Android runtime and will eventually launch the *SecondActivity.*

Now we move on to *SecondActivity.* Naturally, you'd like to extract the data we sent from *MainActivity.* You need to do two things to achieve that. You need to:

1. Get a reference to Intent object; and

2. Call the **getExtra** function from the Intent. That code might look like this:

```
val myintent = getIntent()
val data = myintent.getStringExtra("main_activity_data")
```

But because of Kotlin's magic with getters and setters, the getIntent() function becomes the *intent* property. So, we can rewrite it like this:

```
val data = intent.getStringExtra("main_activity_data")
```

Getting Back Results from Another Activity

In the previous section, we managed to launch a second Activity and send data to it. In this section, we'll build on our previous example, but this time, we will also send some data back to *MainActivity*. To do that, we need to:

1. Create an explicit Intent.

2. Add data to the intent using the **putExtra** method.

3. Launch the other Activity by calling the **startActivityForResult** method. Like the **startActivity** method, we need to pass an Intent object to this method as a parameter. In addition, we also need to pass a *request code* to it. A *request code* acts as some sort of a token. When we start an Activity and we expect some results back, any other Activity can send back any result. If we have a couple of Activities within a project, it could get confusing when we get back the results. We need a way to track who's sending back those results, and the *request code* will help us do that. Once we call startActivityForResult, the *SecondActivity* will launch.

4. Within the **onCreate** method of SecondActivity, we can extract the data from the Intent by using the **getExtra** method.

5. We can do some computation within SecondActivity. When we are ready to send back data, we'll do the following:

   a. Get a reference to the Intent object.

   b. Add data to the Intent using the **putExtra** method.

   c. Call the **setResult** method of SecondActivity. There are two things we need to do in here: (1) set the status of Intent call, if there are no errors, you can set it to *Activity.RESULT_OK*; and (2) pass the intent object containing the extras as the second parameter.

d. Call **finish()** from within *SecondActivity*. This will stop the
SecondActivity and effectively send the Intent to whichever
component called SecondActivity, which is MainActivity

6. Back to MainActivity, whatever results we expect back from
SecondActivity—or any other Activity, for that matter—can be
received from within the **onActivityResult** callback. This method
has three things in its parameter: it has the request code, result
code, and the Intent object that was sent back by SecondActivity.

Figure 12-5 shows a sequence diagram on how to send and get back results from
another Activity.

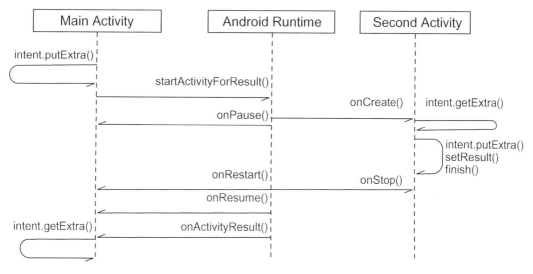

Figure 12-5. *Sequence diagram for getting back results from another Activity*

When you send data to another Activity and you expect to get some data back, you
need to use **startActivityForResult** instead of **startActivity**. The code to do that looks
like this:

```
startActivityForResult(intent, SECOND_ACTIVITY)
```

Like startActivity, you pass the Intent object to **startActivityForResult**, in addition to
the Intent object, you also need to pass a *request code* (SECOND_ACTIVITY). This request
code is important for MainActivity because we will use it to track from whom we are
getting the data back. The request code is an *Int* that you need to define. It doesn't matter

what number you will use for it, as long as if you have multiple request codes, each is different. If you send and expect data back from a couple of Activities, you will use the request code to track which of the other Activities are sending data back to you. This way, when the results come back, we can tell what we were trying to do in the first place.

In SecondActivity, when we are ready to send data back, we need to create another Intent object and load it with data using the **putExtra** method. After that, we call the **setResult** method of SecondActivity. The setResult method takes two parameters: a *result code* and the Intent object. If everything is going fine in the app, use *Activity. RESULT_OK*; otherwise use *Activity.RESULT_CANCELLED*. RESULT_OK is actually -1 and RESULT_CANCELLED is 0, but please don't use the *Int* literals, always use the supplied class constants.

When you call the finish method on SecondActivity, it will enter the stopped state and MainActivity will emerge to the foreground again—so, it will *restart* and *resume*. Whatever data was sent back by SecondActivity, we should be able to pick it up within the **onActivityResult** callback of MainActivity. Listing 12-4 shows a typical overridden onActivityResult callback.

Listing 12-4. onActivityResult

```
override fun onActivityResult(requestCode: Int, resultCode: Int, data:
Intent?) {
  super.onActivityResult(requestCode, resultCode, data)

  if((requestCode == SECOND_ACTIVITY) and (resultCode == Activity.RESULT_
  OK)) {
    // extract data here
  }
}
```

> **Note**   How do you know when you are supposed to override the **onActivityResult** callback? If you launch another Activity using **startActivityForResult**, you should override the onActivityResult callback—it's where you can pick up whatever data was sent back to you.

Implicit Intents

What we've seen in the previous sections are all examples of explicit Intents. An explicit Intent tells the Android runtime precisely which component to Activate. Going back to our analogy, it's like telling somebody to go to the grocery store on 3rd street to buy some sugar. An implicit Intent, on the other hand, simply will give the instruction to "get some sugar"—it doesn't matter where or how. An implicit Intent specifies only the action.

When you use an implicit Intent, the general idea is that you'd like to use a functionality that doesn't exist within your app—if it did exist within your app, you would have used an explicit Intent in the first place;—so, you're asking the Android runtime to find an application somewhere on the device that can service your request.

We know from the previous examples that Intents can carry data; we did that with *Extras*. Extras are one of four things that an Intent can have; the other three are *Action*, *Data,* and *Category*. An Action is the operation that you want to do (e.g., VIEW, DIAL, ANSWER, CALL, etc.). The Data pertains to what kind of information the Action has to work with (is it a URI, a Phone number, a picture, etc.), and Category pertains to what components are eligible to deal with this Intent. Sometimes the runtime needs the Category to filter out or select only those components that can respond to our Intent. You can send Intents to Activities, BroadcastReceivers, and Services, but in this chapter, we'll deal only with Activities.

There's generally four things you need to do to get an implicit Intent off the ground. You need to:

1. Create the Intent object

2. Set its action (e.g., "view a map," "call a number," "take a picture," etc.)

3. Set its data; and

4. Launch the intent

Listing 12-5 shows us how all this might look like in code.

Listing 12-5. Example Intent to Launch a Web Browser

```
val m_intent = Intent() ❶
m_intent = setAction(Intent.ACTION_VIEW)   ❷
m_intent = setData(Uri.parse("https://workingdev.net")) ❸
startActivity (m_intent) ❹
```

❶ Create the Intent using the no-arg constructor.

❷ Set the Intent action. In this example, we'd like to view something; it could be a contact, a web page, a map, a picture somewhere, etc. At this point the Android runtime doesn't know yet what you want to view. ACTION_VIEW is one of the many Intent Actions you can use. You can find other kinds of Action in the official Android's website (`http://bit.ly/ androidcommonintents`).

❸ Set its data. At this point, the Android runtime has a pretty good idea what you're up to. In this example, the Uri is a web page. Android is pretty smart to figure out that we'd like to view a web page.

❹ Android will search every app on the device that will best match this request. If it finds more than one app, it will let the user choose which one. If it finds only one, it will simply launch that app.

We can simply the codes in Listing 12-16 into something like this

```
m_intent = Intent(Intent.ACTION_VIEW,  Uri.parse("https://workingdev.net"))
startActivity(m_intent)
```

The ACTION and DATA can be passed as arguments to the Intent's constructor.

Any component that can answer to our Intent does not need to be running in order to receive the Intent. Remember that all applications need to have a manifest file. Each application declares its capabilities in the manifest file, specifically through the `<intent-filter>` section. Android's package manager has all the info of all the applications installed on the device. Android's runtime only needs the information on the manifest file to see which among the apps are capable and/or eligible to respond to the Intent.

In the following sections, we'll explore implicit and explicit Intents in more details. We'll set up example projects so you can practice on them.

Demo 1: Launch an Activity

We won't do anything fancy with this project. We will simply create two Activities: MainActivity and SecondActivity. We will launch the SecondActivity from MainActivity when a Button is clicked. The project details are shown in Table 12-1.

Table 12-1. *Project Detail for Demo App*

Project Detail	Value
Application name	CH12LaunchAnotherActivity
Company domain	Your website name
Kotlin support	Yes
Form factor	Phone and Tablet only
minimum SDK	API 23 Marshmallow
Type of activity	Empty
Activity name	MainActivity
Layout name	activity_main
Backwards compatibility	Yes. AppCompat

When the project opens in the Main window, create the SecondActivity. One of the ways you can do that is to select the "app" the Project tool window as shown in Figure 12-6, then from the Main toolbar click **File ➤ New ➤ Activity ➤ Empty Activity**.

Figure 12-6. *Select "app" in the Project tool window*

Let's give it the name "SecondActivity," as shown in Figure 12-7.

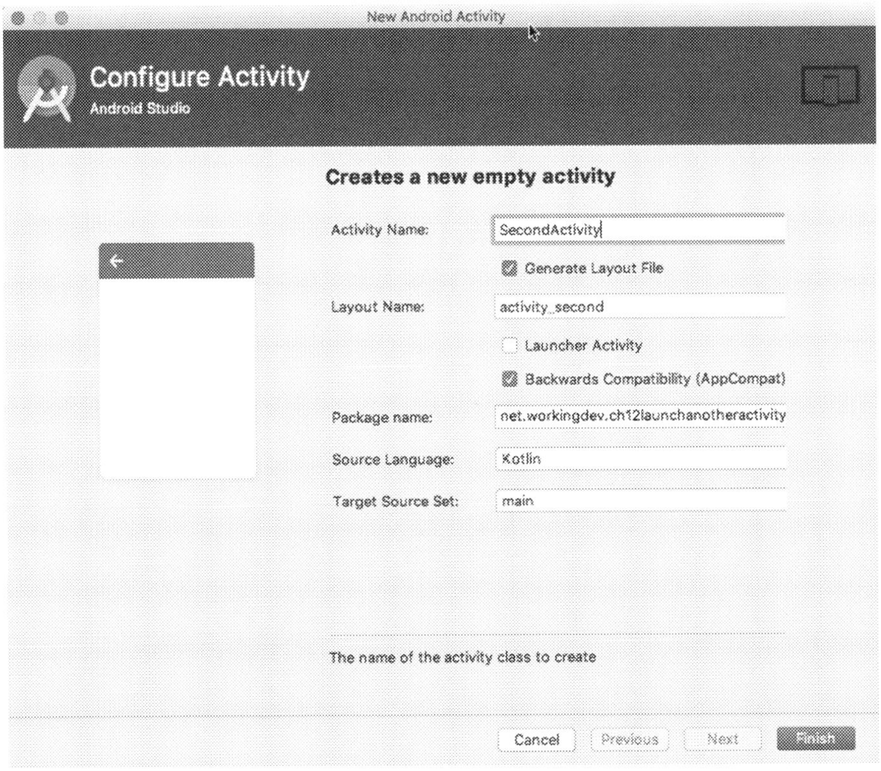

Figure 12-7. *New Android activity*

Next, go to activity_main.xml (design view). Remove the TextView element and replace it with a Button view. Position the Button approximately to the center of the layout, then use the "infer constraint" button, as shown in Figure 12-8.

Next, open activity_second.xml, also in design view, then add a Button view and center it in the layout, just like what you did in activity_main.

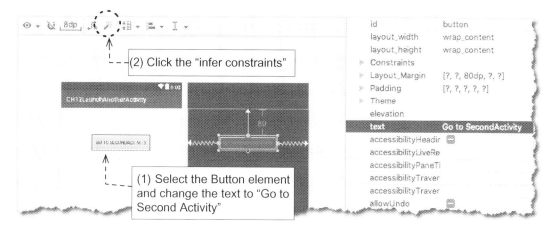

Figure 12-8. *Center the Button view on the layout*

At this point, you should have the following View elements and classes to work with:

- MainActivity.Kt and its associated *activity_main.xml*, this is from the project creation wizard

- SecondActivity.Kt. and its associated *activity_second.xml*, this is from the Activity creation wizard

- A Button view object in *activity_main* whose id is "button"—it's the default id for the first Button element in the project

- Another Button view object in activity_second whose id is "button2"—it's the default id for the second Button element in the project

Listings 12-6 and 12-7 show the codes for activity_main and activity_second, respectively; you may use them as reference or for comparison in case you tried to build the project yourself.

Listing 12-6. /app/res/layout/activity_main.xml

```
<?xml version="1.0" encoding="utf-8"?>
<android.support.constraint.ConstraintLayout xmlns:android=http://schemas.
android.com/apk/res/android
  xmlns:app=http://schemas.android.com/apk/res-auto
  xmlns:tools=http://schemas.android.com/tools
  android:layout_width="match_parent"
```

```
  android:layout_height="match_parent"
  tools:context=".MainActivity">

  <Button
    android:id="@+id/button"
    android:layout_width="wrap_content"
    android:layout_height="wrap_content"
    android:layout_marginTop="80dp"
    android:text="Button"
    app:layout_constraintEnd_toEndOf="parent"
    app:layout_constraintStart_toStartOf="parent"
    app:layout_constraintTop_toTopOf="parent" />
</android.support.constraint.ConstraintLayout>
```

Listing 12-7. /app/res/layout/activity_second.xml

```
<?xml version="1.0" encoding="utf-8"?>
<android.support.constraint.ConstraintLayout xmlns:android=http://schemas.
android.com/apk/res/android
  xmlns:app=http://schemas.android.com/apk/res-auto
  xmlns:tools=http://schemas.android.com/tools
  android:layout_width="match_parent"
  android:layout_height="match_parent"
  tools:context=".SecondActivity">

  <Button
    android:id="@+id/button2"
    android:layout_width="wrap_content"
    android:layout_height="wrap_content"
    android:layout_marginTop="88dp"
    android:text="Button"
    app:layout_constraintEnd_toEndOf="parent"
    app:layout_constraintStart_toStartOf="parent"
    app:layout_constraintTop_toTopOf="parent" />
</android.support.constraint.ConstraintLayout>
```

Listings 12-8 and 12-9 show the annotated codes for MainActivity.Kt and SecondActivity.Kt, respectively.

Listing 12-8. Full Listing and Annotated Code of MainActivity.Kt

```kotlin
import android.content.Intent
import android.support.v7.app.AppCompatActivity
import android.os.Bundle
import kotlinx.android.synthetic.main.activity_main.*
import java.util.logging.Logger

class MainActivity : AppCompatActivity() {

  val Log = Logger.getLogger(MainActivity::class.java.name)  ❶

  override fun onCreate(savedInstanceState: Bundle?) {
    super.onCreate(savedInstanceState)
    setContentView(R.layout.activity_main)

    Log.info("onCreate")  ❷

    button.setOnClickListener {  ❸
      val m_intent = Intent(this@MainActivity, SecondActivity::class.java)  ❹
      startActivity(m_intent)  ❺
    }
  }

  override fun onPause() {
    super.onPause()
    Log.info("onPause")
  }

  override fun onRestart() {
    super.onRestart()
    Log.info("onRestart")
  }

  override fun onResume() {
    super.onResume()
    Log.info("onResume")
  }
}
```

❶   We're defining a simple Logger object. We could have used the **android.util.Log** class, but I
     would think that most of you who will read this book will come from a Java background, so
     this should look familiar. The parameter `MainActivity::class.name` is roughly equivalent
     to Java's `getClass().getName()`. Alternatively, you can also just pass any String to the
     `getLogger()` method—e.g., `getLogger("My Project")`—but the usual practice is to
     use the name of class for the Logger object.

❷   We're just creating a log entry saying that we're on the "onCreate" callback of MainActivity.

❸   This is a basic setup for a Button's click listener; you've done this already.

❹   This line creates an Intent object. First parameter of the Intent object is a Context object; you
     can use an Application Context here, but in our case, we used an Activity context. `this@`
     `MainActivity` is a reference to MainActivity's context. The second parameter is the Intent's
     target object. This is a specific instruction to Android runtime that we want to activate this
     object. The second parameter should be of type **Class**. The notation for MainActivity's class
     object is `MainActivity::class.java`.

❺   We launch the Intent.

Listing 12-9. SecondActivity.Kt

```
import android.support.v7.app.AppCompatActivity
import android.os.Bundle
import kotlinx.android.synthetic.main.activity_second.*
import java.util.logging.Logger

class SecondActivity : AppCompatActivity() {

  val Log = Logger.getLogger(SecondActivity::class.java.name)

  override fun onCreate(savedInstanceState: Bundle?) {
    super.onCreate(savedInstanceState)
    setContentView(R.layout.activity_second)

    Log.info("onCreate")
```

```
  button2.setOnClickListener {
    finish()  ❶
  }
}

override fun onStart() {
  super.onStart()    ❷
  Log.info("onStart")
}

override fun onStop() {
  super.onStop()
  Log.info("onStop")
}
}
```

---

❶   When we call this, SecondActivity will be on a "stopped" state.

❷   When SecondActivity enters the **onStart** callback, it will be visible to the user. Whatever
     Activity was in the foreground, will now be moved to the background; MainActivity will enter a
     "paused" state.

When you call startActivity from MainActivity, the runtime will activate
SecondActivity. When SecondActivity becomes visible to the user, which should happen
during **onStart** of SecondActivity, MainActivity will enter the "paused" state.

When you call finish() from SecondActivity, it will enter the "stopped" state.
MainActivity will be brought to the foreground, so it will re-enter the "resume" and
"restart" states. This interaction is shown in Figure 12-9.

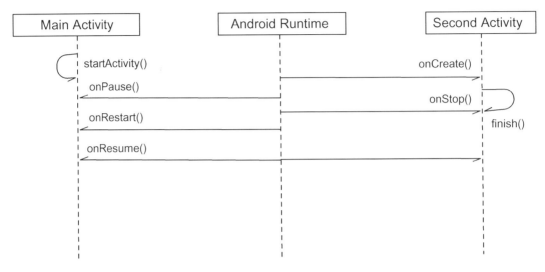

Figure 12-9. *Sequence diagram for MainActivity, SecondActivity, and the runtime*

I've overridden some of the life cycle callbacks for both MainActivity and SecondActivity. You can inspect the logs to see the timing and sequence of when the life cycle methods are called. You can use the Logcat tool window to inspect the application and system logs, as shown in Figure 12-10.

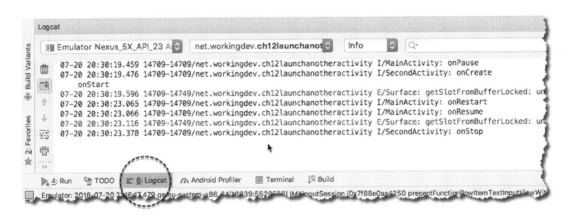

Figure 12-10. *Logcat tool window*

Demo 2: Send Data to an Activity

In this project, we will continue to explore the basic mechanics of explicit Intents. However, instead of just launching another Activity, we will also send some data to it. We'll go through the details on how to put an "Extra" in the Intent and how to extract it. Again, if you want to code along, the details of the project is shown in Table 12-2.

Table 12-2. *Project Details*

Project Detail	Value
Application name	CH12SendDataToAnotherActivity
Company domain	Your website name
Kotlin support	Yes
Form factor	Phone and Tablet only
minimum SDK	API 23 Marshmallow
Type of activity	Empty
Activity name	MainActivity
Layout name	activity_main
Backwards compatibility	Yes. AppCompat

Like in the previous section, we also need to create another Activity. Create another Activity and name it "SecondActivity."

Go back to activity_main and open it in design view. Remove the "Hello" TextView from the layout, then add an EditText and a Button view, as shown in Figure 12-11. Align the elements, center them in the layout, and use the "infer constraint," just like what we did in the previous demo project.

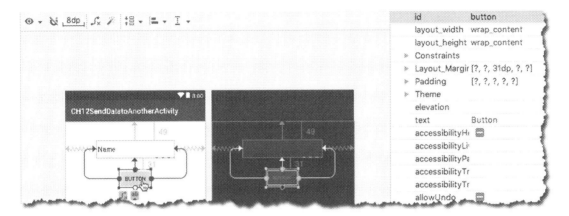

Figure 12-11. *activity_main.xml, design view*

Next, open activity_second in design view, then add A TextView element to it. Use the "infer constraint" (as usual) and adjust some of the attributes like the textSize and text Alignment, as shown in Figure 12-12.

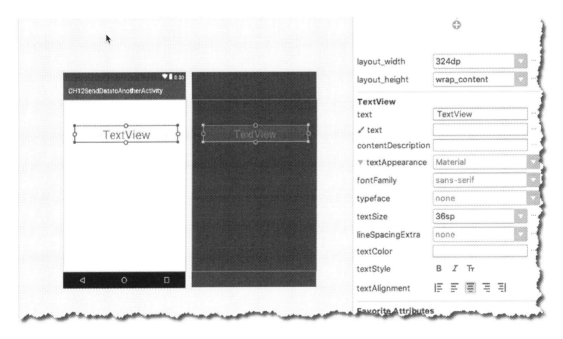

Figure 12-12. *activity_second.xml, design mode*

By now, you should have the following View elements and classes to work with:

- MainActivity.Kt and its associated *activity_main.xml*; this is from the project creation wizard.

- SecondActivity.Kt. and its associated *activity_second.xml*; this is from the Activity creation wizard.

- An EditText and a Button view object in *activity_main* whose ids are "editText" and "button," respectively. editText is the default id for the first PlainText element in the project.

- A TextView view object in activity_second whose id is "textView"—it's the default id for the first TextView element in the project.

Listings 12-10 and 12-11 show the code for activity_main.xml and activity_two.xml, respectively.

Listing 12-10. /app/res/layout/activity_main.xml

```
<?xml version="1.0" encoding="utf-8"?>
<android.support.constraint.ConstraintLayout xmlns:android=http://schemas.
android.com/apk/res/android
  xmlns:app=http://schemas.android.com/apk/res-auto
  xmlns:tools=http://schemas.android.com/tools
  android:layout_width="match_parent"
  android:layout_height="match_parent"
  tools:context=".MainActivity">

  <Button
    android:id="@+id/button"
    android:layout_width="wrap_content"
    android:layout_height="wrap_content"
    android:layout_marginTop="31dp"
    android:text="Button"
    app:layout_constraintEnd_toEndOf="@+id/editText"
    app:layout_constraintStart_toStartOf="@+id/editText"
    app:layout_constraintTop_toBottomOf="@+id/editText" />
```

```
  <EditText
    android:id="@+id/editText"
    android:layout_width="wrap_content"
    android:layout_height="wrap_content"
    android:layout_marginTop="49dp"
    android:ems="10"
    android:inputType="textPersonName"
    android:text="Name"
    app:layout_constraintEnd_toEndOf="parent"
    app:layout_constraintStart_toStartOf="parent"
    app:layout_constraintTop_toTopOf="parent" />
</android.support.constraint.ConstraintLayout>
```

Listing 12-11. /app/res/layout/activity_second.xml

```
<?xml version="1.0" encoding="utf-8"?>
<android.support.constraint.ConstraintLayout xmlns:android=http://schemas.
android.com/apk/res/android
  xmlns:app=http://schemas.android.com/apk/res-auto
  xmlns:tools=http://schemas.android.com/tools
  android:layout_width="match_parent"
  android:layout_height="match_parent"
  tools:context=".SecondActivity">

  <TextView
    android:id="@+id/textView"
    android:layout_width="324dp"
    android:layout_height="wrap_content"
    android:text="TextView"
    android:textAlignment="center"
    android:textSize="36sp"
    tools:layout_editor_absoluteX="35dp"
    tools:layout_editor_absoluteY="78dp" />
</android.support.constraint.ConstraintLayout>
```

Listings 12-12 and 12-13 show the annotated codes for MainActivity and SecondActivity, respectively.

Listing 12-12. MainActivity

```kotlin
import android.content.Intent
import android.support.v7.app.AppCompatActivity
import android.os.Bundle
import kotlinx.android.synthetic.main.activity_main.*

class MainActivity : AppCompatActivity() {

  override fun onCreate(savedInstanceState: Bundle?) {
    super.onCreate(savedInstanceState)
    setContentView(R.layout.activity_main)

    button.setOnClickListener {
      val m_data = editText.text.toString() ❶
      val m_intent = Intent(this@MainActivity, SecondActivity::class.java) ❷
      m_intent.putExtra("main_activity_data", m_data) ❸
      startActivity(m_intent) ❹
    }
  }
}
```

❶   We're getting the value of whatever the user has typed in the EditText object. The syntax to do this is actually `editText.getText().toString()` but Kotlin makes our lives easier with the syntactic sugars of getters and setters. We can use the property "**text**" to either set or get the runtime value of the EditText view. We had to call the `toString()` function because the return type of `EditText.getText()` is **Editable** or **CharSequence**. I needed it to be a of type String because the **putExtra** does not take an Editable nor a CharSequence; it takes in Strings.

❷   We're creating an explicit Intent and its target is **SecondActivity.**

❸   Now we get to put some data to piggyback on the Intent. The two parameters of putExtra look like a *key-value* pair; and they are. The *key* is the first parameter, "main_activity_data" and the *value* is the runtime content of the EditText—converted to String, of course.

❹   We're sending off the Intent object.

Listing 12-13. SecondActivity

```
import android.support.v7.app.AppCompatActivity
import android.os.Bundle
import kotlinx.android.synthetic.main.activity_second.*

class SecondActivity : AppCompatActivity() {

  override fun onCreate(savedInstanceState: Bundle?) {
    super.onCreate(savedInstanceState)
    setContentView(R.layout.activity_second)

    val m_data = intent.getStringExtra("main_activity_data") ❶ ❷
    textView.setText(m_data) ❸
  }
}
```

❶   We're getting a reference to the Intent object that's associated with SecondActivity, we're not creating a new Intent object here. The syntax is actually getIntent() but because of Kotlin's magic sauce, we get to reference it as simply **intent**

❷   The **getStringExtra** method of the Intent object is doing what you think it does. It's extracting some data from the Intent object using a map idiom; you give it a key, you'd get a value. In this case, we gave it the key "main_activity_data—this is the same key we used in MainActivity. We used the **getStringExtra** method because we know that it contains a String. The *get-er* should correspond to the *put-er*. If you put *Byte, Array, or Bundle* then you should get it **getByteExtra**, **getArrayExtra,** and **getBundleExtra**, respectively.

❸   We're changing the runtime value of the TextView. We're setting it to whatever we got from the Intent extra.

Run the program and try typing on the EditText. When you click on the Button, the TextView on SecondActivity should display whatever you typed.

Demo 3: Send and Get Data Back to and from an Activity

In this project, we'll ask the user to input his weight and height and then we'll calculate his BMI (body mass index). The project has two Activities: MainActivity and SecondActivity.

We'll ask the user to input his height and weight on MainActivity. We will send that data to SecondActivity via an Intent. In SecondActivity, we will extract the data from the Intent that was sent to us by MainActivity. We will use the height and weight data to calculate the BMI and then send it back to MainActivity.

If you want to follow along, I've listed the project details in Table 12-3.

Table 12-3. *Project Details for Demo App*

Project Detail	Value
Application name	CH12SendAndGetDataBackFromActivity
Company domain	Your website name
Kotlin support	Yes
Form factor	Phone and Tablet only
minimum SDK	API 23 Marshmallow
Type of activity	Empty
Activity name	MainActivity
Layout name	activity_main
Backwards compatibility	Yes. AppCompat

This project, like the previous demos, also has two Activities, but it has a few more View elements to it. Create the two Activities like how you created them in the previous demos.

The MainActivity has a couple of View elements: two EditTexts for the user input, a Button, and a TextView that we will use to display the BMI. You can find the details for the View objects like *id, height,* and *text size* in Listing 12-14; it's the complete code for activity_main.xml.

I gave the Views a very simple arrangement—I simply packed and centered all of them vertically. I also did not bother much with the layout constraint. After eye-balling an arrangement I thought wasn't so repulsive, I used the "infer constraints" button to automagically fix all the layout constraints, just like what we did in the previous demos. Figure 12-13 illustrates how to manage the layout for activity_main.

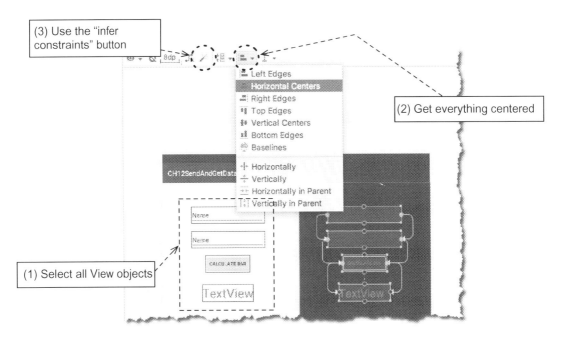

Figure 12-13. *Basic layout for activity_main*

The sample code doesn't go out of its way to validate inputs programmatically, so we'll put some validation mechanism on the EditTexts. The weight and height input fields should take in only numbers—specifically, Float numbers; we can enforce this by setting the *inputType* attribute of the EditText views. Here's how to do it:

1. While editing activity_main on design view, select one the EditText views.

2. On the attributes tool window, click "inputType."

3. Select "numberDecimal."

4. Repeat steps 1-3 for the other EditText.

Figure 12-14 illustrates this process.

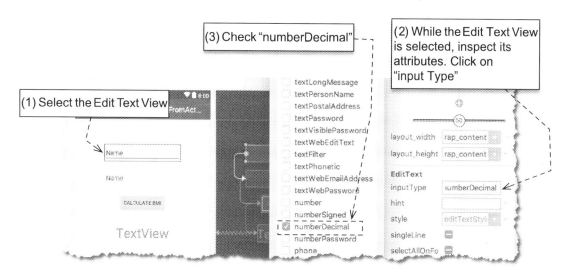

Figure 12-14. *Put a validation constraint on the EditText*

That should take care of MainActivity's UI. Listing 12-14 shows the complete code for activity_main.xml

Listing 12-14. /app/res/layout/activity_main.xml

```xml
<?xml version="1.0" encoding="utf-8"?>
<android.support.constraint.ConstraintLayout xmlns:android=http://schemas.
android.com/apk/res/android
  xmlns:app=http://schemas.android.com/apk/res-auto
  xmlns:tools=http://schemas.android.com/tools
  android:layout_width="match_parent"
  android:layout_height="match_parent"
  tools:context=".MainActivity">

  <EditText
    android:id="@+id/input_weight"
    android:layout_width="wrap_content"
    android:layout_height="wrap_content"
    android:layout_marginTop="68dp"
    android:ems="10"
    android:inputType="numberDecimal"
    android:text="Name"
    app:layout_constraintEnd_toEndOf="@+id/input_height"
```

```
      app:layout_constraintStart_toStartOf="@+id/input_height"
      app:layout_constraintTop_toTopOf="parent" />

  <EditText
      android:id="@+id/input_height"
      android:layout_width="wrap_content"
      android:layout_height="wrap_content"
      android:layout_marginTop="23dp"
      android:ems="10"
      android:inputType="textPersonName"
      android:text="Name"
      app:layout_constraintEnd_toEndOf="@+id/btn_send_data"
      app:layout_constraintStart_toStartOf="@+id/btn_send_data"
      app:layout_constraintTop_toBottomOf="@+id/input_weight" />

  <Button
      android:id="@+id/btn_send_data"
      android:layout_width="wrap_content"
      android:layout_height="wrap_content"
      android:layout_marginTop="21dp"
      android:text="calculate BMI"
      app:layout_constraintEnd_toEndOf="@+id/txt_bmi"
      app:layout_constraintStart_toStartOf="@+id/txt_bmi"
      app:layout_constraintTop_toBottomOf="@+id/input_height" />

  <TextView
      android:id="@+id/txt_bmi"
      android:layout_width="wrap_content"
      android:layout_height="wrap_content"
      android:layout_marginTop="33dp"
      android:text="TextView"
      android:textSize="36sp"
      app:layout_constraintEnd_toEndOf="parent"
      app:layout_constraintStart_toStartOf="parent"
      app:layout_constraintTop_toBottomOf="@+id/btn_send_data" />
</android.support.constraint.ConstraintLayout>
```

You can use the context menu in AS3 to create SecondActivity. Right-click on the "app" in the project folder, then **New ➤ Activity ➤ Empty Activity**, as shown in Figure 12-15.

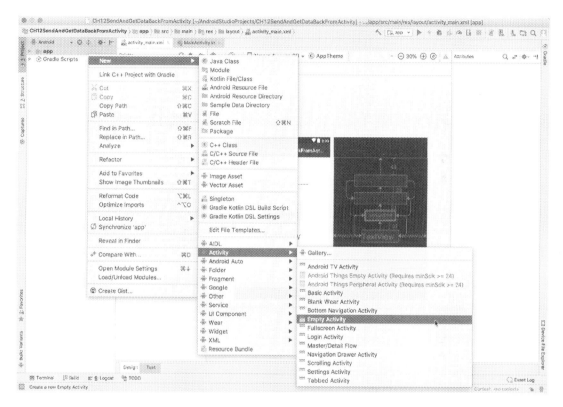

Figure 12-15. *Create a new empty activity*

Fill up the details for the new Activity, as shown in Figure 12-16. Make sure that the name of the new Activity is *SecondActivity* and that you're creating it in the same package as MainActivity.

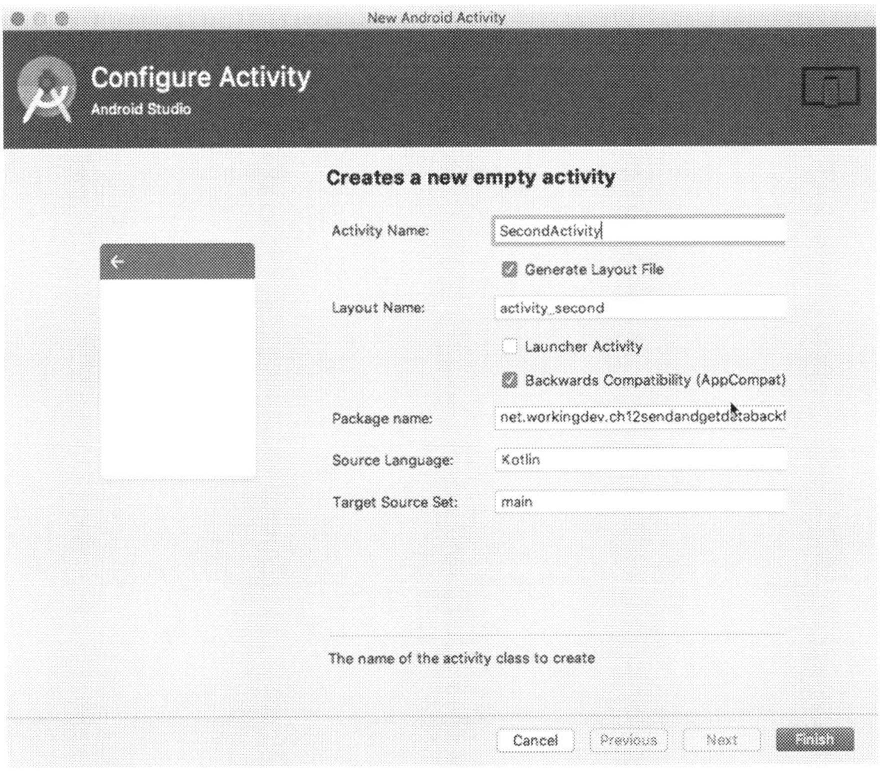

Figure 12-16. *Create SecondActivity*

SecondActivity has two View elements: a TextView to display the contents of the Intent that was passed to it and a Button to trigger the calculation of the BMI. Figure 12-17 show what the UI of SecondActivity looks like. Center the elements in the layout and use the "infer constraints" to anchor the elements into position. You can also adjust *textAlign* and *textSize* attributes of the TextView to fit your liking.

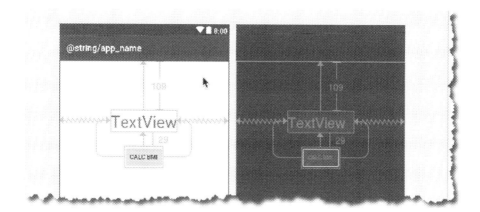

Figure 12-17. *activity_second.xml*

Listing 12-15 shows the full code for activity_second.xml

Listing 12-15. /app/res/layout/activity_second.xml

```
<?xml version="1.0" encoding="utf-8"?>
<android.support.constraint.ConstraintLayout xmlns:android=http://schemas.
android.com/apk/res/android
  xmlns:app=http://schemas.android.com/apk/res-auto
  xmlns:tools=http://schemas.android.com/tools
  android:layout_width="match_parent"
  android:layout_height="match_parent"
  tools:context=".SecondActivity">

  <TextView
    android:id="@+id/txt_intentdata"
    android:layout_width="346dp"
    android:layout_height="wrap_content"
    android:layout_marginTop="109dp"
    android:text="TextView"
    android:textAlignment="center"
    android:textSize="24sp"
    app:layout_constraintEnd_toEndOf="parent"
    app:layout_constraintStart_toStartOf="parent"
    app:layout_constraintTop_toTopOf="parent" />
```

```
<Button
   android:id="@+id/btn_calculate"
   android:layout_width="wrap_content"
   android:layout_height="wrap_content"
   android:layout_marginTop="29dp"
   android:text="calc bmi"
   app:layout_constraintEnd_toEndOf="@+id/txt_intentdata"
   app:layout_constraintStart_toStartOf="@+id/txt_intentdata"

   app:layout_constraintTop_toBottomOf="@+id/txt_intentdata" />
</android.support.constraint.ConstraintLayout>
```

Let's zoom in on MainActivity's onCreate method. As soon as the application opens, the EditText will wait for user inputs. As soon the user clicks the Button, our app will collect the inputs and send it off with an Intent.

Listing 12-16 shows the annotated snippet of MainActivity that contains the event handling code when the Button is clicked.

Listing 12-16. onCreate Method of MainActivity

```
val SECOND_ACTIVITY = 1000  ❶

override fun onCreate(savedInstanceState: Bundle?) {
  super.onCreate(savedInstanceState)
  setContentView(R.layout.activity_main)

  input_weight.setHint("weight (lbs)")      ❷
  input_height.setHint("height (inches)")

  btn_send_data.setOnClickListener {

    val m_intent = Intent(this@MainActivity, SecondActivity::class.java)  ❸
    val m_bundle = Bundle()      ❹

    m_bundle.putFloat("weight", input_weight.text.toString().toFloat())  ❺
    m_bundle.putFloat("height", input_height.text.toString().toFloat())
    m_intent.putExtra("main_activity_data", m_bundle)   ❻

    startActivityForResult(m_intent, SECOND_ACTIVITY)  ❼
  }
}
```

❶   We're declaring and defining a property that will act as some sort of constant. This is what we'll use as the *request code* later on in the code.

❷   We're setting the *hint* attribute of the Plain Text view. A hint appears as greyed place holders for text. If you've used the placeholder attribute in HTML 5, the hint attribute is similar to that. You can use hints as a replacement for labels.

❸   We're defining an explicit Intent, `this@MainActivity` is the Context and the Intent target is a class object (`SecondActivity::class.java`).

❹   We need to send two data points to SecondActivity, when you need to send more than one pair of key-value pair, it's better to use Bundles.

❺   The **Bundle** object, like the Intent, also lets us add data to it in a couple of ways. I used `putFloat()`in this example because I wanted to work with Float numbers. If you need to work String, Byte, Char, Int, etc., just use the appropriate **putXXX** method.

❻   We're loading to bundle to the Intent object. Using bundles with Intents allows us to work with more complex data structures.

❼   We're sending off the Activity, but this time around, we're telling the runtime that we expect some data back—that's why we used **startActivityForResult**. This signals the runtime to invoke MainActivity's **onActivityResult** callback whenever other Activities calls their `finish()` method. The second parameter of startActivityForResult is the request code. The request code will help us route the program logic when we receive the results back. In this call, we used the class constant **SECOND_ACTIVITY** as the request code for launching SecondActivity, which means when SecondActivity calls its `finish()` method, this request code will also be sent back to MainActivity.

The next stage of the exercise happens on the onCreate callback of SecondActivity. After we've sent the height and weight data to the receiving Activity, we must extract and work with that data. Listing 12-17 shows the annotated snippet for that code.

Listing 12-17. onCreate Method of SecondActivity

```
override fun onCreate(savedInstanceState: Bundle?) {
  super.onCreate(savedInstanceState)
  setContentView(R.layout.activity_second)

  val bundle = intent.getBundleExtra("main_activity_data") ❶
```

```kotlin
val height = bundle.getFloat("height")  ❷
val weight = bundle.getFloat("weight")

txt_intentdata.text = "Height: $height | Weight: $weight"  ❸


btn_calculate.setOnClickListener {
    val m_intent = Intent()  ❹
    val m_bmi = 703 * (weight / (height * height))  ❺
    m_intent.putExtra("second_activity_data", m_bmi)  ❻
    setResult(Activity.RESULT_OK, m_intent)  ❼
    finish()  ❽
  }
}
```

❶ We need to get a reference to the Intent object that's associated with SecondActivity. This is the same Intent object that we launched from MainActivity. It's also the same Intent that activated SecondActivity. To get the associated Intent object, we should call getIntent(), but because we're using Kotlin, instead of using the method getIntent(), we simply refer to it as **intent**—a property instead of a method. Just remember that we're not creating a new Intent here, we are simply getting a reference to the Intent associated with SecondActivity. We sent a bundle in MainActivity, so we should use **getBundleExtra** get the data.

❷ Now that we got the bundle out, we need to start getting more data out of the bundle. We used **putFloat** to put data into the bundle, so, we need to use **getFloat** to get it out.

❸ We're setting the *text* attribute of the TextView to the concatenated *height* and *weight* string.

❹ In this line, we are creating a new Intent object. This Activity will send some data back to MainActivity. We need a new Intent to do that.

❺ This is a simplistic way to calculate the BMI, but it should work.

❻ Now that we've calculated the BMI, let's load it up to our newly created Intent object.

❼ The **setResult** method takes in two parameters:

a. **resultCode**. This is either 0 or -1. Generally, if something went wrong, you'd want to return -1, or if everything went well, you'd return 0. But it's a good idea to use the class constants in the Activity class. **Activity.RESULT_OK** is -1 and **Activity.RESULT_CANCELLED** is 0.

b. **intent**. This is the Intent object the contains the calculated BMI.

❽ Finally, to return the result of the calculation to MainActivity, we need to call finish().

The next part of the Intent's journey is back on MainActivity. After SecondActivity calls finish, the runtime will call the onActivityResult callback on MainActivity—it's on this callback that we get the chance to work with whatever data the SecondActivity sent us. Listing 12-18 shows us the annotated snippet of MainActivity's onActivityResult.

Listing 12-18. Annotated onActivityResult of MainActivity

```
override fun onActivityResult(requestCode: Int, resultCode: Int, data:
Intent?) {
  super.onActivityResult(requestCode, resultCode, data)

  if((requestCode == SECOND_ACTIVITY) and (resultCode == Activity.RESULT_
OK)) { ❶
    val bmi = data?.getFloatExtra("second_activity_data", 1.0F) ❷
    txt_bmi.setText(bmi.toString()) ❸
  }
}
```

❶ There are two tests in this expression:

   1. `requestCode == SECOND_ACTIVITY`. We're asking if the data is coming from SecondActivity.
   2. `Activity.RESULT_OK`. We're trying to see if SecondActivity called setResult and actually called finish.

❷ Now that we know that the data came from SecondActivity and everything went well, we can extract the data from the Intent. We used **getFloatExtra** because we know it contains a Float—we put it there after all. We had to use the *safe call* (question mark) in `data?.getFloatExtra()` because the signature of the Intent object as it was passed to onActivityResult is a Nullable type.

❸ We can display the calculated BMI value.

If you're coding along, you should be able to piece the whole application together by now.

Listing 12-19 shows the full code of MainActivity. You might notice some differences between this full listing and Listings 12-16 and 12-18. I omitted a couple of other details in Listings 12-16 and 12-18, for purposes of brevity and clarity. In Listing 12-19, I put back all the omissions, and they're annotated so you can spot them more readily.

Listing 12-19. Full Code Listing for MainActivity

```kotlin
import android.app.Activity
import android.content.Intent
import android.support.v7.app.AppCompatActivity
import android.os.Bundle
import kotlinx.android.synthetic.main.activity_main.*

class MainActivity : AppCompatActivity() {

  val SECOND_ACTIVITY = 1000

  override fun onCreate(savedInstanceState: Bundle?) {
    super.onCreate(savedInstanceState)
    setContentView(R.layout.activity_main)

    input_weight.setHint("weight (lbs)")
    input_height.setHint("height (inches)")

    btn_send_data.setOnClickListener {

      val m_intent = Intent(this@MainActivity, SecondActivity::class.java)
      val m_bundle = Bundle()

      m_bundle.putFloat("weight", input_weight.text.toString().toFloat())
      m_bundle.putFloat("height", input_height.text.toString().toFloat())
      m_intent.putExtra("main_activity_data", m_bundle)

      startActivityForResult(m_intent, SECOND_ACTIVITY)
    }
  }

  override fun onResume() {
    super.onResume()
    clearInputs()  ❶
  }
```

```kotlin
override fun onActivityResult(requestCode: Int, resultCode: Int, data:
Intent?) {
  super.onActivityResult(requestCode, resultCode, data)

  if((requestCode == SECOND_ACTIVITY) and (resultCode == Activity.RESULT_
  OK)) {
    val bmi = data!!.getFloatExtra("second_activity_data", 1.0F) ❷
    val bmiString = "%.2f".format(bmi)
    input_height.setText("")
    input_weight.setText("")
    txt_bmi.setText("BMI : $bmiString ${getBMIDescription(bmi)}")
  }
}

private fun getBMIDescription(bmi: Float) : String { ❸

  return when (bmi) {
    in 1.0..18.5 -> "Underweight"
    in 18.6..24.9 -> "Normal weight"
    in 25.0..29.9 -> "Overweight"
    else -> "Obese"
  }
}

private fun clearInputs() { //  ❹
  input_weight.setText("")
  input_height.setText("")
}
}
```

❶ Let's clear out the input field. We're placing this call inside the **onResume** callback so that every time the Activity becomes visible to the user, the input fields are clear. You might remember that the **onResume** life cycle method could be called several time within the life time of the Activity. It will be called for the first time when the app is started. It will be called the second time when SecondActivity calls **finish**, the MainActivity will be popped out from the back stack, and so on.

❷   Instead of using data?.getExtra(), which would return a Nullable type, I used data!!.
getExtra(), which returned a non-Nullable type. I did this to simplify our codes inside the
gerBMIDescriptionfunction, which expects a non-Nullable type. We could have worked with
Nullables inside **getBMIDescription**, but I chose to use the simpler approach of working with
non-Nullable types.

❸   This function takes in a BMI Float value and returns a weight description.

❹   Implementation of initializeInputs(). We're simply setting the *text* property of the
EditTexts to an empty String.

Demo 4: Implicit Intents

Our last demo app features implicit Intents. In this section, we'll deal with three types
of data: a web URI, a geographic coordinate, and a phone number. Hopefully, these
three examples will give you enough insights and footing to continue your exploration of
implicit Intents. Like always, if you want to code along, the project details are shown in
Table 12-4.

Table 12-4. *Project Details for Demo App*

Project Detail	Value
Application name	CH12ImplicitIntents
Company domain	use your website name
Kotlin support	Yes
Form factor	Phone and Tablet only
Minimum SDK	API 23 Marshmallow
Type of activity	Empty
Activity name	MainActivity
Layout name	activity_main
Backward compatibility	Yes. AppCompat

The app has a simple setup, the only thing I did on activity_main.xml is to remove the "Hello World" TextView. I used the Options Menu to facilitate the user's choices for launching the three sample intents. The Options Menu is on the ActionBar, as shown in Figure 12-18.

Figure 12-18. *MainActivity's menu*

There is nothing to do in UI part so there's no need to show activity_main's XML listing. Everything we need to do is done inside MainActivity.

In earlier chapters, we built the Menu using an XML resource; I built the menu a bit differently in this example. I didn't use an XML resource—instead, I built all the menu items dynamically. Listing 12-20 shows the full and annotated code for MainActivity.

Listing 12-20. MainActivity

```
import android.content.Intent
import android.net.Uri
import android.support.v7.app.AppCompatActivity
import android.os.Bundle
import android.view.Menu
import android.view.MenuItem

class MainActivity : AppCompatActivity() {

  override fun onCreate(savedInstanceState: Bundle?) {
    super.onCreate(savedInstanceState)
    setContentView(R.layout.activity_main)
  }
```

```
  override fun onCreateOptionsMenu(menu: Menu?): Boolean { ❶
    menu?.add("Web") ❷
    menu?.add("Map")
    menu?.add("Phone number")
    return super.onCreateOptionsMenu(menu)
  }

  override fun onOptionsItemSelected(item: MenuItem?): Boolean { ❸

    var m_uri: Uri
    var m_intent: Intent = Intent()

    when (item?.toString()) { ❹
      "Web" -> {
        m_uri = Uri.parse("https://www.apress.com")
        m_intent = Intent(Intent.ACTION_VIEW, m_uri) ❺
      }
      "Map" -> {
        m_uri = Uri.parse("geo:40.7113399,-74.0263469")
//      This would have worked as well
//      m_uri = Uri.parse("https://maps.google.com/maps
        ?q=40.7113399,-74.0263469")
        m_intent = Intent(Intent.ACTION_VIEW, m_uri)

      }
      "Phone number" -> {
        m_uri = Uri.parse("tel:639285083333")
        m_intent = Intent(Intent.ACTION_DIAL, m_uri)
      }

    startActivity(m_intent)
    return true
  }
}
```

❶   The **onCreateOptionsMenu** callback will be called sometime after the **onCreate** method is called. Before API 11 (Honeycomb), **onCreateOptionsMenu** is called only when the user clicks the *Options* button of the phone, but starting from Honeycomb, it's now called onCreate. The main reason for this change of behavior is because the ActionBar was introduced starting with API 11. Since we are using API 23, we can take advantage of this behavior to build a simple menu.

❷   We're adding a Menu Item to dynamically.

❸   Whenever the user clicks on one of the Menu Items, the **onOptionsItemSelected** is called. This is where we will handle the menu clicks.

❹   The **item** parameter can tell us which Menu Item was clicked. We're converting it to String so that we can use it to route our program logic inside the **when** expression.

❺   This is a shortened version of creating an Intent.

Figure 12-19 shows the runtime snapshots of our app.

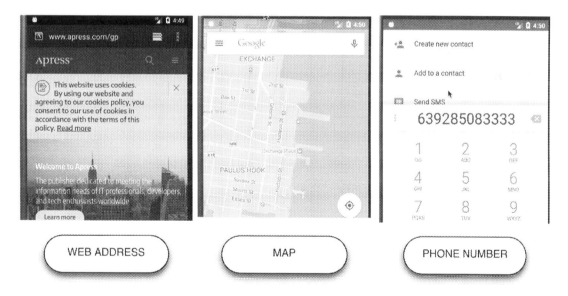

Figure 12-19. *Implicit intent, running*

Chapter Summary

- Intents are used for component activation.

- There are two kinds of Intents: implicit and explicit ones.

- Explicit Intents let us work with multiple activities. You can activate a specific Activity using an explicit Intent.

- Implicit Intent extends the functionality of your application. It lets your application do things that are outside the functionality of your app.

- You can send and receive data via Intents.

In next chapter, we will:

- Peek and dip briefly into Material design (not a lot).

- See how to create and apply Styles and Themes in our app.

- Learn how add menus in the ActionBar.

CHAPTER 13

Themes and Menus

What we'll cover:

- Themes and colors

- Menus

There are nearly 3.5 million apps in the Google Play Store. That's a lot of apps to choose from, which is good for users, but for the developers, that's a lot of competition.

If you will publish an app, you need to polish it—even if it's just cosmetically—so it doesn't come across as shabby. Even if you have a killer app, you should also think about how it looks (and feels) to the user. Remember that no matter how great your code is, the user doesn't see the code, he sees the UI.

Google has published a set of guidelines on user interfaces. They called it Material Design, you can read more about it at `http://material.io`. Material Design is a big topic, it can fill whole books on its own and we don't intend to cover it all, but in this chapter, we'll look at Themes and how to add an AppBar to your apps.

Styles and Themes

The Android platform has concepts like "styles" and "themes". A style is a collection of attributes where you can control how a View looks, what's the background and foreground color, font size, and much more. A theme, on the other hand, is a style that applies to the whole app, not just a single View. When you apply a style as a theme, every View in the app follows the theme. A theme is applied to the application in the Android Manifest's **application** node, as shown in the following snippet:

```
android:theme="@style/AppTheme"
```

© Ted Hagos 2018

T. Hagos, *Learn Android Studio 3 with Kotlin*, https://doi.org/10.1007/978-1-4842-3907-0_13

In this example, "AppTheme" is the name of the style. Styles are written as an XML file in *app ➤ res ➤ styles.xml*—the filename is usually style.xml, but it can change, it's not a hard requirement. Listing 13-1 shows the current styles.xml; this is what we get after the project creation wizard.

Listing 13-1. app/res/values/styles.xml

```
<resources>
 <!-- Base application theme. -->
  <style name="AppTheme" parent="Theme.AppCompat.Light.DarkActionBar">
    <!-- Customize your theme here. -->
    <item name="colorPrimary">@color/colorPrimary</item>
    <item name="colorPrimaryDark">@color/colorPrimaryDark</item>
    <item name="colorAccent">@color/colorAccent</item>
  </style>
</resources>
```

The root node of styles (styles.xml) is "resources," you can define as many styles as you want under this node. A style node has the attributes "name" and "parent." The name attribute is something that you choose, like the name of a variable, class, or function. The parent attribute is something you need to choose from a set of existing Themes. AS3 will you help you out using hints, as shown in Figure 13-1.

Figure 13-1. *Code hinting while editing styles.xml*

Once you have defined a style node, you can start customizing the colors for the app. The colors arc defined as "item" entries inside the "style" element.

Google's Material design brings your brand identity to life by using primary and accent colors that are used throughout the app. These colors are defined as follows:

- **colorPrimary:** The color of the app bar

  colorPrimaryDark: The color of the status bar and contextual app bars; this is the dark version of colorPrimary

- **colorAccent:** The color of Views like check boxes, radio buttons, and edit text boxes

- **windowBackground**: The color of the screen background

- **textColorPrimary:** The color of UI text in the app bar

- **statusBarColor**: The color of the status bar

- **navigationBarColor:** The color of the navigation bar

You don't have to define all of these in styles.xml, but you can if you want to. You may have noticed that the values of the color items are not themselves defined in the styles. xml file but instead are redirected to another resource file. In styles.xml, when you see an entry like this

```
<item name="colorPrimary">@color/colorPrimary</item>
```

It means that the actual value for "colorPrimary" can be found on the colors.xml file, which is in the *app* ➤ *res* ➤ *values* folder. Listing 13-2 shows the current contents of colors.xml.

Listing 13-2. app/res/values/colors.xml

```
<?xml version="1.0" encoding="utf-8"?>
<resources>
  <color name="colorPrimary">#3F51B5</color>
  <color name="colorPrimaryDark">#303F9F</color>
  <color name="colorAccent">#FF4081</color>
</resources>
```

Customizing the Theme

You can edit the colors in two ways. You can either edit the colors.xml file directly or make the color changes using the AS3's theme editor. To use the Theme Editor, open the styles.xml file in the main editor, then click the "Open editor" link in the upper-right corner, as shown in Figure 13-2.

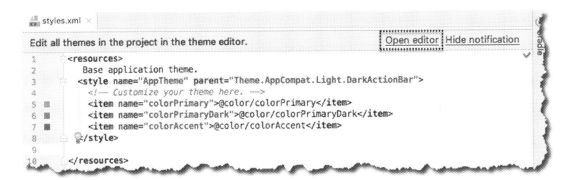

Figure 13-2. *Launch "open editor"*

The Theme editor lets you change the color values for the app. It also shows you how the app will look in a given color scheme. Figure 13-3 shows the various parts of the Theme Editor.

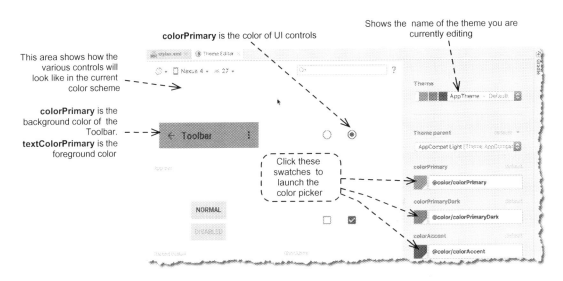

Figure 13-3. *Theme Editor*

To change a color, click the swatch next to the Material color (as shown in Figure 13-3). That will launch the color picker (shown in Figure 13-4).

Figure 13-4. *Color picker*

Google published documentation on Material Design at `http://bit.ly/ materialdesigndox`; it'll be good to read it before making changes to the color scheme. Another web resource you can use is materialPalette.com; it's geared toward Android Material Design. Figure 13-5 shows a screen grab from their website.

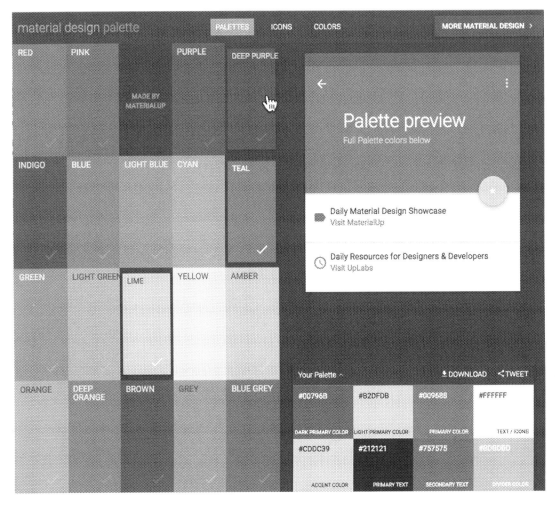

Figure 13-5. *Screen grab from* `https://www.materialpalette.com`

The basic idea is to choose two colors, and the site builds a palette for you. Now you can simply copy the hex values of primary, dark primary, accent, light primary colors, and others.

Menus

Menus are very important in UI design. They allow the user to get to the application's functionality. Traditionally, menu systems are organized hierarchically in intro groups, which means before a user can get to his target action, he needs to traverse the hierarchy of the menu. Android's menu system, at some point in time, has behaved exactly like that—grouped and hierarchical. But that was in the past. Android's approach to menus has changed dramatically over the course of its lifetime.

Menus prior to Android Honeycomb relied on hardware buttons, like the ones shown in Figure 13-6.

 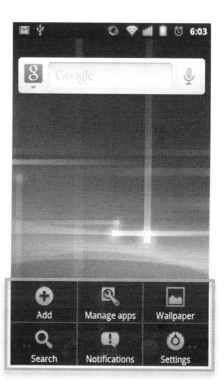

Figure 13-6. *Menus on older Android hardware*

Back then, we could always rely that the "home" and "option" buttons would always be present on any Android phone. We built our apps based on these assumptions because they were reasonable at the time.

Well, times have changed and so has the Android hardware. Screen resolutions have increased dramatically, and the hardware buttons have disappeared. Fortunately, Android's approach to menus has also changed and kept up with the state of hardware capabilities.

When Honeycomb came out, a new kind of menu system was added to Android. Applications whose minimum target SDK is API 11 are now able to use the "ActionBar."

The ActionBar, shown in Figure 13-7, is a dedicated area at the top of the screen and is persistent throughout the app. It's a lot like the main menu bar of AS3 if you think about it.

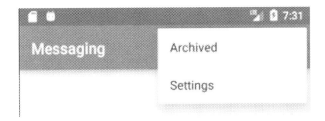

Figure 13-7. *App with an ActionBar*

You can use the ActionBar to display the most important features of your app and make them accessible in a predictable way (e.g., like putting a permanent Search widget on top, etc.). It creates a cleaner look by removing clutter in your menus, and in cases where not all items in the menu fit on the screen, the ActionBar displays an overflow icon. The overflow icon is a vertical ellipsis—three dots arranged vertically, which is always found on the far right of the bar. It also displays the name of the application, so it reinforces brand identity of the app.

Nowadays, the ActionBar has fallen a bit out of fashion and has been eclipsed by the Toolbar. The Toolbar is more versatile because it's not permanently clipped on top of the screen—you can place it anywhere you want—and it has a few more capabilities. The ActionBar, however, remains a viable solution for simple menu systems; in fact, nothing stops you from using both the ActionBar and the Toolbar in your apps. Just work with the best tools you have.

In Android API level 10 or lower, the menu options will appear at the bottom of the screen when the user presses the hardware menu button. In Android API 11 and higher, items from the options menu are available in the app bar. By default, the system places all items in the action overflow, which the user can reveal with the action overflow icon on the right side of the app bar.

To add a menu to an app, you need to do the following:

1. **Create a menu resource file**. We will create a menu folder in the *app/res* folder. Then, we'll create a menu resource file inside it.

2. **Inflate the menu resource in the main program**. We will override the onCreateOptionsMenu of MainActivity and call the *inflate* function of the *Menu* object.

3. **Add event handlers to the menu items**. We'll override the onOptionsItemSelected function of MainActivity, and route the user action depending on which menu item was clicked.

4. Optionally, add vector images to the menu.

Let's create a demo app so we can explore menus. The details of the project are shown in Table 13-1.

Table 13-1. *Project Details for Demo App*

Project Detail	Value
Application name	CH13AppBar
Company domain	use your website name
Kotlin support	Yes
Form factor	Phone and Tablet only
minimum SDK	API 23 Marshmallow
Type of activity	Empty
Activity name	MainActivity
Layout name	activity_main
Backward compatibility	Yes. AppCompat

We won't put any additional View elements in this app because they won't be needed, but we will add and **android:id** to our layout container. Notice the sixth line in Listing 13-3: that ID attribute is not present by default, you'll need to put it in. The IDs of each View element are more important to us now because the Kotlin Android Extension depends on it. The Extension won't be able to synthesize the View IDs if they don't have one.

Listing 13-3. excerpt from activity_main.xml

```
<?xml version="1.0" encoding="utf-8"?>
<android.support.constraint.ConstraintLayout xmlns:android=http://schemas.
android.com/apk/res/android
  xmlns:app=http://schemas.android.com/apk/res-auto
```

```
xmlns:tools=http://schemas.android.com/tools
android:id="@+id/root_layout"
tools:context=".MainActivity">
</android.support.constraint.ConstraintLayout>
```

We also need to edit the module-level build.gradle file. In order to use the Snackbar widget, we need to include the "com.android.support:design" dependency in the gradle file. Figure 13-8 shows you the location of the gradle file in the Project window.

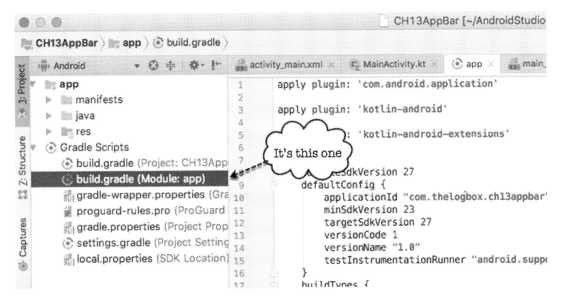

Figure 13-8. *module-level build.gradle*

You need to add the "com.android.support:design" line, as shown in Listing 13-4.

Listing 13-4. excerpt from build.gradle

```
dependencies {
    implementation fileTree(dir: 'libs', include: ['*.jar'])
    implementation"org.jetbrains.kotlin:kotlin-stdlib-jre7:$kotlin_version"
    implementation 'com.android.support:appcompat-v7:27.1.0'
    implementation 'com.android.support.constraint:constraint-layout:1.1.2'
    testImplementation 'junit:junit:4.12'
    androidTestImplementation 'com.android.support.test:runner:1.0.2'
```

```
androidTestImplementation 'com.android.support.test.espresso:espresso-
core:3.0.2'

implementation 'com.android.support:design:27.1.0'
}
```

AS3 will sense that something has changed in build file and it will ask you to "sync" the gradle file. This prompt will appear as a yellow strip on the upper part of the main editor. Click "sync" so you can proceed.

Now we're ready to create the menu file, but before we can do that, let's create a menu folder. Right-click on the **app ➤ res** folder in the Project window, as shown in Figure 13-9. Choose **New ➤ Android Resource Directory**.

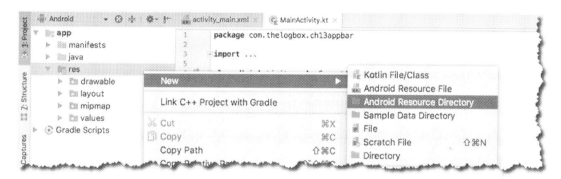

Figure 13-9. *Create a new Android Resource Directory*

Give the newly created folder a name, like the one shown in Figure 13-10.

New Resource Directory

Directory name:	menu
Resource type:	values
Source set:	main
Available qualifiers:	Chosen qualifiers:
Country Code	
Network Code	

Figure 13-10. *New menu folder*

Now that that we have a menu folder, right-click on it and create a new menu resource file, as shown in Figure 13-11.

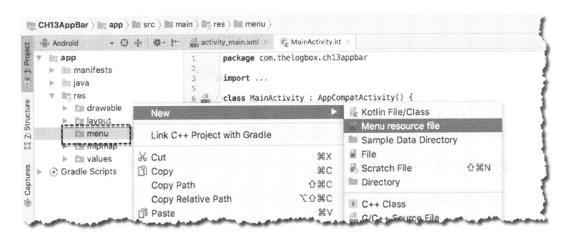

Figure 13-11. *New menu resource file*

Let's give the newly created menu file a name, like how it's shown in Figure 13-12.

Figure 13-12. *main_menu resource file*

Let's add some items in our menu file. Open the file **app/res/menu/main_menu.xml** in the main editor and add the menu items as shown in Listing 13-5.

Listing 13-5. app/res/menu/main_menu.xml

```xml
<?xml version="1.0" encoding="utf-8"?>
<menu xmlns:android="http://schemas.android.com/apk/res/android">

  <item android:id="@+id/menuFile"
    android:title="@string/menuFile"
    />
  <item android:id="@+id/menuEdit"
```

```
    android:title="@string/menuEdit"
    />
  <item android:id="@+id/menuHelp"
    android:title="@string/menuHelp"
    />
  <item android:id="@+id/menuExit"
    android:title="@string/menuExit"
    />
</menu>
```

Each item element in Listing 13-5 represents one menu item. Each element is comprised of two attributes: an **android:id** and an **android:title**. The title is what you will see on the menu itself and the id is a programmatic reference to the menu item. We will use this id later when we want to refer to a menu item from our program.

The **android:id** is written in **@+id** notation so that it will be created in case it doesn't exist yet. The **android:title** is written in **@string** notation so that the value of the title is resolved in the app/res/values/strings.xml file. We could have hard-coded the menu titles like this:

```
<item android:id="@+id/menuFile"
  android:title="File" />
```

But that would be a bad way of doing it. The convention in Android programming is to store and retrieve your string literals in *strings.xml* resource file. Storing your strings in /app/res/values/strings.xml also makes it easier for you to release your app in a non-English version. Imagine if you created a French or Italian version of your app. You'd have to replace all those hard-coded strings manually. But if you stored your strings in the xml file, you would only need to replace it in one file, which makes localization and internationalization a bit easier.

As soon as you're done typing the menu file, you will notice that AS3 complains about the newly created menu items. The android:title entries cannot be resolved or cannot be found in strings.xml. Of course AS3 can't find it—we haven't created it yet.

We can either add the new entries to strings.xml manually, or we can use AS3's Quick Fix to resolve the error. Let's use the Quick Fix. While the main_menu.xml is still on the editor, click on the @string/menuExit, as shown in Figure 13-13, then press **OPTION + ENTER** or **ALT + ENTER**.

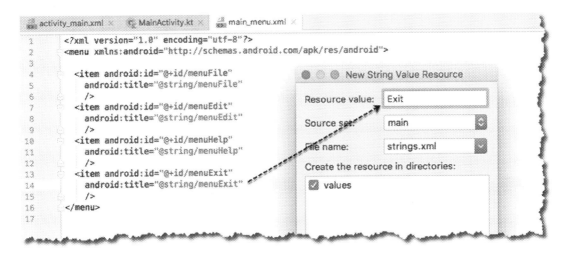

Figure 13-13. *Add the menu titles to strings.xml*

Type the resource value for the item and repeat the steps for each android:title attribute. The resource values will be stored in app ➤ res ➤ values ➤ strings.xml— contents of strings.xml are shown in Listing 13-6.

Listing 13-6. app/res/values/strings.xml

```
<resources>
  <string name="app_name">CH13AppBar</string>
  <string name="menuExit">Exit</string>
  <string name="menuHelp">Help</string>
  <string name="menuEdit">Edit</string>
  <string name="menuFile">File</string>
</resources>
```

The next step is to associate the menu with the MainActivity. To do this, we need to inflate the menu file by overriding the **onCreateOptionsMenu** in MainActivity.

Open MainActivity.Kt in the main editor and start adding a top-level function. As soon as you begin typing the first few characters of the **onCreateOptionsMenu**, AS3 will assist you by giving code hints. Use the autocompletion feature as shown in Figure 13-14 to complete the skeleton of the function.

```
6    class MainActivity : AppCompatActivity() {
7
8        override fun onCreate(savedInstanceState: Bundle?) {
9            super.onCreate(savedInstanceState)
10           setContentView(R.layout.activity_main)
11       }
12
13       override fun onCreateMenu
14               override fun onCreateContextMenu(menu: ContextMenu?, v: View?, …
15   }           override fun onCreateOptionsMenu(menu: Menu?): Boolean {...}    Activity
16              override fun onCreatePanelMenu(featureId: Int, menu: Menu?): Bo…
                 ↑↓ and ↑↑ will move caret down and up in the editor ≫
```

Figure 13-14. *Autocompleting the onCreateOptionsMenu*

Copy the codes in Listing 13-7 to complete the onCreateOptionsMenu.

Listing 13-7. onCreateOptionsMenu

```
override fun onCreateOptionsMenu(menu: Menu?): Boolean {
  menuInflater.inflate(R.menu.main_menu, menu)
  return super.onCreateOptionsMenu(menu)
}
```

The **inflate()** function creates the menu items using the menu XML file we created earlier (first parameter) and attaches it to the Menu object (second parameter of the inflate function). The Android runtime will pass the Menu to us when it invokes onCreateOptionsMenu callback function.

Figure 13-15 shows the menu during runtime; the picture on left shows the overflow icon—it's the three white dots arranged like a vertical ellipsis. Menu items are revealed by clicking or touching the overflow icon. The picture on the right shows our app with all the menu items revealed.

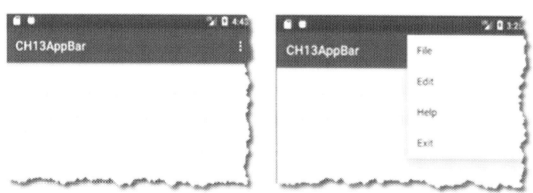

Figure 13-15. *CHAppBar menus*

Right now, the menu items show up, but they don't do anything yet. To handle the events for each menu item, we will override the **onOptionsItemSelected()** function in MainActivity.

Listing 13-8 shows the code for an overridden onOptionsItemSelected. The Android runtime calls this method each time a menu item is clicked by the user. The runtime passes a MenuItem object to the function that represents the menu item clicked.

Listing 13-8. onOptionsItemSelected

```
override fun onOptionsItemSelected(item: MenuItem?): Boolean {
  return true
}
```

We can use the MenuItem to route our program logic by comparing its **itemId** property to the four menu items we defined in main_menu.xml. Listing 13-9 shows how to test if the itemId is equal to one of the menu items in our XML file.

Listing 13-9. comparing itemId with R.id.menuFile

```
override fun onOptionsItemSelected(item: MenuItem?): Boolean {
  if(item?.itemId == R.id.menuFile) {
    showMessage("File Menu ") // user defined function
    return true
  }
}
```

Notice how we are using the safe-call operator (?.) during the test. We need to use the safe-call because MenuItem is declared as nullable in onOptionsItemSelected—also, the function should return a Boolean value. In our example, we returned **true,** which tells the Android runtime that we've consumed this event, and there is no need for other listeners to handle the event any further. We can keep using the if-else construct to route program logic, but the **when** construct might be more appropriate in this situation. Listing 13-10 shows how to use **when** to handle program logic. You might remember from Chapter 3 that Kotlin doesn't have a **switch** statement—the **when** construct is the equivalent of Java's switch.

Listing 13-10. using when to route program logic

```kotlin
override fun onOptionsItemSelected(item: MenuItem?): Boolean {

  when(item?.itemId) {
    R.id.menuFile -> {
      showMessage("File menu")
      return true
    }
    R.id.menuEdit -> {
      showMessage("Edit menu")
      return true
    }
    R.id.menuHelp -> {
      showMessage("Help menu")
      return true
    }
    R.id.menuExit -> {
      showMessage("Exit")
      return true
    }
  }
}
```

Listings 13-11, 13-12, and 13-13 show the full codes for MainActivity, activity_main, and the build.gradle, respectively. You may use for it reference in case you're coding along.

Listing 13-11. complete code for MainActivity.Kt

```kotlin
import android.support.v7.app.AppCompatActivity
import android.os.Bundle
import android.support.design.widget.Snackbar
import android.view.Menu
import android.view.MenuItem

import kotlinx.android.synthetic.main.activity_main.*
```

```kotlin
class MainActivity : AppCompatActivity() {

  override fun onCreate(savedInstanceState: Bundle?) {
    super.onCreate(savedInstanceState)
    setContentView(R.layout.activity_main)
  }

  override fun onCreateOptionsMenu(menu: Menu?): Boolean {
    menuInflater.inflate(R.menu.main_menu, menu)

    return super.onCreateOptionsMenu(menu)
  }

  override fun onOptionsItemSelected(item: MenuItem?): Boolean {

    when(item?.itemId) {
      R.id.menuFile -> {
        showMessage("File menu")
        return true
      }
      R.id.menuEdit -> {
        showMessage("Edit menu")
        return true
      }
      R.id.menuHelp -> {
        showMessage("Help menu")
        return true
      }
      R.id.menuExit -> {
        showMessage("Exit")
        return true
      }
    }
```

```
    return super.onOptionsItemSelected(item)
  }

  private fun showMessage(msg:String) {
    Snackbar.make(root_layout, msg, Snackbar.LENGTH_LONG).show()

  }
}
```

Listing 13-12. complete code for activity_main.xml

```
<?xml version="1.0" encoding="utf-8"?>
<android.support.constraint.ConstraintLayout xmlns:android=http://schemas.
android.com/apk/res/android
  xmlns:app=http://schemas.android.com/apk/res-auto
  xmlns:tools=http://schemas.android.com/tools
  android:id="@+id/root_layout"
  android:layout_width="match_parent"
  android:layout_height="match_parent"
  tools:context=".MainActivity">

  <TextView
    android:layout_width="wrap_content"
    android:layout_height="wrap_content"
    android:text="Hello World!"
    app:layout_constraintBottom_toBottomOf="parent"
    app:layout_constraintLeft_toLeftOf="parent"
    app:layout_constraintRight_toRightOf="parent"
    app:layout_constraintTop_toTopOf="parent" />

</android.support.constraint.ConstraintLayout>
```

Listing 13-13. app/build.gradle

```
apply plugin: 'com.android.application'
apply plugin: 'kotlin-android'
apply plugin: 'kotlin-android-extensions'

android {
    compileSdkVersion 27
    defaultConfig {
        applicationId "com.thelogbox.ch13appbar"
        minSdkVersion 23
        targetSdkVersion 27
        versionCode 1
        versionName "1.0"
        testInstrumentationRunner "android.support.test.runner.
        AndroidJUnitRunner"
    }
    buildTypes {
        release {
            minifyEnabled false
            proguardFiles getDefaultProguardFile('proguard-android.txt'),
            'proguard-rules.pro'
        }
    }
}

dependencies {
    implementation fileTree(dir: 'libs', include: ['*.jar'])
    implementation"org.jetbrains.kotlin:kotlin-stdlib-jre7:$kotlin_version"
    implementation 'com.android.support:appcompat-v7:27.1.0'
    implementation 'com.android.support.constraint:constraint-layout:1.1.2'
    testImplementation 'junit:junit:4.12'
    androidTestImplementation 'com.android.support.test:runner:1.0.2'
    androidTestImplementation 'com.android.support.test.espresso:espresso-
    core:3.0.2'
    implementation 'com.android.support:design:27.1.0'
}
```

Chapter Summary

- Using Styles and Themes can add pizzazz to your app quite instantly. It's the easiest thing to do level up your app's game.

- Menus in the ActionBar can display the most important features of your app.

In the next chapter, we will:

- Look at Fragments. You can use them to make your app adapt to different form factors and device orientation (portrait vs landscape).

- We'll also look at how we can make Fragments talk to each other.

CHAPTER 14

Fragments

What we'll cover:

- Introduction to fragments

- Landscape and portrait orientation

- Interfragment communication

In the early days of Android, when it ran only on phones and there weren't any high-resolution screens, activities were sufficient as a way of composing the UI and interacting with the user. Then came the tablets and high-resolution screens, and it became increasingly difficult to create applications that could run well on both phones and tablets. Developers were faced with hard choices. Either you choose the least capable hardware as the target and make it like the least common denominator or make the app adapt to a range of form factors by removing and adding UI elements in response to the device's capability—which proved to be very difficult to do manually. When API 11 (Honeycomb) came out, Android solved this problem with Fragments.

Introduction to Fragments

Fragments are quite an advanced concept, and beginning programmers may approach it with trepidation, but the basic concept behind it is quite simple. If we think of an activity as a composition unit for our UI, think of a fragment as a mini-activity—it's a smaller composition unit. You will usually show (and hide) fragments during runtime in response to something that a user did (e.g., tilting the device or switching from portrait to landscape orientation, thus making more screen space available). You may even use fragments as a strategy to adapt to device form factors; when the app is running on smaller screen, you will show only some of the fragments.

305

© Ted Hagos 2018
T. Hagos, *Learn Android Studio 3 with Kotlin*, https://doi.org/10.1007/978-1-4842-3907-0_14

A fragment, like an activity, is comprised of two parts: a Java program and a layout file. The idea is almost the same—define the UI elements in an XML file and then inflate the XML file in a program file so that all the view objects in the XML will become an object. After that, we can reference each view object in the XML using the R.class. Once we've wrapped our brains around that concept, just think of a fragment as an ordinary view object that we can drag and drop on the main layout file—except of course, fragments aren't ordinary Views, but they are Views.

To create a Fragment, we generally do the following:

1. Create an XML resource file, put in the **/app/res/layout** folder, just like where we put activity_main.xml .

2. Give the new resource file a descriptive name—say, fragment_booktitles.

3. Create the Fragment class. We used to choose between two classes when creating Fragments—either we inherit from the native **android.app.Fragment** or **android.support.v4.app.Fragment**. You use the former if your target SDK is API 11 or higher and the latter for apps targeted at anything lower than Android 3 (Honeycomb). You can still use android.app.Fragment, but as a heads up, you need to know that Android P (a.k.a. Android 9) has deprecated native Fragments. If you still want to use Fragments, use the support library so you can get consistent behaviors across all API levels.

4. Next, hook up the Fragment class with the XML resource layout. You can do this by inflating the XML resource file in the **onCreate** method of the Fragment class.

5. Add the newly created Fragment.

Let's do them in Android Studio. First, create a project with an empty Activity, just like all the other projects we've created.

Now, create an XML resource file and put it in **/app/res/layout**, as shown in Figure 14-1.

Use the context menu, right click on the **/app/res/layout** folder in the Project tool window (Figure 14-1). Choose **New ➤ Layout Resource File**. This layout resource file will contain all the View elements of our Fragment. You will see a "New Resource File" dialog window; enter the name of the resource file—for the purpose of the exercise, I named it "book_titles."

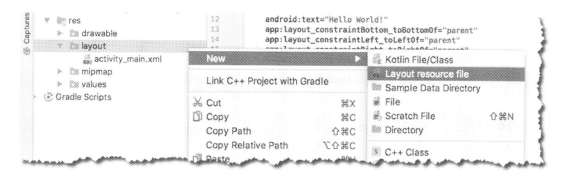

Figure 14-1. *New layout resource file*

You can put whatever View element you need. This fragment resource file is no different than any of the activity resources files we've worked on before. Whatever you can put in an Activity resource file, you can also put in the fragment resource file.

Next, let's create the Fragment class. Use the context menu again to create the class, as shown in Figure 14-2.

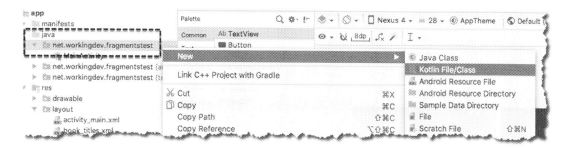

Figure 14-2. *Create new Kotlin class*

If you right-clicked on **java ➤ net.workingdev.fragmentstest** when you created the new Kotlin class, the newly created class will belong to the same package as the rest of your codes. If you right-click just on the **java** folder when you created the new Kotlin class, that class will be on the default package; when that happens, you'll need to add the package statement to the class yourself.

You'll be asked what kind of Kotlin file to create. Choose Class from the drop-down menu, as shown in Figure 14-3.

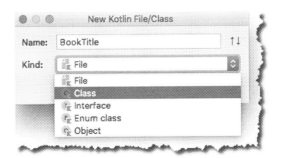

Figure 14-3. *Give the Kotlin class a name*

The Fragment class can be associated with the UI resource file by inflating the resource file and returning it from within the **onCreateView** callback. Listing 14-1 contains the annotated and explained snippet of MainActivity; it shows how to wire the Fragment class with the UI resource file. Bullet ❸, specifically, is the code responsible for associating the Fragment class with the UI resource file.

Listing 14-1. BookTitle Fragment

```
import android.support.v4.app.Fragment    ❶
...

class BookTitle : Fragment() {

  override fun onCreateView(inflater: LayoutInflater, container:
  ViewGroup?, savedInstanceState: Bundle?): View? {              ❷

    val v = inflater.inflate(R.layout.book_titles, container, false) ❸
    return v
  }

  override fun onViewCreated(view: View, savedInstanceState: Bundle?) {
    ❹
  }
}
```

❶   We're using the Fragment class from the Support library because **android.app.Fragment** was deprecated by Android 9. Even if we're usually targeting API 23, it's best to always use supported libraries from now on.

❷   The **onCreateView** callback is similar to the onCreate of the Activity. But be careful not to refer to any View element in here—they won't be available just yet. If you try to refer to an UI element in here (e.g., a Button or TextField), it will return null.

❸   In this example, the name of the UI resource file is **book_titles**. So, presumably, you have a file named **/app/res/layout/book_titles.xml**. Inflate the XML resource file and return it, so that MainActivity can compose the UI on its end. The reason you cannot refer to any UI element while you're inside **onCreateView** is because you haven't inflated the XML resource yet, so none of your UI elements exist at this point. The Android runtime passes the **inflater** and **container** objects to the **onCreateView** method. We need these object to inflate the UI resource.

❹   The runtime calls **onViewCreated** method when all of the UI elements are ready. This is where you can start using and referring to UI elements.

Note   To "inflate" a UI resource file means to take in a UI definition (in XML), create the actual View and ViewGroup objects, and render them. After the inflation process, you will be able to refer to the View objects programmatically.

The final step is to add the Fragment to the Activity. You can add Fragments to an Activity in two ways: during runtime or during design time. For now, we'll add the Fragment during design time.

Open the UI resource file for MainActivity, if it isn't opened yet. From the Project tool window, double-click **/app/res/layout/activity_main.xml**. Open it in "Design" mode. In the Palette, go to **Common**, look for **<fragment>,** as shown in Figure 14-4.

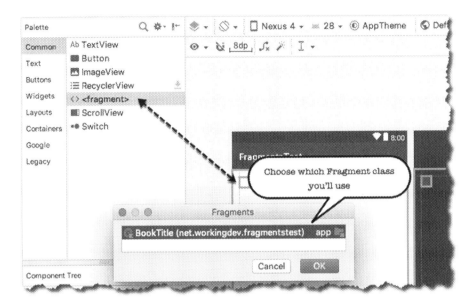

Figure 14-4. *Drag a fragment element into activity_main*

Drag the **<fragment>** element and drop it anywhere in the Activity, just like dragging and dropping any View element. A Fragments dialog will pop up; you'll need to select which Fragment class you would like to add to **activity_main** layout. In our case, there's only one Fragment class—choose the BookTitle fragment.

That's it, we can now run our un-interesting and uninspired Fragment sample. If you run it, it looks like Figure 14-5 in an emulator.

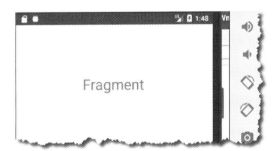

Figure 14-5. *FragmentsTest, running*

Uninteresting as it is, it should ground you well enough on the basics of Fragments. Now, we're ready for something a bit more interesting. In the next section, we'll create a demo project with two fragments.

Book Title and Description, a Fragments Demo

What we'd like to do:

1. Use two fragments in our MainActivity.

2. One of the fragments contains a list of books; we'll let the user choose a book by clicking one of the radio buttons.

3. The other fragment contains a description of the book that's currently selected.

4. The fragments will re-arrange themselves depending on how the user is holding the device—portrait or landscape orientation.

At runtime, the app looks like Figure 14-6 when the device is oriented vertically.

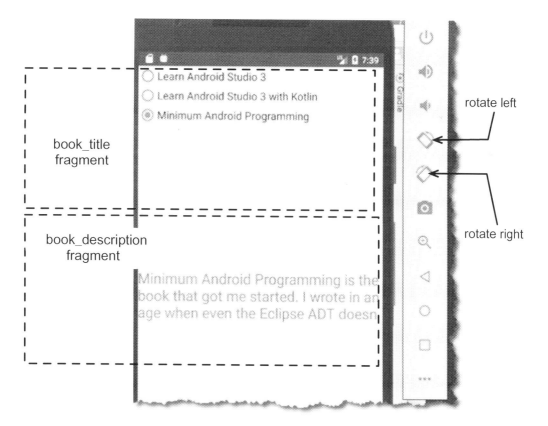

Figure 14-6. *Book titles app, oriented vertically (portrait)*

When the user holds the device in landscape mode, it looks like Figure 14-7.

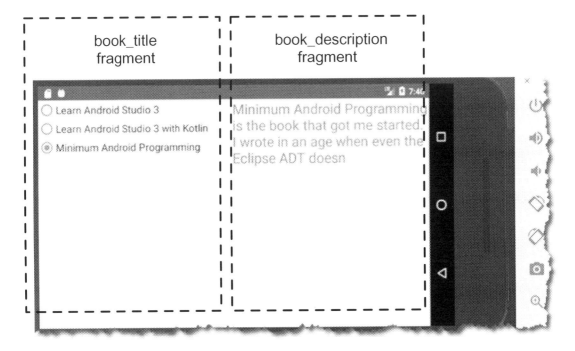

Figure 14-7. Oriented horizontally, landscape

We already know how to create fragments and how to add them to an Activity, but in order to complete this demo project, we'll need to hash a couple more details.

1. **How can we use radio buttons as a selector**, such that when one button is selected, the others are deselected? We'll use a radiogroup and collect all the radio buttons under this group.

2. Where will we **store the text definition of each book**? We will use an XML file and then load it into an array. Each element of the array will contain a book's definition.

3. How are we going to **synchronize the information between the two fragments**? We'll explore interfragment communication. We won't let the fragments communicate with each other directly (although we could, but that's not considered good practice). We will manage the synchronization via the Activity.

4. How are we going to handle the **changes in the device orientation**? We will create another layout folder in /**app**/**res** specifically for landscape layout. It will be named /**app**/**res**/ **layout-land**; this is where we will put our layout files when the device is oriented in landscape.

Let's get to work then. I created a new project for this demo; the details are in Table 14-1.

Table 14-1. *Project Details*

Project Detail	Value
Application name	CH14FragmentsBooks
Company domain	use your website name
Kotlin support	Yes
Form factor	Phone and Tablet only
minimum SDK	API 23 Marshmallow
Type of activity	Empty
Activity name	MainActivity
Layout name	activity_main

Let's create the XML resource file that will hold the text for book descriptions. To do this, you can:

1. Use the context menu, right-click on /**app**/**res**/**values** in the Project tool window, then

2. Click **New ➤ XML ➤ Values XML file**, as shown in Figure 14-8.

3. Name it "bookdescriptions"—don't type the *.xml* extension; Android Studio will take care of that.

Figure 14-8. *Create new XML values file*

Open the bookdescriptions.xml in the editor and copy the contents of Listing 14-2 into it.

Listing 14-2. /app/res/values/bookdescriptions.xml

```
<?xml version="1.0" encoding="utf-8"?>
<resources>
  <string-array name="bookdescriptions">
    <item>
        How to use Android Studio 3, but also teaches you how basic
Android programming. And hey, in case you're also a beginner in Java,
that's covered too.
    </item>
    <item>
      This book is also about how to use Android Studio. Like the first one,
      it also teaches you the basics of the IDE and Android programming; but
```

```
        this time around, you'll use Kotlin. The newest kid in the JVM block
      </item>
      <item>
        Minimum Android Programming is the book that got me started. I wrote
        in an age when even the Eclipse ADT doesn't exist yet. So, this means
        you'll use the Android SDK in all the glory of the CLI tools
      </item>
  </string-array>
</resources>
```

Now we can work on the fragments. Let's create the *book_titles* fragments first. Create a new layout resource file and name it "book_titles."

Listing 14-3 shows the content of **/app/res/layout/book_titles.xml**

Listing 14-3. /app/res/layout/book_titles.xml

```
<?xml version="1.0" encoding="utf-8"?>
<android.support.constraint.ConstraintLayout xmlns:android="http://schemas.
android.com/apk/res/android"
  xmlns:app="http://schemas.android.com/apk/res-auto"
  xmlns:tools="http://schemas.android.com/tools"
  android:layout_width="match_parent"
  android:layout_height="match_parent"
  tools:layout_editor_absoluteY="81dp">

  <RadioGroup                                          ❶
    android:id="@+id/radioGroup"
    android:layout_width="354dp"
    android:layout_height="wrap_content"
    tools:layout_editor_absoluteX="16dp"
    tools:layout_editor_absoluteY="75dp">

    <RadioButton                                       ❷
      android:id="@+id/rlas3"
      android:layout_width="wrap_content"
      android:layout_height="wrap_content"
      android:layout_weight="1"
```

```
      android:text="Learn Android Studio 3"
      android:textSize="18sp" />

  <RadioButton                                            ❸
    android:id="@+id/rlas3kotlin"
    android:layout_width="wrap_content"
    android:layout_height="wrap_content"
    android:layout_weight="1"
    android:text="Learn Android Studio 3 with Kotlin"
    android:textSize="18sp" />

  <RadioButton                                            ❹
    android:id="@+id/rminandroid"
    android:layout_width="wrap_content"
    android:layout_height="wrap_content"
    android:layout_weight="1"
    android:text="Minimum Android Programming"
    android:textSize="18sp" />
  </RadioGroup>
</android.support.constraint.ConstraintLayout>
```

❶	Get a RadioGroup View.
❷	Add the first radio button as a child node of the RadioGroup.
❸	Do the same for the second radio button.
❹	Do the same for the third radio butto.n

Next, let's create the Fragment class for the book_titles UI. Use the context menu, right-click on **/app/java/net.workingdev.ch14fragmentbooks**, then choose **New ➤ Kotlin File/Class**. Create a class and name it BookTitle. In this class, we need to do the following:

1. It's a fragment, so it needs to inherit the Fragment class.

2. Override the **onCreateView** callback, inflate the UI resource file, and return it.

3. Handle the click events for the radio buttons. There are a couple ways to do this. One way is to set up a listener for the radioGroup, and the other way is to set up a click listener for each radio button; we're going for the latter.

The annotated (and explained) BookTitle class is shown in Listing 14-4.

Listing 14-4. BookTitle Fragment Class

```
import android.support.v4.app.Fragment
import android.view.LayoutInflater
import android.view.View
import android.view.ViewGroup

class BookTitle : Fragment(), View.OnClickListener {   ❶

  override fun onCreateView(inflater: LayoutInflater, container:
  ViewGroup?, savedInstanceState: Bundle?): View? {     ❷
    val v = inflater.inflate(R.layout.book_titles, container, false) ❸
    return v
  }

  override fun onViewCreated(view: View, savedInstanceState: Bundle?) {
    rlas3.setOnClickListener(this)              ❹
    rlas3kotlin.setOnClickListener(this)
    rminandroid.setOnClickListener(this)
  }

  override fun onClick(v: View?) {   ❺
    var index:Int = 0
    when(v?.id) {
      R.id.rlas3 -> {                   ❻
        index = 0                       ❼
      }
      R.id.rlas3kotlin -> {
        index = 1
      }
```

```
      R.id.rminandroid -> {
        index = 2
      }
    }
  }
}
```

---

❶   We extend the Fragment class from the support library. We're also implementing the **View. OnClickListener** interface. We will use the class as the **onClick** listener object for the three radio buttons.

❷   The runtime calls **onCreateView** method to compose the UI of the Fragment. At this point, none of UI elements of the Fragment are accessible. You cannot make any UI changes or initialization here.

❸   This will return a View object to the runtime. We're inflating the UI resource file. The **inflate** method takes on three arguments:
1. **UI Resource file**. The XML layout for the fragment, we will use R.layout.book_titles .
2. **This is the would-be parent of the fragment, or root**. We will just use **container** for this.
3. **attachToRoot**. This is a Boolean value. This value will decide whether the inflated View should be attached to the root parameter? If false, root is only used to create the correct subclass of LayoutParams for the root view in the XML.

❹   We're saying that the listener object for the radio button is an instance of the BookTitle class, *this* class.

❺   The **onClick** callback is from the **View.OnClickListener** interface. When one of the radio buttons is clicked, the runtime will call this method and pass along the actual View object that was clicked. This is where we route our program logic. We'll which radiobutton was actually clicked.

❻   The **when** construct is a good fit for routing program logic. We're testing for the runtime value of **View.id** here; *R.id.rlas3*, *R.id.rlas3kotlin*, and *R.id.rminandroid* are the declared *ids* of the radio button in book_title.xml .

❼   We're assigning a zero value to **rlas3** because the description for rlas3 is found on the 0th element of the book description array (we have yet to create this array). Similarly, rlas3kotlin's definition is the 1st element and rminandroid's is the 2nd element of the book description array.

Now that the two components of the *book_titles* fragment are complete, we can work on the *book_description* fragment. You already know how to create a fragment, so I'll skimp on the instructions and jump straight to the codes.

Create a new UI resource and name it **book_description**, and make sure it's in **/app/res/layout** folder. As the for the fragment class, name it **BookDescription**.

Listings 14-5 and 14-6 show the codes for book_description.xml and BookDescription class, respectively.

The book_description fragment is simple. It only has a single TextView element. Note that we're not using a ConstraintLayout for this fragment—we could have, but using a LinearLayout is much simpler. We want the TextView's width to occupy the whole width of the screen. You can simply copy Listing 14-5 and overwrite the contents of your book_description.xml, if you're trying to follow the exercise.

Listing 14-5. /app/res/layout/book_description.xml

```
<?xml version="1.0" encoding="utf-8"?>
<LinearLayout xmlns:android=http://schemas.android.com/apk/res/android
  xmlns:tools=http://schemas.android.com/tools
  android:layout_width="match_parent"
  android:layout_height="match_parent"
  android:orientation="vertical">

  <TextView
    android:id="@+id/txtdescription"
    android:layout_width="match_parent"
    android:layout_height="wrap_content"
    android:text="TextView"
    android:textSize="24sp" />
</LinearLayout>
```

Listing 14-6. BookDescription class

```
class BookDescription : Fragment() {

  lateinit var arrbookdesc: Array<String>
  var bookindex = 0

  override fun onCreateView(inflater: LayoutInflater, container:
ViewGroup?, savedInstanceState: Bundle?): View? {
```

```
    val v = inflater.inflate(R.layout.book_description, container, false)
    arrbookdesc = resources.getStringArray(R.array.bookdescriptions) ❶

    return v
  }

  fun changeDescription(index:Int) : Unit { ❷
    bookindex = index
    txtdescription?.setText(arrbookdesc[bookindex]) ❸
  }

  override fun onViewCreated(view: View, savedInstanceState: Bundle?) {
    changeDescription(bookindex)
  }
}
```

---

❶ This statement reads the file **/app/res/values/bookdescriptions.xml** and creates an array
    out of it.

❷ We created a small function that will take care of changing the text in the description TextView.
    It takes an **Int** value, which we will use as the selector for the description. Each element of the
    array contains a description of a book.

❸ **arrbookdesc[bookindex]** gets a description from the array and then sets the **text** attribute of
    the TextView to it.

Now that the two fragments are built, we can focus on the MainActivity. It needs to
do three things:

1. **Hold the two fragments together**;

2. **Act as a messenger for each fragment.** When the user selects a
    book in book_titles fragment, we need to look up the description
    of that book in *bookdescriptions* array and change the text
    description accordingly in the book_description fragment; and

3. **Adjust the arrangements of the two fragments** depending on the
    orientation of the device. If the device is oriented vertically, the two
    fragments will be arranged stacked from top to bottom. When the
    device is oriented horizontally, the stacking will be from left to right.

Let's work on goal no. 3 first. Right now, we only have one layout folder, the **/app/res/layout** folder is the default location where Android will look for a layout resource. This is the reason why we've always put our **activity_main.xml** in this folder. There is a convention that if we create a folder named **/app/res/layout-land,** Android will look for a layout file in this folder when the device is in landscape mode. We will use this convention to achieve our goal.

Also, we need to solve the top-to-bottom and left-to-right stacking order. The easiest way to achieve this is to change *activity_main's* layout from ConstraintLayout to LinearLayout. The idea is to provide identical *activity_main* xml file for /app/res/layout and /app/res/layout-land, but we will change the LinearLayout orientation such that in the default layout folder, the orientation is vertical (the default) and in the layout-land folder, the orientation is horizontal. We'll make a couple more changes, but we'll get to that in a while.

To convert activity_main's layout to LinearLayout, do the following:

1. Open activity_main.xml in design view.

2. In the "Component Tree" tool window, right-click on "ConstraintLayout, as shown in Figure 14-9.

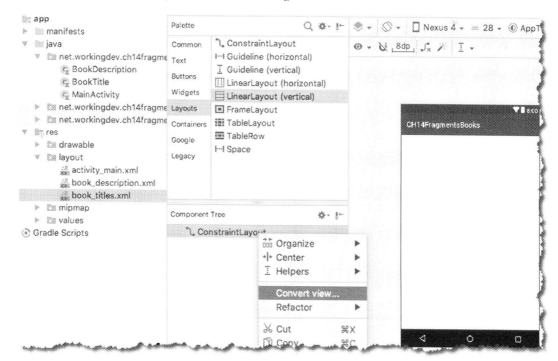

Figure 14-9. *Convert activity_main to LinearLayout*

3. Choose **Convert View**.

4. A dialog box will appear; choose LinearLayout, as shown in
    Figure 14-10.

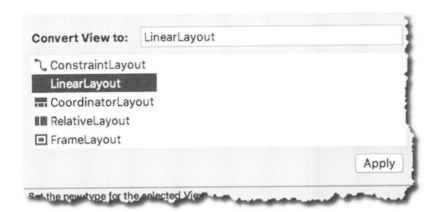

Figure 14-10. *Convert to LinearLayout*

Listing 14-7 shows the code of the revised activity_main (after the conversion to
LinearLayout).

Listing 14-7. Code of activity_main.xml

```
<LinearLayout xmlns:android="http://schemas.android.com/apk/res/android"
  xmlns:app="http://schemas.android.com/apk/res-auto"
  xmlns:tools="http://schemas.android.com/tools"
  android:layout_width="match_parent"    ❶
  android:layout_height="match_parent"   ❷
  android:orientation="vertical"         ❸
  tools:context=".MainActivity">

</LinearLayout>
```

❶ layout_width:"match_parent" means the layout will span the whole width of the screen.

❷ \This means the layout will span the whole height of the screen.

❸ orientation:"vertical" means whatever Views we'll put in this layout will be arranged top to
    bottom.

Next, add the two fragments to activity_main. Open activity_main in design mode, go to the **Palette ➤ Common**, then find the **<fragment>,** as shown in Figure 14-11. Add the BookTitle fragment first. Repeat the process and add BookDescription.

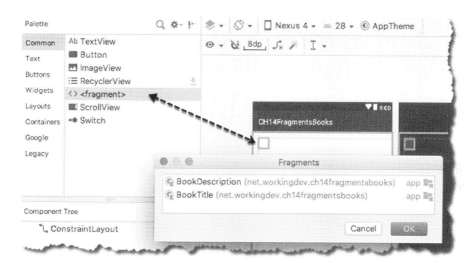

Figure 14-11. *Drag a fragment element into activity_main*

Listing 14-8 shows activity_main.xml with the two fragments added.

Listing 14-8. activity_main With book_titles and book_description Fragments

```xml
<?xml version="1.0" encoding="utf-8"?>
<LinearLayout xmlns:android="http://schemas.android.com/apk/res/android"
  xmlns:app="http://schemas.android.com/apk/res-auto"
  xmlns:tools="http://schemas.android.com/tools"
  android:layout_width="match_parent"
  android:layout_height="match_parent"
  android:orientation="vertical"
  tools:context=".MainActivity">

  <fragment
    android:id="@+id/fragmentbooktitle"
    android:name="net.workingdev.ch14fragmentsbooks.BookTitle"
    android:layout_width="match_parent"    ❶
    android:layout_height="0px"            ❷
    android:layout_weight="1" />           ❸
```

```
<fragment
  android:id="@+id/fragmentbookdescription"
  android:name="net.workingdev.ch14fragmentsbooks.BookDescription"
  android:layout_width="match_parent"    ❹
  android:layout_height="0px"            ❺
  android:layout_weight="1" />           ❻

</LinearLayout>
```

---

❶   We'd like the top fragment to span the whole width.

❷   Just set the height to 0px. We'll let the runtime determine the height for us. We're using layout weights anyway.

❸   Let's give a weight of "1." It doesn't matter what number you use here, as long as the other fragment has the same weight.

❹   We'd also like the bottom fragment to span the whole width.

❺   We're letting the runtime determine the height; set this one to 0px as well.

❻   We want the top and bottom fragments to have equal heights. So, we're setting the weight here to be "1" as well.

That takes care of the default portrait orientation. Now, let's work on the landscape orientation. To control the appearance and behavior of our app when the device is oriented horizontally, we need to do four things. They're outlined as follows:

1.   Create the folder /**app/res/layout-land**.

2.   Create another UI resource file inside **layout-land**; we will name activity_main as well.

3.   Copy the content of /app/res/layout/activity_main to /app/res/layout-land/activity_main.

4.   Make the necessary orientation changes in /app/res/layout-land/activity_main.

First, you need to switch the view of the Project tool window. Right now we're using "Android View," and we need to go to "Project View." Go to the upper area of the Project tool window, click on the downward arrow (as shown in Figure 14-12), then choose "Project."

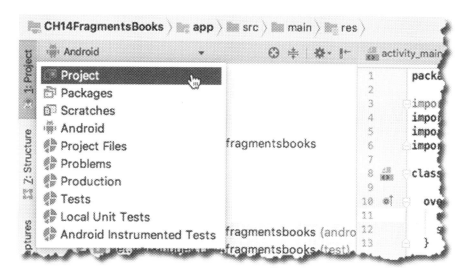

Figure 14-12. *Change from Android view to Project view*

Create the folder layout-land inside the /app/res folder. Right-click on the /app/ res folder, then choose **New ➤ Android Resource Directory**. Name the new directory "layout-land," as shown in Figure 14-13.

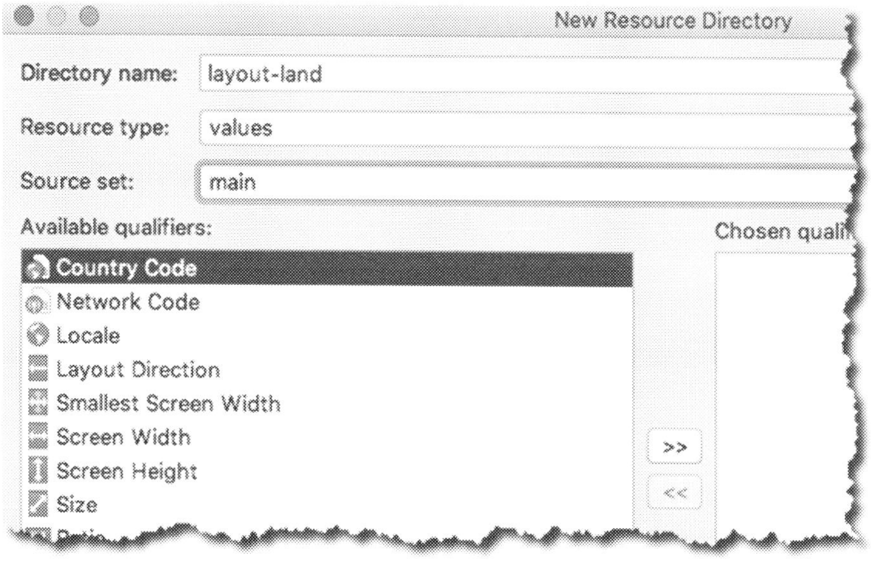

Figure 14-13. *New resource directory*

Right-click on the newly created layout-land folder, then choose **New ➤ Layout Resource File**.

Name the file "activity_main" and choose LinearLayout for the "Root Element," as shown in Figure 14-14.

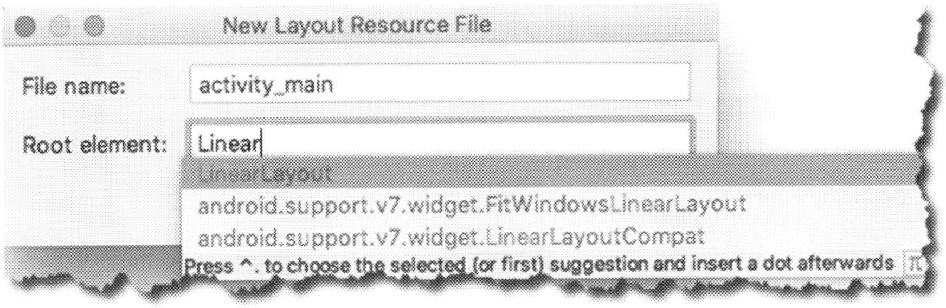

Figure 14-14. *New layout resource file*

Copy the content of /app/res/layout/activity_main.xml to this newly created activity_main in layout-land, and make the appropriate changes, as shown in Listing 14-9.

Listing 14-9. /app/res/layout-land/activity_main.xml

```
<?xml version="1.0" encoding="utf-8"?>
<LinearLayout xmlns:android="http://schemas.android.com/apk/res/android"
  xmlns:app="http://schemas.android.com/apk/res-auto"
  xmlns:tools="http://schemas.android.com/tools"
  android:layout_width="match_parent"
  android:layout_height="match_parent"
  android:orientation="horizontal"      ❶

  tools:context=".MainActivity">

  <fragment
    android:id="@+id/fragmentbooktitle"
    android:name="net.workingdev.ch14fragmentsbooks.BookTitle"
    android:layout_width="0px"                ❷
    android:layout_height="match_parent"      ❸
    android:layout_weight="1" />              ❹
```

```
<fragment
   android:id="@+id/fragmentbookdescription"
   android:name="net.workingdev.ch14fragmentsbooks.BookDescription"
   android:layout_width="0px"
   android:layout_height="match_parent"
   android:layout_weight="1" />

</LinearLayout>
```

---

❶ We're in landscape mode, so this needs to be "horizontal". With this setting, the fragments will be arranged from left to right, instead of top to bottom.

❷ In portrait mode, the layout_width is set to "match_parent and layout_height is set to "0px". We will reverse those settings in landscape mode. So set the layout_width to "0px".

❸ Set the layout_height to "match_parent".

❹ As always, we want to the two fragments to have equal weights, so use "1" in here. Make sure that the layout_weight in the other fragment is also "1."

The last piece of this project is synchronizing the two fragments. Figure 14-15 reminds us of what our small project is supposed to do.

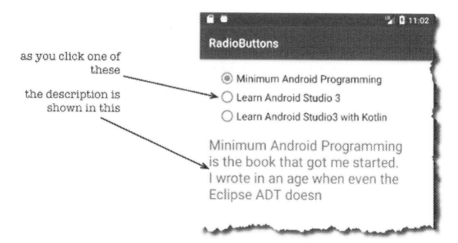

Figure 14-15. *Synchronized fragments*

When the user clicks one of the radio buttons in book_titles fragment, the book_description fragment should change and display the description for the currently selected book. Earlier, we wrote the **changeDescription** function in the BookDescription class; we could simply call this function from the BookTitle class, but that's not considered good practice. Why? Because if we did that, the BookTitle class will know a lot about the BookDescription class—it makes the former depend on the latter. Developers call that "tight coupling," and you should avoid that most of the time.

If we won't call changeDescription directly from BookTitle, how are we going to do it? Figure 14-16 shows us show.

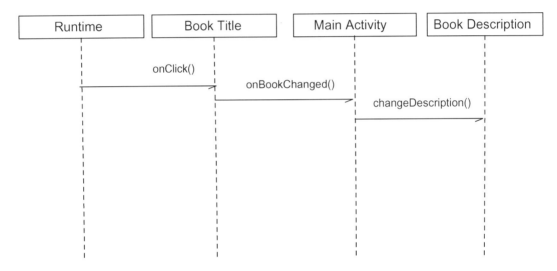

Figure 14-16. *Communication between fragments*

The idea is to course the action through MainActivity. In the sequence diagram, BookTitle calls the **onBookChanged** function in the Activity, then the Activity calls the **changeDescription** function in BookDescription. The astute reader might note that we're simply shifting the dependency away from BookDescription and into MainActivity, and that would make BookTitle dependent on (and tightly coupled with) MainActivity. You would be correct, if we were to couple MainActivity specifically with BookTitle. We won't. We'll use an interface instead; this approach gives us some degree of indirection. It won't be tightly coupled anymore—at least, not that tight. Here's what we'll do.

1. Create a coordinator interface—let's name it Coordinator, why don't we?

2. Implement the Coordinator interface in MainActivity.

3. Use the Coordinator type from within BookTitle. When we need to call the coordinator method within BookTitle, we'll make it against the Coordinator type—not against MainActivity.

To create an interface, right-click on your project's package in the Project tool window (as shown in Figure 14-17), then click **New ➤ Kotlin File/Class**.

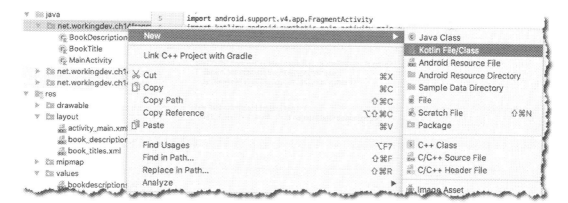

Figure 14-17. *Create new Kotlin file/class*

Name it "Coordinator" as shown in Figure 14-18, then change the "kind" to
"Interface."

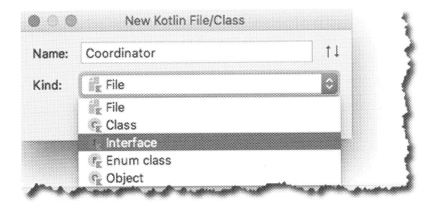

Figure 14-18. *New interface*

Listing 14-10 shows the code for the **Coordinator** interface.

Listing 14-10. Coordinator.Kt

```
interface Coordinator {          ❶
  fun onBookChanged(index:Int)   ❷
}
```

❶ Declare an interface.

❷ Declare an abstract method. It takes an Int parameter. This param stands for the element
number in the bookdescriptions array. Whatever value we receive here, we'll use it to call the
changeDescription method in the BookDescription fragment. By the way, we don't have to
explicitly declare this method as *public* and *abstract*—that's the default for all methods in an
interface.

Next, let's implement this interface in MainActivity. Listing 14-11 shows the
annotated code.

Listing 14-11. MainActivity, Annotated

```
import android.os.Bundle
import android.support.v7.app.AppCompatActivity
import kotlinx.android.synthetic.main.activity_main.*

class MainActivity : AppCompatActivity(), Coordinator {   ❶

  override fun onCreate(savedInstanceState: Bundle?) {
    super.onCreate(savedInstanceState)
    setContentView(R.layout.activity_main)
  }

  override fun onBookChanged(index:Int) {      ❷
    val frag = fragmentbookdescription        ❸
    if (frag is BookDescription) {            ❹
      frag.changeDescription(index)           ❺
    }
  }
}
```

❶   Let's implement the Coordinator interface.

❷   Override the **onBookChanged** method. This was declared as abstract in the Coordinator
       interface; we have to override it in MainActivity so we can provide the concrete behavior.

❸   Let's get a reference to the BookDescription fragment; **fragmentbookdescription** is the **id**
       of the fragment. This call returns a **Fragment** class; *NOT yet* the BookDescription class. If
       you worked with Fragments before, using Java, you might remember that we needed to use
       findFragmentById for doing this kind of thing. We don't have to do it anymore. The Kotlin
       Android Extensions let us refer to the fragments by id, directly—it's already synthesized in
       the MainActivity.

❹   We're casting **frag** (which is still a Fragment class) to **BookDescription**. The **is** operator in
       Kotlin is smart enough to perform the cast automatically for us. We don't have to perform an
       explicit cast anymore. This is one more difference between Java and Kotlin; in the former,
       you to have to cast explicitly. In Kotlin, the **is** operator not only functions as the equivalent of
       instanceof, it also performs as smart cast for us.

❺   Now, we can call the **changeDescription** method of the BookDescription class.

What's left to do is to make the changes in the BookTitle class. When a radiobutton is clicked, we'll do the following:

1. Find out which button was clicked.

2. Depending on the radiobutton's value at the time of the click, we'll assign a value to an index variable; **0**–"Learn Android Studio 3"; **1**– Learn Android Studio 3" with Kotlin; and **2**–"Minimum Android Programming." The integers 0,1, and 2 correspond to the three array elements of **bookdescriptions.xml**.

3. Get a reference to MainActivity using the Coordinator type; then

4. Call the **onBookChanged** method.

Listing 14-12 shows how all this looks in code.

Listing 14-12. BookTitle, Annotated

```
class BookTitle : Fragment(), View.OnClickListener {

  override fun onCreateView(inflater: LayoutInflater, container:
  ViewGroup?, savedInstanceState: Bundle?): View? {
    val v = inflater.inflate(R.layout.book_titles, container, false)
    return v
  }

  override fun onViewCreated(view: View, savedInstanceState: Bundle?) {
    rlas3.setOnClickListener(this)
    rlas3kotlin.setOnClickListener(this)
    rminandroid.setOnClickListener(this)
  }

  override fun onClick(v: View?) {
    var index:Int = 0
    when(v?.id) {                         ❶
      R.id.rlas3 -> {                     ❷
        index = 0
      }
      R.id.rlas3kotlin -> {
        index = 1
```

```
      }
      R.id.rminandroid -> {
        index = 2
      }
    }

    val activity = getActivity()      ❸
    if (activity is Coordinator) {    ❹
      activity.onBookChanged(index)   ❺
    }
  }
}
```

---

❶   Let's find out which button is clicked.

❷   If it's the button for "Learn Android Studio 3," we'll set the value of **index** to 0, and we'll set the value of **index** accordingly for *rlas3kotlin* and *rminandroid*. The **when** construct is essentially translating the runtime value of the radiobutton to an Int, which we can use as an index to our array.

❸   Let's get a reference to the currently running Activity, which is **MainActivity**. Note that **getActivity()** does not return the specific instance of MainActivity; it just returns the supertype of MainActivity (FragmentActivity).

❹   Let's cast **activity** to the **Coordinator** type.

❺   Finally, call the **onBookChanged** method.

We've connected all the dots. Now we can:

- Display books using radiobuttons in one fragment;

- Display a description of the currently selected book in another fragment; and

- Adapt the layout of the fragments in response to changes in device orientation.

Try to run the app in an emulator. Click a few buttons and then try to change the orientation from portrait to landscape. Try to cycle through the radiobuttons in between changes from portrait to landscape mode. Use rotation buttons on the emulator (shown in Figure 14-19) if you want to switch from landscape to portrait and vice versa.

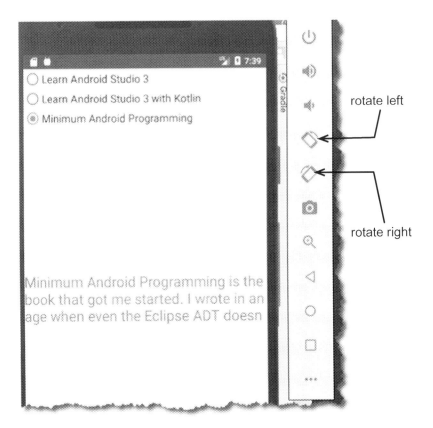

Figure 14-19. *Device rotation buttons, emulator*

You might have noticed that the two fragments go out of sync when you change the device orientation. The **book_description** fragment always goes back to the description of "Learn Android Studio 3" (the first element on the bookdescription array).

The two fragments stay in sync as long as you don't change the device's orientation. Something happens in the fragments when you change the orientation.

As the orientation of the device changes, something happens to MainActivity and its fragments. Remember that an Activity has a life cycle? Fragments have life cycles too—they are similar to that of the Activity but there are notable differences. We won't get into the details of Fragments life cycle nor will we discuss how the Activity life cycle affects the life cycle of Fragments. I'll just point out that as you shift the orientation of the device, the Activity, together with the Fragments, will be torn down and rebuilt again. The Activity may enter and transition through the following states (callbacks):

1. **Activity.onSaveInstanceState.** Fragment's onSaveInstanceState will be called.

2. **Activity.onPause**. Fragment's onPause will be called.

3. **Activity.onStop**. Fragment's onStop will also be called.

4. **Activity.onCreate**. Fragment's onCreate ➤ onCreateView ➤ onViewCreated will be called.

5. **Activity.onStart**. Fragments onStart will be called.

6. **Activity.onRestoreInstanceState**

7. **Activity.onResume**. Fragment's onRestoreInstance will be called.

What's important to take away here is that as you change orientation, the fragments lose their current state. We need to find a way to save the value of the array index (in BookDescription class) before it gets torn down and rebuilt again. Luckily, we know that the runtime will call the Activity's **onSaveInstanceState**, and by extension, it also calls the Fragment's **onSaveInstanceState**; this method lets us save values in a Bundle, so we'll use that to save whatever is the value of the array index when the device is rotated. Listing 14-13 shows the complete and annotated code for the BookDescription class.

Listing 14-13. Complete Code for BookDescription, Annotated

```
import android.os.Bundle
import android.support.v4.app.Fragment
import android.view.LayoutInflater
import android.view.View
import android.view.ViewGroup
import kotlinx.android.synthetic.main.book_description.*

class BookDescription : Fragment() {

  lateinit var arrbookdesc: Array<String>
  var bookindex = 0
```

```kotlin
  override fun onCreateView(inflater: LayoutInflater,
container: ViewGroup?, savedInstanceState: Bundle?): View? {

    val v = inflater.inflate(R.layout.book_description, container, false)
    arrbookdesc = resources.getStringArray(R.array.bookdescriptions)

    bookindex = if(savedInstanceState?.getInt("bookindex") == null) 0    ❶
    else { savedInstanceState.getInt("bookindex")}                       ❷

    return v
  }

  override fun onSaveInstanceState(outState: Bundle) {                   ❸
    outState.putInt("bookindex", bookindex)
  }

  override fun onViewCreated(view: View, savedInstanceState: Bundle?) {
    changeDescription(bookindex)
  }

  fun changeDescription(index:Int) : Unit {
    bookindex = index
    println("BOOK INDEX = $bookindex")
    txtdescription?.setText(arrbookdesc[bookindex])
    println(arrbookdesc[bookindex])
  }
}
```

❶   We need to check if the "bookindex" key isn't null. It will be null the first time we launch the app, because the app hasn't called **onSaveInstanceState** just yet. If it's null, let's make the default **bookindex = 0**; we go with the first description in the array.

❷   If it isn't null, we've already saved a value in the "bookindex" key; so, get the value of "bookindex" and set the value of the **bookindex** variable to it.

❸   Just before the Activity and Fragments are torn and rebuilt, the runtime calls **onSaveInstanceState**. This method gives us access to a Bundle object; this is the same Bundle object that we get during the **onCreateView** callback. Save the current value of **bookindex** to the Bundle using the key "bookindex".

Fragments Demo, Dynamic

Now that we know how to work with fragments during design time, let's see how we can work with fragments dynamically. To add fragments dynamically, we generally have to do the following:

1. Create the layout resource and the corresponding Kotlin class for the fragment; just like what we did in the previous project.

2. In MainActivity, we create an instance of the fragment class.

3. Create an instance of a FragmentManager and a FragmentTransaction object.

4. Create placeholders for the fragments in our Activity's layout file. The placeholders are where we'll put the fragments later on.

5. Using the FragmentTransaction object, add the fragment to the Activity.

This project is almost the same as the previous one. The only difference is the way we'll add the fragments. I think it's best to create a new project for this, so you can keep the previous project untouched for future reference.

Create a new project with the following details (Table 14-2).

Table 14-2. *Project Details*

Project Detail	Value
Application name	CH14FragmentsBooksDynamic
Company domain	use your website name
Kotlin support	Yes
Form factor	Phone and Tablet only
minimum SDK	API 23 Marshmallow
Type of activity	Empty
Activity name	MainActivity
Layout name	activity_main

For the most part, you'll just copy and paste the files from the previous project. I suggest that you don't copy the whole project folder. Create a new project and recreate your steps in the previous project; create the same classes, interfaces, xml resources, and UI resources using exactly the same file names as in the previous project. Then, copy the contents of the file from the previous project and onto the corresponding files in the new project.

Having done that, Table 14-3 shows which file stays unchanged and which file will change in this current project.

Table 14-3. *Summary of Changes in the New Project*

File	Description
MainActivity.Kt	Changes = Yes. We need to add FragmentManager and FragmentTransaction codes .
activity_main.xml	Changes = Yes. We'll remove the <fragment> element and replace it with a placeholder.
book_description.xml	Changes = No. Stays as is. You can copy and paste and then leave it alone.
BookDescription.Kt	Changes = No. Copy, paste, then leave it alone.
book_titles.xml	Changes = No. Copy as is.
BookTitle.Kt	Changes = No. Copy as is.
bookdescriptions.xml	Changes = No. Copy as is.
Coordinator.Kt	Changes = No. Copy as is.

As you can see, the changes are all contained in the main activity files. Listing 14-14 shows the full code and annotates the changes in activity_main.xml.

Listing 14-14. /app/res/layout/activity_main.xml

```
<?xml version="1.0" encoding="utf-8"?>
<LinearLayout xmlns:android="http://schemas.android.com/apk/res/android"
  xmlns:app="http://schemas.android.com/apk/res-auto"
  xmlns:tools="http://schemas.android.com/tools"
  android:layout_width="match_parent"
  android:layout_height="match_parent"
```

```
android:orientation="vertical"
tools:context=".MainActivity">

<LinearLayout                                        ❶
  android:id="@+id/fragtop"                          ❷
  android:layout_width="match_parent"
  android:layout_height="match_parent"
  android:layout_weight="1"
  android:orientation="horizontal">

</LinearLayout>

<LinearLayout                                        ❸
  android:id="@+id/fragbottom"                        ❹
  android:layout_width="match_parent"
  android:layout_height="match_parent"
  android:layout_weight="1"
  android:orientation="horizontal">

</LinearLayout>
</LinearLayout>
```

---

❶   We added a LinearLayout container; and

❷   we named this first container **fragtop**. This is the placeholder for the BookTitles fragment.

❸   We added another LinearLayout container; and

❹   named this one **fragbottom**. This is the placeholder for the BookDescription fragment.

You'll notice that activity_main doesn't contain **<fragment>** elements anymore. Instead, we've put two LinearLayout containers that act as placeholders for the fragments. When we make the call to add the fragments to our Activity, we'll put them in these placeholders. That's the extent of the changes on UI resource layout. Most of the change will actually be on MainActivity.

In the previous project where we added the fragments to the Activity statically, we didn't do much as far as fragments were concerned; but now that we will add fragments dynamically, we'll need to add the necessary codes to add the fragments at runtime.

To work with fragments dynamically, you'll need two objects: a FragmentManager and a FragmentTransaction. You can use the FragmentManager for doing a lot of things like finding fragments by Id and by tag; but for our purpose, we'll only use it as to get a FragmentTransaction object.

A FragmentTransaction is what's responsible for adding, attaching, detaching, and removing fragments at runtime. For our purpose, we will only use it to add fragments.

The full code for MainActivity is shown in Listing 14-15.

Listing 14-15. MainActivity, Annotated

```
import android.support.v7.app.AppCompatActivity
import android.os.Bundle

class MainActivity : AppCompatActivity(), Coordinator {

  lateinit var fragBookDescription: BookDescription
  lateinit var fragBookTitle: BookTitle

  override fun onCreate(savedInstanceState: Bundle?) {
    super.onCreate(savedInstanceState)
    setContentView(R.layout.activity_main)

    fragBookTitle = BookTitle()                                    ❶
    fragBookDescription = BookDescription()                        ❷
    val fragTransaction = supportFragmentManager.beginTransaction() ❸
    fragTransaction.add(R.id.fragtop, fragBookTitle)               ❹
    fragTransaction.add(R.id.fragbottom, fragBookDescription)      ❺
    fragTransaction.commit()                                       ❻

  }

  override fun onBookChanged(index:Int) {                          ❼
    fragBookDescription.changeDescription(index)                  ❽
  }
}
```

❶   Create an instance of the **BookTitle** fragment.

❷   Create an instance of the **BookDescription** fragment.

❸   Let's get a FragmentTransaction object. The **supportFragmentManager** is made available to us as a convenience feature of Android Studio and Kotlin. The actual call is **getSupportFragmentManager()**, but it's synthesized for us already so we don't have to use the actual method. Next, the **beginTransaction()** call is a factory method that gives us a FragmentTransaction object.

❹   Let's use the FragmentTransaction to add a fragment. The **add** method takes two arguments:

1. An id of a View object. This is the id the LinearLayout placeholder that we added in activity_main.xml (fragtop).
2. An instance of a fragment (fragBookTitle)

❺   Similarly, let's add the book description fragment.

❻   We have to call the **commit()** method of the FragmentTransaction to finalize all changes in FragmentTransaction. If you don't call this method, nothing will happen—the fragments won't be added.

❼   You remember this method, when the user clicks one of the radiobuttons in **BookTitle** fragment, that fragment will call the **onBookChanged()** method in MainActivity.

❽   In the previous project, we had to find the id of the book_description fragment and then cast it a BookDescription object before we called **changeDescription**. We don't have to do that anymore, since we can refer to the instance of the **BookDescription** fragment directly.

That concludes the exercise and the chapter. We barely scratched the surface on Fragments—there's more to them than what's presented here; but hopefully, this gives you a good foundation when you further explore them.

Chapter Summary

- Fragments, like Activities, can contain View elements. They are also a composition unit, but smaller.

- You can use Fragments to respond to different device orientation, form factor, or size.

- Fragments, like Activities, also have life cycle callbacks.

- The life cycles of Activities have an effect on Fragments.

- When you change the device's orientation, Activities (and Fragments) get torn down and rebuilt again. They go through a series of life cycle callbacks.

- Android P deprecated **android.app.Fragments**. So, if you want to use Fragments, use the class from the support library.

In the next chapter, we'll learn something about what Android calls "jank" and how to avoid it in your code.

CHAPTER 15

Running in the Background

What we'll cover:

- The UI thread

- Threads and runnables

- Handlers and messages

- AsyncTask

- Anko's doAsync

No one wants to use slow applications. Users want their apps crisp and snappy. Every developer wants this also—no one sets out to build their app and say, "This app is too fast, maybe I should slow it down a bit"; nobody does that. So, how come there are apps that move like molasses? You've probably seen some of these apps I'm talking about—you know those where you try to scroll through a recycler view or a list and then it starts, stops, and sputters. Sluggish.

We can list a number of reasons why some apps are sluggish, but I bet one of the top 10 reasons is that there's too much going on the main thread. It's probably saddled by an I/O routine or a complex calculation—or both—and that's bad.

Does that mean you shouldn't make any I/O calls or do any complex calculation in your app? Not at all. But you should know where to put I/O calls or complex calculation; and it's not on the main thread.

In this chapter, we'll take a look at ways on how to keep slow-moving codes away from the main thread so that apps can respond crisply and snappily.

© Ted Hagos 2018
T. Hagos, *Learn Android Studio 3 with Kotlin*, https://doi.org/10.1007/978-1-4842-3907-0_15

Basic Concepts

A process is created when an app is launched. It's allocated some resources, like memory and some other things that it needs so it can do its job. It's also given at least one thread.

A thread, loosely speaking, is a sequence of instructions. It's the thing that actually executes your code. During the time that the app is alive, the thread will utilize the process' resources. It may read or write data to the memory, to the disk, or, sometimes, even the network I/O. While the thread is interacting with all these, it really is just waiting. It can't take advantage of CPU cycles while it's waiting. We can't let all those CPU cycles go to waste. Can we? What we can do is to create other threads so that when one or more threads are waiting for something, the other threads can utilize the CPU. This is the case for multi-threaded applications.

When the runtime created an instance of the app, that process was given one thread. It's called the main thread; some developers call it the UI thread. The runtime gave us just the one thread and no more. But the good news is we can create more. The UI thread is allowed to spawn other threads.

The UI Thread

Before we dive into the details of spawning or creating child threads, let's talk about the UI thread first. It's the one responsible for launching the main activity and inflating the layout xml so that all the View elements in it turn into actual Java objects (e.g., buttons, text views, etc.). In short, it's the one responsible the UI.

When you make a call like **setText** or **setHint**, it will be done on the main thread; if you thought that these calls executed immediately, that would be wrong. Whatever statements you write in the app will generally follow these steps:

1. The statements will be placed in a MessageQueue, and there it will stay, until

2. a Handler picks it up for execution; and finally

3. it gets executed on the main thread.

You might say, "This is all nice to know, but so what?". Well, you should care about this because the main thread is not only used for drawing UI elements. It's also used for everything else that happens in your app. Remember that the Activity has other methods like **onCreate**, **onStop**, **onResume**, **onCreateOptionsMenu**, **onOptionsItemSelected**, and other similar methods; whenever the code is running on these blocks, the Android runtime cannot process any message in the queue. It's in a *blocked* state; a blocked state is a concurrency jargon that developers use when they mean to say that the app is waiting for something to finish before it can continue to go about its business. Never mind the jargon—just remember that blocking can be bad for the user-experience.

How can this happen? The answer is "because we only have one thread to do all these things." The solution for this problem is to create a background thread or a child thread and do our non-UI tasks in there—but not always. If you think the call is cheap enough in terms of processing resources, say 1 ms to 15 ms, then go ahead and just do it on the main thread. If it's going to take more than 16 ms and up, you should probably do it on background thread.

The 16-ms threshold is a guideline from "Project Butter," which was released at the time of Android 4.1 (Jellybean). It was meant to improve the performance of Android apps. When the runtime senses that you're doing too much on the main thread, it will start dropping frames. When you're not making expensive calls, the app performs at a smooth 60 FPS (frames per second). If you tie up the main thread, you'll start noticing sluggish performance, or what the Android team refers to as "jank." I don't have a clear-cut guideline that can tell you what's an expensive call and what's a cheap one. What I can do, though, is to show you examples of both calls; hopefully, you'll get an idea what an expensive versus cheap call looks like.

Listing 15-1 is a cheap call even if it sets the text attribute to a calculated value. The calculation is simple enough, the UI thread won't break a sweat.

Listing 15-1. Set Text Attribute to a Calculated Value: A Cheap Call

```
button.setOnClickListener {
  txtsecondnumber.setText((2 * 2 * 2).toString())
}
```

Listing 15-2 might seem complicated because it calculates the GCF. What if the numbers are large—wouldn't that be too taxing for the main thread? Not really. Listing 15-2 uses the Euclidian algorithm for finding the GCF. The algorithm performs at constant time or O(1); that's another jargon that developers use when they talk about the time complexity of an algorithm or how long it will take for the code to finish. O(1) or constant time means that the algorithm will perform the same whether the input is large or small; the time complexity doesn't change much whether we're finding the GCF of 12 and 15 or 16,848,662 and 24. So, it's quite okay to put this in the main thread.

345

> **Note**   Time complexity of algorithms can be expressed as either O(1), O(N), O(N²), O(2ᴺ), or O(log N), where N stands for the size of the input. This is a called Big O notation. It's good to know something about it—especially if you want to write performant codes.

Listing 15-2. Calculate GCF: Still a Cheap Call

```kotlin
button.setOnClickListener {

  val numfno = txtfirstnumber.text.toString().toInt()
  val numsno = txtsecondnumber.text.toString().toInt()

  var numbig = if(numfno > numsno) numfno else numsno
  var numsmall = if(numfno < numsno) numfno else numsno

  var rem = numbig % numsmall

  while(rem != 0) {
    numbig = numsmall
    numsmall = rem
    rem = numbig % numsmall
  }
  Toast.makeText(this@MainActivity, "GCF is $numsmall", Toast.LENGTH_LONG).
  show()
}
```

Listing 15-3 is considered expensive because it makes a call to the network I/O. The code, in fact, won't even compile at all because it will result in a **NetworkOnMainThreadException**. The IDE won't even let us through the compilation process. As a rule of thumb, if your code will make I/O calls, whether local file or the network, you should do it in a background thread.

Listing 15-3. Read Something from GitHub: Expensive Call

```
button.setOnClickListener {
  val url = "https://api.github.com/users/tedhagos"
  println("inside doGetHttp")
  val client = OkHttpClient()
  val request = Request.Builder().url(url).build()
  val response = client.newCall(request).execute()

  val bodystr = response.body().string()
}
```

Listing 15-4 doesn't do any I/O, but the function **killSomeTime** simulates an expensive call.

Listing 15-4. Do Something That Blocks: Expensive Call

```
button.setOnClickListener {
    killSomeTime()
  }
}

private fun killSomeTime() {
  for (i in 1..20) {
    textView.text = i.toString()
    println("i:$i")
    Thread.sleep(2000)
  }
}
```

The **Thread.sleep** call in Listing 15-4 is a dead giveaway that the code will block, but it can simulate something that can take 2 seconds to complete. At first glance, you might think that the **textView** will update every 2 seconds to show the current value of *i*, but that won't happen because the runtime will drop the framerates already. The UI thread can't update the textView because it's tied up waiting for the Thread to wake up and resume.

Imagine if you have a code like Listing 15-5—it doesn't have any I/O call or **Thread. sleep**, but it won't update the text field (in the second level of the loop) like you expect—again, because the main thread is busy calculating the Cartesian product.

Listing 15-5. Deeply Nested Calculation: Expensive Call

```
button.setOnClickListener {
  for (i in 1..100000) {
    for (j in 1..10000) {
      txtfirstnumber.setText((i*j).toString())
      for (k in 1..10000) {
        println("i: $i | j: $j | k$k | i*j*k = ${i*j*k}")
      }
    }
  }
}
```

Note   A Cartesian product is a mathematical set that is the result of multiplying other sets.

In earlier versions of Android, before Project Butter, the codes shown in Listings 15-3, 15-4, and 15-5 may have resulted in the ANR error (Android Not Responding). Nowadays, they may not draw the ANR anymore, but the bigger concern is **jank**. To avoid jank, we should move those expensive calls to a background thread. There are many ways to do that in Android. Some solutions are found on the framework level like the Loader API or AsyncTaskLoader; however, these things were deprecated starting with API 28, so it's best to stay away from them. There's also a couple of low-level ways to do some task in the background, they are:

- **Threads and Runnables**, from Java
- **AsyncTask**, this is part of Android framework
- **Handlers and Messages**, also part of the Android framework
- **Anko's doAsync**, Anko is a third-party library written in Kotin

Threads and Runnables

Let's use Listing 15-14 as a use-case for our exploration. To run that code, you'll need a UI that looks like Figure 15-1; the xml code for our basic UI is in Listing 15-6.

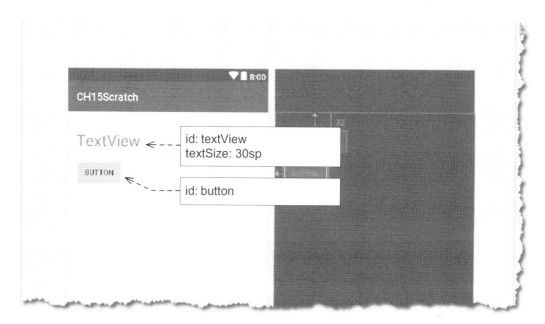

Figure 15-1. *Our basic activity_main layout*

Listing 15-6. /app/res/layout/activity_main.xml

```
<?xml version="1.0" encoding="utf-8"?>
<android.support.constraint.ConstraintLayout xmlns:android=http://schemas.
android.com/apk/res/android
  xmlns:app=http://schemas.android.com/apk/res-auto
  xmlns:tools=http://schemas.android.com/tools
  android:layout_width="match_parent"
  android:layout_height="match_parent"
  tools:context=".MainActivity">

  <Button
    android:id="@+id/button"
    android:layout_width="wrap_content"
    android:layout_height="wrap_content"
```

```
        android:layout_marginStart="16dp"
        android:layout_marginTop="16dp"
        android:text="Button"
        app:layout_constraintStart_toStartOf="parent"
        app:layout_constraintTop_toBottomOf="@+id/textView" />

    <TextView
        android:id="@+id/textView"
        android:layout_width="wrap_content"
        android:layout_height="wrap_content"
        android:layout_marginStart="16dp"
        android:layout_marginTop="32dp"
        android:text="TextView"
        android:textSize="30sp"
        app:layout_constraintStart_toStartOf="parent"
        app:layout_constraintTop_toTopOf="parent" />
</android.support.constraint.ConstraintLayout>
```

If you try to run Listing 15-4 as it stands right now, it will run; but it won't run well. You will notice the following:

1. You expect that the **textView** will refresh every 2 seconds to show the current value of *i*. It won't. The frames are going to drop, so you won't see any UI activity.

2. But you will see the value of *I* as it gets updated every 2 seconds in the **Logcat** window. This is because **println** isn't affected by the reduction in framerate—the output is in the console, not in the UI.

3. You might see a message like this from the runtime's **Choreographer:**

   ```
   07-31 15:51:29.646 13403-13403/net.workingdev.
   ch15scratchasynctask I/Choreographer: Skipped 2402 frames!
   The application may be doing too much work on its main
   thread.
   ```

Though the app didn't draw an ANR, it significantly slowed down. You can definitely feel some jank. To fix this, let's move the janky code to a background thread.

To create a thread and start it, you need to do the following:

1. Create a class that implements the Runnable type.

2. Anything that you want to run in the background, put it inside the overridden **run** method.

3. Create a Thread object, then pass the Runnable object that you just created in step 1 to the Thread's constructor.

4. Call the start method of Thread.

5. Every time the value of the variable i changes, we update the TextView.

In code, it looks like the following (see Listing 15-7).

Listing 15-7. Threads and Runnables

```kotlin
class MainActivity : AppCompatActivity() {

  override fun onCreate(savedInstanceState: Bundle?) {
    super.onCreate(savedInstanceState)
    setContentView(R.layout.activity_main)

    button.setOnClickListener {
      val runnable = Worker()
      val thread = Thread(runnable)
      thread.start()
    }
  }

  inner class Worker : Runnable {
    override fun run() {
      killSomeTime()
    }
  }
}
```

```kotlin
private fun killSomeTime() {
  for (i in 1..20) {
    Thread.sleep(2000)
    println("i: $i")
  }
}
}
```

By now, in Chapter 15 of this book, you already know about anonymous objects, lambdas, and how to chain function calls. We should be able to whip up something like this:

```kotlin
button.setOnClickListener {
  Thread(Runnable {         ❶ ❷
    killSomeTime()
  }).start()                    ❸
}
```

---

❶   A Runnable anonymous object is created using Kotlin lambda expressions. It's passed to the constructor of a Thread class.

❷   We don't have to write the **run** method anymore. Runnable is a SAM class (a class with a Single Abstract Method). You don't need to explicitly write the name of the abstract method when you use a SAM class in a lambda expression.

❸   Calling **start** kicks the thread into high gear.

Our code should work fine right now if all we want to do is println to the console. But remember that we need to set the value of the TextField to the current value of *i*.

A background thread is not allowed to change anything in the UI. That responsibility belongs only to the UI thread. So, the next problem we need to solve is how to come back to the UI thread so we can update the TextView. There are a couple of ways to do that, but the simplest is to call the **runOnUiThread** method of Activity class.

The **runOnUiThread** method takes a Runnable object and executes the code of the Runnable object in the main thread. Listing 15-8 shows the full, annotated, and explained code for MainActivity.

Listing 15-8. Full Code of MainActivity, With Annotations

```kotlin
import android.os.AsyncTask
import android.support.v7.app.AppCompatActivity
import android.os.Bundle
import kotlinx.android.synthetic.main.activity_main.*

class MainActivity : AppCompatActivity() {

  override fun onCreate(savedInstanceState: Bundle?) {
    super.onCreate(savedInstanceState)
    setContentView(R.layout.activity_main)

    button.setOnClickListener {
      Thread(Runnable {                    ❶
        killSomeTime()                     ❷
      }).start()                           ❸
    }
  }

  private fun killSomeTime() {
    for (i in 1..20) {
      runOnUiThread(Runnable{              ❹
        textView.text = i.toString()
      })
      println("i:$i")
      Thread.sleep(2000)
    }
  }
}
```

❶   To create a background thread, you need to create an instance of Runnable type (Thread) and
      start it. The **Thread** constructor takes a Runnable type and executes whatever is inside the
      run method. I used an object expression in this line to create an instance of a Runnable type
      without creating a *named subclass*—kinda like Java's anonymous classes.

❷   We are inside the Runnable's **run** method now. We're in a background thread.

❸   Don't forget to call **start** on the Thread object.

❹   One of the limitations of a background thread is that it **cannot** do anything that modifies the
      UI. Any UI modification code has to run from the original thread that created the UI—which is
      the UI Thread. If you need to change the UI from a background thread (like this), you can call
      the **runOnUiThread** method of the **Activity** class. It takes a Runnable type (again), you can put
      all the UI modification code on the **run** method of this Runnable type.

When you run this code, you should see the updated value of the variable *i* every 2
seconds. The **Choreographer** will also stop bugging us about dropped frames because
we're back to the buttery smooth rate of 60 FPS.

Using the Handler Class

The Handler class, unlike the Thread, is part of the Android framework—not part of Java.
Handler objects are used mainly to manage threads. Remember the discussion earlier
about your code being put in MessageQueue; it waits there until it gets picked up and
executed—it's the Handler that does the picking and the executing.

The basic idea is to get a reference to the Handler of the main thread, then, while
we're inside the background thread (where we can't make any UI changes), send a
Message to the handler object. Use the Message object to convey data between the
background thread and the main thread.

To use a Handler object, you need to do the following:

1.   Get the Handler object that's associated with the UI Thread.

2.   Somewhere in your code, when you're about to do something that
       may cause jank, run that instead on a background thread.

3. While you're inside the background thread, when you need to change something in the UI, do the following:

    a. Create a **Message** object, best way to do this is to call **Message. obtain()**.

    b. Send a message to the Handler object by calling the **sendMessage** method. Message objects can carry data. The **data** attribute of the Message object is a Bundle object, so you can use the various putXXX() methods on it (e.g., **putString, putInt, putBundle, putFloat**, etc.).

4. You can do the UI changes in the **handleMessage** callback of the Handler object.

Listing 15-9 shows how all these come together in code.

Listing 15-9. Full Listing for MainActivity, Annotated and Explained

```kotlin
import android.support.v7.app.AppCompatActivity
import android.os.Bundle
import android.os.Handler
import android.os.Message
import kotlinx.android.synthetic.main.activity_main.*

class MainActivity : AppCompatActivity() {

  lateinit var mhandler: Handler                         ❶

  override fun onCreate(savedInstanceState: Bundle?) {
    super.onCreate(savedInstanceState)
    setContentView(R.layout.activity_main)

    mhandler = object : Handler() {                      ❷
      override fun handleMessage(msg: Message?) {
        textView.text = msg?.data?.getString("counter")  ❸
      }
    }
```

```
  button.setOnClickListener {
    Thread(Runnable {
      killSomeTime()                                    ❹
    }).start()
  }
}

private fun killSomeTime() {
  for (i in 1..20) {
    var msg = Message.obtain()                          ❺
    msg.data.putString("counter", i.toString())         ❻
    mhandler.sendMessage(msg)                           ❼
    Thread.sleep(2000)
  }
}
}
```

❶   Declare a Handler object as a property of the class. We need access to this from two of our
     top-level functions. We're using **lateinit** here because were not yet ready to define the object.

❷   We're defining the Handler object now. We're getting the Handler object that's associated with
     the UI Thread.

❸   It's safe to make UI changes in here. This is the Handler that's associated with the UI
     Thread. The **handleMessage** callback will be called by the runtime when we invoke the
     sendMessage. The Message parameter of this method carries the data.

❹   **killSomeTime** is representative of any I/O or time-consuming task. Always run it in a
     background thread to avoid jank.

❺   Create a Message object. This is what we will send to the Handler later.

❻   The **data** property of the Message object is like a **Bundle**—you can put things in it. It's like
     a dictionary, each item is a pair—a key and a value. We passed two things to the putString()
     method, these are:

     1.   "counter", the **key**
     2.   i.toString(), the **value**

❼   Send the Message to the Handler object.

When you run this code, it performs just as well as our earlier Thread example.

AsyncTask

Another way to run codes in the background is to use the AsyncTask class. AsyncTask, like the Handler class, is part of the Android framework. Like the Handler, it has a mechanism for doing the work on the background, and it also provides a (cleaner) way to update the UI.

To use the AsyncTask, you generally need to do the following:

1. Extend the AsyncTask class.

2. Override AsyncTask's **doInBackground** method so you can accomplish the background work.

3. Override a couple more of AsyncTask's life cycle methods so you can update the UI and report on the overall status of the background task.

4. Create an instance of AsyncTask subclass and call the **execute**—that's how you kickstart the background operation.

One of the reasons why AsyncTask is less preferred than simple Threads is that it uses generics. The AsyncTask class is parameterized. You have to specify three types before you can use it. Listing 15-10 shows us how to subclass the AsyncTask class.

Listing 15-10. Subclassing the AsyncTask

```
AsyncTask<Void, String, Boolean> {                            ❶

  override fun doInBackground(vararg p0: Void?) : Boolean {   ❷
    // statement
    publishProgress("status of anything")                     ❸
  }
  override fun onProgressUpdate(vararg values: String?) {
    // update the UI                                          ❹
  }
  override fun onPostExecute(result: Boolean?) {
    println(result)                                           ❺
  }
}
```

❶   The AsyncTask is a parameterized class. You have to specify three types before you can use it. The three types, in the order they appear, are the following:

    a. Params. This is the information you need to pass to the AsyncTask so that it can do the background task. It could be anything, like a list of URLs, View object(s), or String(s). To make it a bit more challenging for us, it's a *vararg* parameter. Typically, developers use this parameter to pass the View elements so the AsyncTask can reference the View objects of the Activity. But in our example, I will make the AsyncTask an inner class—that way, it can refer to any View element in MainActivity (this is reason why I used **Void** as the first type parameter—I simply don't need it).

    b. Progress. The type of information that you want the background thread to pass to the UI thread so you can tell the user what's going on.

    c. Result. The kind data you want to indicate the result of the background operation; most of the time, this is either *true* or *false*. If the operation succeeds, then it's *true,* otherwise it'*s false.*

❷   This is the only mandatory function to override. As the name suggests, this is where you'll do things in the background. Whenever you need to read/write to a file or a network I/O, you'd want to do it here. This function takes in a *vararg* **Void** parameter, it corresponds to the first *type parameter* we defined for our class. If you made the first type parameter as String, then **doInBackground** should take a String. Notice also that this method returns a Boolean; that's because we passed a **Boolean** as the third parameter type.

❸   Periodically, you may want to inform the user of what's going on in your app, especially if it's a lengthy operation. The **publishProgress** method lets you do that. While you are inside **doInBackground**, you cannot make any changes to the UI. UI changes needs to happen on the UI Thread. When you call **publishProgress**, the Android runtime will call **onProgressUpdate**— that's where you can make UI changes. Whatever argument you pass to **publishProgress**, the **onProgressUpdate** receives it.

❹   When you're inside this method, all the statements will be executed on the UI Thread. This is where you make changes to your View objects. The method takes a String parameter because we passed **String** as the second type parameter of the AsyncTask class, and it corresponds to that. This method will be called after we've invoked **publishProgress** from the **doInBackground** method; whatever data you pass to **publishProgress** will be received by **onProgressUpdate.**

❺   When **doInBackground** finishes, the runtime will call this method. The **result** parameter was returned by doInBackground.

Now that were acquainted with the structure of the AsyncTask, let's see how we can use it for our counting example. Listing 15-11 shows the full and annotated code for AsyncTask when used within MainActivity.

Listing 15-11. Full Code for MainActivity, Annotated and Explained

```kotlin
import android.os.AsyncTask
import android.support.v7.app.AppCompatActivity
import android.os.Bundle
import android.view.View
import kotlinx.android.synthetic.main.activity_main.*

class MainActivity : AppCompatActivity() {

  override fun onCreate(savedInstanceState: Bundle?) {
    super.onCreate(savedInstanceState)
    setContentView(R.layout.activity_main)

    button.setOnClickListener {
      Worker().execute()                                    ❶
    }
  }

  inner class Worker : AsyncTask<Void, String, Boolean>() {  ❷

    override fun doInBackground(vararg p0: Void?) : Boolean {
      for (i in 1..20) {
        publishProgress(i.toString())                      ❸
        Thread.sleep(2000)                                 ❹
      }
      return true
    }

    override fun onProgressUpdate(vararg values: String?) {
      textView.text = values[0]                            ❺
    }
```

```
    override fun onPostExecute(result: Boolean?) {
      println(result)
    }
  }
}
```

❶   Create an instance of **Worker**, then **execute** it.

❷   Define an AsyncTask as an inner class, so we can refer to the View objects of the enclosing MainActivity. The *type parameters* are explained below.

   a. Void. I don't really need to pass anything to the AsyncTask, so, Void.

   b. String. The **onProgressUpdate** method will update the TextView. Since we'll use this second Type to update the value TextView, String seems like a good choice.

   c. Boolean. When we're done with **doInBackground**, we want to set a status to indicate failure or success; Boolean seems to be good choice for that.

❸   Let's tell the user what the current value of *i* is. The onProgressUpdate takes a String argument; that's why we're converting *i* to an Int.

❹   This simulates a length operation.

❺   Now that were in the UI Thread, we can safely set the *text* attribute of TextView to the current value of *i*. We only passed one parameter from **publishProgress**, so if we want to get that, it's the 0th element of the **values** parameter.

The AsyncTask, like the Handler and the Thread classes, will free up the UI thread. When you run this, the app purrs at a smooth 60 FPS.

Anko's doAsync

Anko is an Android library written in Kotlin by JetBrains (the same company that created Kotlin). You can use it for a wide variety of tasks, but for our purpose, we only need the **doAsync** portion. As its name implies, Anko's doAsync will let us run codes asynchronously or in the background.

Before you can use Anko, you need to add it to the dependencies of the project's Gradle file, as shown in Listing 15-12.

Listing 15-12. /app/build.gradle

```
dependencies {
  ....
  implementation 'org.jetbrains.anko:anko-common:0.9'
}
```

The syntax for using doAsync is shown in Listing 15-13.

Listing 15-13. Syntax for doAsync

```
doAsync {
  // do things in the background   ❶
}
```

---

❶   In here, you can read or write to large files, download a file from the internet, or do a task that will take a long time to complete. This block will execute in a background thread.

The next challenge is how to go back to the UI Thread. Remember that a background thread is not allowed to change anything in the UI. Anko's approach is probably the simplest of all the other options we've discussed in the previous sections. Listing 15-14 shows a sample code on how doAsync runs code in the background and how it gets back to the UI thread.

Listing 15-14. doAsync and activityUiThread

```
doAsync {
  // do things in the background   ❶
  activityUiThread {
    // make changes to the UI    ❷
    textView.text = "Hello"
  }
}
```

---

❶   Background processing.

❷   Now, you're back to the UI Thread. It's that simple. Whenever you need to go back to the UI Thread, you can do it inside the **activityUiThread**block.

Listing 15-15 shows the full code example for MainActivity. It uses Anko's doAsync to perform a long computation and then write something back to the UI.

Listing 15-15. Full Code for MainActivity Using doAsync, Annotated and Explained

```
import android.support.v7.app.AppCompatActivity
import android.os.Bundle
import kotlinx.android.synthetic.main.activity_main.*
import org.jetbrains.anko.activityUiThread
import org.jetbrains.anko.doAsync

class MainActivity : AppCompatActivity() {

  override fun onCreate(savedInstanceState: Bundle?) {
    super.onCreate(savedInstanceState)
    setContentView(R.layout.activity_main)

    button.setOnClickListener {                ❶
      doAsync {
        for(i in 1..15) {                      ❷
          Thread.sleep(2000)                   ❸
          activityUiThread {
            textView.text = i.toString()       ❹
          }
        }
      }
    }
  }
}
```

❶   Let's set up a basic OnClickListener. This will trigger the background task.

❷   Let's just count from 1 to 15.

❸   This simulates a long running task. Our loop will come around 15 times, so the task will take a total of 30 seconds to complete.

❹   Let's tell the user what's going on with the app. Update the TextView object with the current value of *i*.

The doAsync, like the Thread, Handler, and AsyncTask examples before it, should perform equally well. When you run this code, the app will run smoothly at 60 FPS.

You've seen four low-level techniques to execute tasks in the background. Hopefully the code examples gave you enough ideas to continue on your own.

A Real-World Example

Before we close the chapter, let's work on something that you might actually use in your projects. Let's pull some user info from GitHub using their public API. GitHub allows anyone access to **https://api.github.com/users/<username>**. If you have a GitHub account, try calling this URL using you GitHub login so you can be familiar with what it returns. Listing 15-16 shows a partial output of the HTTP call using my own GitHub id (tedhagos).

Listing 15-16. Sample JSON Response from GitHub API

```
{
  "login": "tedhagos",
  "id": 1287584,
  "node_id": "MDQ6VXNlcjEyODc1ODQ=",
  "avatar_url": "https://avatars1.githubusercontent.com/u/1287584?v=4",
  "gravatar_id": "",
  "url": "https://api.github.com/users/tedhagos",
  "html_url": "https://github.com/tedhagos",
  "followers_url": "https://api.github.com/users/tedhagos/followers",
  "following_url": "https://api.github.com/users/tedhagos/following{/other_
                   user}",
  "gists_url": "https://api.github.com/users/tedhagos/gists{/gist_id}",
  "starred_url": "https://api.github.com/users/tedhagos/starred{/owner}{/
                 repo}",
  "subscriptions_url": "https://api.github.com/users/tedhagos/
                       subscriptions",
  "organizations_url": "https://api.github.com/users/tedhagos/orgs",
  "repos_url": "https://api.github.com/users/tedhagos/repos",
  "events_url": "https://api.github.com/users/tedhagos/events{/privacy}",
```

```
"received_events_url": "https://api.github.com/users/tedhagos/received_
                        events",
"type": "User",
"site_admin": false,
"name": "Ted Hagos",
"company": null,
"blog": "https://workingdev.net",
"location": null,
"email": null,
"hireable": null,
"bio": "Currently CTO and Data Protection Officer of RenditionDigital
        International. Sometimes a writer and tech trainer."
}
```

What we'd like to do is as follows:

1. Prompt the user to input a GitHub account; it's the login id. We'll use the hint attribute of the EditText to tell the user what to input.

2. Compose the HTTP request using the login id we got from the user. We can DIY our approach to this by using low-level java.net classes, but that will distract us from the main topic, so we'll use OkHttp. It's a third-party library, but it's very easy to use—and, most importantly, easy to understand.

3. Make an HTTP call to GitHub API and run it in a background thread. We'll use Anko's doAsync for this project. It's the easiest to use. Don't you think?

4. The HTTP call returns a JSON object, as you can see from Listing 15-16. We'll parse the JSON message and get only the value of the name property.

5. We'll go back to UI thread by using the method **activityUiThread**, and there, we'll update the textView with the value of the name property (the one we got from the JSON object).

Table 15-1 shows the details of the demo project.

Table 15-1. *Project Details*

Project Detail	Value
Application name	CH15GetGitHubInfo
Company domain	use your website name
Kotlin support	Yes
Form factor	Phone and Tablet only
minimum SDK	API 23 Marshmallow
Type of activity	Empty
Activity name	MainActivity
Layout name	activity_main
Backwards compatibility	Yes. AppCompat

A screenshot of the UI is shown in Figure 15-2. We'll use an EditText to take the user's input and we'll use a TextView to display the **name** attribute of the returned JSON file.

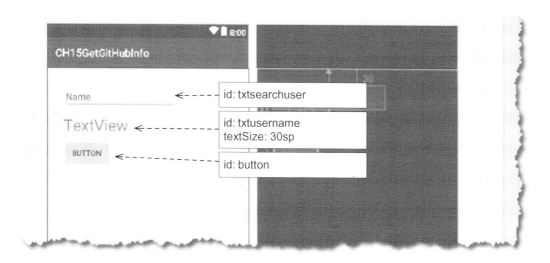

Figure 15-2. *UI for CH15GetGitHubInfo*

Listing 15-17 shows the full listing for activity_main.xml

Listing 15-17. /app/res/layout/activity_main.xml

```
<?xml version="1.0" encoding="utf-8"?>
<android.support.constraint.ConstraintLayout xmlns:android=http://schemas.
android.com/apk/res/android
  xmlns:app=http://schemas.android.com/apk/res-auto
  xmlns:tools=http://schemas.android.com/tools
  android:layout_width="match_parent"
  android:layout_height="match_parent"
  tools:context=".MainActivity"
  tools:layout_editor_absoluteY="81dp">

  <Button
    android:id="@+id/button"
    android:layout_width="wrap_content"
    android:layout_height="wrap_content"
    android:layout_marginTop="8dp"
    android:text="Button"
    app:layout_constraintStart_toStartOf="@+id/txtusername"
    app:layout_constraintTop_toBottomOf="@+id/txtusername" />

  <TextView
    android:id="@+id/txtusername"
    android:layout_width="wrap_content"
    android:layout_height="wrap_content"
    android:layout_marginTop="8dp"
    android:text="TextView"
    android:textSize="30sp"
    app:layout_constraintStart_toStartOf="@+id/txtsearchuser"
    app:layout_constraintTop_toBottomOf="@+id/txtsearchuser" />

  <EditText
    android:id="@+id/txtsearchuser"
    android:layout_width="wrap_content"
    android:layout_height="wrap_content"
    android:layout_marginStart="31dp"
```

```
        android:layout_marginTop="30dp"
        android:ems="10"
        android:inputType="textPersonName"
        android:text="Name"
        app:layout_constraintStart_toStartOf="parent"
        app:layout_constraintTop_toTopOf="parent" />
</android.support.constraint.ConstraintLayout>
```

Before you can use OkHttp and the Anko library, you need to add their dependencies to the project's module level gradle file. Listing 15-18 shows what you need to add to the **dependencies** section of **/app/build.gradle**.

Listing 15-18. Add OkHttp and Anko to /app/build.gradle

```
dependencies {
    implementation fileTree(dir: 'libs', include: ['*.jar'])
    implementation"org.jetbrains.kotlin:kotlin-stdlib-jre7:$kotlin_version"
    implementation 'com.android.support:appcompat-v7:28.0.0-alpha3'
    implementation 'com.android.support.constraint:constraint-layout:1.1.2'
    testImplementation 'junit:junit:4.12'
    androidTestImplementation 'com.android.support.test:runner:1.0.2'
    androidTestImplementation 'com.android.support.test.espresso:espresso-
    core:3.0.2'
    implementation 'com.squareup.okhttp:okhttp:2.5.0'     ❶
    implementation 'org.jetbrains.anko:anko-common:0.9' ❷
}
```

---

❶   You need to add this in order to use OkHttp.

❷   You need to add this so you can use Anko's doAsync.

After you've added Anko and OkHttp in the gradle file, you have to sync the file. Click the "Sync Now" link, which is in the upper-right corner of the screen, as shown in Figure 15-3.

```
Gradle files have changed since last project sync. A project sync may be necessary for the IDE to work properly.          Sync Now
1    apply plugin: 'com.android.application'
2    apply plugin: 'kotlin-android'
3    apply plugin: 'kotlin-android-extensions'
4
5    android {
6        compileSdkVersion 28
7        defaultConfig {
8            applicationId "net.workingdev.ch15getgithubinfo"
```

Figure 15-3. *Sync the gradle file after making your edits*

The OkHttp website has a sample code that shows the basic usage—it's shown in Listing 15-19. It's in Java, but it's easy to adapt it for our use.

Listing 15-19. Sample Code from `http://square.github.io/okhttp/`

```java
OkHttpClient client = new OkHttpClient();

String run(String url) throws IOException {
  Request request = new Request.Builder()
      .url(url)
      .build();

  Response response = client.newCall(request).execute();
  return response.body().string();
}
```

Listing 15-20 shows our Kotlin version of OkHttp's code sample.

Listing 15-20. Our Kotlin Version of OkHttp Code

```kotlin
private fun fetchGitHubInfo(login_id: String): String {
  val url = https://api.github.com/users/$login_id
  val client = OkHttpClient()
  val request = Request.Builder().url(url).build()
  val response = client.newCall(request).execute()
  val bodystr =  response.body().string() // this can be consumed only once

  return bodystr
}
```

That's close enough. By the way, I hope you noticed the second to the last line of Listing 15-20—I even commented it. When you call **response.body.string,** you can consume it only once, so you can't make calls like this:

```
println(response.body.string())          // consumes the content
val bodystr =  response.body().string().  // no more JSON file here
```

The **response.body.string** call is not *idempotent*. You can't make repeated calls to it and expect that it will return the same results on each call.

Now that we've got everything we need, it's time to code the MainActivity. Listing 15-21 shows the full and annotated code for MainActivity.

Listing 15-21. MainActivity, Annotated and Explained

```
import android.support.v7.app.AppCompatActivity
import android.os.Bundle
import com.squareup.okhttp.OkHttpClient
import com.squareup.okhttp.Request
import kotlinx.android.synthetic.main.activity_main.*
import org.jetbrains.anko.activityUiThread
import org.jetbrains.anko.doAsync
import org.json.JSONObject

class MainActivity : AppCompatActivity() {

  override fun onCreate(savedInstanceState: Bundle?) {
    super.onCreate(savedInstanceState)
    setContentView(R.layout.activity_main)

    button.setOnClickListener {
      doAsync {                                                      ❶
        val mgithubinfo = fetchGitHubInfo(txtsearchuser.text.toString())  ❷
        val jsonreader = JSONObject(mgithubinfo)                    ❸
        activityUiThread {                                          ❹
          txtusername.text = jsonreader.getString("name")          ❺
        }
      }
    }
  }
}
```

```
private fun fetchGitHubInfo(login_id: String): String {
  val url = "https://api.github.com/users/$login_id"
  val client = OkHttpClient()
  val request = Request.Builder().url(url).build()
  val response = client.newCall(request).execute()
  val bodystr =  response.body().string() // this can be consumed only once

  return bodystr
}

override fun onResume() {
  super.onResume()

  txtsearchuser.setText("")
  txtsearchuser.setHint("Enter GitHub username")
}
}
```

❶ Anko's **doAsync** block starts here. Everything inside this block will run in a background thread.

❷ Let's pass the current value of the **txtsearchuser** EditText to **fetchGitHubInfo** and assign the resulting JSON object to the *mgithubinfo* variable.

❸ Let's parse *mgithubinfo* with the built-in **JSONObject**.

❹ Now we need to go to back to the UI thread so we can write the result of the http call to the UI.

❺ The **activityUiThread** block lets us come back to the UI thread and make some changes. We're setting the **text** attribute of **txtusername** to the name property of the JSON file.

One more thing to do before we can run the app: we need the add the INTERNET permission to the manifest file.

Listing 15-22. AndroidManifest.xml

```
<?xml version="1.0" encoding="utf-8"?>
<manifest xmlns:android="http://schemas.android.com/apk/res/android"
  package="net.workingdev.ch15getgithubinfo">
  <uses-permission android:name="android.permission.INTERNET"/> ❶
```

```
<application
....
</application>=
</manifest>
```

❶   You should add this to the project's AndroidManifest file.

Figure 15-4 shows the running application.

Figure 15-4. *CH15GetGitHubInfo on an emulator*

Chapter Summary

- **What is jank?** When you try to do too much on the UI Thread, the Android runtime will start dropping frames. When your app's FPS drops, the UI will stutter, it will be sluggish and annoying to use. This is **jank.**

- **How do we avoid it?** Don't try to do too much on UI Thread. **Don't:**

  - Read from a large file, or write a large amount of info to a file.

  - Connect to the network and read from it (or write).

  - Compute a complex routine Do these things in background thread.

- **What is the UI Thread?** It's the original Thread that's responsible for creating (and modifying) View elements in your app. Some developers refer to UI Thread as the "Main Thread."

- **What is a background thread**? Any thread that isn't the UI Thread. You generally create a background thread for your app.

- **What are the ways to create a background thread**? Java Threads, Handlers, AsyncTask, and Anko's doAsync

In the next chapter:

- We'll learn about the kinds of errors that devs face day-to-day.

- We'll also get some tips on how to avoid them.

- We will learn what to do if we get knee-deep in errors.

CHAPTER 16

Debugging

What we'll cover:

- Kind of errors you will encounter
- Logging debug statements
- Walk through codes with the inteactive debugger

Very soon, you will outgrow the simple structure of the example codes presented in this book. Your programs will grow in complexity, number of files, and number of components. As that happens, the number of errors you will face will also grow; and they might be harder to detect by then.

In this chapter, we'll look at the three main types of errors you might encounter and what kinds of tools or techniques could help cope.

Syntax Errors

Syntax errors are exactly what you thought they were: errors in the syntax. It happens because you wrote something in the code that's not allowed in the set-rules of the Kotlin compiler. In other words, the compiler doesn't understand it. This could be as benign as forgetting the closing curly brace or closing parenthesis in an expression. It can also be slightly more complex, such as passing the wrong type of argument to a function or a parameterized class when using generics. In the early days of Android development when all you had to work with the was the bare SDK, you can only know if you have syntactic error when you try to compile your code—this is the reason why other programmers also call this kind of error a "compile time" error. Of course, Android development has come a long way since. We have a very competent IDE that can spot and point out syntax errors even before you try to compile your code. It's almost as if the IDE is continuously reading the code and compiling it.

© Ted Hagos 2018
T. Hagos, *Learn Android Studio 3 with Kotlin*, https://doi.org/10.1007/978-1-4842-3907-0_16

Figure 16-1 shows a snippet of an inner AsyncTask subclass. The IDE draws your attention to it by highlighting the offending code in red squiggly lines.

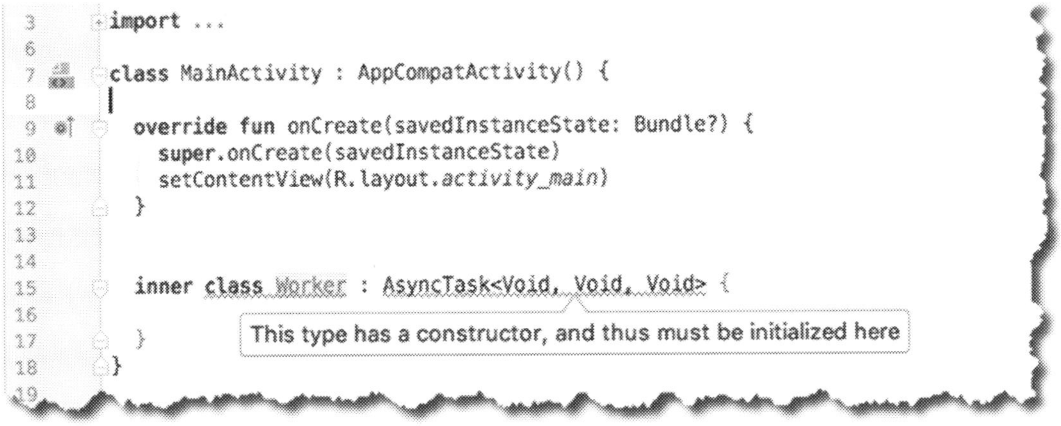

Figure 16-1. *AsyncTask class, missing a constructor*

Hover the mouse long enough in the area where the squiggly lines appear, and you should see AS3's balloon tips. It says the AsyncTask class has a type constructor that must be initialized. To fix it, put the constructor call—a paired parentheses—next to the class definition, as shown in Figure 16-2.

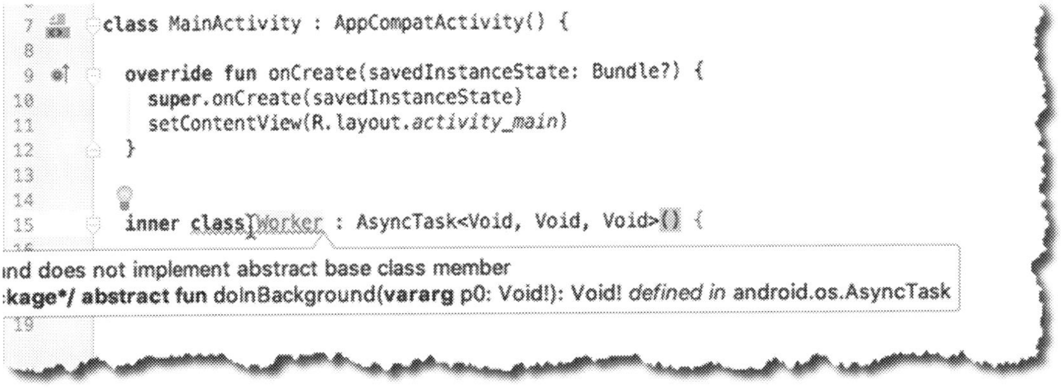

Figure 16-2. *AsyncTask class missing a mandatory implementation*

The squiggly lines are disappearing one by one. That's a good sign—it means we're fixing the errors, but we're not done yet. Did you notice line 15 in Figure 16-2? We still have an error. It says our class doesn't implement a base class member. The AsyncTask class is abstract; it declares the abstract method **doInBackground**. We have to override this method and write our implementation, unless we make class Worker an abstract class also—that's not our intention. Use Android Studio's Quick Fix feature (**option + Enter** in Mac, **alt + Enter** in Windows and Linux) to solve the problem, as shown in Figure 16-2.

Figure 16-3 shows the Quick Fix in action. It's offering some suggestions on how we can fix it. The first option is what we want—to implement and override the abstract member of AsyncTask.

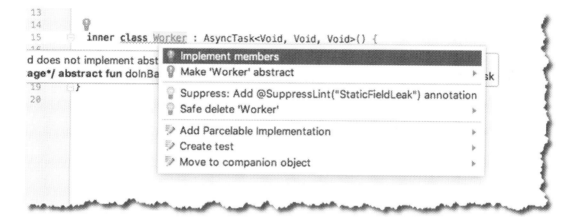

Figure 16-3. *Quick fix on the AsyncTask class*

Click **OK**. What follows next is the dialog window for implementing members, as shown in Figure 16-4. AsyncTask only has one abstract member that needs to be overridden by child classes. Choose **doInBackground** and click **OK** to proceed.

Figure 16-4. *Implement members*

Android Studio will give you a structural skeleton of the **doInBackground** function. Now, you can write your implementation.

There will be times when the error isn't very obvious, even with help of the squiggly lines. Figure 16-5 shows you an example of this problem.

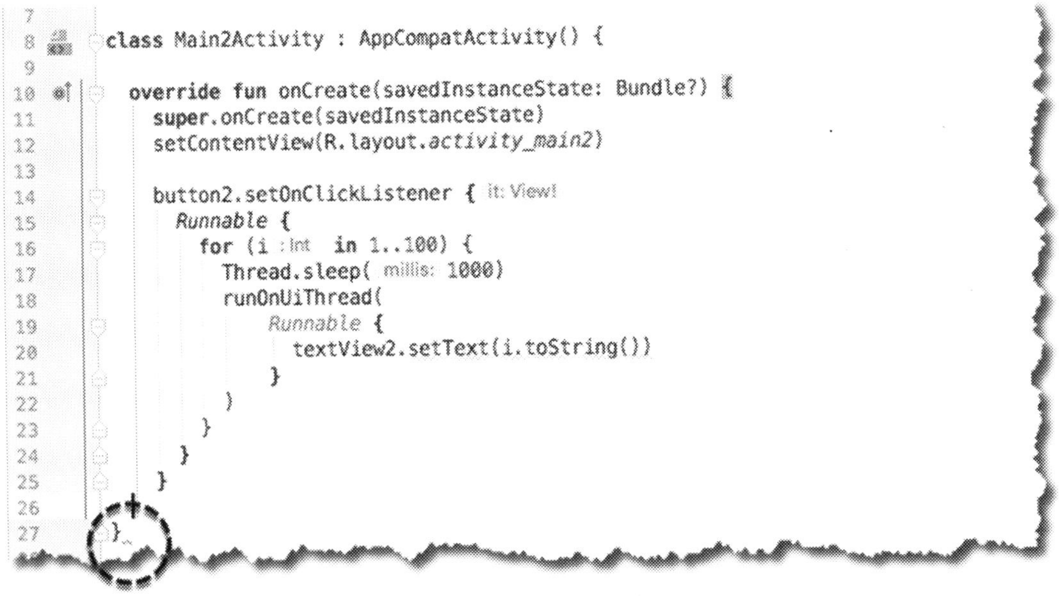

```
 7
 8    class Main2Activity : AppCompatActivity() {
 9
10       override fun onCreate(savedInstanceState: Bundle?) {
11          super.onCreate(savedInstanceState)
12          setContentView(R.layout.activity_main2)
13
14          button2.setOnClickListener { it: View!
15             Runnable {
16                for (i :Int  in 1..100) {
17                   Thread.sleep( millis: 1000)
18                   runOnUiThread(
19                      Runnable {
20                         textView2.setText(i.toString())
21                      }
22                   )
23                }
24             }
25          }
26       }
27    }
```

Figure 16-5. *Nested blocks*

The code between lines 14 and 27 in Figure 16-5 shows a deeply nested block. This can happen sometimes when you use anonymous objects, as you can see from the structure of the example code.

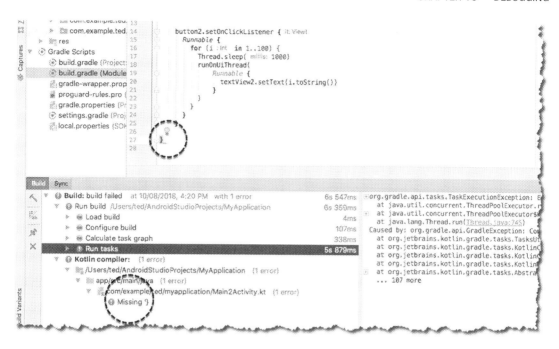

Figure 16-6. *Code with error*

If you try to *Make* the project (from the main menu bar ➤ **Build** ➤ **Make**) the IDE will give you more information, lots more, as you can see in Figure 16-6; but it may not give you more insights. This is one of those situations where you really need to do the heavy lifting. You have to inspect the code structure manually. Notice that the squiggly line appears at the tail-end of class (line 27 in Figure 16-6) and the error message that tells us we're missing a curly brace; start there and inspect the pairs of curly braces manually. This problem has something to do with how we structure our codes. You just need to be careful with those braces—Python programmers are probably gloating right now saying, "That's what you get for using braces, indentation rocks."

Runtime Errors

Runtime errors happen when your code encounters a situation it doesn't expect; and as its name implies, that errant condition is something that appears only when the program is running—it's not something you or the compiler can see at the time of compilation. Your code will compile without problems, but it may stop running when something in the runtime environment doesn't agree with what your code wants to do. There are many examples of these things, for example:

- The app gets something from the Internet—a picture or a file, etc. —so it assumes that the Internet is available and there is network connection. Always. Experience should tell you that isn't always the case. Network connections go down sometimes, and if you don't factor this in your code, it may crash.

- The app needs to read from a file. Just like our first case earlier, your code assumes that the file will always be there. Sometimes, files get corrupted and may become unreadable. This should also be factored in the code.

- The app performs Math calculations. It uses values that are input by users, and sometimes it also uses values that are derived from other calculations. If your code happens to perform a division and in one of those divisions the divisor is zero, that will also cause a runtime problem.

Here are some code samples that may look okay at first glance—and will compile— but when it encounters a condition in the runtime that it's not prepared for, you will get runtime error.

Listing 16-1 shows the basic code for opening a file and reading its contents to a String variable. If the code tries to open a file that exists, there's no problem—the code will work fine and as expected. The problem will come if it tries to open a file that isn't there or is unreadable for some reason.

Listing 16-1. Possible FileNotFoundException or Other IOException

```
override fun onCreate(savedInstanceState: Bundle?) {
  super.onCreate(savedInstanceState)
  setContentView(R.layout.activity_main)

  button.setOnClickListener {
      openFile("doesnotexist.txt")
  }
}
```

```
private fun openFile(file: String) {
  val strFile = File(file).readText()
}
```

Listing 16-2 may look contrived, but imagine if you were getting the input from a user or you're reading the inputs from somewhere else and the divisor becomes zero. You will encounter an ArithmeticException error.

Listing 16-2. Possible ArithmeticException

```
override fun onCreate(savedInstanceState: Bundle?) {
  super.onCreate(savedInstanceState)
  setContentView(R.layout.activity_main)

  button.setOnClickListener {
      divide(10, 0)
  }
}

private fun divide(a:Int, b:Int) : {
  return a / b
}
```

By the way, the **ArithmeticException** is thrown only for Integer values. It doesn't happen for Floats and Doubles. If you try to divide a Float number by zero, it will just yield an Infinity value, but it won't throw an exception.

Another example of a code that will encounter a runtime problem is shown in Listing 16-3. It looks contrived right now because you can obviously see that there's no fifth element of the array. But imagine if you're reading the array from an API (you didn't create the array, somebody else did) and you're not using Integer literals to access the array; instead you're using variables. The error won't be so obvious by then.

Listing 16-3. ArrayIndexOutOfBounds Exception

```
val arr = arrayOf(1,2,3,4)
println(arr[5])
```

The only way to address runtime errors is to:

1. Know your code. You need to know what calls may encounter a runtime exception; and

2. Use proper exception handling in your codes.

Like Java, Kotlin also uses the try-catch structure for handling exceptions; but unlike Java, all of Kotlin's exceptions are *unchecked*. Exception handling is effectively optional in Kotlin—**throws** isn't even a keyword in Kotlin, but the **throw** keyword still is. This may be a good or a bad thing, depending on how you look at it; and there's a lively discussion about this topic on popular coding forums. The opinion of the Kotlin team regarding checked exceptions can be found on the Kotlin docs online (`https://kotlinlang.org/docs/reference/exceptions.html`).

According to the Kotlin team, Kotlin is aimed at large development projects, and there is little evidence that using checked Exceptions contributes to developer productivity; quite the contrary, it lessens it.

Exception handling in Kotlin is, for the most part, exactly like the way you would do it in Java. You can do it with a **try-catch** or **try-catch-finally**. In Java 7, the concept of **try-with**-resources was introduced. Kotlin doesn't have try-with-resources, but it does have the **use** extension; it's the equivalent of try-with-resources.

Just to jog our memories, the basic form of a try-catch block is shown in Listing 16-4.

Listing 16-4. The Try-Catch-Finally Structure

```
try {
  ... ❶
}
catch(mexception: theException) { ❷
  ... ❸
  throw mexception ❹
}
finally {
  ... ❺
}
```

❶ This is the body of the **try** block. This is where you should write calls that may throw Exceptions.

❷ You have to provide, as much as possible, the exact type of Exception in the catch clause (e.g., if you're dealing with FileNotFoundException, then that is what you should write in here in place of **theException).**

❸ This is the body of the **catch** clause. This is where you should write the things you want to do when an exception happens (e.g., log to a file, ask the user repeat the input, etc.).

❹ Occasionally, you may not want to handle the Exception. You can **throw** it back to the caller of the function (next level up the call-stack), and let it be their problem.

❺ The body of the **finally** clause is where you put codes that you want to execute whether or not an exception happens. The body of finally clause is *guaranteed* to be executed always.

Now, let's see how we can use try-catch to prevent a crash when opening a file. See Listing 16-5.

Listing 16-5. How to Handle the FileNotFoundException

```
private fun openFile(file: String) {
  try {                                    ❶
    File(file).useLines {
      println(it)
    }
  }
  catch (fe: FileNotFoundException) {      ❷
    println("do your error handling here")
  }
}
```

❶ The **File** constructor can actually throw a FileNotFoundException, so we put them inside a try-catch block.

❷ We know that **FileNotFoundException** can be thrown by **File** constructor, so that's what we put in the **catch** clause. If you want to match a more general type of Exception, you may also use **IOException** in here. IOException is the parent class of **FileNotFoundException.**

Listing 16-6 shows how to prevent a crash when working with Integer arithmetic.

Listing 16-6. How to Handle the ArithmeticException

```kotlin
private fun divideInt(a:Int, b:Int): Int {
  var result = 0
  try {
    result = a /b
  }
  catch (ae: ArithmeticException) {
    println("handle your exception here")
  }
  finally {
    return result
  }
}
```

Logic Errors

Logic errors are the hardest to find. As its name suggests, it's an error on your logic. When your code is not doing what you thought it should be doing, that's logic error. There are many ways to cope with it, but in this section, we'll take a look at two: printing debugging statements in certain places of your code and code walkthrough using breakpoints.

As you inspect your codes, you will recognize certain areas where you're pretty sure what's going on, and then there are areas where you are less sure—you can place debugging statements in these areas. It's like leaving breadcrumbs for you to follow. There are a couple of ways to print debugging statements. You can either use **println**, **Log,** or the **Logger** class in Java.

Figure 16-7 shows the output of a println statement in Logcat tool window.

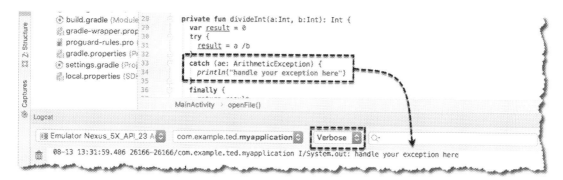

Figure 16-7. println as shown in the Logcat tool window

println is the simplest and the easiest thing you can do to print debugging statements, but remember that you will only see these statements in Logcat if Logcat's mode is set to "verbose," "info," or "debug." If you set the mode to anything else, like warn, error, or assert, you won't see println statements.

When you set Logcat's mode to verbose, info, or debug, you will see all the messages that Android's runtime generates. If you only want to see warn messages or errors, then you need to use either the Log or the Logger class.

The Log class has five static methods; the usage is shown below.

```
Log.v(tag, message) // verbose
Log.d(tag, message) // debug
Log.i(tag, message) // info
Log.w(tag, message) // warning
Log.e(tag, message) // error
```

In each case, **tag** is a String literal or variable. You can use the tag for filtering the messages in the Logcat window. The **message** is also String literal or variable, which contains what you actually want to see in the log. Listing 16-7 shows a sample code on how to use the Log class.

Listing 16-7. How to Use the Log Class

```
val TAG = this@MainActivity::class.toString() ❶

private fun divideInt(a:Int, b:Int): Int {
  var result = 0
  try {
```

```
      Log.d(TAG, "Inside the try")                    ❷
      result = a /b
    }
    catch (ae: ArithmeticException) {
      Log.w(TAG, "Sample log message")                ❸
    }
    finally {
      return result
    }
  }
}
```

---

❶   You can define the TAG anywhere in the class, but in this example, it's defined as class
     property.

❷   We're printing a DEBUG message.

❸   We're printing a WARN message.

Alternatively, we can also use the Logger class from Java; as shown in Listing 16-8.

Listing 16-8. How to Use the Logger Class

```
val Log = Logger.getLogger(MainActivity::class.java.name)

private fun divideInt(a:Int, b:Int): Int {
  var result = 0
  try {
    Log.info("inside try")
    result = a /b
    }
  catch (ae: ArithmeticException) {
    Log.warning("Sample log message")
    println("handle your exception here")
  }
  finally {
    return result
  }
}
```

When you run your app, you can see the Log messages in the Logcat tool window. You can launch it either by clicking its tab in the menu strip at the bottom of the AS3 window or from the main menu bar, **View ➤ Tool Windows ➤ Logcat**. Figure 16-8 shows the Logcat Tool Window.

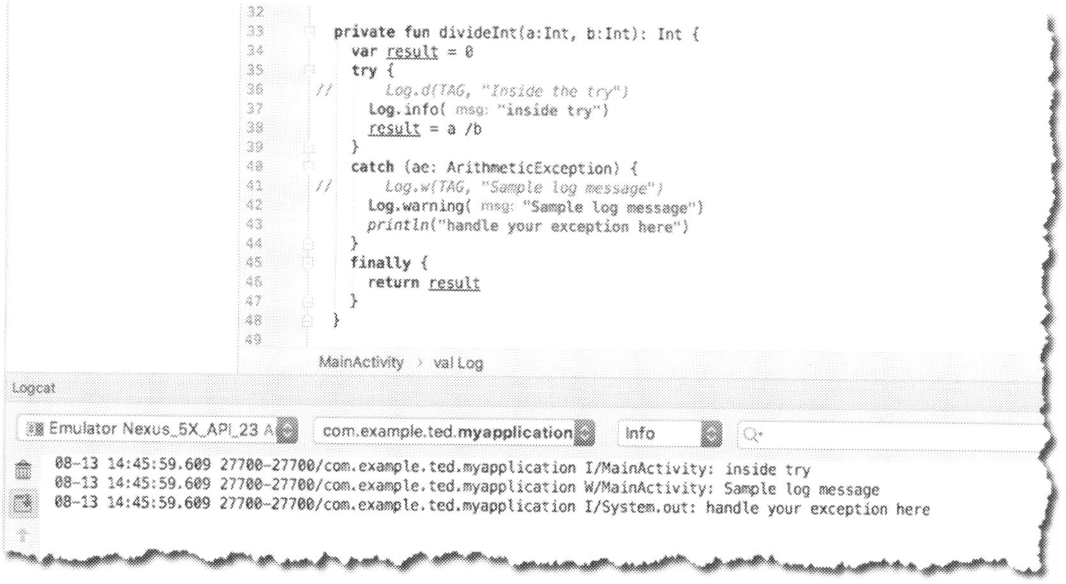

```
32
33          private fun divideInt(a:Int, b:Int): Int {
34              var result = 0
35              try {
36      //          Log.d(TAG, "Inside the try")
37                  Log.info( msg: "inside try")
38                  result = a /b
39              }
40              catch (ae: ArithmeticException) {
41      //          Log.w(TAG, "Sample log message")
42                  Log.warning( msg: "Sample log message")
43                  println("handle your exception here")
44              }
45              finally {
46                  return result
47              }
48          }
49
            MainActivity  ›  val Log
```

```
Logcat

Emulator Nexus_5X_API_23 A    com.example.ted.myapplication    Info    Q-

08-13 14:45:59.609 27700-27700/com.example.ted.myapplication I/MainActivity: inside try
08-13 14:45:59.609 27700-27700/com.example.ted.myapplication W/MainActivity: Sample log message
08-13 14:45:59.609 27700-27700/com.example.ted.myapplication I/System.out: handle your exception here
```

Figure 16-8. *Logcat Tool Window*

Walking Through Code

AS3 includes an interactive debugger that allows you to walk and step through your code as it runs. With the interactive debugger, we can inspect snapshots of the application—values of variables, running threads, etc.—at specific locations in the code and at specific points in time. These specific locations in the code are called *breakpoints*; you get to choose these breakpoints.

To set a breakpoint, choose a line that has an executable statement, then click its line number in the gutter. When you set a breakpoint, there will be a pink circle icon in the gutter, and the whole line is lit in pink, as shown in Figure 16-9.

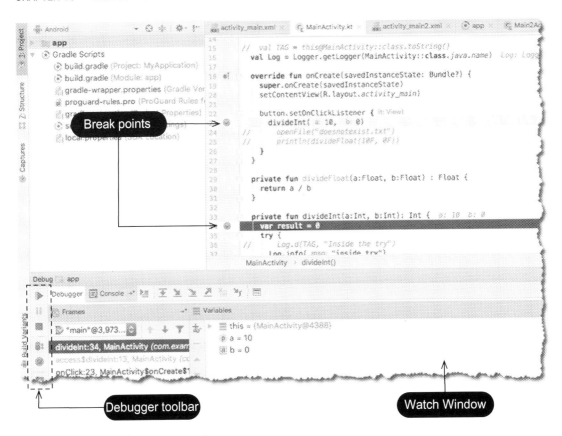

Figure 16-9. *Debugger window*

After the breakpoints are set, you have to to run the app in debug mode. Stop the app if it is currently running, then from the main menu bar, click **Run ➤ Debug App.**

Note   Running the app in debug mode isn't the only way to debug the app. You can also attach the debugger process in a currently running application. There are situations where this second technique is useful—for example, when the bug you are trying to solve occurs on very specific conditions, you may want to run the app for a while, and when you think you are close to the point of error, you can then attach the debugger.

Use the application as usual. When the execution comes to a line where you set a breakpoint, the line turns from pink to blue. This is how you know code execution is at your breakpoint. At this point, the debugger window opens, the execution stops, and AS3 gets into interactive debugging mode. While you are here, the state of the application is displayed in the **Debug tool window**. During this time, you can inspect values of variables and even see the threads running in the app.

You can even add variables or expression in the Watch window by clicking the plus sign with the spectacles icon. There will be a text field where you can enter any valid expression. When you press **Enter**, Android Studio will evaluate the expression and show you the result. To remove a watch expression, select the expression and click the minus sign icon on the watch window.

To resume program execution, you can click the "Resume program" button at the top of the debugger toolbar—it's the green arrow pointing to the right. Alternatively, you can also resume the program from the main menu bar, **Run ➤ Resume Program**. If you want to halt the program before it finishes naturally, you can click the "Stop app" button on the debugger toolbar—it's the red square icon. Alternatively, you can do this also from the main menu bar, **Run ➤ Stop app**

Other Notes

In the early days of Android development, when there were no IDEs yet, developers used a tool called "adb," which is short for Android Debug Bridge. It's a nifty command-line tool that lets you communicate with Android devices (virtual or real). It lets you do things like:

- install apps

- debug apps

- gets you access to shell terminal; Remember that Android is based on Linux, having access to a terminal can be very handy (e.g., when you're doing some white-box testing on a sqlite database, etc.).

Android Studio has taken over some of the things that **adb** used to do (e.g., displaying logs, installing apps, debugging apps, etc.). But, if you need to do things at a linux command line level, you really have to use **adb**—you can find this tool in the **ANDROID_HOME/sdk/platform-tools** folder; where ANDROID_HOME is the folder where you installed the Android SDK.

Another tool we didn't cover in this chapter is the *Android Profiler*, it's new in Android Studio 3.0. It replaced a tool called *Android Device Monitor*. You can use this tool to look at your app's real-time data. You can find out how much CPU, memory, network, and I/O resources your app consumes. You can capture heap dumps, view memory allocations, and inspect the details of network-transmitted files.

Chapter Summary

- The three kinds of errors you may encounter are compile type or syntax errors, runtime errors, and logic errors.

- Syntax errors are the easiest to fix. Android Studio itself bends over backward for you so you can quickly spot syntax errors. There are various ways to fix syntax errors with AS3, but most of the time, the **Quick Fix** should do it.

- Kotlin doesn't have checked Exceptions like Java does. The Kotlin team has good reasons for doing this. If you're a beginner in Kotlin but quite an old hat in Java, then this shouldn't affect you—use your knowledge of the old Java APIs when dealing with possible exceptions. If you're a newcomer to both Kotlin and Java, you should invest a little bit more time in learning about unit testing; that way, you get to see the "happy path" and the "not-so-happy path" of your apps; then you can act accordingly.

- Logic errors are the toughest to find, but Android Studio makes this activity more bearable because of the tools available for us—you can literally walk through the code and inspect things while the program is running.

In the next chapter, we'll look at the following:

- How to save data using SharedPreferences.

- We'll work with the Bundle object so we can save some basic types into a file.

- We'll also look at how we can pass data around among Activities.

CHAPTER 17

SharedPreferences

What we'll cover:

- Introduction to SharedPreferences
- How to put and get data from a preferences file
- How to share a preferences file between Activities

Android apps do not persist your data by default. It's your responsibility to make the data durable and resilient throughout the app's life cycle. Let's say you're collecting data from the user, then midway into your workflow, the application gets interrupted by another app. There is no guarantee that whatever data the user has already input will be there when your app comes back.

Making data durable means storing data in one form or another. You can store data in a couple of ways. They're listed below:

- **SharedPreferences**. This is the simplest option. It's just a dictionary object, it uses the familiar key-value pair mechanics. This is useful if your data is simple enough to be structured as a key-value pair. Android stores these files internally as XML files. You can only store simple data types, like String and basic types. This is usually used for storing user's preferences like sort order on a list, the last page you were reading on an ebook application, etc.

- **Internal or external storage**. Uses the internal or media storage in the device (e.g., sdcard). You can use this to store data that has more complexity in structure (e.g., audio or video files). If you worked with File I/O before, this is no different from that.

© Ted Hagos 2018
T. Hagos, *Learn Android Studio 3 with Kotlin*, https://doi.org/10.1007/978-1-4842-3907-0_17

- **SQLite database**. This one uses a relational database. If you have worked with other databases before like MS SQL server, MySQL, PostgreSQL, or any other relational database, this is essentially the same. Data is stored in tables, and you need to use SQL statements to create, read, update, and delete data.

- **Network Storage**. If you can assume that your users will always have internet access and you have a database server that is hosted on the Internet, then you can use this option. This setup can get a bit complicated because you will need to host the database somewhere (Amazon, Google, any other cloud provider), provide a REST interface for the data, and use an HTTP library as a client in the Android app. We won't cover this topic in this book.

- **ContentProviders**. Content Provider is another component on the Android platform; it's right up there with Activities, Services, and BroadcastReceivers. This component makes data available to applications other than itself. Think of it like a database that has public HTTP API layer. Any application that communicates over HTTP can read and write data to it. By the way, ContentProviders use SQLite databases internally—they just wrap and serve the data in neat HTTP API. If you've worked on RESTful apps that expose some underlying data via API, this is kinda like that.

In this chapter, we'll take a look at SharedPreferences.

A SharedPreferences object lets you store and retrieve data in the form of *key-value* pairs, like a dictionary. It uses XML files for storage. Using a SharedPreferences object to store basic data can be done with the following steps:

1. Get SharedPreferences object. You can do this by calling the **getPreferences** method from within an Activity.

2. Next, we get a **SharedPrefences.Editor** object by using a factory method of the SharedPreferences object.

3. Now we can insert data with the **editor** object.

4. Finally, to store the data permanently, we use either the **commit** or **apply** method on the editor.

Listing 17-1 shows how all these look in code.

Listing 17-1. Basic Steps to Save Data

```
val pref = getPreferences(Context.MODE_PRIVATE) ❶
val editor = pref.edit()  ❷

editor.putString("lastname", "Breslav") ❸
editor.putString("firstname", "Andrey")
editor.apply() ❹
```

❶ The **Activity.getPreferences** method gives us a **SharedPreferences** object that's private to the Activity. We're using the `Context.MODE_PRIVATE` because we'd like the preferences file to allow access only to our app—other apps are off limits.

❷ We need a **SharedPreferences.Editor** object, we can get it by calling **edit** method on a SharedPreferences object.

❸ Now, we can use the various **putXXX** methods to store key-value pairs. The first parameter is the key, this should be a String. The second parameter can be any of the basic types like Int, Float, Double, String, etc.

❹ None of our **putString** calls will be stored permanently to a file if we don't call **apply**. Alternatively you can also call **commit**. The **apply** method saves the data *asynchronously*, while **commit** does it *synchronously*. So, to persist the data, call either apply or commit.

In case you're wondering about the other Context mode options, here they are.

- **MODE_PRIVATE**: the default mode, where the created file can only be accessed by the calling application. This is probably what you want most of the time.

- **MODE_WORLD_READABLE**: Any application can read the preference data. This may cause security holes in applications. Unless you have a very good reason, stay away from this. If you want to make the data available to any application, consider building a ContentProvider instead.

- **MODE_WORLD_WRITEABLE**: Any application can edit the preference data. This may cause security holes in applications. Again, unless you have a good reason, stay away from this.

- **MODE_APPEND**: This will append the new preferences with the already existing preferences.

Let's make a small demo project for this. Table 17-1 shows the details for the project.

Table 17-1. *Details for the Demo Project*

Project Detail	Value
Application name	CH17Preferences
Company domain	use your website name
Kotlin support	Yes
Form factor	Phone and tablet only
Minimum SDK	API 23 Marshmallow
Type of activity	Empty
Activity name	MainActivity
Layout name	activity_main

What we want to do:

1. Let the user input his lastname and firstname—we'll use two EditTexts for this.

2. When the user clicks the "Save" button, we'll store the lastname and firstname to the preferences file.

3. When the user clicks the "Load" button, we'll read the lastname and firstname from the preferences file.

4. We'll display them in a TextView object.

Figure 17-1 shows a screenshot of the running app.

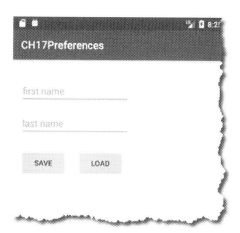

Figure 17-1. *Snapshot of our project, running*

Listing 17-2 contains the full code for the XML layout file, so you can see the attribute settings of the View objects. Listing 17-3 shows the full and annotated code for MainActivity.

Listing 17-2. /app/res/layout/activity_main.xml

```
<?xml version="1.0" encoding="utf-8"?>
<android.support.constraint.ConstraintLayout xmlns:android=http://schemas.
android.com/apk/res/android
  xmlns:app=http://schemas.android.com/apk/res-auto
  xmlns:tools=http://schemas.android.com/tools
  android:layout_width="match_parent"
  android:layout_height="match_parent"
  tools:context=".MainActivity">

  <EditText
    android:id="@+id/txtfirstname"
    android:layout_width="wrap_content"
    android:layout_height="wrap_content"
    android:layout_marginStart="16dp"
    android:layout_marginTop="36dp"
    android:ems="10"
    android:inputType="textPersonName"
    android:text="Name"
```

```
    app:layout_constraintStart_toStartOf="parent"
    app:layout_constraintTop_toTopOf="parent" />

  <EditText
    android:id="@+id/txtlastname"
    android:layout_width="wrap_content"
    android:layout_height="wrap_content"
    android:layout_marginStart="16dp"
    android:layout_marginTop="16dp"
    android:ems="10"
    android:inputType="textPersonName"
    android:text="Name"
    app:layout_constraintStart_toStartOf="parent"
    app:layout_constraintTop_toBottomOf="@+id/txtfirstname" />

  <TextView
    android:id="@+id/txtoutput"
    android:layout_width="wrap_content"
    android:layout_height="wrap_content"
    android:layout_marginBottom="183dp"
    android:layout_marginStart="16dp"
    android:text="TextView"
    android:textSize="36sp"
    app:layout_constraintBottom_toBottomOf="parent"
    app:layout_constraintStart_toStartOf="parent" />

  <Button
    android:id="@+id/btnsave"
    android:layout_width="wrap_content"
    android:layout_height="wrap_content"
    android:layout_marginStart="16dp"
    android:text="save"
    app:layout_constraintBaseline_toBaselineOf="@+id/btnload"
    app:layout_constraintStart_toStartOf="parent" />

  <Button
    android:id="@+id/btnload"
```

```
    android:layout_width="wrap_content"
    android:layout_height="wrap_content"
    android:layout_marginEnd="11dp"
    android:layout_marginTop="27dp"
    android:text="load"
    app:layout_constraintEnd_toEndOf="@+id/txtlastname"
    app:layout_constraintTop_toBottomOf="@+id/txtlastname" />
</android.support.constraint.ConstraintLayout>
```

Listing 17-3. MainActivity, Annotated

```
import android.content.Context
import android.content.SharedPreferences
import android.support.v7.app.AppCompatActivity
import android.os.Bundle
import android.widget.Toast
import kotlinx.android.synthetic.main.activity_main.*

class MainActivity : AppCompatActivity() {

  override fun onCreate(savedInstanceState: Bundle?) {
    super.onCreate(savedInstanceState)
    setContentView(R.layout.activity_main)

    val pref = getPreferences(Context.MODE_PRIVATE)               ❶

    btnsave.setOnClickListener {
      val editor = pref.edit()                                    ❷

      editor.putString("lastname", txtlastname.text.toString())   ❸
      editor.putString("firstname", txtfirstname.text.toString())
      editor.apply()                                              ❹

      Toast.makeText(this, "Saved data", Toast.LENGTH_LONG).show()
    }

    btnload.setOnClickListener {
      val mlastname = pref.getString("lastname", "")              ❺
      val mfirstname = pref.getString("firstname", "")
```

```
      val moutput = "$mfirstname $mlastname"                            ❻

      txtoutput.text = moutput                                         ❼

    }
  }

  override fun onResume() {                                            ❽
    super.onResume()

    txtfirstname.setText("")
    txtlastname.setText("")
    txtfirstname.setHint("first name")
    txtlastname.setHint("last name")

    txtoutput.setText("")
  }
}
```

❶ Get a **SharedPreferences** object.

❷ Get a **SharedPreferences.Editor** object.

❸ Save the runtime value of the EditText (txtlastname); let's use "lastname" as key.

❹ Save the data asynchronously by calling **apply** instead of **commit.**

❺ We're inside the "Load" button listener now. Let's get the value of the "lastname" key and save it to a temporary variable.

❻ Concatenates the lastname and firstname variables

❼ Sets the **text** attribute of the TextView (txtoutput) to the concatenated lastname and firstname

❽ Inside the **onResume** callback, we initialized the text attributes of txtlastname, txtfirstname, and txtoutput. We also set the hint attributes of the textfields.

Android will create an XML file to store the preference, and it will be named after the Activity that created it; in our case, it's MainActivity.

If you want to inspect the file, you can download it using the Device File Explorer (it used to be called Android Device Monitor). Go to the main menu bar, then **View ➤ Tool Windows ➤ Device File Explorer.** You should see a screen similar to Figure 17-2.

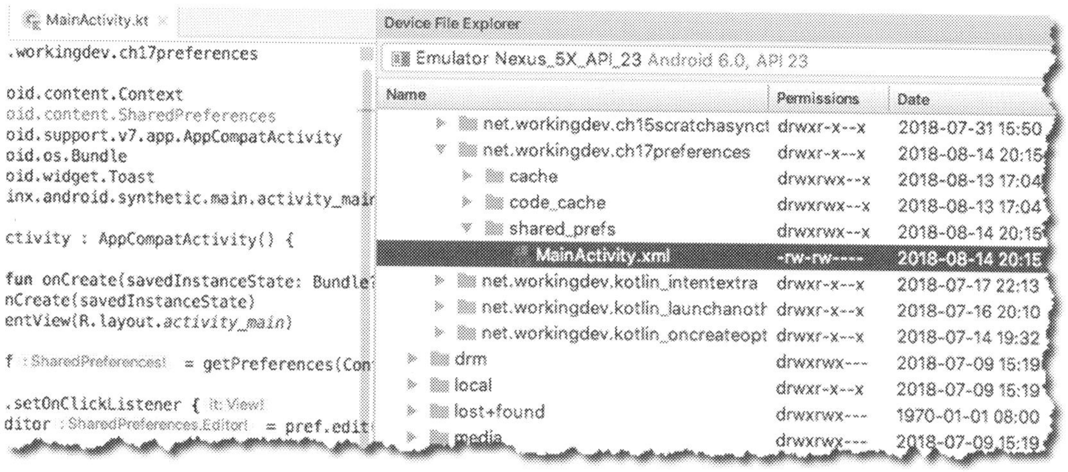

Figure 17-2. *MainActivity.xml file in Device File Explorer*

Next, drill down to **data ➤ data ➤ fullyQualifiedNameOfProject** (which in my case is net.workingdev.ch17preferences; substitute your own project name); then, drill down further to **shared_prefs ➤ MainActivity.xml**, as shown in Figure 17-2.

If you double-click the MainActivity.xml file, Android Studio will display its contents in the main editor. Alternatively, you can also download it to your PC. Use the context-sensitive menu (right-click) on MainActivity.xml, as shown in Figure 17-3, then "Save As." You can then open the XML file with your program editor.

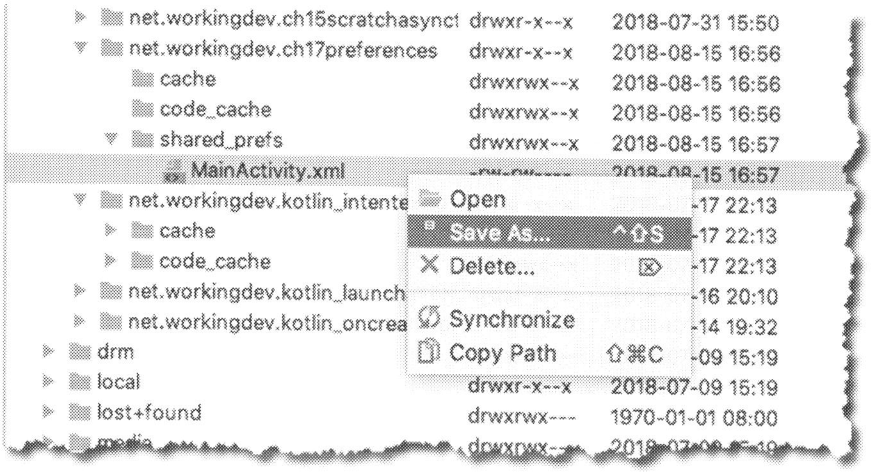

Figure 17-3. *Save the XML file to a computer*

Listing 17-4 shows the contents of the MainActivity.xml preferences file.

Listing 17-4. Contents of MainActivity.xml

```
<?xml version='1.0' encoding='utf-8' standalone='yes' ?>
<map>
    <string name="lastname">hagos</string>
    <string name="firstname">ted</string>
</map>
```

Keep in mind that the preference file we created here can only be accessed by the MainActivity class. If you need to share the preference file with other Activities in the app, you need to create an application level preferences.

Sharing Data Between Activities

To make a preference file available to all Activities in app, we only need to make a minor change in our code.

Listing 17-5. How to Create an Application Level Preferences File

```
val filename = "$packageName TESTFILE"                    ❶
val pref = getSharedPreferences(filename, Context.MODE_PRIVATE)    ❷
val editor = pref.edit()

editor.putString("lastname", "Breslav")
editor.putString("firstname", "Andrey")
editor.apply()
```

---

❶ **packageName** is actually a call to **getPackageName()**. We're just constructing a file name in this line.

❷ **This is the only change we need to make**; instead of calling **getPreferences**, let's use **getSharedPreferences**. This function takes in two parameters. You already know the second one, and it's easy to guess what the first parameter is for. The first parameter specifies a filename for the preferences file.

Actually, **getPreferences** (our example in the previous section) is just a wrapper call to **getSharedPreferences**, the former simply passes the name of current Activity as the first parameter to the latter.

To retrieve data from the shared preferences file, use the **getSharedPreferences** again, specifying which file to read from, then use the **getString** methods, as shown in Listing 17-6.

Listing 17-6. How to Read From an Application Preferences File

```kotlin
val pref = getSharedPreferences("$packageName TESTFILE", Context.MODE_
PRIVATE)  ❶

val mlastname = pref.getString("lastname", "")  ❷
val mfirstname = pref.getString("firstname", "")
```

❶   Get a SharedPreferences object. Specify the name of the preferences file by passing it as a the first parameter.

❷   First parameter is the key; it's the name of the preference to retrieve. The second parameter is a default value, in case the key doesn't exist.

Let's do another small demo project for this. Table 17-2 shows the project details.

Table 17-2. *Project Details*

Project Detail	Value
Application name	CH17SharedPreferences
Company domain	use your website name
Kotlin support	Yes
Form factor	Phone and Tablet only
Minimum SDK	API 23 Marshmallow
Type of activity	Empty
Activity name	MainActivity
Layout name	activity_main

What we want to do:

1. Let the user input his lastname and firstname; we'll use two EditTexts for this.

2. When the user clicks the "Go to 2nd Activity" button, we'll create an Intent that will launch "SecondActivity."

3. Before MainActivity enters the paused state, we'll save the lastname and firstname data into the specified preferences file.

4. We'll display the "Click LOAD DATA" hint into a TextView, as the SecondActivity comes to the user's view.

5. As the "Load Data" button is clicked, we'll retrieve the preferences file and display it as the text attribute of the TextView.

Figure 17-4 shows us a basic storyboard for our app.

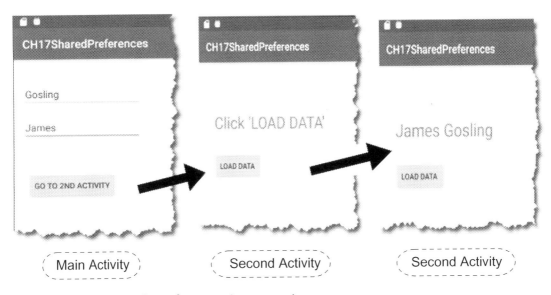

Figure 17-4. *Snapshot of our project, running*

Listings 17-7 and 17-8 show the full codes for activity_main.xml and activity_second. xml, so you can see the attributes of the View objects.

Listing 17-7. /app/res/layout/activity_main.xml

```xml
<?xml version="1.0" encoding="utf-8"?>
<android.support.constraint.ConstraintLayout xmlns:android=http://schemas.
android.com/apk/res/android
  xmlns:app=http://schemas.android.com/apk/res-auto
  xmlns:tools=http://schemas.android.com/tools
  android:layout_width="match_parent"
  android:layout_height="match_parent"
  tools:context=".MainActivity"
  tools:layout_editor_absoluteY="81dp">

  <EditText
    android:id="@+id/txtlastname"
    android:layout_width="wrap_content"
    android:layout_height="wrap_content"
    android:layout_marginStart="16dp"
    android:layout_marginTop="40dp"
    android:ems="10"
    android:inputType="textPersonName"
    android:text="Name"
    app:layout_constraintStart_toStartOf="parent"
    app:layout_constraintTop_toTopOf="parent" />

  <EditText
    android:id="@+id/txtfirstname"
    android:layout_width="wrap_content"
    android:layout_height="wrap_content"
    android:layout_marginStart="16dp"
    android:layout_marginTop="15dp"
    android:ems="10"
    android:inputType="textPersonName"
    android:text="Name"
    app:layout_constraintStart_toStartOf="parent"
    app:layout_constraintTop_toBottomOf="@+id/txtlastname" />
```

```
    <Button
      android:id="@+id/button"
      android:layout_width="wrap_content"
      android:layout_height="wrap_content"
      android:layout_marginStart="24dp"
      android:layout_marginTop="57dp"
      android:text="Go to 2nd Activity"
      app:layout_constraintStart_toStartOf="parent"
      app:layout_constraintTop_toBottomOf="@+id/txtfirstname" />

</android.support.constraint.ConstraintLayout>
```

Listing 17-8. /app/res/activity_second.xml

```
<?xml version="1.0" encoding="utf-8"?>
<android.support.constraint.ConstraintLayout xmlns:android=http://schemas.
android.com/apk/res/android
  xmlns:app=http://schemas.android.com/apk/res-auto
  xmlns:tools=http://schemas.android.com/tools
  android:layout_width="match_parent"
  android:layout_height="match_parent"
  tools:context=".SecondActivity"
  tools:layout_editor_absoluteY="81dp">

    <Button
      android:id="@+id/btnloaddata"
      android:layout_width="wrap_content"
      android:layout_height="wrap_content"
      android:layout_marginStart="34dp"
      android:layout_marginTop="33dp"
      android:text="Load data "
      app:layout_constraintStart_toStartOf="parent"
      app:layout_constraintTop_toBottomOf="@+id/txtoutput" />

    <TextView
      android:id="@+id/txtoutput"
      android:layout_width="wrap_content"
      android:layout_height="wrap_content"
```

```
    android:layout_marginStart="34dp"
    android:layout_marginTop="87dp"
    android:text="TextView"
    android:textSize="30sp"
    app:layout_constraintStart_toStartOf="parent"
    app:layout_constraintTop_toTopOf="parent" />
</android.support.constraint.ConstraintLayout>
```

That takes care of the layout. In MainActivity, all we need to do are the following:

1. Take some input from the user, the lastname and firstname.

2. When the button is clicked, launch SecondActivity using an explicit Intent.

3. Before MainActivity gets into the "paused" state, let's save the preferences file.

Listing 17-9 shows the full and annotated code for MainActivity.

Listing 17-9. MainActivity, Annotated

```
import android.content.Context
import android.content.Intent
import android.content.SharedPreferences
import android.support.v7.app.AppCompatActivity
import android.os.Bundle
import android.widget.Toast
import kotlinx.android.synthetic.main.activity_main.*

class MainActivity : AppCompatActivity() {

  override fun onCreate(savedInstanceState: Bundle?) {
    super.onCreate(savedInstanceState)
    setContentView(R.layout.activity_main)

    button.setOnClickListener {
      val intent = Intent(this@MainActivity, SecondActivity::class.java) ❶
      startActivity(intent)
    }
  }
```

```kotlin
override fun onPause() {
  super.onPause()
  saveData()        ❷
}

private fun saveData() {    ❸

  val filename = "$packageName TESTFILE"
  val pref = getSharedPreferences(filename, Context.MODE_PRIVATE)
  val edit = pref.edit()

  edit.putString("lastname", txtlastname.text.toString())
  edit.putString("firstname", txtfirstname.text.toString())
  edit.apply()

  Toast.makeText(this, "Saved data", Toast.LENGTH_LONG).show() ❹
}

override fun onResume() { ❺
  super.onResume()

  txtfirstname.setText("")
  txtlastname.setText("")
  txtfirstname.setHint("first name")
  txtlastname.setHint("last name")
}
}
```

---

❶ We're creating an explicit Intent that will launch SecondActivity. We won't save the preferences file in here—we'll do that later in the **onPause** callback.

❷ Let's call the **saveData** function from here. The onPause function will be called by the Android runtime before MainActivity disappears from the user's view, and eventually enter the "paused" state.

❸ The **saveData** function is where we do the actual persisting of the preferences file. You've seen all these codes before, so we won't annotate them anymore.

❹   A simple Toast message to tell the user that we've saved the data

❺   Android runtime will call the **onResume** function before MainActivity becomes fully visible to the user again, if it's coming from a "paused" state. I thought it was best to reinitialize all the UI elements in here.

That's all we need to do in MainActivity. In SecondActivity, we need to read the specified preferences file when the button is clicked. Listing 17-10 shows the full and annotated code for SecondActivity.

Listing 17-10. SecondActivity

```
import android.content.Context
import android.support.v7.app.AppCompatActivity
import android.os.Bundle
import kotlinx.android.synthetic.main.activity_second.*

class SecondActivity : AppCompatActivity() {

  override fun onCreate(savedInstanceState: Bundle?) {
    super.onCreate(savedInstanceState)
    setContentView(R.layout.activity_second)

    btnloaddata.setOnClickListener {
    val filename = "$packageName TESTFILE"
    val pref = getSharedPreferences(filename, Context.MODE_PRIVATE) ❶

      val mlastname = pref.getString("lastname", "") ❷
      val mfirstname = pref.getString("firstname", "")

      txtoutput.text = "$mfirstname $mlastname " ❸
    }
  }

  override fun onResume() {
    super.onResume()

    txtoutput.text = "Click 'LOAD DATA'"
  }
}
```

❶   When the button is clicked, let's read the specified preferences file.

❷   Let's extract the lastname (and the firstname as well).

❸   Concatenate the lastname and firstname data, and show it as the text attribute of the TextView.

That should get you started with SharedPreferences. Before we close the chapter, I'd like to leave you with a couple more pieces of information about the *SharedPreferences.Editor* object. You already know that it's **commit** or **apply** function is the one responsible for actually persisting the file. It also has other functions such as clear and remove. Here's what they do:

- **remove(String parameter).** This call deletes a named preference. The String parameter stands for the key. So, a call like remove("lastname") will remove the lastname key from the preferences file.

- **clear().** Removes all the keys in the preference file.

I'll leave it up to you to experiment on these two Editor functions.

Chapter Summary

- Android has a couple of ways to persist data. It ranges from simple mechanisms SharedPreferences up until the robust and a couple more complicated ContentProviders and HTTP databases like FireBase.

- SharedPreferences uses a dictionary-like or a Map-like idiom. It stores the data in key-value pairs.

- You can make a preference file private to an Activity, or you can make it available to all Activities in the app.

In the next chapter, we'll look at another way to save data into files; however, it won't be limited to basic types. You'll learn how to work with file without an imposed structure (like key-value pairs).

CHAPTER 18

Internal Storage

What we'll cover:

- Introduction to file I/O of Android

- Internal vs External storage

- How to use internal storage

We learned how to use the preferences file in the previous chapter. SharedPreferences use a dictionary-like structure, you can save rows of data in key-value format; but you can only save basic types in it. When you need to work with file structures that are not limited to key-value pair and basic types, you can use the good ole file classes from Java I/O (input/output). That's the topic of this chapter.

Overview of File Storage

When you need to work with video, audio, json, or just plain text files, you can use the Java file I/O for local files. You'll use the same **File**, **InputStream,** and **OutputWriter** and other **I/O** classes in Java—if you've worked with them before. What will be different in Android is where you save them. In a Java desktop application, you can put your files practically anywhere you want. That's not the case in Android. Just like in a Java web application, Android apps are not free to create and read files just about anywhere. There are certain places where your app has read and write access.

Don't worry if you haven't used Java I/O before, we won't use any codes that are difficult to follow. All I/O routines we will use will be within the capabilities of a beginner.

© Ted Hagos 2018
T. Hagos, *Learn Android Studio 3 with Kotlin*, https://doi.org/10.1007/978-1-4842-3907-0_18

Internal and External Storage

Android differentiates between internal and external storage. The *internal* storage refers to that part of a flash drive that's shared among all installed applications. The *external* storage refers to a storage space that can be mounted by the user—it's typically an sdcard, but it doesn't have to be. As long as it can be mounted by the user, it could be anything; it could even be a portion of the internal flash drive.

Each option has pros and cons, so you need to consider your app's needs and the limitation of each option. The following list shows some of these pros and cons.

Internal storage

- The memory is always available to your app. There is no danger of a user unmounting the sdcard or whatever device. It's guaranteed to be there always.

- The storage space will be smaller in size than an external storage because your app will be allocated only a portion of the flash storage that is shared by all the other apps. This was a concern in earlier versions of Android, but it's less of a concern now. According to the Android Compatibility Definition, as of Android 6.0, an Android phone or tablet must have at least 1.5 GB of non-volatile space reserved for user space (the/data partition). This space should be plenty for most apps. You can read the compatibility definition here `https://bit.ly/android6compatibilitydefinition`.

- When your app creates files in this space, only your app can access them. Except when the phone is rooted, but most users don't root their phones, so generally, it isn't much of a concern.

- When you uninstall your app, all the files it created will be deleted.

External Storage

- It typically has more space than internal storage; but

- it may not always be available (e.g., when the user removes the sdcard or if it's mounted as USB drive.

- All files in here are visible to all applications and to the user. Anybody and any app can create and save files here. They can also delete files.

- When an app creates a file in this space, it can outlive the app; by that I mean when you uninstall the app, the file won't be removed.

Cache Directory

Whether you choose internal or external storage, you may still have to make one more decision on file location. You can put your files on a cache directory or somewhere more permanent. Files in a cache directory may be reclaimed by the Android OS or third-party apps, if the space will be needed. All files that are not in the cache directory are pretty safe, unless you delete them manually. In this chapter, we won't work with cache directories or external storage. We will use only the internal storage, and we'll put the files in the standard location.

How to Work with Internal Storage

As said earlier, working with file storage in Android is like working with the usual classes in Java I/O. There are few options to use like **openFileInput()** and **openFileOutput(),** or some other ways where you can use **InputStreams** and **OutputStreams**. You just need to remember that these calls will not let you specify the file paths. You can only provide the filename, if you're not concerned with that, go ahead and use them—it's what we will use in this chapter, actually. If, on the other hand, you need more flexibility, you can use the **getFilesDir()** or **getCacheDir()** to get a **File** object that points to the root of your file locations—use **getCacheDir()** if you want to work with the cache directories of the internal storage. When you have a **File** object, you can create your own directory and file structure from there.

That's the general lay of the territory when it comes to Android file storage. Again, in this chapter, we'll only work with internal storage in the standard location (not cache).

Writing to a file requires a few simple steps. You need to:

1. Decide on a file name

2. Get a FileOutputStream object

3. Convert your content to a ByteArray

4.   Write the ByteArray using the FileOutputStream

5.   Don't forget to close the file

Listing 18-1 shows us how it looks in code.

Listing 18-1. How to Save to a File

```
val filename = "ourfile.txt"
val out = openFileOutput(filename, Context.MODE_PRIVATE) ❶
out.use { ❷
  out.write(txtinput.text.toString().toByteArray()) ❸
}
```

❶   **openFileOutput** returns a FileOutputStream; we need this object so we can write to a file. The first parameter of the call is the name of the file you want to create. The second parameter is a Context mode; you already know this from the previous chapter. We're using MODE_PRIVATE because we want the file to be private to the app.

❷   The **use** extension means I don't have to close the file explicitly or manually. As soon as we're done using it, the Android runtime will close it for us. This is pretty handy considering that a lot of developers forget to close files. Leaving a file handle open until the app terminates causes memory leak. The **use** extension is Kotlin's equivalent of Java's **try-with-resources.**

❸   The **write** method expects a ByteArray. So, we need to convert the Editable (data type of EditText) to a String, then convert it to a ByteArray.

Reading from a file involves more steps than writing to it. You generally need to do the following:

1.   Get a FileInputStream

2.   Read from the stream, one byte at a time

3.   Keep on reading until there's nothing more to read. You'll know when you're at the end of the file if the value of the last byte you've read is **-1**. It's time to stop by then.

4.   As you work your way to the end of the file, you need to store the bytes you're taking from the stream into a temporary container. A StringBuilder or a StringBuffer should do the trick. Building a

String object using the plus operator is wasteful and inefficient because Strings are immutable. Each time you use the plus operator, it creates a new String object; if your file has 2,000 characters in it, you would have created 2,000 String objects.

This will be the case if you're reading a text file. If you're reading something else like an audio or video file, you'll use a different data structure.

5. When you reach the end of the file, stop reading. Do what you need to do with what you've read and don't forget to close the file.

Listing 18-2 shows us how this looks in code.

Listing 18-2. How to Read From a File

```
val filename = "ourfile.txt"
val input = openFileInput(filename) ❶

input.use {
  var buffer = StringBuilder() ❷
  var bytes_read = input.read() ❸
  while(bytes_read != -1) { ❹
    buffer.append(bytes_read.toChar()) ❺
    bytes_read = input.read() ❻
  }
  println(buffer.toString()) ❼
}
```

❶ **openFileInput** returns a FileInputStream; this is the object we need so can read from a file. The only parameter it takes is the name of the file to read.

❷ We won't be able to read the entire file in one fell swoop. We'll read it by chunks. As we get some chunks, we'll store them inside the StringBuilder object.

❸ The **read** method reads a byte of data from the input stream and returns it as an integer. We need to keep reading from the stream one byte at a time until we reach the end of file (EOF) marker.

❹ When there are no more bytes to read from the stream, the EOF is marked as **-1**. We will use this as the condition for the **while** loop. Until **bytes_read** isn't equal to **-1** yet, just keep on reading.

❺   The **read** method returns an int; it's the ASCII value of each letter in the file, returned as integer. We have to convert it to a **Char** before we can put it in the StringBuilder.

❻   If we're not at EOF yet, let's read another byte.

❼   When we run out of bytes to read, we'll get out of the loop and print the content of StringBuilder.

Of course, we'll do small demo project. It solidifies our learning. Table 18-1 shows the details for the demo project.

Table 18-1. *Project Details*

Project Detail	Value
Application name	CH18InternalStorage
Company domain	use your website name
Kotlin support	Yes
Form factor	Phone and Tablet only
Minimum SDK	API 23 Marshmallow
Type of activity	Empty
Activity name	MainActivity
Layout name	activity_main

What we want to do:

1.   We'll set up two activities: MainActivity and SecondActivity.

2.   In MainActivity, the user can freely type text in a multiline EditText.

3.   When the button "2ⁿᵈ Activity" is clicked, we'll launch an explicit Intent to open SecondActivity.

4.   But before we leave MainActivity, we'll create a file and save the contents of the EditText to that file. This call isn't terribly expensive, but we'll run this code in background thread because it's an I/O call. You can never be sure if an I/O call will be more or less than 16 ms, so err in the side of caution.

5. In SecondActivity, as soon as it becomes visible to the user, we will read the contents of the file (that one we just saved in MainActivity) and show it to the user using a multiline TextEdit.

6. Still in SecondActivity, when the user clicks the button "1st Activity," we'll launch an explicit Intent to go back to the MainActivity.

7. In MainActivity's onResume, we'll try to read the file and make it available for editing.

Figure 18-1 shows the two screens of our app.

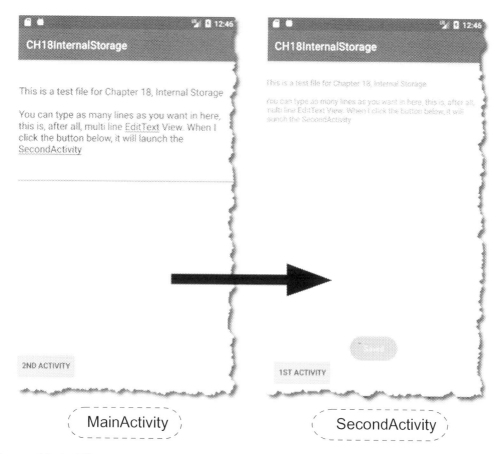

Figure 18-1. *The app, at runtime*

Listings 18-3 and 18-4 show the full codes for activity_main.xml (UI for MainActivity. Kt) and activity_second.xml (UI for SecondActivity.Kt), respectively.

Listing 18-3. /app/res/layout/activity_main.xml

```xml
<?xml version="1.0" encoding="utf-8"?>
<android.support.constraint.ConstraintLayout xmlns:android=http://schemas.
android.com/apk/res/android
  xmlns:app=http://schemas.android.com/apk/res-auto
  xmlns:tools=http://schemas.android.com/tools
  android:layout_width="match_parent"
  android:layout_height="match_parent"
  tools:context=".MainActivity">

  <EditText
    android:id="@+id/txtinput"
    android:layout_width="0dp"
    android:layout_height="wrap_content"
    android:layout_marginTop="34dp"
    android:ems="10"
    android:inputType="textMultiLine"
    app:layout_constraintEnd_toEndOf="parent"
    app:layout_constraintStart_toStartOf="parent"
    app:layout_constraintTop_toTopOf="parent" />

  <Button
    android:id="@+id/btnsecondactivity"
    android:layout_width="wrap_content"
    android:layout_height="wrap_content"
    android:layout_marginBottom="16dp"
    android:layout_marginTop="8dp"
    android:text="2nd Activity"
    app:layout_constraintBottom_toBottomOf="parent"
    app:layout_constraintTop_toBottomOf="@+id/txtinput"
    app:layout_constraintVertical_bias="0.963"
    tools:layout_editor_absoluteX="16dp" />
</android.support.constraint.ConstraintLayout>
```

Next comes the xml definition for activity_second.

Listing 18-4. /app/res/layout/activity_second.xml

```xml
<?xml version="1.0" encoding="utf-8"?>
<android.support.constraint.ConstraintLayout xmlns:android=http://schemas.
android.com/apk/res/android
  xmlns:app=http://schemas.android.com/apk/res-auto
  xmlns:tools=http://schemas.android.com/tools
  android:layout_width="match_parent"
  android:layout_height="match_parent"
  tools:context=".SecondActivity">

  <Button
    android:id="@+id/btnmainactivity"
    android:layout_width="wrap_content"
    android:layout_height="wrap_content"
    android:layout_marginBottom="18dp"
    android:layout_marginStart="16dp"
    android:text="1st activity"
    app:layout_constraintBottom_toBottomOf="parent"
    app:layout_constraintStart_toStartOf="parent" />

  <TextView
    android:id="@+id/txtoutput"
    android:layout_width="0dp"
    android:layout_height="wrap_content"
    android:layout_marginTop="29dp"
    android:inputType="textMultiLine"
    android:text="TextView"
    app:layout_constraintEnd_toEndOf="parent"
    app:layout_constraintStart_toStartOf="parent"
    app:layout_constraintTop_toTopOf="parent" />

</android.support.constraint.ConstraintLayout>
```

There's a couple of things going on for MainActivity. Before we look at the full code, let's look at its important sections first.

When MainActivity opens, we run some code that checks if "ourfile.txt" (the name of the file) already exists. If it does, we'll read it and display the contents in the EditText, so the user can edit it. This code is inside the **onResume()** callback, this is a good place to put the code because the runtime calls it as soon as the Activity is visible to the user.

Listing 18-5 shows the **onResume** callback and the **loadData** function. I annotated three points only—from where to call **loadData** and the beginning/ending lines of all the codes related to file input/output. You're already familiar with the rest of the codes since they've been explained earlier in this chapter and/or in earlier chapters.

The code is straightforward, but it may be structurally challenging for a beginner. So, let's take it step by step.

Listing 18-5. loadData Function

```kotlin
val Log = Logger.getLogger(MainActivity::class.java.name)

override fun onResume() {
  super.onResume()
  loadData()                                              ❶
}

private fun loadData() {

  val filename = "ourfile.txt"
  Thread(Runnable{
    try {
      val input = openFileInput(filename)             ❷
      input.use {
        var buffer = StringBuilder()
        var bytes_read = input.read()

        while(bytes_read != -1) {
          buffer.append(bytes_read.toChar())
          bytes_read = input.read()
        }
        runOnUiThread(Runnable{
          txtinput.setText(buffer.toString())
        })
      }                                                 ❸
    }
```

```
    catch(fnfe:FileNotFoundException) {
      Log.warning("file not found, occurs only once")
    }
    catch(ioe: IOException) {
      Log.warning("IOException : $ioe")
    }
  }).start()
}
```

❶ Let's call **loadData()** as soon as the Activity is visible to the user; this happens inside the **onResume** callback.

❷ Start of I/O code

❸ End of I/O code. The rest is boiler-plate for Threading and Exception.

Focus on the codes between points ❷ and ❸ of Listing 18-5. They are the only ones important for reading the file. The **Thread**, **Runnable**, **runOnUiThread**, **try,** and **catch** are all housekeeping codes. They're there because we're trying to code defensively. We're running in the background because the I/O code might take some time to complete. We're using the try-catch block because the I/O codes might throw an Exception. We used the **runOnUiThread** because we can't write anything to the UI while we're inside a background thread. Those are the reasons for the structural acrobatics.

Listing 18-6 shows the **loadData** function again, but this time without the I/O codes. You only get to see the housekeeping codes.

Listing 18-6. loadData Without the I/O Codes

```
Thread(Runnable {
  ...                            ❶
  try {
    ...                          ❷
    runOnUiThread(Runnable {
      ...                        ❸
    })
  }
```

```
catch(ioe:IOException) {
   ...                              ❹
}
}).start()                         ❺
```

---

❶   Run your background code here. All of our file input/out codes are here.

❷   This is where you write codes that **can throw Exceptions**. Java I/O calls can throw Exceptions—that's why we need to put them here.

❸   If you need to update the UI, you have to come back to the UI Thread. You cannot make changes to the UI while in a background thread.

❹   If an Exception does happen, do whatever you need to do here so the app can recover. At the very least, log something here, so you'll see what errors occurred when you look at the logs later. The benefit of handling Exceptions explicitly (like this) is that the app won't crash if it encounters something unfavorable during runtime. This way, you have a chance to recover gracefully.

❺   The **start** method kicks the Thread into high gear. It gets the Thread, well, started.

Points ❶ to ❺ contain everything that's running in a background thread. The basic structure of that overstretched statement is this `Thread(Runnable { ... }).start()`. All the I/O codes and the try-catch block are written in place of the ellipsis.

Next, when the app is fully visible to the user, it waits for input. The user can add text in the multiline EditText. If the user clicks the "2nd Activity" button, we'll launch SecondActivity with an explicit Intent. MainActivity transitions from "running" to "paused" state, but before that happens, the runtime will call MainActivity's **onPause** method. This is where we'll write our codes to save the data to a file. Listing 18-7 shows the annotated saveData function.

Listing 18-7. annotated saveData function

```
private fun saveData() {
  val filename = "ourfile.txt"
  Thread(Runnable {                                              ❶
    try {
      val out = openFileOutput(filename, Context.MODE_PRIVATE)   ❷
      out.use {
        out.write(txtinput.text.toString().toByteArray())        ❸
      }
```

```
      runOnUiThread(Runnable {                                   ❹
        Toast.makeText(this, "Saved", Toast.LENGTH_LONG).show()
      })
    }
    catch(ioe:IOException) {
      Log.warning("Error while saving ${filename} : ${ioe}")
    }
  }).start()
}

override fun onPause() {
  super.onPause()
  saveData()
}
```

---

❶   We'll run in a background thread because it's an I/O call.

❷   Let's open a file for input. This gives us a **FileInputStream**. Pass the name of the file as first parameter and the context mode for the second parameter.

❸   Now we can write to the file. Remember that you can only write an array of bytes in a FileInputStream object, so you have to convert the runtime value of the EditText to a ByteArray.

❹   Now we have to go back to the UI thread, even if we're only going to show a Toast message.

Hopefully that clarifies the structure of MainActivity. SecondActivity is much simpler but it also follows the same structural flow as MainActivity. Listings 18-8 and 18-9 show the complete and annotated codes for MainActivity and SecondActivity, respectively.

Listing 18-8. MainActivity, Annotated

```
import android.content.Context
import android.content.Intent
import android.support.v7.app.AppCompatActivity
import android.os.Bundle
import android.widget.Toast
import kotlinx.android.synthetic.main.activity_main.*
import java.io.FileNotFoundException
import java.io.IOException
```

```
import java.util.logging.Logger

class MainActivity : AppCompatActivity() {

  val Log = Logger.getLogger(MainActivity::class.java.name)
  override fun onCreate(savedInstanceState: Bundle?) {
    super.onCreate(savedInstanceState)
    setContentView(R.layout.activity_main)

    btnsecondactivity.setOnClickListener {
      startActivity(Intent(this, SecondActivity::class.java))      ❶
    }
  }

  private fun saveData() {                                          ❷
    val filename = "ourfile.txt"
    Thread(Runnable {
      try {
        val out = openFileOutput(filename, Context.MODE_PRIVATE)
        out.use {
          out.write(txtinput.text.toString().toByteArray())
        }
        runOnUiThread(Runnable {
          Toast.makeText(this, "Saved", Toast.LENGTH_LONG).show()
        })
      }
      catch(ioe:IOException) {
        Log.warning("Error while saving ${filename} : ${ioe}")
      }
    }).start()
  }

  override fun onPause() {                                          ❸
    super.onPause()
    saveData()
  }
```

```kotlin
    override fun onResume() {                                    ❹
      super.onResume()
      loadData()
    }

    private fun loadData() {

      val filename = "ourfile.txt"
      Thread(Runnable{
        try {
          val input = openFileInput(filename)
          input.use {
            var buffer = StringBuilder()
            var bytes_read = input.read()

            while(bytes_read != -1) {
              buffer.append(bytes_read.toChar())
              bytes_read = input.read()
            }
            runOnUiThread(Runnable{
              txtinput.setText(buffer.toString())
            })
          }
        }
        catch(fnfe:FileNotFoundException) {
          Log.warning("file not found, occurs only once")
        }
        catch(ioe: IOException) {
          Log.warning("IOException : $ioe")
        }
      }).start()
    }
}
```

❶   When the button is clicked, we'll simply launch an explicit Intent to open SecondActivity. We won't do any I/O codes here.

❷   The **saveData** function contains all the I/O code to write the runtime contents of the EditText to a file.

❸   Before MainActivity enters the "paused" state and disappears from the user's view, the runtime will call **onPause;** this is where we'll call **saveData.**

❹   When MainActivity first comes to the user's view, the runtime calls **onResume**. This is where we'll call the **loadData** function. It'll read the file and show its contents in a TextView object.

Let's move on to SecondActivity.

Listing 18-9. SecondActivity, Annotated

```
import android.content.Intent
import android.support.v7.app.AppCompatActivity
import android.os.Bundle
import kotlinx.android.synthetic.main.activity_second.*

class SecondActivity : AppCompatActivity() {

  override fun onResume() {                        ❶
    super.onResume()
    loadData()
  }

  private fun loadData() {                         ❷
    val filename = "ourfile.txt"
    Thread(Runnable {
      val input = openFileInput(filename)
      input.use {
        var buffer = StringBuilder()
        var bytes_read = input.read()
        while(bytes_read != -1) {
          buffer.append(bytes_read.toChar())
          bytes_read = input.read()
        }
        runOnUiThread(Runnable{
```

```
        txtoutput.setText(buffer.toString())
      })
    }
  }).start()
}

override fun onCreate(savedInstanceState: Bundle?) {
  super.onCreate(savedInstanceState)
  setContentView(R.layout.activity_second)

  btnmainactivity.setOnClickListener {              ❸
    startActivity(Intent(this, MainActivity::class.java))
  }
}
}
```

---

❶ When SecondActivity comes to the user's view, we'll call **loadData.**

❷ You've seen this code before. This is the same code in MainActivity. It reads the file and shows its contents using the TextView object. I suppose we could have refactored the code and abstracted this function somewhere so that we could follow the DRY (don't repeat yourself) principle, but that means we have more code and concept to explain. I violated the DRY principle in here in favor of readability. Just remember not to do this on production code.

❸ When the "1st Activity" button is clicked, we go back to the MainActivity. We could have called **finish()** in here as well, but I didn't want to completely destroy SecondActivity, so I used an explicit Intent to go back to MainActivity instead.

That draws the chapter to a close. I've said this a couple of times in the chapter, but it's worth repeating. The I/O codes are not the ones that are difficult—it's the boiler-plate codes that makes the program look more complicated than it really is. But you can't get away with that, you need the threading and exception handling codes to observe good housekeeping in your codes.

Chapter Summary

- When your need for storage exceeds the simple structure of key-value pairs and basic data type, use the Java I/O classes.

- You can store your file either in the always-available-but-limited internal storage or in the larger-but-may-be-dismounted external storage.

- Even if you think the I/O call will be less than 16 ms, run the codes in background thread. You never know what can happen in an I/O call.

- Java I/O calls throw Exceptions; handle them appropriately.

In the next chapter, we'll look at another important component of Android apps: BroadcastReceivers. They actually do, what you think they do—receive broadcasts. We'll look at some types of broadcast, and as always, we'll do a small demo project on it.

CHAPTER 19

BroadcastReceivers

What we'll cover:

- Introduction to BroadcastReceivers

- Custom and system broadcasts

- Manifest and context registered receivers

Android's application model is unique in many ways, but what makes it stand out is the way it lets you build an app using the functionalities of other apps that you didn't make yourself—I don't mean just libraries, I mean full apps. You already know about Intents—what they are and what they can do. We've looked at how to use Intents to launch other components, and we even used it to pass data around and in-between components.

There's one more way we can use Intents. We can use it to send a broadcast to all components. A broadcast is an Intent that is sent either by the Android runtime or other apps (your own apps included) so that every application or component can hear it. Most applications will ignore the broadcast but you can make your app listen to it. You can tune in to the message so you can respond to the broadcast. That is the topic of this chapter.

Introduction to BroadcastReceivers

So, we can launch Intents that are sent (broadcasted) to all apps and components. But what good does that do? To answer that, we need to jog our memories a bit and talk about Android's philosophy on interoperability and pluggability. Remember in Chapter 12 when we first talked about Intents? We looked at the picture in Figure 19-1.

© Ted Hagos 2018

T. Hagos, *Learn Android Studio 3 with Kotlin*, https://doi.org/10.1007/978-1-4842-3907-0_19

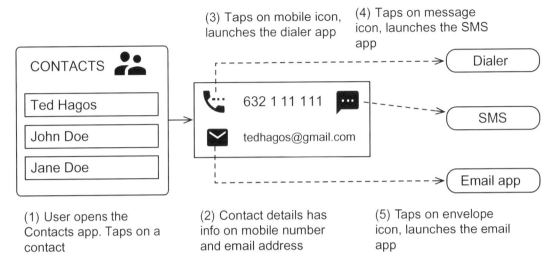

(3) Taps on mobile icon, launches the dialer app

(4) Taps on message icon, launches the SMS app

(1) User opens the Contacts app. Taps on a contact

(2) Contact details has info on mobile number and email address

(5) Taps on envelope icon, launches the email app

Figure 19-1. *How a user interacts with the Contacts app*

The user doesn't care which app to use to send an e-mail, SMS, or make a phone call. When a user clicks on the e-mail, it launches an implicit intent that says, "Hey, I wanna send an e-mail. Who's interested?" every app in the device will hear this but only those who are tuned-in will be able to respond. That's the whole idea about BroadcastReceivers—a message is published to all and if some apps are subscribed to it, then they can respond. It uses a **publish-subscribe** model.

System Broadcast vs. Custom Broadcast

An Intent broadcast can be sent either by the OS (system broadcast) or by applications (custom broadcast). A system broadcast is sent by the OS whenever something interesting happens (e.g., when WiFi is turned on [or off], when the battery goes down to a specified threshold, a headset is plugged, or the device was switched to airplane mode, etc.). Some examples of broadcast actions from the system are as follows:

- `android.app.action.ACTION_PASSWORD_CHANGED`

- `android.app.action.ACTION_PASSWORD_EXPIRING`

- `android.bluetooth.a2dp.profile.action.CONNECTION_STATE_ CHANGED`

- `android.bluetooth.a2dp.profile.action.PLAYING_STATE_CHANGED`

- android.bluetooth.adapter.action.CONNECTION_STATE_CHANGED

- android.intent.action.BATTERY_CHANGED

- android.intent.action.BATTERY_LOW

- android.intent.action.BATTERY_OKAY

There's about 150+ of these listed on the documentation. You can find them on the **BROADCAST_ACTIONS.TXT** file in the Android SDK.

A custom broadcast, on the other hand, is something you make up. These are intents that you send in order to notify some of your app's components (or other apps that are tuned in) that something "interesting" happened (e.g., a file has finished downloading or you've finished calculating prime numbers, etc.).

Manifest Registration vs. Context Registration

If you want to do something as a response to a broadcast, you need to listen for it, and in order to do that, you need to register a receiver. There are two ways to register: via the manifest and via the context.

A receiver registered in the manifest looks like Listing 19-1.

Listing 19-1. BroadcastReceiver Declared in AndroidManifest.xml

```
<?xml version="1.0" encoding="utf-8"?>
<manifest xmlns:android="http://schemas.android.com/apk/res/android"
  package="net.workingdev.ch19broadcastreceiverdosomething">
<application
  android:allowBackup="true"
  android:icon="@mipmap/ic_launcher"
  android:label="@string/app_name"
  android:roundIcon="@mipmap/ic_launcher_round"
  android:supportsRtl="true"
  android:theme="@style/AppTheme">
  <activity android:name=".MainActivity">
    <intent-filter>
      <action android:name="android.intent.action.MAIN" />
      <category android:name="android.intent.category.LAUNCHER" />
```

```
    </intent-filter>
  </activity>

  <receiver                                    ❶
    android:name=".MyReceiver"                 ❷
    android:enabled="true"
    android:exported="true">
    <intent-filter>                            ❸
      <action android:name="com.workingdev.DOSOMETHING"/>
    </intent-filter>
  </receiver>

</application>
```

---

❶　Just like an Activity, a **BroadcastReceiver** needs to be declared in the manifest. You have to declare it in its own node. Like an Activity declaration, it needs to be a child node of **application.**

❷　".MyReceiver" is the name of the BroadcastReceiver class. So, presumably, there is a class in your app named MyReceiver and it inherits BroadcastReceiver. We simply write it as ".MyReceiver," just like the Activity above it, ".MainActivity". The complete form is actually **net.workingdev.ch19broadcastreceiverdosomething.MyReceiver**, but we can use the short form because the **package** name is already declared earlier; look at the second line of the manifest, and you'll find the complete name of the package. Any subsequent classes that need to be declared in the manifest can simply use the short form, like ".MyReceiver" or ".MainActivity".

❸　The **intent-filter** is how we actually register. We're telling the OS that we're interested in the event **com.workingdev.DOSOMETHING**. In case that Intent is sent as a broadcast, this app would like to respond to it.

Receivers that were registered via the manifest don't need to be currently running in order to respond to the broadcast. The fact that a receiver is registered on the manifest is enough to resolve an intent.

When a receiver is programmatically registered—via a Context object—it looks like Listing 19-2.

Listing 19-2. How to Register and Unregister a BroadcastReceiver

```kotlin
val Log = Logger.getLogger(javaClass.name)

override fun onCreate(savedInstanceState: Bundle?) {

  super.onCreate(savedInstanceState)
  setContentView(R.layout.activity_main)

  val action_filter = IntentFilter("com.workingdev.DOSOMETHING") ❶
  val receiver = MyReceiver()

  btnregister.setOnClickListener {
    registerReceiver(receiver, action_filter)  ❷
  }

  btnunregister.setOnClickListener {
    try {
      unregisterReceiver(receiver)               ❸
    }
    catch(iae:IllegalArgumentException) {
      Log.warning("IllegalArgument\n ${iae}")
    }
    catch(e:Exception) {
      Log.warning("IllegalArgument\n ${e}")
    }
  }
}

inner class MyReceiver : BroadcastReceiver() {                    ❹
  override fun onReceive(context: Context?, intent: Intent?) {
    println("got it");
    Toast.makeText(this@MainActivity, "Got it", Toast.LENGTH_LONG).show()
  }
}
```

❶   This is the programmatic equivalent of the `<intent-filter>` node we've seen earlier. To create an **IntentFilter** object, pass a broadcast action to its constructor. The broadcast action is the event you'd like to subscribe to. In this case, we'd like to be notified when the Intent whose action is **com.workingdev.DOSOMETHING** is sent out; this Intent is an example of a custom broadcast, not a system broadcast.

❷   Use the **registerReceiver** method of the Activity to register the receiver. The method takes two arguments:
   a. An instance of BroadcastReceiver, and
   b. An instance of an IntentFilter

❸   When you register a receiver programmatically, make sure you also unregister it. That's what we're doing here. It's inside a **try-catch** structure because it can throw an exception. If you try to unregister a receiver that isn't registered yet (or a receiver that's been unregistered already), the runtime will throw the **IllegalArgumentException**. I didn't do this for the registration part because **registerReceiver** doesn't throw any exception, even if you (accidentally) register the same receiver more than once. Once a receiver is registered, the runtime will ignore any further attempts to register the same.

❹   This is the bare-bones definition of a BroadcastReceiver class.

Receivers that are registered programmatically can only respond to broadcasts while the app (which was used to register the receiver) is still running.

Basics of BroadcastReceivers

There are a couple of steps to follow when creating broadcast receivers. They are:

1. **Decide which broadcast action** you'd like to tune into. Do you want to listen to a system broadcast or a custom broadcast? Custom broadcast is typically used if you'd like to facilitate some messaging between your app's components. One use-case for using a BroadcastReceiver is when you use the DownloadManager system service to download large files, the service sends out a broadcast when it finishes the download—you'd want to listen to that so you can take action right after.

2. **Decide how you will register the receiver**, via the context or through the manifest? You can listen to custom broadcasts either way (manifest or context), but there are some broadcast actions that are restricted—you cannot listen to them via manifest registration. We will discuss this shortly.

3. **Create a class** that inherits from the BroadcastReceiver class.

4. **Override and implement the onReceive** method of the new class. When a broadcast is sent, the intent-filter is matched with the action, the OS resolves the Intent to your app, and eventually the specific BroadcastReceiver class, the runtime calls the **onReceive** method. The **onReceive** method is the meat and potatoes of the BroadcastReceiver class. Whatever you want to do when the broadcast is matched, this is the place where you need to write it.

Generally, you can listen to broadcasts if you register a BroadcastReceiver either via the Android manifest or via a Context object. Let's segue a little bit. Earlier, I used the term "register via the context" and "register programmatically"—they are one and the same, they mean the same. "Register via the context" means to call the **registerReceiver** method on the **Context** object. So the statement

```
registerReceiver(receiver, intent_filter)
```

is the same as the statement

```
this.registerReceiver(receiver, intent_filter)
```

They are both called on Context of the current Activity—the Activity class actually inherits from the Context object, and so does the Service class. So, you can call the registerReceiver method from within an Activity or Service. If you're inside a class that doesn't inherit from Context, you may still be able to register a receiver by getting the Application's context. The code looks something like this:

```
getApplicationContext().registerReceiver(receiver, intent_filter)   // or
applicationContext.registerReceiver(receiver, intent_filter)
```

Going back to manifest versus context registration, there are some broadcast actions that you cannot register in the manifest; but you can register them via the Context.

One example is `android.intent.action.TIME_TICK`, this is a protected intent that can only be sent by the system. It's sent every 60 seconds and you can only listen to it if you registered via the Context.

In earlier versions of Android, there were already a couple of broadcast that were off limits from the manifest. At the time of this writing, Android 9 (or API level 28) came out. In this book, we've always used API level 23 as the target, but you will benefit from reading the behavior changes documents for each Android version. I've listed some links to the official Android documentation below. These documentations affect BroadcastReceivers in one way or another.

- **Android 9 (API 28) behavior changes**. `http://bit.ly/ behaviorchanges9`. Talks about all the changes in the API that developers should know if we want to target Android 9. This doc has something to say about BroadcastReceivers.

- **Background execution limits**. `http://bit.ly/bgexeclimit`. This talks about the things your app can and can't do while it's running in the background. Don't think that because you're not in the UI thread, you can run around and do whatever you want. This doc talks about those limitations; it also talks about the limitations imposed on BroadcastReceivers.

- **BroadcastReceiver exceptions**. `http://bit.ly/ broadcastexceptions`. Starting with Android 8 (continuing to 9), all implicit broadcast actions are now off-limits from the manifest, with the exception of some. This document itemizes those actions that are exempted. If you want to know which implicit broadcast actions can still be registered via the manifest, read this doc.

Implicit vs. Explicit Broadcast Actions

Android makes a distinction between implicit and explicit broadcast actions. It defines an explicit broadcast as something that target just one application, no matter how many other apps are listening for it. An explicit broadcast, on the other hand, can be heard by any app that registered for it. For our purpose and to make our lives simpler, the documentation is telling us not to listen to system broadcast via the manifest. Starting

Android 8, all implicit broadcasts (with the exception of those listed at `http://bit.ly/broadcastexceptions`) cannot be heard by receivers that were registered via the manifest. But you may still listen for these broadcast actions if you register via the context.

The main reasons for all the new restrictions have to do with performance optimization and saving power. Consider this: when a device's WiFi connectivity goes up or down, the CONNECTIVITY_ACTION broadcast is sent. If there are a dozen apps listening for this broadcast, all of them will wake up and take action. This is going to happen every time the WiFi drops and reconnects. Remember that manifest-registered receivers don't need to be alive to receive the broadcast; in fact, they will come alive when they get the broadcast. This behavior can cause significant power drain. If your app doesn't need to be informed on WiFi connectivity when it's not running, it's more responsible to do the registration via the context.

Demo App: Custom Broadcast

Let's build a small project so you can try the BroadcastReceivers yourself. Table 19-1 shows the details for this project.

Table 19-1. *Project Details*

Project Detail	Value
Application name	CH19ContextRegistration
Company domain	use your website name
Kotlin support	Yes
Form factor	Phone and tablet only
Minimum SDK	API 23 Marshmallow
Type of activity	Empty
Activity name	MainActivity
Layout name	activity_main

What want to do:

1.   Create a BroadcastReceiver that will respond to an implicit custom broadcast

2.   We'll register the receiver as soon as the Activity becomes visible to the user; and

3.   We'll unregister the receiver before the Activity gets into the "paused" state.

4.   The MainActivity's UI will only have one button. When the button is clicked, it will send a custom broadcast intent.

Listing 19-3 shows minimalistic code for the UI.

Listing 19-3. /app/res/layout/activity_main.xml

```
<?xml version="1.0" encoding="utf-8"?>
<android.support.constraint.ConstraintLayout xmlns:android=http://schemas.
android.com/apk/res/android
  xmlns:app=http://schemas.android.com/apk/res-auto
  xmlns:tools=http://schemas.android.com/tools
  android:layout_width="match_parent"
  android:layout_height="match_parent"
  tools:context=".MainActivity">

  <Button
    android:id="@+id/button"
    android:layout_width="wrap_content"
    android:layout_height="wrap_content"
    android:layout_marginStart="26dp"
    android:layout_marginTop="43dp"
    android:text="send broadcast"
    app:layout_constraintStart_toStartOf="parent"
    app:layout_constraintTop_toTopOf="parent" />
</android.support.constraint.ConstraintLayout>
```

We need to add a class that inherits from BroadcastReceiver. One way to do this is from the main menu bar **File ➤ New ➤ Kotlin File/Class**. Alternatively, we can also use the context menu from the **app ➤ java** folder of the Project tool window, as shown in Figure 19-2. From there, you can go to **New ➤ Other ➤ BroadcastReceiver**.

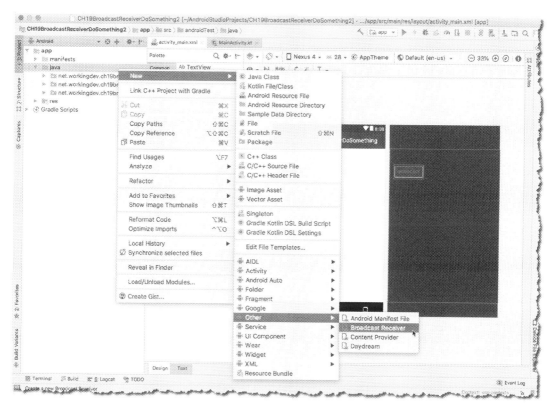

Figure 19-2. *New BroadcastReceiver*

You need to fill in the name of the class. In this example, I named the class "MyReceiver."

We won't do anything special in the receiver. We'll simply display at toast message print something in the Logger. Listing 19-4 shows the code for MyReceiver.

Listing 19-4. MyReceiver.java

```
import android.content.BroadcastReceiver
import android.content.Context
import android.content.Intent
import android.widget.Toast
import java.util.logging.Logger

class MyReceiver : BroadcastReceiver() {

  val Log = Logger.getLogger(javaClass.name)

  override fun onReceive(context: Context, intent: Intent) {  ❶
    Toast.makeText(context, "Got it", Toast.LENGTH_LONG).show()
    Log.info("Got it")
  }
}
```

❶ When a broadcast intent is matched to a receiver, the OS calls the BroadcastReceiver's
   onReceive method. This is where you should write your app's business logic for the receiver
   (e.g., save a file, route program logic depending on WiFi conditions, etc.).

In MainActivity, we will do the following:

1. Create an instance of MyReceiver. We need to do this only once.
   That's why we will create the instance inside the **onCreate**
   callback.

2. Register the receiver each time it becomes visible to the user. We'll
   put this code inside the **onResume** callback of MainActivity.

3. Unregister the receiver when the user is no longer interacting with
   MainActivity.

4. When the button is clicked, we'll send a custom broadcast intent.

Listing 19-5 shows the full and annotated code for MainActivity.

Listing 19-5. MainActivity.java

```
import android.content.Intent
import android.content.IntentFilter
import android.support.v7.app.AppCompatActivity
import android.os.Bundle
import kotlinx.android.synthetic.main.activity_main.*
import java.util.logging.Logger

class MainActivity : AppCompatActivity() {

  lateinit var receiver:MyReceiver                          ❶
  val Log = Logger.getLogger(javaClass.name)                ❷

  override fun onCreate(savedInstanceState: Bundle?) {
    super.onCreate(savedInstanceState)
    setContentView(R.layout.activity_main)

    receiver = MyReceiver()                                 ❸

    button.setOnClickListener {
      val intent = Intent("com.workingdev.DOSOMETHING") ❹
      sendBroadcast(intent)                                 ❺
    }
  }

  override fun onResume() {                                  ❻
    super.onResume()

    val filter = IntentFilter("com.workingdev.DOSOMETHING")
    registerReceiver(receiver, filter)
    Log.info("Registered receiver")
  }

  override fun onPause() {                                   ❼
    super.onPause()

    try {
      unregisterReceiver(receiver)
      Log.info("Unregistered receiver")
    }
```

```
    catch(iae: IllegalArgumentException) {
      Log.warning(iae.toString())
    }
  }
}
```

---

❶ The **receiver** variable holds the instance of the **MyReceiver** class (our BroadcastReceiver). We're declaring the variable as a property because we will refer to it in the **onResume** and **onPause** methods. We used the **lateinit** keyword because we won't define it just yet.

❷ Let's use a basic Logger object.

❸ Now that we're inside **onCreate**, let's define the MyReceiver object.

❹ When the button is clicked, we'd like to create a broadcast intent and set its *action* to DOSOMETHING.

❺ Launch the intent.

❻ We're inside the **onResume** callback. The OS will call this method every time MainActivity is becomes visible to the user. This is good place to register the receiver. We only want to be notified when we're using the app.

❼ We're inside **onPause**, the OS calls this method before MainActivity enters a "paused" state and then disappears from the user's view. This is a good place to unregister the receiver. We don't want to be notified when we're not using the app.

Figure 19-3. *Our app, running*

Another way to send a broadcast intent is via the Android Debug Bridge or **adb,** for short. It's a command-line tool that lets you communicate to a device—physical or emulated. The adb can do quite a range of things like installing/uninstalling APKs, displaying logs, running Linux commands on the device, simulating phone calls, and many more. For our purpose, we'll use to send out a broadcast intent.

adb is in the platform tools folder of the Android SDK. Open a command-line window and switch to the directory of the Android SDK. If you've forgotten where it is, go to Android Studio's *Settings* (Windows and Linux) or *Preferences* (macOS). You can do that by the pressing the keys **CTRL + ALT + S**, for Windows and Linux, or **Command + ,** (comma) for macOS.

From there, go to Appearance and Behavior ➤ System Settings ➤ Android SDK, as shown in Figure 19-4. The Android SDK location is found there.

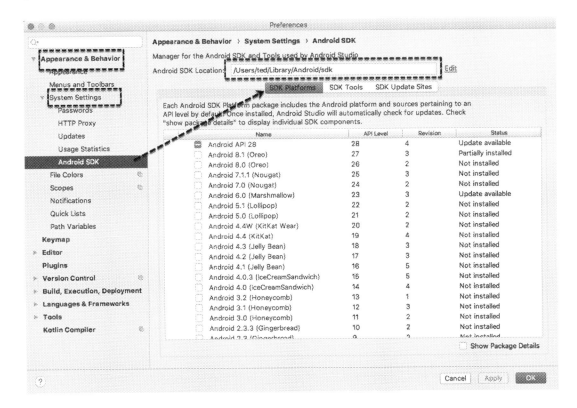

Figure 19-4. *Preferences, Android SDK*

Go back to the command-line window, and switch to the Android SDK folder. From there, switch to the **platform-tools** folder, then run the following command:

```
adb shell am broadcast -a com.workingdev.DOSOMETHING
```

If you're on macOS or Linux, you may have to prepend the command with dot and forward slash, like this:

```
./adb shell am broadcast -a com.workingdev.DOSOMETHING
```

Demo App: System Broadcast

The next project will be similar to the previous project, but we'll listen for a system broadcast. We will listen for the ACTION_TIME_TICK, which is sent out by the system every 60 seconds. This is a protected intent, so we really have to register the receiver at runtime. Table 19-2 shows the details for this project.

Table 19-2. *Project Details for System Broadcast*

Project Detail	Value
Application name	CH19SystemBroadcast
Company domain	use your website name
Kotlin support	Yes
Form factor	Phone and tablet only
Minimum SDK	API 23 Marshmallow
Type of activity	Empty
Activity name	MainActivity
Layout name	activity_main

The app is very simple. There are no UI elements to set up. Here's what we'd like to do:

1. Create a BroadcastReceiver that will listen for the ACTION_TIME_ TICK intent. We'll implement this one as an inner class—the only reason for this is to make the presentation of the code a bit more compact. You can definitely implement the receiver class as stand-alone class if you wish.

2. We want to listen to broadcast only when the user is interacting with the app. So we will register the receiver in the **onResume** callback of MainActivity; we'll unregister it in the **onPause** callback.

3. Whenever the ACTION_TIME_TICK is received, we'll simply print out a message to the console and also to the user screen using a Toast object.

Listing 19-6. MainActivity

```
import android.content.BroadcastReceiver
import android.content.Context
import android.content.Intent
import android.content.IntentFilter
import android.support.v7.app.AppCompatActivity
import android.os.Bundle
import android.widget.Toast

import java.util.logging.Logger

class MainActivity : AppCompatActivity() {

  lateinit var intentfilter:IntentFilter
  lateinit var timereceiver:TimeReceiver
  var current_count = 0

  val Log = Logger.getLogger(javaClass.name)

  override fun onCreate(savedInstanceState: Bundle?) {
    super.onCreate(savedInstanceState)
    setContentView(R.layout.activity_main)

    timereceiver = TimeReceiver()                             ❶
    intentfilter = IntentFilter(Intent.ACTION_TIME_TICK)      ❷
  }
  override fun onResume() {
    super.onResume()
    Log.info("App is resuming")
    registerReceiver(timereceiver,intentfilter)               ❸
  }
  override fun onPause() {
    super.onPause()
    Log.info("App is paused")
    try {
```

```
      unregisterReceiver(timereceiver)                        ❹
    }
    catch(iae:IllegalArgumentException) {
      Log.warning(iae.toString())
    }
  }

  inner class TimeReceiver : BroadcastReceiver() {          ❺
    override fun onReceive(context: Context?, intent: Intent?) {
      current_count += 1
      var message = "Counter:${current_count}"
      Log.info(message)
      Toast.makeText(this@MainActivity, message, Toast.LENGTH_LONG).show()
    }
  }
}
```

❶   Creates an instance of the BroadcastReceiver

❷   Creates the **intentfilter** that'll listen for the ACTION_TIME_TICK broadcast

❸   Register the receiver inside **onResume**; this method is called by the runtime when the app is seen by the user.

❹   Unregister the receiver before the app goes to a "paused" state. This way, the receiver only listens for broadcast whenever our app is in view of the user. When the app is no longer in the user's view, we don't want to be notified of any broadcast.

❺   Here's the class definition for the BroadcastReceiver. It's implemented as inner class, and it's just as effective. This works for us because we're not trying to do anything substantial in the **onReceive** callback. If the program logic gets too involved or complex, the BroadcastReceiver might be better implemented outside MainActivity.

Other Notes

BroadcastReceivers and Intents do an effective job of making decoupled components talk to each other. It's good to use BroadcastReceivers if you want to facilitate communication between apps; they're a good solution for inter-process communication.

But if the communication is limited among the components of your own app, BroadcastReceivers are an expensive solution. It's not appropriate to use global broadcast.

If you simply want to facilitate some messaging between your app's components, you might want to consider a LocalBroadcastManager class. When you use this, the broadcast data doesn't leave your application. It's not interprocess. Unfortunately, LocalBroadcastManager won't be discussed in this chapter. But hopefully you've gained some good grounding on the concept and use of BroadcastReceivers.

Chapter Summary

- You can use BroadcastReceivers and Intents to create truly decoupled apps.

- You can make your app listen to a specific broadcast and do something interesting when the broadcast is sent.

- BroadcastReceivers can be used to route program logic in your app. You can make the app behave in certain ways as a response to the changes in the runtime environment (e.g., low battery, no WiFi connection).

- BroadcastReceivers can be registered via the manifest or via a Context object. If you will target Android 9.0, make sure to read on the broadcast actions that are allowed to be registered via the manifest. There is a push from the Android team that discourages apps to register via the manifest and use context registration instead.

In the next chapter, you'll learn how to prepare your app for distribution.

CHAPTER 20

App Distribution

What we'll cover:

- Cleaning up
- Preparing for release
- Signing the app
- Google Play

At some point, you might want to distribute your application to a wide audience. Android apps can be distributed quite freely and without much restriction; you can make it available as a download on your website or even e-mail the app directly to the users, but many developers choose to distribute their app on a market place like Google Play Store or Amazon App Store to maximize reach. Regardless of how you intend to distribute, there are things you need to do before you release the app.

Publishing an app can be a very involved activity, and it's not limited to the technical and procedural aspects of app distribution such as creating an account on **developer.android.com**, making polished icons, and signing your app. It may also involve creating copy and promotional text, social media activities, and many other things that have nothing to do with tech at all. This chapter will only focus on the technical requirements of app distribution.

Generally, there are two stages when you publish an app:

1. **Prepare the app for release**. This is where we do some clean up. You'll need to sanitize the app before the release. This is where we remove all debug information and other settings or log what we used during development. You certainly don't want your users accidentally seeing all those "got it" or "I am here" breadcrumbs you left for yourself while you were coding. You may also want to think about icons and other visual assets for the app. It's a good

© Ted Hagos 2018
T. Hagos, *Learn Android Studio 3 with Kotlin*, https://doi.org/10.1007/978-1-4842-3907-0_20

idea to invest on an actual device at this stage and test your app on it. Most importantly, in this stage, we'll build a developer certificate.

2. **Releasing the app**. You'll need to publicize the app, sell it, and distribute it. If you will release the app in the Google Play Store, you will need to sign up for a publisher account and use developer console of Google play to publish.

Preparing the App for Release

The three major things we need to do here are:

1. Prepare the material and assets for release

2. Configure the app for release

3. Build a release-ready app

Prepare Materials and Assets for Release

No matter how nifty or clever your codes are, the user will never see it. What he will see are your View objects, the icons, and other graphical assets of the app. Make sure they are polished.

You'd be remiss if you didn't think about your app's icon. This icon helps users identify your app as it sits on the home screen. This icon also appears on a couple of other areas such as the launcher window, the downloads section, and, more importantly, if you are publishing your app in the Google marketplace, this icon will be displayed there too. The app icon may play a major role in creating the first impressions to your would-be users, so it is a good idea to put some work into this and to read Google's guidelines for app icons, which can be found at `http://bit.ly/androidreleaseiconguidelines`.

Other things to consider if you will publish the app in Google's marketplace are graphical assets, like screen captures and the text for promotional copy. Make sure to read Google's guideline for graphical assets, which can be found at `http://bit.ly/androidreleasegraphicassets`

Configure the App for Release

This is the part where you clean-up and sanitize the app. The things we mention here are by no means mandatory, but it's a good idea to go through them before building a release version.

Check the Package Name

In previous chapters, you have used *"com.example.myapp"* for package names. That's alright for test or practice apps, but that's not alright when you will release the app to the public. The package name makes the app unique across the marketplace, and once you decide on a package name, you can't change it anymore. So, give it some thought.

Remove Logging and Debug Information

Debug and log information are useful—indispensable even—during development, but you must not let your users see them. Before releasing the app, strip your app of all debug and log information.

The debugging information is easy enough to deal with, you simply need to remove the **android:debuggable** attribute in the **<application>** tag of the Manifest file. The same cannot be said about the logging information, unfortunately.

There are various approaches to the log issue; the solutions can be as simple (but tedious) as manually removing all Log statements or as sophisticated as writing sed or awk programs to automatically strip away the Log calls. Some people deal with the log issues by configuring ProGuard (which is outside the scope of this book), and some others would go as far as using a third-party library like Timber (a GitHub project) to replace Android's Log class. Regardless of what approach you take, just be mindful that you need to strip away the Log statements before you build for release.

Check the Application Permissions

Sometime during development, you may have experimented on some features of the application and you may have set permissions on the manifest like permission to use the network, write to external storage, etc. Review the **<uses-permission>** tag on the manifest and make sure that you don't grant permissions that the application does not need.

Remote Servers and URLs

If your application relies on web APIs or cloud services, make sure that the release build of the app is using production URLs and not test paths. You may have been given sandboxes and test URLs during development; you need to switch them up to the production version.

Build a Release-Ready Application

All of the projects and samples we did in this book were deployed in the emulator with a simple procedure. We clicked the **Run** button. Android Studio built and assembled the app into an APK, which was deployed in the target device. After that, the app ran. Throughout this process, there was one step that Android Studio did for us, and you didn't know it. You weren't aware of it at all.

Android Studio performed a very important task that is required before any APK can be delivered or installed on any device (emulated or actual device). Android Studio signed that APK.

Before you can install and run an app in any device, the application's APK has to be signed digitally. Android Studio automatically signs all apps when we click the Run button. But it uses a debug certificate, which is good only for development and testing. You cannot use the same certificate when you release the app. Most app stores, including Google, won't accept an application that is signed with a debug certificate.

Before we distribute the app, we have to sign it with a proper certificate—not a debug certificate. We don't need to go to a certificate authority like Thawte or Verisign for this—a self-signed certificate will do.

Launch Android Studio, if it isn't open yet. Open your project. From the main menu bar, go to **Build ➤ Generate Signed APK**, as shown in Figure 20-1.

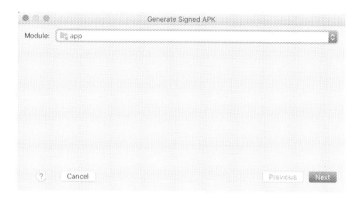

Figure 20-1. *Generate signed APK*

Click the "Next" button. You should see the "Keystore" dialog, as shown in Figure 20-2.

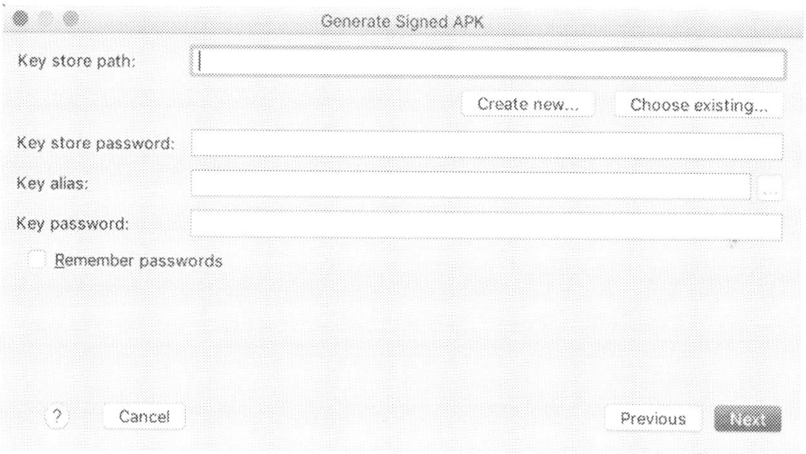

Figure 20-2. *Keystore dialog*

The **Key store path** is asking where our Java Keystore (JKS) file is. At this point, you don't have it yet. So, click **Create New**. You'll see the dialog window for creating a new Keystore, as shown in Figure 20-3.

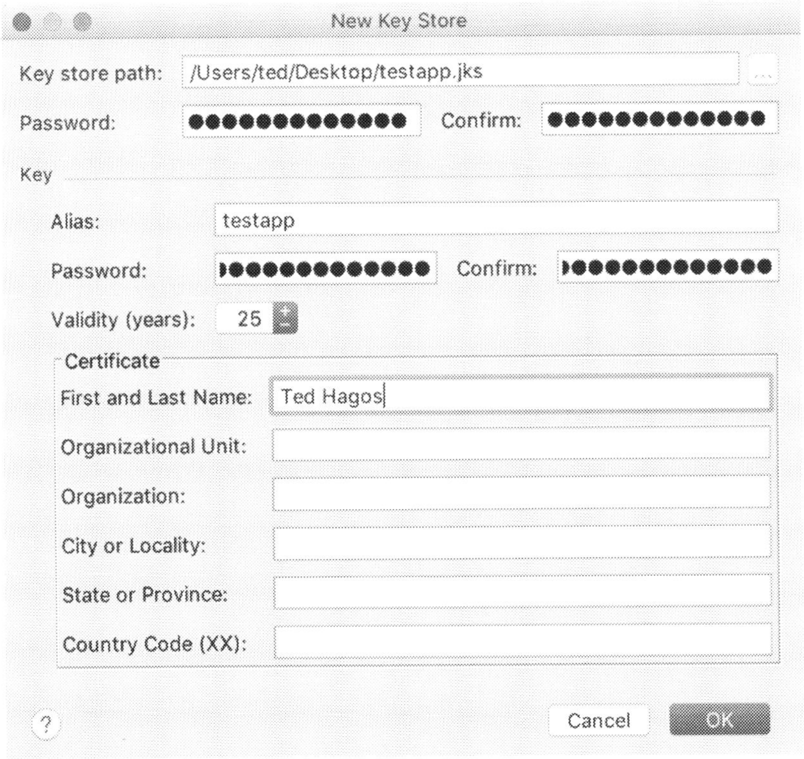

Figure 20-3. *New Keystore*

Note   In Java, a keystore is a repository of security certificates—either authorization certificates or public key certificates.

Table 20-1 shows the description for the input items of the Keystore.

Table 20-1. *Keystore Items and Description*

Keystore items	Description
Keystore path	The location where you want to keep the keystore. This is entirely up to. Just make sure you remember this location.
Password	This is the password for the keystore.
Alias	This alias identifies the key. It's just a friendly name for it.
(Key) Password	This is the password for the key. This is **NOT** the same password as the keystore's (but you can use the same password if you like).
Validity, in years	The default is 25 years; you can just accept the default. If publish on Google Play, the certificate must be valid until October of 2033—so, 25 years should be fine.
Other information	Only the first and last name fields are required.

When you're done filling up the New Keystore dialog, click "OK." This will bring you back to the Generate Signed APK window, as shown in Figure 20-4; but now, the JKS file is created and Keystore dialog is populated with it.

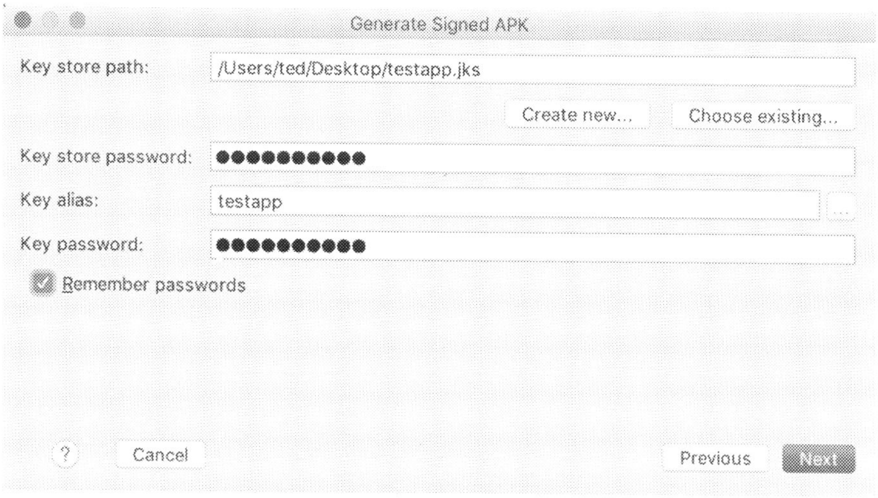

Figure 20-4. *Generate signed APK, populated*

Click "Next."

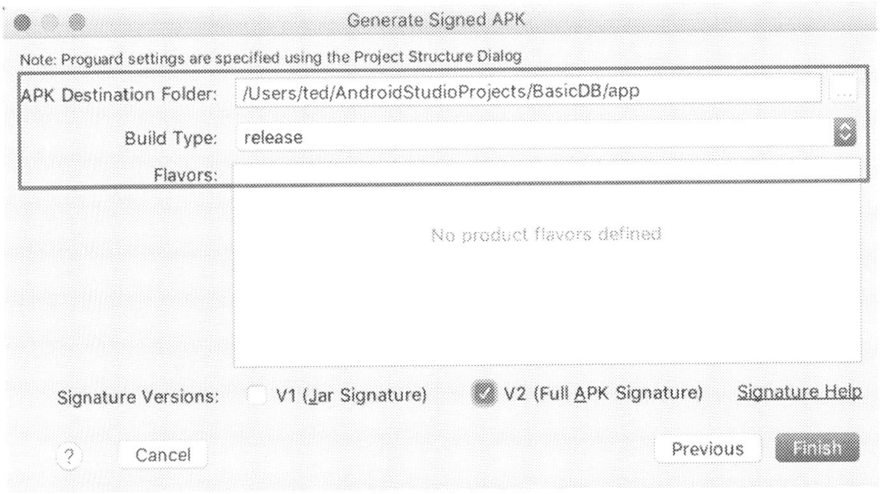

Figure 20-5. *Signed APK, APK destination folder*

Next, we choose the destination of the signed APK, as shown Figure 20-5. You need to remember this location. This is where Android Studio will store the signed APK. Also, make sure that the **Build type** is set to "release."

When you click Finish, Android Studio will generate the signed APK for your app. This is the file that you will submit to Google Play. You can even sell this APK on your website or some other marketplace—it ready for release.

Releasing the App

Before you can submit an app to Google Play, you'll need a developer account. If you don't have one yet, you can sign up at `https://developer.android.com`. There's a lot of assumptions I'm making about the next activities. I'm assuming that:

1. You already have a Google account (Gmail);

2. You're using Google Chrome to go to `https://developer.android.com`; and

3. You're Google account is logged on to Chrome.

If you're Google account isn't logged on to Chrome, you might see something like Figure 20-6. Chrome will ask you go select an account (or create one).

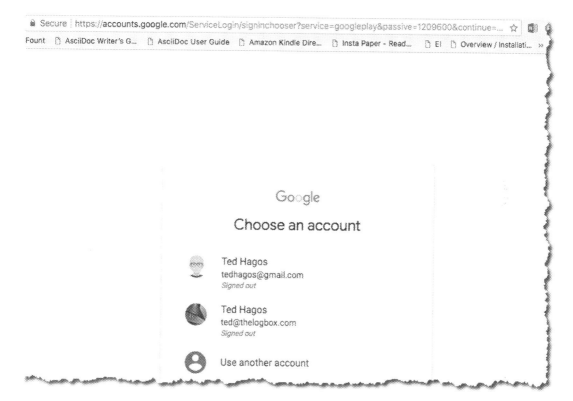

Figure 20-6. *Choose an account*

When you get your Google account sorted out, you'll be taken to the developer. android.com website, as shown in Figure 20-7.

Note The screenshots shown here are as they appear at the time of writing. Google makes changes to the websites from time to time. The Google Play website may not look like these screenshots anymore by the time you read this book.

Click **Google Play**, as shown in Figure 20-7.

Figure 20-7. *developer.android.com*

Click **Launch Play Console**, as shown in Figure 20-8.

Figure 20-8. *Launch Play Console*

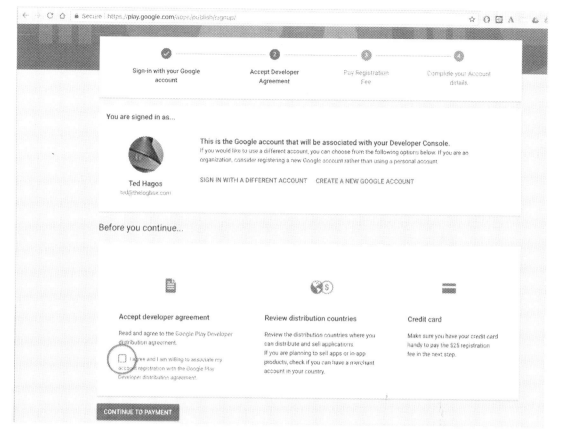

Figure 20-9. *Google Play console, sign up*

You need to go through four steps to complete the registration (shown in Figure 20-9):

1. Sign-in with your Google account.

2. Accept the developer agreement.

3. Pay the registration fee.

4. Complete your account details.

Once you have completed the registration and payment, you will now have access to the Google Play console, as shown in Figure 20-10.

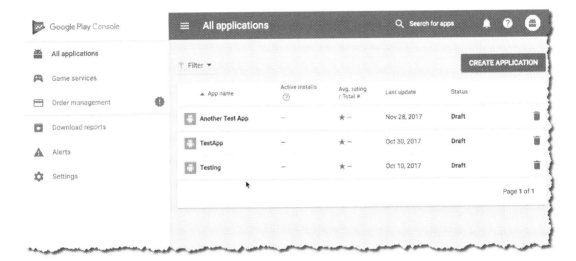

Figure 20-10. *Play Console*

This is where you can start the process of submitting your app to the store. Click the "Create application" button to get started.

Chapter Summary

- Your codes may be great, but the user will never see them. Pay attention (also) to the things the user will see, like icons and other graphical assets.

- Clean up your code before you release them. Remove all those log and debug info.

- Code-review your own work. If you have buddies or other people who can review the code with you, that's much better. If your app uses servers, RESTful URLs, etc., make sure they are production-ready and not sandboxes.

- You can't use debug certificates if you want to release your app into marketplaces like Google Play or Amazon.

- You'll need a Google Play account if want to sell your apps on Google Play. I paid a one-time fee of $25 USD, but that was a couple of years ago.

- Don't forget to test your app on a real device.

- We tried to distill and simplify the process of putting your app in the Play Store,\ but this chapter isn't a subsitute to Android Developer's launch checklist. You should still read that. You can find at `https://bit.ly/appstorelaunchchecklist`.

Index

A

Access modifiers, 102
Accessor methods, 94–96
ADTs, *see* Android development
       tools (ADTs)
Android
    architecture of, 158–160
    history, 157–158
    Studio (*see* Android Studio)
Android app
    AndroidManifest, 175–176
    AS3 IDE (*see* AS3 IDE)
    components
        activities, 174
        BroadcastReceivers, 174–175
        Contacts app, 176
        ContentProviders, 174–175
        Intents, 176–177
        Services, 174–175
    EXE files, 173
    logical structure, APK, 173
    project creation
        AS3 welcome screen, 177–178
        AVDs, 183, 188, 190
        choosing activity, 181
        Component installer, 186
        configure activity, 182
        "Include Kotlin support"
          tick box, 179
        Instant apps, 180
        Instant run, 189
        launching AS3, 177
        location, 178
        main AS3, 182–183
        new project, 178
        package name, 178
        Run icon, 183
        Select Deployment Target
          screen, 183, 189
        selecting hardware, 184
        system image, 185, 187
        target Android devices, 179
Android Debug Bridge (adb), 387, 439
Android development tools (ADTs), 160
Android Device Monitor, 387
Android Honeycomb, 289
Android Not Responding (ANR), 348
Android Studio
    in 2013, 161
    ADTs, 160
    AS3 installer, 161
    AVD, 169
    32-bit libraries, Linux, 162
    commercial Java IDE, 161
    configuration
        API levels, 165
        changes, channel, 168
        coding, 163
        SDK tools, 166–167
        SDK window, 165
        updates, 167–168

© Ted Hagos 2018
T. Hagos, *Learn Android Studio 3 with Kotlin*, https://doi.org/10.1007/978-1-4842-3907-0

E

F

W, X, Y

Z

Printed in the United States
By Bookmasters